Arbitrability

International Arbitration Law Library

Series Editor Dr. Julian D.M. Lew QC

In the series *International Arbitration Law Library* this book, *Arbitrability: International & Comparative Perspectives* is the Nineteenth title

The titles published in this series are listed at the end of this volume

KLUWER LAW INTERNATIONAL

Arbitrability

International & Comparative Perspectives

Edited by

Loukas A. Mistelis & Stavros L. Brekoulakis

Wolters Kluwer
Law & Business

AUSTIN BOSTON CHICAGO NEW YORK THE NETHERLANDS

Published by:
Kluwer Law International
PO Box 316
2400 AH Alphen aan den Rijn
The Netherlands
Website: www.kluwerlaw.com

Sold and distributed in North, Central and South America by:
Aspen Publishers, Inc.
7201 McKinney Circle
Frederick, MD 21704
United States of America
Email: customer.care@aspenpubl.com

Sold and distributed in all other countries by:
Turpin Distribution Services Ltd.
Stratton Business Park
Pegasus Drive, Biggleswade
Bedfordshire SG18 8TQ
United Kingdom
Email: kluwerlaw@turpin-distribution.com

Printed on acid-free paper.

ISBN 978-90-411-2730-3

Printed in Great Britain.

FOREWORD

Since the introduction of the New York Convention on the Recognition and Enforcement of Foreign Arbitral Awards in 1958, a great deal has been achieved towards the creation of uniform rules and practices relating to international arbitration. There were some areas, however, where uniformity was impossible or, indeed undesired, to achieve, and were reserved for the domain of national laws: most prominently, public policy, mandatory rules and arbitrability. All three topics have received significant attention by scholarly writing, arbitral and judicial practice. One can nowadays safely argue that as far as public policy and mandatory rules of law are concerned, certain international and even transnational standards have been developed and are in the meantime widely accepted.

This is not the case with arbitrability where, despite significant debate, the focus is on national laws and national practices. Arbitrability is a multi-facetted and multi-purpose concept which despite national origins has an international dynamic. It defines the classes of disputes that *may* be removed from the scope of arbitral reference and be placed at the exclusive jurisdiction of given national courts. This does not automatically imply that an arbitration tribunal will be barred from determining whether a particular issue can be adjudicated in arbitration. In other words, national laws typically retain for national courts the determination of limited legal rights; such a jurisdictional retention, however, would not cover all disputes arising out of these rights. It is unclear to what extent one could argue that even in the context of arbitrability there are certain international and even transnational standards.

L Mistelis & S Brekoulakis (eds), Arbitrability: International & Comparative Perspectives, v - vi

Several questions relating to arbitrability are pertinent and are explored in this book. More specifically, the book discusses first the notions and rationale of arbitrability in international arbitration, as well as the laws applicable to the issue of arbitrability (Part I), and second, specific national and international substantive rules on arbitrability (Part II).

This volume originates from a conference organised by the Hellenic Arbitration Initiative, the Greek chapter of the alumni of the School of International Arbitration, in September 2005. Seven of the sixteen chapters in this volume were originally presented at the 2005 conference. As these papers were finalised, we thought we had to expand the collection of contributions by inviting leading academics and practitioners from Europe and the United States to write on the arbitrability and addressing aspects of the topic not encompassed by the Athens conference.

We owe a number of debts. First, to our authors: this book could not have been published without the generosity of the contributors who enthusiastically gave their time to prepare their contributions. Second, to the Hellenic Arbitration Initiative: for organising the arbitrability conference and for inviting us and the other speakers to contribute. Third, to John Ribeiro who has assisted with the technical and linguistic editing of this volume.

As always, it has been a pleasure to work with Kluwer Law International.Our publishers, Eleanor Taylor and Vincent Verschoor, have shown patience as deadlines have passed. Their encouragement and support are much appreciated.

Loukas A Mistelis
Clive M Schmitthoff Professor of
Transnational Law and Arbitration

Stavros L. Brekoulakis
Lecturer in International Dispute
Resolution

20 DECEMBER 2008

TABLE OF CONTENTS

TABLE OF ABBREVIATIONS

INSTITUTIONS, ORGANIZATIONS, RULES AND JOURNALS

AAA	American Arbitration Association
ABA	American Bar Association
AC	Law Reports, House of Lords (Appeal Cases)
ADRLJ	Arbitration and Dispute Resolution Law Journal
Akron L. Rev.	Akron Law Review
Alb. L. Rev	Albany Law Review
ALI	American Law Institute
All ER	All England Law Reports
Am. J. Comp. L.	American Journal of Comparative Law
Am. J. Int'l L.	American Journal of International Law
Am. Rev. Int'l Arb.	American Review of International Arbitration
Ann IDI	Annuaire de l'Institut de droit international
Ann. Rev. Banking L.	Annual Review of Banking Law
Arab L. Q.	Arab Law Quarterly
Arb. Int'l	Arbitration International
Arbitration (Arb.)	Arbitration, Journal of the Chartered Institute of Arbitrators
ASA	Swiss Arbitration Association
ASA Bulletin	Swiss Arbitration Association Bulletin
Asian DR	Asian Dispute Review

L Mistelis & S Brekoulakis (eds), Arbitrability: International & Comparative Perspectives, xvii - xxiv

Asian Pac. L. Rev.	Asian Pacific Law Review
ATF	Arrêts du Tribunal Fédéral Suisse
BC L. Rev.	Boston College Law Review
Berkeley J. Emp. & Lab. L.	Berkeley Journal of Employment and Labor Law
Berkeley J. Int'l L	Berkeley Journal of International Law
BGB	Bürgerliches Gesetzbuch (German Civil Code)
BGE	Entscheidungen des schweizerischen Bundesgerichts
BGHZ	Sammlung der Entscheidungen des Bundesgerichtshofs in Zivilsachen
BIT	Bilateral Investment Treaty
Brook. J. Int'l L.	Brooklyn Journal of International Law
BU Int'l L. J.	Boston University International Law Journal
BULR	Boston University Law Review
BYIL	British Yearbook of International Law
BYU L. Rev.	Brigham Young University Law Review
CA	Court of Appeal
Cardozo L. Rev.	Cardozo Law Review
Cass. Civ.	Cour de cassation (civil chamber)
Cass. Com.	Cour de cassation (Chambre commerciale et financière)
CC	Code civil, codice civile, civil code
CCLS	Centre for Commercial Law Studies
CCP	Code of Civil Procedure
CIETAC	China International Economic and Trade Arbitration Commission
CISG	United Nations Convention on the International Sale Goods
CLR	Commonwealth Law Reports
Clunet	Journal de droit international
Columbia J. Transnat'l L.	Columbia Journal of Transnational Law
Con. LR	Construction Law Reports

Cornell Int'l L.J.	Cornell International Law Journal
CPR	Civil Procedure Rules (England)
CRCICA	Cairo Regional Centre For International Commercial Arbitration
DIS	Deutsche Institution für Schiedsgerichtsbarkeit
Disp. Res. J.	Dispute Resolution Journal
Duke L. J.	Duke Law Journal
EAA	English Arbitration Act
EC	European Community
ECHR	European Convention on Human Rights
ECJ	Court of Justice of the European Communities
ECR	Report of Cases before the Court of Justice of the European Communities
EDNY	Eastern District of New York
EEC	European Economic Community
EHRR	European Human Rights Reports
EHRR	European Human Rights Reports
Electronic J. Comp. L.	Electronic Journal of Comparative Law
ER	English Reports
EU	European Union
EWCA Civ	Neutral citation for England and Wales Court of Appeal civil division decisions
EWHC	High Court of England and Wales
F 2d	The Federal Reporter Second Series
F 3d	The Federal Reporter Third Series
F Supp	Federal Supplement
FAA	United States Federal Arbitration Act
FS	Festschrift
FSR	Fleet Street Reports
Ga. J. Int'l & Comp. L.	Georgia Journal of International and Comparative Law
Gaz. Pal.	Gazette du Palais

Geo. Wash. J Int'l L. & Eco.	George Washington University Journal of International Law and Economics
Hague Yearbook of Int'l L.	Hague Yearbook of International Law
Hastings Int'l & Comp. L. Rev.	Hastings International and Comparative Law Review
HKHC	Hong Kong High Court
HKIAC	Hong Kong International Arbitration Centre
HL	House of Lords
IBA	International Bar Association
IBA Rules	IBA Rules on the taking of Evidence in International Commercial Arbitration, 1999
ICC	International Chamber of Commerce
ICC Bulletin	International Chamber of Commerce International Court of Arbitration Bulletin
ICCA	International Council for Commercial Arbitration
ICDR	American Arbitration Association International Center for Dispute Resolution
ICL Rev.	International Construction Law Review
ICLQ	International and Comparative Law Quarterly.
ICSID	International Centre for the Settlement of Investment Disputes
ICSID Rev-FILJ	ICSID Review – Foreign Investment Law Journal
IECL	International Encyclopaedia of Comparative Law
IFCAI	International Federation of Commercial Arbitration Institutions
ILA	International Law Association
ILM	International Legal Materials
ILR	International Law Reports
InsO	InsolvenzOrdnung
Int'l ALR	International Arbitration Law Review
Int'l Bus. Law.	International Business Lawyer

Int'l Law	International Lawyer
IPRax	Praxis des internationalen Privat- und Verfahrensrechts
Iran-US CTR	Iran-US Claims Tribunal Reports
IStR	Internationales Steuerrecht – Zeitschrift für europäische und internationale Steuer- und Wirtschaftsberatung
J. Am. Arb.	Journal of American Arbitration
J. Disp. Res.	Journal on Dispute Resolution
J. Int'l Arb.	Journal of International Arbitration.
J. Pat. Off. Soc'y	Journal of the Patent and Trademark Office Society
J. Trans'l. Law & Policy	Journal of Transnational Law & Policy
JBL	Journal of Business Law
JCAA	Japan Commercial Arbitration Association
Law & Policy in Int'l Bus.	Law & Policy in International Business
LCIA	London Court of International Arbitration
Lewis & Clark L. Rev.	Lewis & Clark Law Review
LGDJ	Librairie Générale de Droit et de Jurisprudence
Lloyd's Rep.	Lloyd's Law Reports
LNTS	League of Nations Treaty Series
Louisiana L. Rev	Louisiana Law Review
Loy. LA Int'l. & Comp. L.J.	Loyola Los Angeles International and Comparative Law Journal
Managing IP	Managing Intellectual Property
Mealey's IAR	Mealey's International Arbitration Reports
Miami L. Rev.	Miami Law Review
Michigan J. Int'l L.	Michigan Journal of International Law
Minn. L. Rev.	Minnesota Law Review
Model Law	UNCITRAL Model Law on International Commercial Arbitration adopted 21 June 1985
MR	Master of the Rolls

NC J. Int'l L. & Com. Reg.	North Carolina Journal of International Law and Commercial Regulation
NCPC	French Code of Civil Procedure (Nouveau Code de Procedure Civile)
New York Convention	1958 New York Convention on the Recognition and Enforcement of Foreign Arbitral Awards
NILR	Netherlands International Law Review
NW. J. Int'l L. & Bus.	Northwestern Journal of International Law & Business
NY	New York
NY. L. Sch. J. Int'l & Comp. L.	New York Law School Journal of International and Comparative Law
NYAD	New York Appellate Division
NYLJ	New York Law Journal
NZLR	New Zealand Law Review
OECD	Organisation for Economic Co-operation and Development
Ohio St. J. Disp. Res.	Ohio State Journal on Dispute Resolution
OJ	Official Journal of the European Communities
OLG	Oberlandesgericht
PC	Privy Council
PCA	Permanent Court of Arbitration (The Hague)
PECL	Principles of European Contract Law
Pepperdine Disp. Res. L.J.	Pepperdine Dispute Resolution Law Journal
PILA	(Swiss) Private International Law
QBD	Queen's Bench Division
RCADI	Recueil des Cours de l'Académie de Droit International de la Haye / Collected Courses of the Hague Academy of International Law
RCJB	Revue Critique de Jurisprudence Belge
RDAI/IBLJ	Revue de droit des affaires internationales / International Business Law Journal
Rep	Report

Rev. Arb.	Revue de l'arbitrage
Rev. Brasileira Arb.	Revista Brasileira de Arbitragem
Rev. Crit. Dip.	Revue critique de droit international privé
Rome Convention	EC (Rome) Convention on the Law Applicable to Contractual Obligations 1980
S Ct	Supreme Court
S. Tex. L. Rev.	South Texas Law Review
SCC	Stockholm Chamber of Commerce Arbitration Institute
SchiedsVZ	Zeitschrift für Schiedsverfahren – German Arbitration Law Journal
SDNY	Southern District of New York
SIA	School of International Arbitration, Queen Mary University of London
SIAC	Singapore International Arbitration Centre
Stanford J. Int'l L.	Stanford Journal of International Law
Stockholm Int'l Arb. Rev.	Stockholm International Arbitration Review
Suffolk U. L. Rev.	Suffolk University Law Review
Syracuse L. Rev.	Syracuse Law Review
Tex. L. Rev.	Texas Law Review
Texas Int'l L.J.	Texas International Law Journal
Tul. Int'l & Comp. L.	Tulane Journal of International and Comparative Law
Tul. L. Rev.	Tulane Law Review
Tul. Mar. L.J.	Tulane Maritime Law Journal
Tulsa J. Comp. & Int'l L.	Tulsa Journal of Comparative and International Law
U. Cin. L. Rev.	University of Cincinnati Law Review
U. Ill. L. Rev.	University of Illinois Law Review
UKHL	United Kingdom House of Lords Decisions
UKPC	Neutral citation for decisions of the Privy Council
UNCITRAL	United Nations Commission for International Trade Law

UNCITRAL Notes	UNCITRAL Notes on Organizing Arbitral Proceedings
UNIDROIT	International Institute for the Unification of Private Law
Unif L. Rev.	Uniform Law Review
UNTS	United Nations Treaty Series
Va. J. Int'l L.	Virginia Journal of International Law
Va. L. Rev	Virginia Law Review
Vand. J. Transnat'l L.	Vanderbilt Journal of Transnational Law
Vanderbilt L. Rev.	Vanderbilt Law Review
Vienna	Austrian Federal Economic Chamber in Vienna
WAMR	World Arbitration and Mediation Report
Washington Convention	Washington Convention on the Settlement of Investment Disputes between States and Nationals of other States 1965
WIPO	World Intellectual Property Organisation
WIPO Expedited Rules	WIPO Expedited Rules
WL	Westlaw
WLR	The Weekly Law Reports
WTAM	World Trade and Arbitration Materials
Yale LJ	Yale Law Journal
YBCA	Yearbook of Commercial Arbitration
YJIL	Yale Journal of International Law
ZPO	German Code of Civil Procedure (ZPO)

PART I

FUNDAMENTAL OBSERVATIONS AND APPLICABLE LAW

*Loukas A. Mistelis**

CHAPTER 1

ARBITRABILITY – INTERNATIONAL AND COMPARATIVE PERSPECTIVES

Is Arbitrability a National or an International Law Issue?

1. INTRODUCTION

1-1 The success of the 1958 New York Convention on the Recognition and Enforcement of Foreign Arbitral Awards is the most important achievement in the world of international arbitration in the last 50 years. The Convention celebrated in 2008 its golden jubilee and has received to-date 143 ratifications,[1] including most, if not all, jurisdictions in the world which have decided to take part in international trade. The Convention established uniform rules in respect of (a) the validity and enforcement of arbitration agreements (the Convention sets maximum standards, while national laws may introduce more lenient standards); (b) the formalities for enforcement of foreign arbitral awards (although the actual procedure of execution is left to domestic laws); and (c) the grounds for which recognition or enforcement of awards may be refused (again these are maximum standards while domestic regimes may be more lenient).

1-2 In relation to the listed grounds on which enforcement may be resisted, the Convention succeeded in creating – to a great extent – autonomous concepts. For example, Article V(1)(b) introduces an autonomous concept of due process[2] and

* LLB (Athens), MLE (magna cum laude), Dr. juris (summa cum laude) (Hannover), Advocate; Clive M Schmitthoff Professor of Transnational Commercial Law and Arbitration and Director of the School of International Arbitration, Centre of Commercial Law Studies, Queen Mary, University London.

[1] See www.uncitral.org for more details and updates of status of the New York Convention.

[2] See, recently, Emmanuel Gaillard & Domenico Di Pietro (eds), *Enforcement of Arbitration Agreements and International Arbitral Awards: The New York Convention in Practice* (Cameron May, Ltd. 2008).

L Mistelis & S Brekoulakis (eds), Arbitrability: International & Comparative Perspectives, 1-17

Article V(1)(d) confirms the primacy of party autonomy as far as issues of procedure are concerned. Where the Convention cannot show the same level of harmony is with respect to Article V(2) dealing with arbitrability and public policy.[3]

1-3 Public policy, whatever it means, pursuant Article V(2)(b), must be construed narrowly. In fact, only violation of the enforcement state's public policy with respect to international relations (international public policy) ought to be a valid defence.[4] This defence is only available "where the enforcement would violate the forum state's most basic notions of morality and justice."[5] The public policy exception set out in Article V(2)(b) is an acknowledgment "of the right of the State and its courts to exercise ultimate control over the arbitral process."[6] It is difficult, if not impossible, to define the concept of public policy. In 2000 and 2002 the International Law Association Committee on International Commercial Arbitration published a well received report and a resolution on public policy as a bar to the enforcement of foreign arbitration awards.[7] It is an intriguing complication that public policy has by its very nature, a dynamic character, so that any classification may crystallise public policy only at a certain period of time.

3 Bernard Hanotiau & Oliver Caprasse, "Public Policy in International Commercial Arbitration" in Gaillard & Di Pietro (eds), *ibid.*, 805 et seq.

4 Distinctions between domestic and international public policy have been recorded, e.g., in Bundesgerichtshof, (1992) XVII YBCA 503 (18 January 1990), where the court held that New York Convention Article V(2)(b) requires violation of international public policy; and *General Electric Co (U.S.) v. Renusagar Power Co (India)*, (1990) XV YBCA 465 (High Court Bombay, 21 October 1988). References to international public policy are made in all laws which have been influenced by the French NCPC Articles 1498 and 1502. Followers of this model include Portugal, Algeria, and Lebanon. See also, e.g., Tunisia, Arbitration Code 1993 Articles 78(2)(II) and 81(II); 1992 Romania, Law on Settlement of Private International Law Disputes Articles 168(2) and 174; U.S., FAA sections 201 (incorporation of New York Convention) and 301 (incorporation of the Panama Convention) and *Sherk v. Alberto Curver*, 417 U.S. 506 (1974) which distinguishes between domestic and international public policy.

5 See, e.g., *Parsons and Whittemore Overseas Co, Inc v. Société générale de l'industrie du papier (RAKTA)*, 508 F. 2d 969, 974 (2nd Cir., 1974).

6 See ILA Committee on International Commercial Arbitration, *Public Policy as a Bar to the Enforcement of International Arbitral Awards*, London Conference Report (2000), 2. The final Report was presented at the 2002 New Delhi conference and published in the 2002 Proceedings and at <www.ila-hq.org>.

7 ILA Committee on International Commercial Arbitration, *supra* note 6. See also L. Mistelis, "Keeping the Unruly Horse in Control or Public Policy as a Bar to the Enforcement of Foreign Arbitral Awards", 2(4) *International Law FORUM du droit international* (2000) 248.

1-4 The other aspect of Article V, namely V(2)(a), has also attracted and continues to attract the interest of scholarly writing as the discussion on the matter is far from settled yet.[8] While it may be argued that the issue of what disputes are arbitrable has now become less of a problem, the question is ultimately still in the control of national courts and national laws, and it is still unclear as to whether an international or transnational concept of arbitrability exists.

1-5 Several questions relating to arbitrability are pertinent, if not pervasive and are explored in this chapter and this book. More specifically, we will discuss first the notion and rationale of arbitrability in international arbitration (infra, 2), then we will explore the laws applicable to the issue of arbitrability (infra, 3), before turning our attention to national and international substantive rules on arbitrability (infra, 4).

2. The Notion and Rationale of Arbitrability

1-6 Arbitrability is one of the issues where the contractual and jurisdictional natures of international commercial arbitration collide head on.[9] It involves the

[8] See H. Arfazadeh, "Arbitrability under the New York Convention: the Lex Fori Revisited", 17 *Arb. Int'l* (2001) 73; M. Blessing, "Arbitrability of Intellectual Property Disputes", 12 *Arb. Int'l* (1996) 191; K.-H. Böckstiegel, "Public Policy and Arbitrability" in P. Sanders (ed), *ICCA Congress Series No.3* (Deventer: Kluwer Law & Taxation 1987) at 177; G. Born, *International Commercial Arbitration: Commentary and Materials* (2nd ed, Kluwer 2001) Chapter 3 (D), at 343 et seq; T. Carbonneau, *The Law and Practice of Arbitration* (2nd ed, Juris 2007) para 23-26; T. Carbonneau & F. Janson, "Cartesian Logic and Frontier Politics: French and American Concepts of Arbitrability", 2 *Tul. Int'l & Comp. L.* (1994) 193; Fouchard, Gaillard & Goldman, *On International Commercial Arbitration*, E. Gaillard & J. Savage (eds) (1999), para 532 et seq; B. Hanotiau, "What law governs the issue of arbitrability?", 12(4) *Arb. Int'l* (1996) 391; B. Hanotiau, "The Law Applicable to Arbitrability", in A. van den Berg (ed), *ICCA Congress Series No. 9* (Kluwer 1999) at 146; B. Hanotiau, "L'arbitrabilité", in *Recueil des Cours - Collected Courses of The Hague Academy of International Law* (2002) Tome 296, at 165-166 (The Hague Boston London, Martinus Nijhoff Publishers, 2003); J. Lew, L. Mistelis & S. Kröll, *Comparative International Commercial Arbitration* (Kluwer 2003) Chapter 9; J. Paulsson, "Arbitrability, Still Through a Glass Darkly", in *Arbitration in the Next Decade* (ICC Bulletin, Special Supplement 1999) at 95; Pilar Perales Viscasillas, *Arbitrabilidad y convenio arbitral. Ley 60/2003 de Arbitraje y Derecho Societario* (Thomson-Aranzadi 2005); Redfern & Hunter (with N. Blackaby & C. Partasides), *Law and Practice of International Commercial Arbitration* (4th ed, Sweet & Maxwell 2004), para 3-13 et seq.

[9] See Lew, Mistelis & Kröll, *ibid.*, at 9-1 and Chapter 5. See also the definition by Carbonneau & Janson, *ibid.*, at 194: arbitrability "determines the point at which the exercise of contractual freedom ends and the public mission of adjudication begins."

simple question of what types of issues can and cannot be submitted to arbitration and whether specific classes of disputes are exempt from arbitration proceedings. While party autonomy espouses the right of parties to submit any dispute to arbitration, national laws often impose restrictions or limitations on what matters can be referred to and resolved by arbitration. This is referred to in literature as "objective arbitrability."[10] Certain disputes may involve such sensitive public policy issues that it is felt that they should only be dealt with by the judicial authority of state courts. An obvious example is criminal law which is generally the domain of the national courts: it is undisputed that the sanctioning of criminal activity is in the power of the judiciary.

1-7 For example, historically, the mere allegation of bribery or other illegal activity associated with a dispute referred to arbitration was sufficient to shock arbitration tribunals and to render the dispute inarbitrable. In 1963, in a very well known award, which was only published in 1994,[11] Judge Gunnar Lagergren decided that a dispute where bribery was involved was outside the jurisdiction of international arbitration tribunals. He concluded:

> [23] … I am convinced that a case such as this, involving such gross violations of good morals and international public policy, can have no countenance in any court either in the Argentine or in France or, for that matter, in any other civilised country, nor in any arbitral tribunal. Thus, jurisdiction must be declined in this case. It follows from the foregoing, that in concluding that I have no jurisdiction, guidance has been sought from general principles denying arbitrators to entertain disputes of this nature rather than from any national rules on arbitrability. Parties who ally themselves in an enterprise of the present nature must realise that they have forfeited any right to ask for the assistance of the machinery of justice (national courts or arbitral tribunals) in settling their disputes.

1-8 This restriction on party autonomy may be justified in *exceptional* cases and must not be the norm. Consequently, arbitration agreements covering those

[10] For distinction between subjective and objective arbitrability see Emmanuel Gaillard & John Savage (eds), *Fouchard Gaillard Goldman on International Commercial Arbitration* (Kluwer Law International 1999), para 533 (hereinafter referred to as Fouchard Gaillard Goldman). See also Lew, Mistelis & Kröll, *supra* note 8 at paras 9-35 et seq. See also Pilar Perales Viscasillas, *Arbitrabilidad y Convenio Arbitral* (Thompson Aranzadi 2005) at 15 et seq.

[11] Award published in 3 *Arb. Int'l* (1994) 282 with note J. Gillis Wetter at 277-281. Subsequently the award was also published in XXI YBCA 47 (1996). The award was first made publicly available via a summary in Julian DM Lew, *Applicable Law in International Commercial Arbitration* (Oceana 1978), at 553-555 and 574-575.

matters will, in general, not be considered valid, will not be able to establish the jurisdiction of the arbitrators and leave the subsequent award unenforceable.[12]

2.1. The Notion(s) of Arbitrability

1-9 Is the notion of "arbitrability" as simple as the New York Convention suggests? The Convention provides for disputes "capable of settlement by arbitration". [13] However, it should be noted that in the U.S. the term "arbitrability" is often used in a wider sense, covering the whole issue of the tribunal's jurisdiction.[14] In line with the prevailing international understanding, this chapter only deals with the restrictions imposed on the parties' freedom to submit certain types of disputes to arbitration.

1-10 In this book several definitions have been offered. Brekoulakis highlights the functions of arbitrability in suggesting a definition to the effect that

> "[a]rbitrability is ... a specific condition pertaining to the jurisdictional aspect of arbitration agreements ... a condition precedent for the tribunal to assume jurisdiction over a particular dispute (a jurisdictional requirement), rather than a condition of validity of an arbitration agreement (a contractual requirement)".[15]

1-11 Youssef emphasises the contractual nature of arbitration:

> "an objective notion, arbitrability is ... the fundamental expression of the freedom to arbitrate. It defines the scope of the parties' power of reference or the boundaries of the right to go to arbitration in the first place."[16]

1-12 Shore distinguishes

> "Internationally, arbitrability refers to whether specific classes of disputes are barred from arbitration either because of public policy or because they are outside the scope of the arbitration agreement ... arbitrability refers to whether the specific claims raised are of [a] subject matter capable of

[12] See, e.g., Arts. II(1) and V(2)(a) New York Convention and Art. 34 UNCITRAL Model Law.

[13] New York Convention Arts. II(1) and V(2)(a).

[14] See, e.g., *First Options of Chicago v. Manuel Kaplan et and MK Investment, Inc*, 115 S Ct 1920, 1943 (1995); *Smith Enron Cogeneration Limited Partnership, Inc et al v. Smith Cogeneration International, Inc*, XXV YBCA 1088 (2000) para 28 (2nd Cir.); see also Carbonneau & Janson, supra note 8, at 194.

[15] S. Brekoulakis, Chapter 2, infra at para 2-63.

[16] Youssef, Chapter 3, infra at para 3-6.

> settlement by arbitration, and are not subject to the exclusive jurisdiction of ... courts."[17] ... "the term in the U.S. further includes the jurisdictional question that asks whether an arbitrator or a court should decide if a given dispute should be submitted to arbitration."[18]

1-13 Di Pietro, in light of the New York Convention, points out that arbitrability

> "is a "*ratione materiae*" notion, which is normally referred to as "objective" arbitrability as it is independent of the quality of the parties or their will. It is distinguished from the so-called "*ratione personae*" or "subjective" arbitrability, which is concerned with the capacity of the parties to submit disputes to arbitration."[19]

1-14 Finally, Carbonneau pertinently stresses that

> "Arbitrability establishes the respective domains of law and arbitral adjudication. It is the essential dividing line between public and private justice."[20]

1-15 This book does not specifically address the issue of subjective arbitrability. This may be relevant to disputes involving states and their instrumentalities[21] or disputes involving parties linked in elaborate corporate arrangements, as well as in certain multi-party, multi-contract or multi-action disputes.[22] Generally, it is understood that restrictions on the capacity of a party to enter into arbitration agreements aim to protect the party itself. By contrast, the restrictions on the state's entitlement to enter into arbitration agreements are based on policy considerations.[23]

1-16 To a certain extent, most of these restrictions are influenced by the old concept that it is against sovereign dignity to submit to any type of dispute resolution system not controlled by the state itself. These restrictions are the expression of a deep-rooted distrust of arbitration in countries which historically considered arbitration to be a dispute settlement favouring parties (often multi-

17 Shore, Chapter 4, infra at para 4-2.

18 *Ibid.*, at para 4-3.

19 Di Pietro, Chapter 5, infra at para 5-18. See also Pamboukis, Chapter 7, infra at para 7-2.

20 Carbonneau, Chapter 8, infra at para 8-1.

21 See Emmanuel Gaillard & Jennifer Younan (eds), *State Entities in International Arbitration* (Juris Publishing 2008).

22 For a detailed discussion of complex, see Bernard Hanotiau, *Complex Arbitration – Multiparty, Multicontract, Multi-issue and Class Actions* (Kluwer 2006).

23 See Lew, Mistelis & Kröll, *supra* note 8 at paras 27-7 et seq.

national corporations) from industrialised countries.[24] However, the rapid growth of investment treaty arbitration, as well as the lively debate on arbitration and non-signatories, gradually (albeit slowly) diminish the areas of subjective inarbitrability.

1-17 It follows that arbitrability is a multi-facetted and multi-purpose concept which despite national origins has an international dynamic. It defines the classes of disputes that *may* be removed from the scope of arbitral reference and placed at the exclusive jurisdiction of given national courts. This does not automatically imply that an arbitration tribunal will be barred from determining whether a particular issue can be adjudicated in arbitration. In other words, national laws typically retain for national courts the determination of limited legal rights; such a jurisdictional retention, however, does not cover all disputes arising out of these rights. The typical example is that while the validity of a patent in Europe is a matter for the exclusive jurisdiction of the courts at the place of registration of the patent, the commercial use of the patent may well be the subject matter of arbitral proceedings.

1-18 Given that arbitration is a creature of party autonomy, one could argue that arbitration tribunals are not part of any national judicial system and therefore do not owe any allegiance to a particular state. As long as the parties want to have their dispute decided by arbitration, the tribunal should be prepared to hear the case irrespective of the fact that its award may later be set aside for lack of arbitrability. The duty towards the parties to render an enforceable award only exists as long as the parties have not renounced it. It appears that the preferred view is that an arbitration tribunal should on its own initiative deny jurisdiction if the dispute is inarbitrable on the basis of the facts submitted by the parties. By declaring certain disputes inarbitrable, the legislator has removed these from the disposal of the parties. Accordingly, the arbitration tribunal, despite being a creation of the parties, not only owes a duty to the parties but also the public; it would also serve the parties better if tribunals were apprehensive (and even proactive in cases) of inarbitrability issues. The success of arbitration as a dispute settlement mechanism rests on the fact that it is not being abused to circumvent the policy of states in areas which are considered to be so crucial that they are reserved for adjudication by state courts.[25]

[24] M. Sornarajah, *The Settlement of Foreign Investment Disputes*, 110; see also J. Paulsson, "Third World Participation in International Investment Arbitration", 3(1) *ICSID Rev-FILJ* (1987) 19, who considers that such a view was justified in the early 1950s.

[25] Lew, Mistelis & Kröll, *supra* note 8 at para 9-97.

2.2. The Rationale of Arbitrability

1-19 The next main issue intrinsically linked to the notion of arbitrability is the underlying rationale justifying restrictions to party autonomy. The fact that the New York Convention deals with the issue of arbitrability in Article V(2)(a) together with the public policy defence to the enforcement of awards, provided for in Article V(2)(b) led most readers to the conclusion that arbitrability is also based on public policy.

1-20 Although, in general, limits on arbitrability of disputes arise from public policy, only few laws make express reference to the notion of "public policy".[26] Not only is the notion often too vague to give clear guidance, but also in the contemporary arbitration-friendly environment, not every rule of public policy justifies reserving the disputes involved for determination by state courts.[27] Therefore, despite the underlying public policy considerations, different criteria are adopted in determining arbitrability, and as a result different grounds have been offered for the justification of inarbitrability.

1-21 For example, Brekoulakis concludes

> "... the relevance of public policy to the discussion of arbitrability is essentially very limited, and therefore, the scope of inarbitrability should not be determined by reference to public policy."[28]

He further points out that:

> "Arbitration ... has inherent limitations. Based on consent, arbitration has intrinsic difficulties to affect a circle of persons other than the contractual parties to an arbitration agreement. This type of conceptual boundaries of arbitration may have repercussions on the scope of arbitrability. ... Eventually, arbitrability should be determined on the basis of efficiency: whether an arbitral tribunal can get disposed of the pending dispute in an effective manner."[29]

[26] See, e.g., France, NCPC Article 2060.
[27] See Antoine Kirry, "Arbitrability: Current Trends in Europe", 12 *Arb Int'l* (1996) 373 at 374-379.
[28] Brekoulakis, Chapter 2, infra at para 2-39.
[29] Brekoulakis, *ibid.*, at para 2-84.

1-22. Youssef adds that

> "the *problematique de base* of the arbitrability of rights involving public interest relates to the nature of the arbitrator's mandate as a limited delegation of power. Constrained by the *privity* inherent in the source of his jurisdiction, an arbitrator has authority to dictate legal effects *inter partes* and not *vis-à-vis* third parties. To the extent it would dictate effects with respect to third parties, the arbitrability of mixed/public rights would simply conflict with the contractual nature of arbitration."[30]

1-23 There is little doubt that the juridical natural of arbitration is determinative of the extent of jurisdictional powers of arbitrators and the question of arbitrability. Tribunals should only be dealing with disputes specifically referred to them by the disputing parties and should exercise self-restraint if certain matters before them are *manifestly* inarbitrable.

1-24 It is a matter of the efficiency and effectiveness of the arbitration process that one should assume and imply the consent of the parties that an arbitral reference is limited to matters that are arbitrable. In this respect, it is consistent with the mandate and functions of arbitration tribunals, and indeed with the nature of arbitration, that not all matters can be arbitrated. In real terms, such a limit is rather very narrow: most matters can and could be arbitrated; inarbitrability should be triggered in very few occasions and such occasions should typically be relevant for domestic, and only rarely for international disputes. In this respect arbitrability provides the delineation between public and private adjudication.

3. Law Applicable to the Issue of Arbitrability

1-25 The determination of the law governing the arbitrability of disputes is of considerable significance. Despite the generally prevailing tendency to increase the scope of arbitrable disputes, national laws may differ from each other significantly. A number of disputes, which are not arbitrable under the law of one country, are arbitrable in another country where the interests involved are considered to be less important. The approach to bribery is an example of existing differences. In many countries, whilst bribery is a vitiating factor in all contracts, it can be considered by arbitrators. In other countries not only is bribery illegal, but also to preclude it from being legitimised, by a commercial or

[30] Youssef, Chapter 3, infra at para 3-10.

consultancy arrangement, if allegations of bribery are raised they cannot be considered by arbitrators. Consequently, in some countries, consultancy contracts relating to public procurement are not arbitrable because of the prevalence of excessive commissions considered to be bribes.[31]

1-26 The determination of arbitrability may well be a matter for national law or matter of international law, depending on where the basis of sanction for a particular conduct (or the treatment for a class of disputes) is to be found. It may also be based on international standards, rather than specific violation of statutory provisions. The law governing the arbitrability of a dispute may depend on where and at what stage of the proceedings the question arises. Tribunals may apply different criteria than courts in determining this law, and the criteria applied by courts at the post-award stage may differ from those at the pre-award stage.

1-27 Most national arbitration laws do not regulate which law governs the question of arbitrability; rather they determine directly which disputes are arbitrable or inarbitrable. Indeed, every national law determines which types of disputes are reserved for the exclusive domain of national courts and which can be referred to arbitration. This differs from state to state, reflecting the political, social and economic prerogatives of the state, as well as its general attitude towards arbitration. This is a balancing act between the largely domestic importance of reserving certain matters for the exclusive decision of courts and the more general public interest of promoting trade and commerce through an effective means of dispute settlement.[32]

1-28 Generally, national laws sometimes contain a specific arbitrability provision in their arbitration law: such provisions are invariably permissive and reassuring in declaring that most disputes are arbitrable.[33] The other option is to include arbitrability provisions in other domestic law: such provisions are typically restrictive but are also expressed in narrow terms.[34] Some national laws refer to

[31] Lew, Mistelis & Kröll, *supra* note 8 at paras 9-5 to 9-7.

[32] For a description of the relevant issues in the balancing process in the context of arbitrability of disputes involving allegations of bribery see the decision of the English Commercial Court of 19 December 1997, *Westacre Investments Inc v. Jugoimport-SPDR Ltd* [1998] 2 Lloyd's Rep 111, 129.

[33] Switzerland, PILA Art. 177; Germany, ZPO section 1030(1); Belgium, Judicial Code Art. 1676(1).

[34] See, for example, Article 22 of the EC Regulation 44/2001 on the International Jurisdiction in Civil and Commercial Matters.

very broad notions such as "disputes involving economic interest"[35] or "disputes involving property."[36] Other national laws rely on the narrower concept of "capability of the parties to reach an agreement."[37]

1-29 The UNCITRAL Model Law on International Commercial Arbitration does not contain any definition of which disputes are arbitrable. Quite to the contrary Article 1(5) provides that it is not intended to affect other laws of the state that preclude certain disputes being submitted to arbitration. In implementing the Model Law, national legislators are completely free to determine which disputes are arbitrable and which are not. This may be done expressly where arbitrability of certain disputes is excluded by statute. The exclusion may also result from conferring exclusive jurisdiction on specialised tribunals[38] or national courts.[39] Therefore, the decision may be different in cases arising in a purely national context from that in relation to an international transaction.

1-30 International conventions may also directly or indirectly address the issue of arbitrability. The New York Convention, for example, provides for the obligation of national courts to enforce arbitration agreements and awards, where the dispute is arbitrable.[40] Indirectly and unambiguously these provisions generally regulate which law governs arbitrability, and in this sense are choice-of-law provisions. If a dispute is arbitrable according to this law, courts may not rely on the inarbitrability of the dispute under a different law to refuse enforcement of the arbitration agreement or award.[41]

1-31 In respect of the pre-award (jurisdictional) stage, Article II(1) merely stipulates that arbitration agreements have to be recognised and that national

35 Germany, ZPO section 1030(1).

36 Switzerland, PILA Article 177.

37 Belgium, Judicial Code Article 1676(1). See Lew, Mistelis & Kröll, *supra* note 8 at paras 9-20 – 9-21.

38 For an overview of the importance of "exclusive jurisdiction" and other criteria see Vesna Lazic, *Insolvency Proceedings and Commercial Arbitration* (Kluwer 1998) 146-158.

39 See, e.g., EC Regulation 44/2001 Article 22.

40 See New York Convention Article II(1) and (3).

41 See New York Convention Article V(2)(a). An identical provision is contained in Inter-American Convention Article 5(2)(a):

> Recognition and enforcement of an arbitral award may also be refused if the competent authority in the country where recognition and enforcement is sought finds that:
> (a) The subject matter of the difference is not capable of settlement by arbitration under the law of that country…

courts have an international obligation to deny jurisdiction (typically by staying the proceedings) under Article II(3) unless the dispute is not capable of settlement by arbitration. According to which law the dispute has to be capable of settlement by arbitration, however, is not expressly provided for, and has given rise to a number of divergent views in national court practices.

1-32 It is not uncommon that courts support the application of different criteria depending on whether the question arises at the referral or at the enforcement stage. In the majority of cases, courts have determined the question of arbitrability at the pre-award stage according to their own national law.[42] While this is frequently done without any proper conflict of laws analysis,[43] courts which have reviewed the issue properly have in general applied Article V(2)(a) of the New York Convention. This approach, and the underlying rationale of applying the national law, are well illustrated by two Italian cases.[44]

1-33 The New York Convention clearly and pertinently distinguishes between the law applicable to the issue of arbitrability and the law governing the validity of the arbitration agreement. While the latter is primarily submitted to the choice

[42] See, e.g., Belgium, Tribunal de Commerce, Brussels, 20 September 1999, *Matermaco SA v. PPM Cranes Inc et al*, XXV YBCA 673 (2000) 675; Switzerland, Tribunal Fédéral, 28 April 1992, XVIII YBCA 143 (1993) 146.

[43] In relation to U.S. see Gary Born, *International Commercial Arbitration* (Kluwer 2001) 244.

[44] Corte di Appello Genoa, 7 May 1994, *Fincantieri - Cantieri Navali Italiani SpA and Oto Melara SpA v. Ministry of Defence, Armament and Supply Directorate of Iraq, Republic of Iraq*, 4 Rev. Arb *505* (1994), XXI YBCA (1996), specifically para 13:

> "The answer must be sought in Italian law, according to the jurisprudential principle that, when an objection for foreign arbitration is raised in court proceedings concerning a contractual dispute, the arbitrability of the dispute must be ascertained according to Italian law as this question directly affects jurisdiction, and the court seized of the action can only deny jurisdiction on the basis of its own legal system. This also corresponds to the principles expressed in Arts. II and V of the [New York Convention]. Hence, the answer to the question [of arbitrability] can only be that the dispute was not arbitrable due to [Italian embargo legislation]."

The other case is Corte di Appello Bologna, 21 December 1991, XVIII YBCA 422 (1993), reversing the decision of the Court of First Instance, 18 July 1987, XVII YBCA 534 (1992). The case considered the arbitrability of disputes relating to EC Competition law:

> Art. II(3) … becomes even clearer if … read in conjunction with Art. V(2)(a) ..., which subordinates the efficacy of the arbitral award to the requirement that its subject matter be capable of settlement by arbitration, according to the law of the State where recognition and enforcement are sought. … It would be totally useless to recognize the jurisdiction of the arbitrator if the award, when rendered, could in no way be enforced in the legal system of the court which has jurisdiction.

of the parties and in the absence of such a choice to the law of the place of arbitration, each national court determines the arbitrability of a dispute according to its own law.[45]

1-34 Of course, the New York Convention is primarily directed to courts and not to tribunals. It is unclear to what extent the Convention and national laws bind an international arbitration tribunal. It should not be surprising that the practice of arbitration tribunals concerning the issue of arbitrability varies considerably.[46] In the majority of cases, however, tribunals determine the arbitrability of a dispute on the basis of the provisions of the place of arbitration (*lex loci arbitri*):[47] the justification seems to be that the in respect of the *lex loci arbitri* the applicable rules and standards are easy to identify, and fishing expeditions are eliminated. Moreover, in other cases, arbitrators have avoided a definitive decision where the disputes were arbitrable according to all possible applicable laws.[48]

1-35 There is an alternative view that maintains that as arbitration tribunals are not organs of a particular state's legal order, they should determine arbitrability on the basis of a genuinely international public policy.[49] The main thrust of this approach is that arbitrators derive their power from the disputing parties and they are to be guided by the parties' legitimate expectations.[50] Whilst this view is intellectually convincing, it may lead to unwanted consequences in cases where the law of the place of arbitration contains a narrower concept of arbitrability than the "genuinely international public policy". In those cases, necessary measures of support from the courts of the place of arbitration may not be

[45] H. Arfazadeh, "Arbitrability under the New York Convention: The *Lex Fori* Revisited", 17 *Arb Int'l* (2001) 73 at 80. See also Lew, Mistelis & Kröll, *supra* note 8 at paras 9-16 to 9-18. See also Brekoulakis, Chapter 2 infra, paras 2-58 et seq. and Di Pietro, Chapter 5 infra, para 5-17 et seq.

[46] See M. Blessing, "Arbitrability of Intellectual Property Disputes", 12 *Arb Int'l* (1996) 191 at 192 and J. Lew, "Intellectual Property Disputes and Arbitration, Final Report of the Commission on International Arbitration", 9 *ICC Arbitration Bulletin* (1998) 37 at 41 et seq.

[47] See, e.g., ICC case no. 6162, *Consultant v. Egyptian Local Authority*, XVII YBCA 153 (1992); ICC case no. 4604, X YBCA 973 (1985) 975; Partial Award ICC case no. 8420, XXV YBCA 328 (2000), 330 et seq.

[48] ICC case no. 6149, XX YBCA 41(1995) 144; for the tendency of ICC tribunals to ascertain the arbitrability of a dispute according to all laws concerned, see E. Schwartz, "The Domain of Arbitration and Issues of Arbitrability: The view from the ICC", *ICSID Rev-FILJ* (1994) 17 at 27.

[49] Fouchard Gaillard Goldman, see *supra* note 10, para 559. See also Lew, Mistelis & Kröll, *supra* note 8 at paras 9-30 et seq.

[50] See Pamboukis, Chapter 7, infra, particularly, paras 7-5 et seq., 7-31 et seq.

available and the award may be open to challenge. In this respect, it is noteworthy that many of the relevant arbitrability rules are only applicable to domestic arbitration; accordingly, the fewer connections the dispute has with a country the greater the likelihood that the considerations underlying the rules are not applicable to the case.[51]

1-36 Some authors argue that a tribunal should additionally consider arbitrability according to the law of the probable enforcement state.[52] This is on the basis that enforcement of an award can be resisted if the dispute is not arbitrable according to the law of the state of enforcement.[53] Nevertheless, tribunals have been reluctant to deny jurisdiction on the basis that the dispute is not arbitrable under the law of the possible place of enforcement or even another interested country:[54] while enforcement may not be possible in the country originally envisaged, assets may be available in a different country.

1-37 Reference to domestic law, especially the *lex fori* of the court that has to make an arbitrability determination, should not lead to putting excessive emphasis on *lex fori*. Pamboukis[55] and Brekoulakis[56] make the point very convincingly in their chapters of this book. Perales further suggests that a higher level of predictability is needed and hence the UNCITRAL Arbitration Working Group should consider arbitrability in their future work.[57]

1-38 It is worth exploring whether there is a genuine transnational concept of arbitrability. Arbitration has achieved a level of acceptance and uniformity that it is timely to formulate a process of identifying arbitrability rules, written or unwritten. There is also a substantial body of arbitral decisions as well as a

[51] See W. Laurence Craig, William W Park & Jan Paulsson, *ICC Arbitration* (Oceana 2000) para 5-07, with reference to a number of court decisions where rules restraining arbitrability in the domestic context were considered to be not applicable to international cases.

[52] Fouchard Gaillard Goldman, see *supra* note 10, para 559; see also ICC Rules Article 35; for a detailed discussion of whether an arbitration tribunal having its seat in Geneva should take into account the provisions of the *lex causae*, see Partial Award ICC case no. 8420, XXV YBCA 328 (2000) 330 et seq.

[53] See New York Convention, Article V(2)(a); Model Law, Article 36(1)(b)(i).

[54] See, e.g., ICC case no. 2476, 104 Clunet 936 (1977) 937; ICC case no. 4604, X YBCA 973 (1985) 975.

[55] Pamboukis, Chapter 7, infra.

[56] Brekoulakis, Chapter 6, infra.

[57] Chapter 14 infra at 14-33. See also Report of UNCITRAL on the work of its 39th session, 19 June to 7 July 2006, General Assembly Official Records sixty-first session, Supplement no. 17, A/61/17, no. 183.

number of national provisions that could be used as a starting point for such an exercise. The basic tenet of a transnational concept of arbitrability is the fact that unless there are strong domestic interests (which is arguably the case mostly in domestic disputes), arbitration tribunals ought to be allowed to determine their own jurisdiction. Ultimately, national courts have the right to review the award at a later stage and it would be unhelpful for tribunals to attempt to fortune-tell what national courts may later decide!

4. National and International Substantive Rules on Arbitrability

1-39 Over the years, several issues have been identified as matters which may, under very specific circumstances, be considered inarbitrable. Some of these themes, such as family law, personal status, criminal offences carrying sentences restrictive of personal freedom, are universally accepted as inarbitrable. Many other matters are borderline, and in developed arbitral jurisdictions are considered arbitrable while in some states may be inarbitrable. In the second part of this book, several such areas have been identified and discussed.

1-40 Carbonneau discusses in Chapter 8 general rules on arbitrability in U.S. Law and focuses on the practice of the Supreme Court and on the example of Labour Arbitration; he specifically alerts readers of the danger associated with the proposed U.S. Arbitration Fairness Act.

1-41 Liebscher, in Chapter 9, explores the likelihood of synergies between insolvency and arbitration. Insolvency may impact on both the validity of arbitration agreements and the arbitrability of disputes involving insolvent parties. His comparative survey identifies where synergy may work and where no such likelihood exists.

1-42 Park, in Chapter 10, focuses on the issue of arbitrability and tax, a topic which increasingly becomes the subject matter of investment arbitrations. He provides a thorough analysis of relevant arbitral practice and identifies problems arbitrators may face in the future.

1-43 Mourre, in Chapter 11, looks at arbitration and criminal law. He points out the relevant issues of jurisdiction and arbitrability and explores specific issues of procedure, illegality and the need for more arbitral self-regulation in the future. There is a delicate balance to be drawn in this regard and examples of good court practice are highlighted.

1-44 Lew, in Chapter 12, discuses Competition laws as potential limits to the authority of arbitrators. He particularly looks at arbitration and competition law in the EU and the U.S., but he also presents differing scenarios for arbitration tribunals as well as the nature of arbitral decision-making.

1-45 Mantakou, in Chapter 13, focuses on arbitrability and intellectual property disputes. Her particular stand is to revisit the work of a related ICC Report produced in the late 1990s, and to identify what has happened in the last ten years. She distinguishes between intellectual property rights requiring national action and restriction-free rights.

1-46 Perales, in Chapter 14, explores the arbitrability of intra-corporate disputes. She employs comparative methodology to discuss a number of recent statutory and jurisprudential developments. She identifies the different national approaches and calls for more international work towards uniformity and predictability.

1-47 Bantekas, in Chapter 15, discusses arbitrability in finance and banking, both domestic and international. He particularly refers to the existence of general rules and principles and their application, before turning his attention to securities transactions, selected financial arrangements, corporate disputes and matters arising out of banking activities (including issues of Islamic finance and consumer disputes). He concludes that there are different trends in developed and developing countries.

1-48 Kröll, in Chapter 16, focuses on the "arbitrability" of disputes arising from commercial representation. He specifically looks at distribution agreements, commercial agency and identifies different approaches in national legal systems but also in arbitral practice and provides a critical appraisal of different possible approaches.

1-49 The discussion of the various substantive rules on arbitrability reveals a clear tension: while it seems that many systems have been liberalised over the last thirty or forty years, there still remain some areas of controversy. On the one hand, national legal systems with developed and confident arbitration practice are liberal and lenient in their approach of the issue of arbitrability. On the other hand, countries which manifest a scepticism towards the private sector and the establishment and development of arbitration resort to "public policy" and introduce extensive restrictions to arbitration practice.

1-50 The harsh reality is that in cases where there are no real "public policy" reasons, or legitimate restrictions as to what disputes may be referred to arbitration, it is inevitable that disputing parties will seek to identify a convenient venue to place their arbitration. There will always be jurisdictions which are more favourable to arbitration with the consequence that arbitral forum shopping would be a more frequent occurrence in years to come. Arbitral forum shopping is not a new phenomenon nor a negative one: competition amongst national regulators of arbitration is potentially a very positive development. If arbitration is the alternative to national courts, as it is, it will have to be market driven and prepared to respond to the legitimate expectations of the users of the process.

1-51 Another positive feature of the competition amongst regulators could well be the increased transnationalisation of the issue of arbitrability, the formulation of soft law rules dealing with what justifiable restrictions may exist to the authority of arbitrators to deal with disputes referred to them.

Stavros L. Brekoulakis[*]

CHAPTER 2

ON ARBITRABILITY: PERSISTING MISCONCEPTIONS AND NEW AREAS OF CONCERN

1. INTRODUCTION

2-1 More than twenty years after the seminal decision of the U.S. Supreme Court in *Mitsubishi Motors Corp v. Soler Chrysler Plymouth Inc*,[1] it can safely be argued that the argument for the arbitrability of the vast majority of commercial disputes has largely been won.[2] Nevertheless, the subject of arbitrability continues to attract the interest of scholarly writing as the discussion on the matter is far from settled yet.[3]

* LLB (Athens), LLM (KCL), PhD (QMUL), Advocate; Lecturer in International Dispute Resolution, Centre of Commercial Law Studies, Queen Mary, University London. I would like to thank Dr Stefan Kröll, in particular, for the very useful discussion we had on an earlier draft of this paper. Many of his comments have been incorporated here. My thanks are also extended to Maarten Draye, Associate Hanotiau & van den Berg, who critically read this paper.

1 473 U.S. 614 S Ct 3346 (1985) (U.S. Supreme Court, 2 July 1985).

2 *Cf* K. Youssef, in Chapter 3 *infra*, who goes as far as proclaiming "The Death of Inarbitrability". *Cf* however, T. Carbonneau, in Chapter 8, *infra*, in "Conclusions", who draws the attention to a possible backlash against arbitration coming from the U.S. and a change in power configurations in the U.S. Congress. This backlash would restrict the scope of arbitrability, especially in the areas of employment contracts and consumer transactions.

3 See for example articles H. Arfazadeh, "Arbitrability Under the New York Convention: the Lex Fori Revisited", 17 *Arb. Int'l* (2001) 73; M. Blessing "Arbitrability of Intellectual Property Disputes", 12 *Arb. Int'l* (1996) 191; K.-H. Böckstiegel, "Public Policy and Arbitrability" in P. Sanders (ed), *ICCA Congress Series No.3* (Deventer: Kluwer Law & Taxation 1987) at 177; G. Born, *International Commercial Arbitration: Commentary and Materials,* (2nd ed, Kluwer 2001) Chapter 3 (D), at 343 et seq; T. Carbonneau, The *Law and Practice of Arbitration* (2nd ed, Juris 2007) para 23-26; T. Carbonneau & Janson "Cartesian Logic and Frontier Politics: French and American Concepts of Arbitrability", 2 *Tul. Int'l & Comp. L.* (1994) 193; Fouchard, Gaillard & Goldman, *On International Commercial Arbitration*, E. Gaillard & J. Savage (eds)

L Mistelis & S Brekoulakis (eds), Arbitrability: International & Comparative Perspectives, 19-45

2-2 While the issue of what disputes are arbitrable has now become less of a problem, some basic misconceptions about the subject of arbitrability still persist. In particular, two areas on arbitrability require further analysis.

2-3 First, the rationale behind inarbitrability and the role of public policy in particular. Despite the remarkable expansion of the scope of arbitrability in the last two decades, the prevailing view is still that public policy considerations underpin inarbitrability.[4] The paper argues that in the limited types of disputes that are still considered inarbitrable, inarbitrability relates to the natural limitations of arbitration as a dispute resolution mechanism of consensual character rather than to public policy. The latter, as argued here, is effectively irrelevant to the discussion of arbitrability.

2-4 Secondly, the sanctions of inarbitrability, and especially whether it has any impact on the validity of an arbitration agreement. Here the prevailing view is that inarbitrability of the subject matter of an arbitration agreement renders the arbitration agreement invalid.[5] This paper argues that inarbitrability is an issue concerning the jurisdiction of an arbitral tribunal rather than the validity of an arbitration agreement. This discussion has important practical relevance. In fact, as will be shown, it pertains to the much debatable matter of which forum, national courts or arbitral tribunals, should have priority in determining whether a dispute is arbitrable or not.

(1999), para 532 et seq; B. Hanotiau, "What law governs the issue of arbitrability?", 12(4) *Arb. Int'l* (1996) 391; B. Hanotiau, "The Law Applicable to Arbitrability", in A. van den Berg (ed), *ICCA Congress Series No.9*, (Kluwer 1999) at 146; B. Hanotiau, "L'arbitrabilité", in *Recueil des Cours - Collected Courses of The Hague Academy of International Law*, (2002) Tome 296, at 165-166 (The Hague Boston London, Martinus Nijhoff Publishers, 2003); A. Kirry, "Arbitrability: Current Trends in Europe", 12 *Arb. Int'l* (1996) 373; J. McLaughlin, "Arbitrability: Currents Trends in the United States", 59 *Alb. L. Rev.* (1996) 905; P. Level, "L'arbitrabilité" 2 *Rev. Arb.* (1992) 213; J. Lew, L. Mistelis & S. Kröll, *Comparative International Commercial Arbitration*, (Kluwer 2003), Chapter 9; J. Paulsson, "Arbitrability, Still Through a Glass Darkly", in *Arbitration in the Next Decade (ICC Bulletin, Special Supplement 1999)* at 95; Redfern & Hunter (with N. Blackaby & C. Partasides), *Law and Practice of International Commercial Arbitration,* (4th ed, Sweet & Maxwell 2004), para 3-13 et seq; A. Rogers, "Arbitrability", 10 *Arb. Int'l* (1994) at 263; E. Schwartz, "The Domain of Arbitration and Issues of Arbitrability: The View from the ICC", 9(17) *ICSID Rev-FILJ* (1994) at 27.

4 See section A(a) below, and *supra* notes 9 and 10 in particular.

5 See section B below, and *supra* note 33 in particular.

2. THE RATIONALE BEHIND INARBITRABILITY

2.1 The limited relevance of public policy

2-5 The argument for arbitrability is now won principally because a series of court decisions in various jurisdictions demonstrated that arbitrators should not be excluded from applying national rules of public policy nature.[6] In their decisions, national courts at the highest level clearly accepted that arbitrators might not only examine, but also apply national provisions of public policy.[7]

2-6 Notwithstanding the above decisions, the view that inarbitrability is founded upon public policy persistently prevails in international arbitration.[8] More

[6] In the U.S., *Mitsubishi Motors Corp v. Soler Chrysler Plymouth Inc*, *supra* note 1 (with regard to anti-competition claims); in France, CA Paris, 29 March 1991, *Ganz v. Nationale des Chemins de Fer Tunisiens (SNCFT)*, (1991) Rev. Arb. 478, (with regard to fraud allegations) – with note L. Idot; also CA Paris, 19 May 1993 *Labinal v. Mors*, (1993) Rev. Arb. 645, (with regard to anti-competition claims) – with note Jarrosson; in England, CA, *Fiona Trust & Holding Corporation and Others v. Privalov and Others*, [2007] 2 Lloyd's Rep. 267 (with regard to fraud allegations) confirmed by the House of Lords, *Premium Nafta Products Limited (20th Defendant) and others v. Fili Shipping Company Limited (14th Claimant) and others*, [2007] UKHL 40; in Switzerland, Federal Tribunal, 23 June 1992, *Fincantieri-Cantieri Navali Italiiani and Oto Melara v. M and arbitration tribunal*, (1995) XX YBCA 766 (with regard to claims arising out of illegal activities); in the context of the European Union, ECJ, 1 June 1999, C- 126/97, *Eco Swiss China Time v. Benetton International*, [1999] ECR I 3055 (with regard to anti-competition claims).

[7] In *Ganz v. SNCFT*, *ibid*, the court held that:

> in international arbitration, an arbitrator [...] is entitled to apply the principles and rules of public policy and to grant redress in the event that those principles and rules have been disregarded

In, *Fincantieri-Cantieri Navali Italiiani and Oto Melara v. M and arbitration tribunal*, *ibid*, the court stressed that:

> The fact that the said claim affects public policy would not suffice, in itself, to rule out the arbitrability of the dispute [...] Arbitrability cannot be denied for the only reason that mandatory provisions of law or a given material public policy make the claim null and void or its execution impossible

[8] See for example, Redfern & Hunter, *supra* note 3, para 3-13, who argue: "Whether or not a particular type of dispute is "arbitrable" under a given law is in essence a matter of public policy for that law to determine." In the same vein, K.-H. Böckstiegel, *supra* note 3 at 177 et seq.; Y. Fortier, "Arbitrability of Disputes" in *Global Reflections on International Law, Commerce and Dispute Resolution, Liber Amicorum in honour of Robert Briner*, G. Aksen, K.-H. Böckstiegel, M. Mustill, P.M. Patocchi & A.-M. Whitesell (eds) (ICC 2005) at 276; Lew, Mistelis & Kröll, *supra note* 3, para 9-2; Fouchard, Gaillald & Goldman, *supra* note 3 at 332-333; Carbonneau &

importantly, with the exception of some arbitration laws that define arbitrability by reference to "economic interest"[9] or "property",[10] many arbitration laws still delineate inarbitrability on the basis of criteria related to public policy.[11]

2-7 Moreover, in the U.S., the suggested Arbitration Fairness Act of 2007 and Fair Arbitration Act of 2007[12] constitute the latest legislative effort to severely

---

Janson, *supra* note 3 at 195 et seq; *cf*, however, Kirry, *supra* note 3 at 374, who argues that the role of public policy in arbitrability is diminishing; the same D. Cohen, *Arbitrage et Société*, tome 229 (LGDJ 1993), para 238 et seq.

9 German ZPO Art. 1030

10 Swiss Private International Law Act (PILA) Art. 177

11 See for example, arbitration laws that define inarbitrability on the basis that the dispute is "permissible to compromise" (Belgian Judicial Code Art. 1676(1)), or that the legal consequences which "the parties cannot freely dispose" (The Netherlands Arbitration Act Art. 1020(3)) or that the rights in question "cannot be disposed by the parties" (Italian Code of Civil Procedure Art. 806 and Greek Code of Civil Procedure Art. 867). See also, French Civil Code 2060

> One may not enter into arbitration agreements in matters of status and capacity of the persons, in those relating to divorce and judicial separation or on controversies concerning public bodies and institutions and more generally in all matters in which public policy is concerned. However, categories of public institutions of an industrial or commercial character may be authorized by decree to enter into arbitration agreements.

In Singapore arbitrability is also defined by reference to public policy, see Singapore's International Arbitration Act Art. 11 providing that

> Any dispute which the parties have agreed to submit to arbitration under an arbitration agreement may be determined by arbitration unless it is contrary to public policy to do so.

In China, administrative disputes, disputes over personal rights, labour disputes and disputes concerning agricultural projects are excluded from arbitration (Chinese Arbitration Law 1995 Art. 2, 3 and 77). *Cf* also the A/CN.9WG.II/WP.150 Annotated Provisional Agenda (9 July 2008) of the UNCITRAL working group on the revision of UNICTRAL Arbitration Rules (available at:
http://daccessdds.un.org/doc/UNDOC/LTD/V08/554/48/PDF/V0855448.pdf?OpenElement) para 10:

> The topic of arbitrability was said to be an important question, which should also be given priority. It was said that it would be for the Working Group to consider whether arbitrable matters could be defined in a generic manner, possibly with an illustrative list of such matters, or whether the legislative provision to be prepared in respect of arbitrability should identify the topics that were not arbitrable. It was suggested that studying the question of arbitrability in the context of immovable property, unfair competition and insolvency could provide useful guidance for States. It was cautioned however that the topic of arbitrability was a matter raising questions of public policy, which was notoriously difficult to define in a uniform manner, and that providing a pre-defined list of arbitrable matters could unnecessarily restrict a State's ability to meet certain public policy concerns that were likely to evolve over time.

restrict the scope of arbitrability on public policy considerations. The above drafts would amend the U.S. Federal Arbitration Act to invalidate any pre-dispute arbitration agreement requiring arbitration of an employment, consumer or franchise dispute, or any dispute arising under any statute "intended to protect civil rights or to regulate contracts or transactions between parties of unequal bargaining power".

2-8 It is still too early to safely say whether the Arbitration Fairness Act and the Fair Arbitration Act will eventually pass through, and whether they will trigger similar legislation in other jurisdictions. Nevertheless, it seems that the argument for arbitrability has not been won after all. Inarbitrability forces driven by public policy concerns are bound to revise the subject in the near future. Public policy remains defiantly pertinent to the discussion on arbitrability.

2-9 Thus, it is entirely timely to look into the reasons that keep the discussion of inarbitrability entangled with public policy. Why is it that arbitration is still perceived as not to be well equipped to address specific types of public policy disputes? There are three different possible types of objections against the arbitrability of public policy disputes

2-10 First, there are concerns that have due process implications. Specific characteristics of arbitration proceedings have often been mentioned as reasons related to inarbitrability of public policy disputes. Less intensive fact-finding process and less rigorous evidential proceedings, for example. In *Alexander v. Gardner-Denver,* the U.S. Supreme court noted that:

> Moreover, the fact-finding process in arbitration usually is not equivalent to judicial fact-finding. The record of the arbitration proceedings is not as

[12] Arbitration Fairness Act of 2007, H.R. 3010, S. 1782 (110th Congress, 1st Session) (July 12, 2007); Fair Arbitration Act of 2007, S. 1135 (110th Congress, 1st Session) (April 17, 2007). Arbitration Fairness Act of 2007 declares that no pre-dispute arbitration agreement shall be valid or enforceable if it requires arbitration of: (1) an employment, consumer, or franchise dispute, or (2) a dispute arising under any statute intended to protect civil rights or to regulate contracts or transactions between parties of unequal bargaining power. It declares, further, that the validity or enforceability of an agreement to arbitrate shall be determined by a court, under federal law, rather than an arbitrator, irrespective of whether the party resisting arbitration challenges the arbitration agreement specifically or in conjunction with other terms of the contract containing such agreement. It also exempts arbitration provisions in collective bargaining agreements from this Act. The latest news on that front is that on the 15th July 2008 the House Subcommittee on Commercial and Administrative Law voted to report favourably the Arbitration Fairness Act of 2007 (H.R. 3010) to the full Judiciary Committee. See the full text at http://www.govtrack.us/congress/billtext.xpd?bill=h110-3010 (last visited 3 September 2008).

complete; the usual rules of evidence do not apply; and rights and procedures common to civil trials, such as discovery, compulsory process, cross-examination, and testimony under oath, are often severely limited or unavailable.[13]

2-11 Or the limited or lack of reasoning of the awards. Justice Douglas, dissenting in *Scherk v. Alberto-Culver*,[14] pointed out that:

> An arbitral award can be made without explication of reasons and without development of a record, so that the arbitrator's conception of our statutory requirement may be absolutely incorrect yet functionally unreviewable, even when the arbitrator seeks to apply our law.[15]

2-12 Or, the fact that there is usually no appeal process in arbitration combined with the limited review of arbitral awards by national courts. Justice Stevens, dissenting in *Mitsubishi v. Soler* stated characteristically:

> Arbitration awards are only reviewable for manifest disregard of the law [...] and the rudimentary procedures which make arbitration so desirable in the context of a private dispute often mean that the record is so inadequate that the arbitrator's decision is virtually unreviewable. Despotic decision-making of this kind is fine for parties who are willing to agree in advance to settle for a best approximation of the correct result in order to resolve quickly and inexpensively any contractual dispute that may arise in an ongoing commercial relationship. Such informality, however, is simply unacceptable when every error may have devastating consequences for important businesses in our national economy and may undermine their ability to compete in world markets.[16]

13 415 U.S. 36, 94 S Ct 1011, 39 L.Ed.2d 147 (1974). The same view was taken by the U.S. Supreme Court in *Bernhardt v. Polygraphic Co.,* 350 U.S. 198, 203, 76 S Ct 273, 276, 100 L.Ed. 199 (1956) and in *Wilko v. Swan,* 346 U.S., at 435-437, 74 S Ct, at 186-188.

14 417 U.S. 506 (U.S. Supreme Court 1974).

15 *Ibid*, at 533.

16 *Supra* note 1 at 657-658. *Cf* also the preamble of the text of the bill Arbitration Fairness Act of 2007, *supra* note 13, as it was written by its sponsor and submitted to the House for consideration:

> S. 2(5) Mandatory arbitration undermines the development of public law for civil rights and consumer rights, because there is no meaningful judicial review of arbitrators' decisions. With the knowledge that their rulings will not be seriously examined by a court

2-13 Finally, the fact that arbitration proceedings are usually private and confidential. The U.S. Supreme Court in *Merrill Lynch* in rebutting an argument forwarded by Merrill Lynch that the public adjudication of disputes may jeopardise the confidence of the investors and the market in general, noted in regard to the private character of arbitration:

> There is no explanation of why a judicial proceeding, even though public, would prevent lessening of investor confidence. It is difficult to understand why *muffling a grievance in the cloakroom of arbitration* would undermine confidence in the market. To the contrary, for the generally sophisticated investing public, market confidence may tend to be restored *in the light of impartial public court adjudication.*[17] (emphasis added)

2-14 It is true that arbitration proceedings have procedural characteristics different from national litigation. However, this does not make arbitration a *compromised dispute resolution mechanism* in terms of due process, which is unfit to deal with public policy disputes. Otherwise, if that was the case, all disputes – public policy and non public policy ones – should be excluded from arbitration altogether. Even pure commercial disputes require uncompromised procedural safeguards. Thousands of "private disputes" arise every year, which *prima facie* have no public policy implications. However, they are collectively worth billions of dollars and, in fact, they have a far-reaching impact on economy and society that goes beyond the parties to a private contract. This is why the protection of the fundamental principle of due process is accorded to any type of dispute, be that a private or a public policy one. The European Convention of Human Rights Art. 6 is not limited to public policy disputes.[18] Similarly, parties to non public policy disputes are not permitted to waive fundamental due process guarantees.[19]

> applying current law, arbitrators enjoy near complete freedom to ignore the law and even their own rules.
>
> (6) Mandatory arbitration is a poor system for protecting civil rights and consumer rights because it is not transparent. While the American civil justice system features publicly accountable decision makers who generally issue written decisions that are widely available to the public, arbitration offers none of these features.

17 *Merrill Lynch, Pierce, Fenner & Smith, Inc. v. Ware,* 414 U.S. 117, 136, 94 S Ct 383, 394, 38 L.Ed.2d 348 (1973), at 136.

18 See Lew, Mistelis & Kröll, *supra* note 3, paras 5-54 et seq. for a detailed review of the matter of application of basic human rights and due process, in particular, to arbitration.

19 In the *Dutco* case (French Cour de cassation, 7 January 1992, *Siemens AG/BKMI Industrieanlagen v. Dutco Construction Company*, (1993) XVII YBCA, p.140), for example, the

2-15 The conclusion here is that arbitration, despite its unique procedural character, meets all due process standards necessary to safeguard rigorous and uncompromised proceedings.

2-16 A second, and arguably more pervasive, set of reservations relates to arbitrators as *decision makers* rather than to the procedural characteristics of arbitration proceedings. The *ability* of the arbitrators to correctly apply public policy rules seems to be under question.[20]

2-17 In another oft-cited extract, the U.S. Second Circuit in *American Safety Equipment Corp. v. J.P. Maguire & Co.*[21] noted that as

> issues of war and peace are too important to be vested in the generals, ... decisions as to antitrust regulation of business are too important to be lodged in arbitrators chosen from the business community-particularly those from a foreign community that has had no experience with or exposure to our law and values.[22]

2-18 Whereas, In *University Life Insurance Co. v. Unimarc Ltd.*, Judge Posner wrote:

> [Federal anti-trust issues] are considered to be at once too difficult to be decided competently by arbitrators-who are not judges, and often not even lawyers-and too important to be decided otherwise than by competent tribunals.[23]

2-19 More pertinently, it is believed that arbitrators are unfit to address issues arising out of the economic power disparity between corporations and specific social groups, such as consumers or employees. In this respect, consumers and employees are often portrayed in simplistic, if not demagogic terms, as economically weak, inexperienced or even commercially naïve parties, who are

---

dispute that arose out of a consortium agreement in the context of a construction contract had no public policy connotations. However, the Cour de cassation held that the parties cannot waive fundamental procedural safeguards, such as the principle of the equality of the parties in arbitral proceedings.

20 Here note that public policy rules will be understood in a wide sense, including mandatory rules.

21 391 F. 2d 821 (2d Cir. 1968).

22 *Ibid*, at 826-827.

23 699 F. 2d 846 (CA 1983) at 850-851.

coerced by powerful and sophisticated corporations to sign adhesion arbitration agreements, and relinquish their right to resort to a national judge.

2-20 The argument implies that arbitrators, as private judges, are by nature in alliance with the interests of private corporations. Thus, arbitrators are necessarily unfit to take into account, or even acknowledge, the interests of economically weak parties.

2-21 It is worth looking into the preamble of the text of the bill of 2007 Arbitration Fairness Act[24] as it was written by its sponsor and submitted to the House for consideration:

> "Sec.2- Findings: The Congress finds the following: […]
>
> (2) A series of United States Supreme Court decisions have changed the meaning of the Act so that it now extends to disputes between parties of greatly disparate economic power, such as consumer disputes and employment disputes. As a result, a large and rapidly growing number of corporations are requiring millions of consumers and employees to give up their right to have disputes resolved by a judge or jury, and instead submit their claims to binding arbitration.
>
> (3) Most consumers and employees have little or no meaningful option whether to submit their claims to arbitration. Few people realize, or understand the importance of the deliberately fine print that strips them of rights; and because entire industries are adopting these clauses, people increasingly have no choice but to accept them. They must often give up their rights as a condition of having a job, getting necessary medical care, buying a car, opening a bank account, getting a credit card, and the like. Often times, they are not even aware that they have given up their rights.
>
> (4) Private arbitration companies are sometimes under great pressure to devise systems that favor the corporate repeat players who decide whether those companies will receive their lucrative business."

2-22 There are, thus, apparent concerns that arbitrators, as private adjudicators, are not necessarily suitable to reveal the real meaning of public policy statutory provisions, which can properly be applied by national judges only. The private viewpoint that arbitrators are expected to adopt towards a dispute, automatically

[24] See *supra* note 12.

renders them inappropriate to apply national rules set out to protect society or a group of people larger than the parties that have instructed the arbitrators.

2-23 This argument is based on the assumption that the policy behind consumer or labour legislation, for example, set out to protect specific social groups (i.e. consumers or employees) and may only be implemented by a forum that is *biased towards those social groups*. In other words, the materialisation of the objective of public policy legislation requires a forum that is predisposed, namely a forum that takes a public rather than a private perspective to the dispute.

2-24 Indeed, in *Barrentine v. Arkansas-Best Freight System,*[25] it was noted with regard to the application of national labour legislation that:

> Because the arbitrator is required to effectuate the intent of the parties, rather than to enforce the statute, he may issue a ruling that is inimical to the public policies underlying the [US Fair Labor Standards Act], thus depriving an employee of protected statutory rights.[26]

2-25 However, it is questionable whether the above assumption is correct. First, it would be difficult to readily accept that all national judges, as opposed to all arbitrators, are positively predisposed to specific social groups, such as consumers, for example.

2-26 Second, and more importantly, public policy rules are not drafted in *neutral* moral and social terms. Rather, the public policy objective underpinning the relevant rules is *clearly reflected in the wording* of the relevant provisions, in the form of specific conditions. For example, a provision drafted to protect the interests of employees will typically provide that for an employer to terminate an employment contract, proper notice and compensation has to be given to the

25 *Barrentine v. Arkansas-Best Freight System, Inc.*, 450 U.S. 728, 101 S Ct 1427, 67 L.Ed.2d 641 (1981), at 744-45.

26 Similarly, in *Alexander v. Gardner-Denver Co.*, 415 U.S. 36, 94 S Ct 1011, L.Ed.2d 147 (1974), at 39:

> Arbitral procedures, while well suited to the resolution of contractual disputes, make arbitration a comparatively inappropriate forum for the final resolution of rights created by Title VII. This conclusion rests first on the special role of the arbitrator, whose task is to effectuate the intent of the parties rather than the requirements of enacted legislation.

employee. The amount of the compensation and the minimum period of the notice required are also provided in detail in the relevant provision.[27]

2-27 Thus, the objective of such a provision, which is set out to protect the interests of employees and which reflects valid public policy considerations, is achieved as soon as the conditions of 'compensation' and 'specific notice' are met. The materialisation of the public policy objection does not depend on the external condition that the decision maker would be favourably predisposed towards employees. Otherwise the relevant provision would have been dangerously ill drafted.

2-28 In general, the proper application of public policy rules does not depend on the whims of the person applying the provision. For the public policy purpose to be attained, the decision maker is not required to be biased; they are required to *correctly* apply the relevant rules. In principle, rules can be correctly applied by both a person hired by a state (i.e. a judge) and a person hired by parties (i.e. an arbitrator). Therefore, it can be argued, that allegiance to a national state is not a condition precedent for the correct application of a public policy provision.

2-29 This is not to argue that the question of who applies a legal rule is irrelevant. A decision maker does not mechanically apply the rules simply going through a checklist. The application of a legal provision requires the judge or the arbitrator to perform a complicated analysis, which to some extent is subjective. For example, the analysis of whether an agreement would restrict competition or not by reference to EC Art. 81(1) seems to provide the decision maker with plenty of discretion. However, this analysis as well as the final determination on the issue would have to be performed by reference to facts, evidence, and possibly, previous relevant case law, rather than by reference to abstract principles or to the personal beliefs of the decision maker.[28]

2-30 Eventually, any discretion allowed by legal provisions to a decision maker cannot overturn their original drafting purpose, which is reflected in the wording of the rules. It can thus be argued that the fact that arbitrators, as opposed to

[27] See for example, in England, the Employment Rights Act 1996 s. 86 et seq.

[28] Unless the parties in arbitration have expressly authorised the arbitrator to decide *ex aequo et bono*, in which case too the decision may not violate public policy, see Lew, Mistelis & Kröll, *supra* note 3, para 18-91.

national judges, may take a private rather than public perspective to the dispute, does not make them, as a matter of principle, unfit to apply public policy rules.

2-31 The third area of concern pertains to whether arbitrators will *ever actually apply* the public policy or mandatory provisions of a national law, rather than to whether arbitrators *are fit* to apply them in accordance with their drafting purpose.

2-32 This objection is possibly the most valid one. The arbitration dealing with the resolution of a dispute relating to the public policy of a particular country may well take place in a different country. Thus, the question here is whether the arbitrators would have the duty to take the public policy rules of the former country into account. Here, it is feared that choice-of-forum clauses operating in tandem with choice-of-law clauses can be used as a vehicle for the parties to escape the public policy of a specific state. This is an objection based on a typical *Mitsubishi v. Soler* case scenario.[29]

2-33 An obvious possible response here would be that, in principle, arbitrators are not bound to apply the rules of any other country than the one whose rules the parties have expressly agreed on.[30] One could also refer to the well-known "second look", advanced by the *Mitsubishi v. Soler* in this context: national courts of the country whose public policy provisions are at stake will have the chance to examine whether the award has actually disregarded their public policy at the stage of the enforcement.[31]

2-34 Arguably, this is not the most satisfactory answer, and in this respect, the *Mitsubishi* dictum has been validly criticised on two grounds: first, it is not at all

[29] Where the dispute arose in connection with the U.S. Sherman Act, but the seat of the arbitration was agreed to be in Japan, while the law applicable to the merits of the dispute was agreed to be the law of Switzerland.

[30] As the U.S. Supreme Court in *Mitsubishi v. Soler, supra* note 1 at 637 noted

> the international arbitral tribunal owes no prior allegiance to the legal norms of particular states; hence, it has no direct obligation to vindicate their statutory dictates. The tribunal, however, is bound to effectuate the intentions of the parties. Where the parties have agreed that the arbitral body is to decide a defined set of claims which includes, as in these cases, those arising from the application of American antitrust law, the tribunal therefore should be bound to decide that dispute in accord with the national law giving rise to the claim.

[31] *Ibid*, at 638-639.

certain that the award will be brought for enforcement before the courts of the state whose public policy was relevant in the dispute; second, the review of an award by national courts at the enforcement stage might not be thorough enough to reveal any public policy infringement.[32]

2-35 However, the *Mitsubishi* scenario is a matter related more to the application of mandatory or public policy rules by the arbitrators than to the inarbitrability of public policy provisions altogether. In other words, it is a matter on how arbitrators can efficiently resolve a dispute relating to the public policy of a particular country, rather than a matter relating to an inherent flaw of the arbitration mechanism, which would render arbitration unfit to deal with public policy disputes in general.

2-36 Indeed, it is within the duties of the arbitrator to balance all the relevant factual circumstances of a dispute and decide whether to apply, or at least take into account, the public policy or mandatory rules of a country other than the one whose rules the parties have agreed on. The ultimate goal of the arbitrators is to resolve the dispute as efficiently as they can,[33] which of course would require that the award is enforceable after all.[34]

2-37 Ultimately, it is upon the arbitrator deciding the particular case whether to take the enforcement factor into account or not. However, there is nothing to indicate that arbitrators are inherently incapable of exercising this kind of balance. After all, the arbitrators in the *Mitsubishi* case did take the U.S. anti-

[32] See for example, WW Park, "Private Adjudicators and the Public Interest: The Expanding Scope of International Arbitration" (1986) 12 *Brook. J. Int'l L.* 642:

> The 'second look' doctrine is a problematic safety valve for ensuring that public law issues receive proper consideration. If it calls for review on the merits, it disrupts the arbitral process. But if it calls only for a mechanical examination of the face of the award, it may not provide an effective check on an arbitrator who mentions the Sherman Act before he proceeds to ignore it.

A possible response to this criticism could be in the *Mitsubishi v. Soler* itself:

> While the efficacy of the arbitral process requires that substantive review at the award-enforcement stage remain minimal, it would not require intrusive inquiry to ascertain that the tribunal took cognizance of the antitrust claims and actually decided them

Ibid., at 639.

[33] *Cf* EAA s. 1 (a).

[34] *Cf* ICC Art. 35.

competition rules into account, despite the fact that the parties in their contract had expressly agreed on the application of Swiss law.

2-38 Equally, there is nothing to suggest that national judges that are "bound" to apply the mandatory rules of their country, or even the mandatory rules of a different country by reference to the Rome Convention[35], will eventually apply these rules rightly.

2-39 To conclude on the issue of arbitrability and public policy, it can be argued that the prohibition of arbitrability on public policy grounds is to a large extent unsubstantiated. In fact the relevance of public policy to the discussion of arbitrability is essentially very limited, and therefore, the scope of inarbitrability should not be determined by reference to public policy.

2.2. Inarbitrability and inherent characteristics of arbitration: redefining the theory of inarbitrability

2-40 The previous section argued that public policy has limited relevance to inarbitrability. This section examines whether there are other considerations that relate to the scope of inarbitrability. The main question here, in effect, remains unanswered: why do state laws still restrict arbitrability? To what extent are these restrictions acceptable?

2-41 One could argue that prohibition of arbitrability is based on persisting prejudice against arbitration. Prejudice might still have a role to play in inarbitrability. However, its role is much more limited than two decades ago,[36] and, in any case, prejudice alone could not sufficiently explain the theory of inarbitrability.

2-42 Inarbitrability should be examined in light of the inherent limitations of arbitration as a dispute resolution mechanism of contractual origins. Based on consent, arbitration has intrinsic difficulties to affect a circle of persons other

[35] 1980 Rome Convention On The Law Applicable To Contractual Obligations. *Cf* also the latest Regulation (EC) No 593/2008 of the European Parliament and of the Council of 17 June 2008 On The Law Applicable To Contractual Obligations (Rome I).

[36] A series of progressive court decisions in different countries, see *supra* note 7, played a significant role in this respect, raising awareness about arbitration and fighting old myths and prejudice against it.

than the contractual parties to an arbitration agreement. This conceptual limitation of arbitration has repercussions on the scope of arbitrability.

2-43 For example, an insolvency dispute would most likely involve several claims (some unsecured, some secured or preferred, some even contested) and several parties (for example, the insolvent, the trustee, several creditors).[37] Invariably, the several claims would normally arise out of completely different contracts, which would have been concluded at different stages, and which would provide for different dispute resolution agreements. In such a scenario, it would be virtually impossible to bring all the several claims and the several parties involved in insolvency disputes under the jurisdiction of a single arbitral tribunal. If the several claims were allowed to be submitted to different bilateral proceedings (some before arbitral tribunals and some others before national courts), the outcomes of the several bilateral proceedings would most likely be incompatible, if not conflicting. A decision to satisfy one creditor would necessarily affect the legal position of another creditor. Given the fact that third-party proceedings are generally not accepted in arbitration,[38] third-party creditors would not be able to take part in bilateral proceedings between the trustee or the administrator and one of the several creditors. Therefore, it would be very difficult to determine the order in which the several creditors would be paid, and the allocation of the available funds to the several creditors, especially if some of the claims are contested. Thus, the purpose of the insolvency legislation (namely, the allocation of the limited funds to the several creditors in accordance with the security that each of the creditors had originally obtained) might be defeated, because of the contractual limitations of arbitration.

2-44 Therefore, national laws often provide that insolvency disputes will collectively be submitted to the exclusive jurisdiction of specially designated national courts.[39] To the extent that insolvency disputes are considered inarbitrable,[40] the rationale of the inarbitrability of insolvency disputes is exactly that the resolution of this type of disputes can more efficiently be achieved by

[37] See, in detail, C. Liebscher, Chapter 9 *infra*.

[38] See for example, Lew, Mistelis & Kröll, *supra* note 3, para 16-74; Born, *supra* note 3, Chapter 10; Redfern & Hunter, *supra* note 3, para 3-73.

[39] See for example, Austrian Bankruptcy Code s. 43(5) and s. 111(1) or the French Code of Commerce, R 662-3.

[40] See Liebscher, Chapter 9 *infra*, referring to list of "non-core" insolvency disputes that are considered arbitrable.

collective litigation proceedings where all the relevant parties may be brought before the same court.[41]

2-45 This is why, insolvency disputes involving the debtor, but not affecting the collective insolvency proceedings, are in general considered arbitrable.[42] Here, the scope of inarbitrability of insolvency disputes is defined by reference to the consensual limitations of arbitration, which constitute, thus, the underpinning rationale of inarbitrability.

2-46 A similar theory underpins the inarbitrability of some intra-company disputes. Here, the main concern militating against the arbitrability of disputes regarding shareholders resolutions is that the decision of an arbitral tribunal, constrained by the boundaries of the arbitration agreement upon which it is based, would be binding only upon those shareholders that were parties to the arbitration agreement.[43] By contrast, those shareholders not bound by an arbitration agreement would be left unaffected by the arbitral award. Thus, the dispute would in effect remain partially resolved, if submitted to an arbitral tribunal. Therefore, it is questionable whether arbitration is fit to deal with this type of intra-corporate disputes, which would be better addressed by national courts.[44]

2-47 Arbitration has a natural limitation to accommodate disputes that involve several parties. It would defeat the principle goal of arbitration, namely the effective resolution of commercial disputes, to have only some of the several claims submitted to arbitration and others to a different court.

2-48 'Inarbitrability' can thus be read 'inability of arbitration to provide for an effective resolution of a specific dispute'. In fact, this is a limitation that is not exclusively related to arbitration and arbitration agreements. It equally applies to jurisdiction (choice of courts) agreements. Similar issues, for example, would arise in relation to a jurisdiction agreement between a creditor and a debtor, who becomes insolvent. Or, in relation to a jurisdiction agreement binding some of the

[41] See Cohen, *supra* note 9, para 243.

[42] See V Ancel "Arbitation et procédure collectives", *Rev. Arb* (1983) at 255; and Cohen, *idem*.

[43] See in detail P. Perales, Chapter 14 *infra*; see also Trittman/Hanefeld in K.-H. Böckstiegel, S. Kröll, P. Nacimiento (eds), *Arbitration in Germany - The Model Law in Practice* (Wolters Kluwer 2007), s. 1030, para 17-19.

[44] See EC Regulation 44/2001 Art. 22(2)

shareholders in an intra-company dispute. In such cases, the jurisdiction agreement would most likely be inoperative too, in favour of collective court proceedings.

2-49 Two reasonable questions may arise from the above thoughts: first, if inarbitrability mainly relates to the contractual constraints of arbitration, why are not other types of multiparty disputes considered inarbitrable too? In other words, why are mandatory collective proceedings provided only for insolvency disputes, for example, and not for other multiparty interrelated contracts, such as construction or maritime contracts?[45]

2-50 One possible explanation here would be that collective proceedings in insolvency disputes (to remain in the same example) directly relate to the fundamentals of our commercial system: they relate to the securitisation of contractual claims. More specifically, collective insolvency proceedings are required to ensure that secured claims will be given priority over unsecured claims. If secured claims were not preferentially satisfied, the securitisation and financial system would be undermined.

2-51 The negative repercussions of non-collective proceedings in this case would extend way further than in the case of other types of multiparty disputes, such as construction or maritime disputes. The mandatory centralisation of insolvency disputes seems more reasonable. This does not mean that "public policy" considerations would enter again "through the back door". The primary reason for inarbitrability remains the fact that arbitration has inherent difficulties to reach out beyond its contractual boundaries. As is accepted, if all the relevant parties agreed to submit to arbitration, insolvency or intra-companies disputes would be perfectly arbitrable.[46]

2-52 This brings us to the second question, namely, why not have all disputes centralised before an arbitral tribunal then? As just mentioned, there is nothing to suggest that an arbitral tribunal would not be capable to hear and determine collective insolvency or intra-company disputes. However, this would also go

[45] Although it should be noted that there have been cases that have held arbitration agreements "inoperative" on the basis that they did not cover all the parties concerned in the dispute, see for example British Columbia Supreme Court, *Prince George (City) v. McElhanney Engineering Services Ltd and Al Sims and Sons*, (1997) 6 ADRLJ 315 (BCSC 30 December 1994).

[46] See also Trittman/Hanefeld in Böckstiegel, Kröll & Nacimiento, *supra* note 43, s. 1030, para 27. The same in Liebscher, Chapter 9 *infra*.

against the consensual nature of arbitration: only those parties that have consented to arbitration may be submitted to the jurisdiction of an arbitral tribunal. Thus, creditors or shareholders not bound by an arbitration agreement could not be brought before a tribunal against their own volition. By contrast, the jurisdiction of national courts does not depend on the agreement of the parties; national courts have default jurisdiction over them.

2-53 From this perspective, the reasoning behind national laws restricting arbitrability in some areas could be re-examined. For example, inarbitrability of disputes over the validity of intellectual property rights, such as patents or trademarks, which require registration with a public authority.

2-54 Except for Switzerland, where the relevant governmental agency accepts an arbitral award as a basis for altering the ownership status of a patent or a trademark, national laws usually provide that disputes regarding ownership rights on patents and trademarks may only be submitted to the exclusive jurisdiction of specific national courts.[47] A typical example of legislation restricting arbitrability on this subject is the EC Regulation 44/2001 Art. 22(4).

2-55 Is the prohibition of arbitrability of this type of dispute reasonable? One could argue in the affirmative: effectively, it depends on whether the relevant public authorities are ready to accept an arbitral award as a valid cause for them to alter their public records. This principle is feasible, as is provided in Switzerland. There is nothing inherently wrong with an arbitral award, that would render it unfit to be taken as a basis for the annulment of a patent, for example. In this context, a national judgement may produce exactly the same effects as an arbitral award.[48] A national judgment on the validity of a patent acquires an *erga omnes* effect because it can be registered or deposited with the relevant public authority, which eventually alters the ownership status of a trademark or a patent in accordance with the dictum of the judgment.[49] An arbitral award could equally obtain such an *erga omnes* effect, if the relevant public authorities were willing to accept an arbitral award as a basis for them to

[47] See A. Mantakou, Chapter 13, *infra*.

[48] See S. Brekoulakis, "The Effect of an Arbitral Award and Third Parties in International Arbitration: *Res Judicata* Revisited", 1 (16) *Am. Rev. Int'l Arb.* (2005) 180, notes 9-10.

[49] See the in detail about the effect of national court decisions in patent litigation in the European context, ECJ case C- 4/03 *GAT v. Luk* [2006] FSR 45.

alter the ownership status of an IP right. Arbitral awards and national judgments can operate equally in this respect.

2-56 Nevertheless, inarbitrability of this type of patent and trademark disputes is arguably justified by reference to the *inter partes* effect of the *arbitral proceedings*, rather than the *inter partes* effect of *arbitral awards*. The bilateral arbitration proceedings between two parties disputing over the ownership of a patent or a trademark, would naturally exclude any third party, who might actually be the true owner of the right at stake.

2-57 Court litigation over these disputes, where third parties, possibly real owners, have extensive opportunities to take part into the proceedings can reduce the risk of collusion, and ensure that the public record would reflect the actual ownership status of patents and trademarks. The consensual limitations of arbitration most likely lies behind inarbitrability here too: the resolution of disputes involving ownership rights registered on public records may be more efficiently resolved by national courts rather than arbitral tribunals.

3. Effects of Inarbitrability on the Validity of Arbitration Agreement

2-58 The prevailing view here is that inarbitrability of the subject matter of an arbitration agreement renders the arbitration agreement null and void.[50] However, it is questionable whether inarbitrability relates to the validity of an arbitration agreement. Indeed, the following indicate that inarbitrability relates to tribunal's jurisdiction and should be distinguished from arbitration agreement's invalidity:

[50] See for example, B. Hanotiau, "What law governs the issue of arbitrability?", *supra* note 3 at 391: "Arbitrability is indeed a condition of validity of the arbitration agreement and consequently, of the arbitrators' jurisdiction."; Böckstiegel, "Public Policy and Arbitrability", *supra* note 3 at 180:

> The final effect for the arbitration agreement and for the arbitration procedure is identical: the arbitration agreement is invalid and the arbitrators lack jurisdiction if either one of the two is missing

Switzerland, Federal Tribunal, 23 June 1992, *Fincantieri- Cantieri Navali Italiiani and Oto Melara v. M and arbitration tribunal*, *supra* note 7: "Arbitrability is a requirement for the validity of the arbitration agreements". Also, Redfern & Hunder, *supra* note 3, examine the subject of arbitrability under the section "The Validity of an Arbitration Agreement" in Chapter 3, para 3-13 et seq; *Cf* Lew, Mistelis & Kröll, *supra* note 3, para. 9-18: "though arbitrability is often considered to be a requirement for the validity of the arbitration agreement it is primarily a question of jurisdiction."

2-59 First, many arbitration provision draw a distinction between inarbitrability and invalidity. In the New York Convention, for example, invalidity of an arbitration agreement is provided in Art. V(1)(a), whereas inarbitrability is provided as a distinct ground for non-enforcement in Art. V(2)(a). Similarly, in many arbitration laws arbitrability is not included in the provisions dealing with the validity requirements of arbitration agreements. This is, for example, the case for the UNCITRAL Model Law Art. 7, the English Arbitration Act 1996 s. 6, the German ZPO s. 1029 or the Swiss PILA Art. 178. Arbitrability is usually dealt with at a separate provision.[51]

2-60 Second, and more importantly: as is generally accepted, arbitration agreements are *sui generis* contracts with both contractual and jurisdictional features.[52] Arbitration agreements differ from ordinary contracts, as they produce unique jurisdictional effects, namely they establish the jurisdiction of a particular arbitral tribunal, excluding the default jurisdiction of national courts.[53]

2-61 However, as regards their validity requirements, arbitration agreements are on the same footing as any other substantive contract (contractual nature). Indeed, for an arbitration agreement to be validly concluded, the only conditions to be met are: consent (meeting of minds), capacity of the parties and the formal requirements provided in the New York Convention (NYC) and the other arbitration laws.[54] No additional requirements of validity may be provided for an arbitration agreement, or else the principle of the contractual nature of arbitration agreements would be violated. If further conditions of validity were required for them in particular, arbitration agreements would be put in a disadvantageous position compared to other substantive contracts, and, therefore, the principle of the contractual nature of arbitration agreements would be violated.

2-62 True, the arbitration agreement's validity and a tribunal's jurisdiction are closely interrelated; however, the latter has a wider scope. Whether a tribunal has jurisdiction over a particular claim would usually depend on more factors than arbitration agreement's validity. For example, an arbitration agreement may be valid, but the tribunal might still not have jurisdiction to look into the dispute,

[51] See for example, the Swiss PILA Art. 177, or the German ZPO s. 1030.

[52] Lew, Mistelis & Kröll, *supra* note 3, para 6-2.

[53] See S. Brekoulakis, "The Notion of the Superiority of Arbitration Agreements over Jurisdiction Agreements: Time to Abandon It?", 24(4) *J. Int'l Arb.* (2007) 361.

[54] Lew, Mistelis & Kröll, *supra* note 3, para 7-3.

because, for example, the claim falls outside the scope of the arbitration agreement; or because the main claim is covered by *res judicata* of a previous award or a national judgement, which would preclude the tribunal to determine the merits of the claim. Equally, arbitrability belongs to this group of additional factors related to jurisdiction that go beyond the validity of an arbitration agreement.

2-63 Arbitrability is, thus, a specific condition pertaining to the jurisdictional aspect of arbitration agreements, and therefore, it goes beyond the discussion on validity. Arbitrability is a condition precedent for the tribunal to assume jurisdiction over a particular dispute (a jurisdictional requirement), rather than a condition of validity of an arbitration agreement (contractual requirement).

2-64 When a particular claim is considered to be inarbitrable, the tribunal is prevented from assuming jurisdiction over the particular claim only. The inarbitrability of this claim would not render the arbitration agreement *ab initio* null and void. The same tribunal might well have jurisdiction to determine another claim falling under the same arbitration agreement. Indeed, as is accepted, different claims may arise out of the same dispute, some of which might be inarbitrable, whereas some others might perfectly be arbitrable.[55]

2-65 In fact, it would be difficult to determine with certainty at the time of the conclusion of an arbitration agreement whether an arbitration agreement deals with a subject matter that is inarbitrable. In the majority of the cases, it is not the subject matter of an arbitration agreement that is *in abstracto* inarbitrable; rather, it is the specific dispute that arises after the arbitration agreement is concluded that is *ad hoc* determined inarbitrable by a tribunal or a national court.

2-66 For example, an arbitration agreement in a contract for the licensing of a patent providing that "any dispute arising out of this contract will be referred to arbitration", would not provide for a non-arbitrable subject matter *per se*, and thus it could never be held as null or void from the outset. If, however, a specific dispute arose out of this contract, which touched upon issues of ownership and validity of the patent, the tribunal would probably decline jurisdiction over the specific dispute. However, the particular arbitration agreement would remain valid and active and, if another dispute, relating to the licensing contract this time

[55] See in general A. Buzbee, "When arbitrable claims are mixed with nonarbitrable ones: What's a court to do?", 39 *S. Tex. L. Rev.* (1997-98) 663 et seq.

arose between the same parties, the tribunal would have no difficulties to confirm its jurisdiction over the licensing dispute.

2-67 The same would apply to insolvency disputes. The fact that a debtor becomes insolvent would not retrospectively render an arbitration agreement, signed by the debtor, null and void.[56] This is why specific insolvency disputes (for example, disputes that do not affect the collective insolvency proceedings) may be submitted to arbitration even after the debtor becomes insolvent.[57] The subject matter of the arbitration agreement as such cannot be held arbitrable or inarbitrable at the time of its conclusion. It is the specific dispute or claim that will be arbitrable (if it does not affect the collective insolvency proceedings) or not (if it does affect the insolvency proceedings).

2-68 In this respect, some provisions on arbitrability are more accurately drafted than others. For example, the Swiss PILA[58] and the German ZPO[59] refer to "dispute" and "claim" respectively, whereas the New York Convention[60] refers to "subject matter".

2-69 The conclusion that can be drawn from the above analysis is that inarbitrability should not be considered as a condition of arbitration agreement's validity. Arbitrability pertains to the unique jurisdictional character of arbitration agreements, and it is thus a condition precedent of the jurisdiction of an arbitral tribunal.

4. Practical Relevance of the Discussion on the Rationale behind Arbitrability

2-70 The above is not mere academic discussion. The issue of whether arbitrability relates to the validity of an arbitration agreement or to the tribunal's jurisdiction has important practical repercussions. It may, in particular, influence

56 See Trittman/Hanefeld in Böckstiegel, Kröll & Nacimiento, *supra* note 43, s. 1030, para 27.

57 *Idem*; The same Liebscher, Chapter 9 *infra*.

58 Art. 177 "Any *dispute* involving property …"

59 S. 1030 (1): "Any claim involving an economic interest". The provision has in fact been influenced by the Swiss PILA; see, Trittman/Hanefeld in Böckstiegel, Kröll & Nacimiento, *supra* note 43, s. 1030, para 3.

60 Art. II(1): "….concerning a subject matter capable of settlement by arbitration".

the discussion of which forum should be given priority, or even exclusivity, in determining arbitrability: national courts or arbitral tribunals?

2-71 While different approaches have been taken on this issue,[61] the prevailing view seems to be that courts and tribunals have concurrent power to review arbitrability at a pre-award stage.[62]

2-72 It is worth noting that the suggested U.S. Arbitration Fairness Act of 2007 intents to take the issue completely out of the domain of arbitration, providing that U.S. Courts will have the exclusive jurisdiction to determine the issue of arbitrability under federal law. The provision seems to apply to all issues relating to arbitrability, not just to the arbitrability of employment, consumer, or franchise disputes.[63]

2-73 However, if, as argued above, arbitrability is a matter related to jurisdiction rather than a matter related to the validity of arbitration agreements, it seems less reasonable for the courts to review arbitrability at a pre-award stage.

2-74 Indeed, at the stage of referral of the dispute to the tribunal, national courts should limit their review to what pertains to the contractual requirements of an arbitration agreement: capacity of the parties, consent to arbitrate, and formal requirements. Once a national court is satisfied that an arbitration agreement, as a substantive contract, is validly concluded, the "baton will be handed" to the tribunal.[64] It should then be for the tribunal to exclusively review any issue

[61] See in general on the discussion L. Shore, Chapter 4 *infra*. See also Y. Fortier, *supra* note 8 at 274 et seq., who argues that the *First Option* dictum on arbitrability, taken in the U.S. wide sense (i.e. covering the scope of the arbitration agreement), should apply equally to the issue of objective arbitrability. Thus, according to Fortier, the issue of which forum should determine arbitrability is eventually a matter that would depend on the parties' agreement.

[62] See Lew, Mistelis & Kröll, *supra* note 3, para 14-49 et seq, who however refer to the matter in more general terms, including all issues related to the jurisdiction of an arbitral tribunal, and not just arbitrability.

[63] See note *supra* 12 above. As is mentioned in the suggested s. 2(c):

> An issue as to whether this chapter applies to an arbitration agreement shall be determined by Federal law. Except as otherwise provided in this chapter, the validity or enforceability of an agreement to arbitrate shall be determined by the court, rather than the arbitrator, irrespective of whether the party resisting arbitration challenges the arbitration agreement specifically or in conjunction with other terms of the contract containing such agreement.

[64] To refer to the Lord Mustill's well-know comparison of the relationship between courts and arbitrators to a relay race:

relating to the jurisdictional effects of that arbitration agreement: for example, arbitrability or the scope of the arbitration agreement.[65]

2-75 As long as the parties have validly concluded an arbitration agreement, a tribunal is established as the forum that assumes the exclusive jurisdiction to address all questions relating to the parties' relationship, including, of course, the question of arbitrability of their dispute. National courts may have concurrent jurisdiction to review the foundations of the jurisdiction of the tribunal, namely the validity of the arbitration agreement.[66] However, anything more than the validity of the arbitration agreement should be reviewed exclusively by the tribunal at the pre-award stage.

2-76 In this sense, arbitrability would be effectively disconnected from NYC Art. II(3),[67] which will have to read along the lines of:

> once the court of a Contracting state is seized of an action in a matter in respect of which the parties have made an agreement *which is valid, in terms of substantive and formal validity*, the court shall, at the request of one of the parties, refer the parties to arbitration, unless it finds that the said agreement is null and void, inoperative or incapable of being performed.

> Ideally, the handling of arbitrable disputes should resemble a relay race. In the initial stages, before the arbitrators are seized of the dispute, the baton is in the grasp of the court; for at that stage there is no other organisation which could take steps to prevent the arbitration agreement from being ineffectual. When the arbitrators take charge they take over the baton and retain it until they have made an award. At this point, having no longer a function to fill, the arbitrators hand back the baton so that the court can in case of need lend its coercive powers to the enforcement of the award.

Mustill, "Comments and Conclusions" in *Conservatory and Provisional Measures in International Arbitration* (ICC ed, 1993) at 119.

65 *Cf* Cour de cassation, 18 May 1971, *Impex v. P.A.Z. Produzione Lavorazione*, (1972) Rev. Arb. at 3:

> arbitral tribunals have exclusive jurisdiction to rule on disputes falling within the terms of the brief conferred upon them, subject to review by the courts hearing the application for an enforcement order [or to set the award aside...] if ... a party claims that public policy has been contravened.

66 *Cf* Fouchard, Gaillard & Goldman, *supra* note 3 at 569:

> Disputes concerning matters that remain non-arbitrable (such as divorce) can be brought directly before the courts, even where they are the subject of an existing arbitration agreement. In that case, the court will establish its jurisdiction by carrying out a *prima facie* review of the arbitration agreement and determining that it is patently void

67 See Born, *supra* note 3 at 243 and note 102-103.

2-77 True, it is not easy to bring this view into conformity with the wording in NYC Art. II(3) and in particular with the phrase "within the meaning of this article" which is a reference to NYC Art. II(1), which seems to include arbitrability within the essential meaning of an arbitration agreement.[68] Equally, it is not easy to overlook the last line of NYC Art. II(3), which is widely drafted and which refers not only to arbitration agreements that are "null and void", but also to arbitration agreements that are "inoperative or incapable of being performed", a phrase that would on the face of it include arbitrability.

2-78 However, it is certainly easier to uphold this argument in the context of more favourable national provisions that first, do not include arbitrability within the essential meaning of validity[69] and second, avoid the wording "inoperative, or incapable of being performed". This is the case, for example, with the French NCPC Art. 1458,[70] or with the English Arbitration Act 1996 ss. 72.[71]

2-79 By reference to such national provisions, which are directly applicable at the referral stage, a national court would have to be satisfied that only the minimum requirements for the valid conclusion of an arbitration agreement are met. Thus, once all the formal and substantive requirements of the validity of an arbitration agreement are confirmed, the court shall have the duty to refer the parties to the tribunal, which will have the exclusive power to determine issues related to its own jurisdiction.

2-80 This argument based on the distinction between contractual and jurisdictional features of arbitration agreements can provide clear-cut guidance on the troublesome issue of conflict of jurisdiction between national courts and arbitral tribunal: national courts, at the stage of referral, may review only whatever is related to the formation of arbitration agreements as substantive contracts (the contractual aspect of an arbitration agreement). Issues related to the jurisdictional aspect of an arbitration agreement should be under the exclusive jurisdiction of arbitral tribunals.

[68] "Each Contracting State shall recognise an agreement in writing under which the parties undertake to submit to arbitration all or any differences which have arisen or which may arise between them in respect of a defined legal relationship, whether contractual or nor, *concerning a subject matter capable of settlement by arbitration*" (emphasis added).

[69] See *supra* para 2-59.

[70] NCPC Art. 1458(2) only refers to invalidity "à moins que la convention d'arbitrage ne soit manifestement nulle".

[71] EAA s. 72 only refers to validity of arbitration agreement, rather than arbitrability.

2-81 This view is further supported by the argument, explained above, that public policy is not relevant to arbitrability. Thus, if public policy of a state is not at stake when the arbitrability of a dispute is in question, it seems less reasonable for the national courts of that state to have the right to review arbitrability at the stage of referral.[72] Finally, this view is in line with the recorded trend of the last two decades, favouring the expansion of the scope of arbitrability.[73]

5. Conclusions

2-82 Despite the significant progress of the arbitration theory in the last three decades, the discussion on inarbitrability remains today more pertinent than ever. New anti-arbitration forces from different ideological perspectives seem to have re-emerged seeking to revisit, and eventually, restrain the scope of arbitrability.

2-83 It is thus critical to put the discussion on arbitrability in the right context, which does not include considerations of public policy. As was argued in this paper, arbitration theory should oppose recurring arguments that arbitration cannot address public policy disputes on the basis that it is a compromised – in due process terms – dispute resolution system or that arbitrators owe allegiance to the private interests of the parties rather than to the public interests of the state.

2-84 At the same time, it is equally important to define the boundaries of arbitrability on a realistic basis. Arbitration as consensual dispute resolution system has inherent limitations. Based on consent, arbitration has intrinsic difficulties to affect a circle of persons other than the contractual parties to an arbitration agreement. This type of conceptual boundaries of arbitration may have repercussions on the scope of arbitrability. Thus, for example, some types of patent or insolvency or intra-company disputes may be addressed by national courts more efficiently than by an arbitral tribunal. Eventually, arbitrability

[72] *Cf* Fouchard, Gaillard & Goldman, *supra* note 3 at 569:

> Under the previous approach, where the criterion was a breach of public policy in the disputed contract, determining the arbitrability of the dispute entailed examining often complex aspects of the merits of the case. By contrast, using a criterion based on the subject-matter of the dispute enables the courts to determine the arbitrability or non-arbitrability of a dispute with ease. French law has thus returned to the simple technique of "non-arbitrable blocks

[73] See Lew, Mistelis & Kröll, *supra* note 3, para 9-36; Fouchard, Gaillard & Goldman, *supra* note 3, para 568.

should be determined on the basis of efficiency: whether an arbitral tribunal can get disposed of the pending dispute in an effective manner.

2-85 Finally, in this discussion it is always relevant to note that arbitrability is an issue exclusively related to jurisdiction. As this paper argued, all arbitrability provisions are in essence jurisdictional rather than substantive rules. They are conflict of jurisdiction rules, whose objective is to delineate the area of exclusive jurisdiction of its national courts. From this jurisdictional viewpoint, the role of the national state and the *lex fori,* in particular in the discussion on arbitration is diminished. As was shown above, the *lex fori* would only be relevant if the actual dispute pending before the tribunal had any territorial or other jurisdictional connection with the national state of the *lex fori.*

2-86 Inarbitrability is not dead; at least, not yet. As the matter pertains to the fundamentals of arbitration and its relation with the state courts, the scope of inarbitrability will always remain a relevant subject matter. However, arbitration doctrine must win the argument that inarbitrability should be defined by reference to the specific characteristics of arbitration, rather than old prejudices.

Karim Youssef[*]

CHAPTER 3

THE DEATH OF INARBITRABILITY

1. INTRODUCTION

3-1 The significant expansion of the domain of arbitration, in the last few decades, has greatly undermined the relevance of the notion of arbitrability, in international matters. Back in 1999, Redfern & Hunter wrote:

> the significance of "arbitrability" should not be exaggerated. It is important to be aware that it may be an issue, but in broad terms most commercial disputes are arbitrable under the laws of most countries.[1]

In recent years, the scope of rights amenable to arbitration has grown to such an extent that, the concept of arbitrability (or its mirror image, inarbitrability) as central as it may be to arbitration theory, has virtually died in real arbitral life.

3-2 Gradually, the issue of arbitrability faded in disputes on jurisdiction. The defence that a particular subject matter is not arbitrable has almost disappeared in the practice of developed *fora*, and arises less frequently in emerging ones. Arbitrability seems to be the least of a modern practitioner's problems; while other issues, including third-party involvement, consolidation of proceedings and conflict between commercial and investment jurisdiction occupy the top of the

[*] Doctor of the Science of Law (J.S.D.); Masters of Laws (LL.M), Yale Law School. Associate, Cleary, Gottlieb, Steen & Hamilton LLP, Paris.
The views expressed in this article are exclusively those of the author and do not necessarily reflect the opinions of Cleary, Gottlieb, Steen & Hamilton LLP or its clients.
The author wishes to thank Professor W. Michael Reisman, Myres S. McDougal Professor of International Law, and Professor Ahmed El Kosheri, Vice-Chairman of the ICC Court of Arbitration for discussions of ideas and comments on an earlier version of this article.

[1] Redfern & Hunter, *Law and Practice of International Commercial Arbitration* (1999) at 154.

L Mistelis & S Brekoulakis (eds), Arbitrability: International & Comparative Perspectives, 47-67

list of the most frequent objections to arbitral jurisdiction and the more problematic issues in reform agendas.

2. A Notion in Flux

3-3 Arbitrability is a key concept of arbitration law. "What is arbitrable and what is not" is a ubiquitous question, which faces policy makers, contract drafters, judges and arbitrators.[2]

3-4 Arbitrability is also the *primordial* question, which precedes all other matters in the regulation of arbitration. National laws establish *a priori* the domain of arbitration[3] *vis-à-vis* State justice. The scope of arbitrable claims is thus a central *policy* decision, which involves beyond the purely *legal,* essential reflections of a *pragmatic* nature, and the legislative or judicial arbitration of competing policy considerations.[4] This *political essentiala* of arbitrability adds to the fascination of its study, but also to the complexity of decision-making and the incessant dynamism of the concept.[5] This also makes arbitrability *national* by nature,[6] and thus a subject with respect to which the international unification or harmonisation of arbitration rules is at its lowest.[7]

2 Craig, Park & Paulsson, *International Chamber of Commerce Arbitration* (3rd ed, 2000) 60.

3 See P. Sanders, "The Domain of Arbitration", in *Encyclopedia of International & Comparative Law*, Vol. XVI, chapter 12, at 113.

4 Arbitrable claims and the subsequent reception of expansive notions of arbitrability "depend on the judgment of the respective community at a particular time." Douglas Jones, "Arbitration and Party Autonomy: How free is the Choice to Arbitrate?", in *The Commercial Way to Justice*, G.M. Beresford Hartwell (ed), (Kluwer 1997) at 121-149. In international arbitration, national perceptions of the role of private justice, the sphere of private autonomy versus social norms, and the ordering of global and local values are decisive factors.

5 "L'arbitrabilité est une question abstraite, mal cernée, fuyante, et qui suscite un certain nombre de malentendus, voire de contresens." Ch. Jarosson, "L'arbitrabilité: Présentation Méthodologique", JCP, Droit Int. *Cited in* J-B. Racine, *L'Arbitrage Commercial International et L'ordre Public* (LGDJ 1999) 27.

6 "Each State may decide, in accordance with its own economic and social policy, which matters may be settled by arbitration and which may not." Redfern & Hunter, *supra* note 1 at 148. The New York Convention and the UNCITRAL Model Law treat arbitrability as a matter which belongs to the *lex fori,* respectively *the law of the country where enforcement is sought* (Art. V(2)(a)) or *the law of the place of arbitration* (Art. 34(2)).

7 "Uncertainty about and differences among definitions of which disputes are arbitrable may cause considerable difficulties in practice." U.N. General Assembly Document A/CN.9/460 (April 6, 1999) 32–34.

3-5 *Primordial,* arbitrability thus precedes *jurisdiction,* conceptually and usually also in time.[8] Arbitrability involves a *general* enquiry as to what types of disputes are "capable of settlement by arbitration." Jurisdiction comes at a *post-design* stage, as a more specific issue: the authority to rule on the particular dispute. It is decided by reference to the existence, validity and scope, under the applicable law, of the specific source of the tribunal's jurisdiction (the particular arbitration agreement, or other source of authority, such as legislative arbitration provisions).

3-6 An *objective* notion, arbitrability is also the fundamental expression of freedom to arbitrate. It defines the scope of the parties' power of reference or the boundaries of the right to go to arbitration in the first place. With respect to all non-arbitrable matters, courts retain exclusive jurisdiction and parties lack jurisdictional autonomy about *where* they can settle their dispute. The modern history of arbitration has been one of expansion of the parties' freedom to arbitrate.

3. From Restriction to Expansion

3-7 National laws traditionally defined arbitrability in terms of *public policy.*[9] Legal systems would only accept the arbitration of rights of a private nature or those that "can be compromised."[10] Rights which the parties could not dispose of were outside the domain of arbitration and within *exclusive* judicial jurisdiction. The nature of arbitrability: as restriction to party autonomy, its source: as national policy decision and its essential role: as *technique of* demarcation of the spheres of two jurisdictional orders, State and private justice, all supported this initial –and apparently inescapable attachment of arbitrability to *public policy.* In

[8] Unfortunately, legal systems do not always distinguish the two notions. In the U.S. and elsewhere, arbitrability is often used to refer to jurisdiction. Courts would describe the dispute as being not "arbitrable" when they mean that it falls outside the scope of the arbitration agreement. Redfern & Hunter, *supra* note 1 at 20.

[9] Germany, ZPO, s 1030; France, Art. 2060-1 of the *Code Civil* (and its predecessors Art. 83 and 1004 Ancien Code de Procedure Civile) both now unwritten by judicial practice; Japan, Code of Civil Procedure, Art. 786; Dutch Arbitration Act of 1986, Art. 1020(3)); Art. 1 Spanish Arbitration Act; In Italy, rights that may not be freely alienated (*diriti indisponibili*) are not arbitrable, Italian Code of Civil Procedure Art. 806. *Cf* Art. 11 of the 1994 Egyptian Arbitration Law.

[10] Rights that "can be compromised lawfully by way of accord and satisfaction" para 503, Halsbury's Laws of England 32 (4th ed).

fact, public policy was more than an element of the definition of arbitrability. Arbitrability was the *jurisdictional* reflection of public policy.

3-8 With arbitrable claims defined on the private-public divide, rights of a purely private nature did not pose particular problems with respect to their arbitrability. The main uncertainty existed regarding cases where the private right of action is entangled with elements of public interest or involves public law. Traditionally, legal systems excluded the arbitrability of these rights; and the arguments advanced to exclude their arbitrability revolved around the idea of *national public interest.*

3-9 Because the private right is entangled with the public interest, its enforcement has public effects external to the parties. Society at large has an interest in the proper enforcement of these rights; and arbitrators would fail to do that. The fear that private arbitrators would under-enforce public laws has very widely served as the reason to consider certain matters non-arbitrable. The image of arbitrators as "commercial men" biased to business and hostile to public regulation of commercial activity, or presumably unable to deal with complex public law issues[11] has nourished this classic fear. Furthermore, if arbitrators did not correctly apply public laws, there is no remedy, since awards are final.

3-10 On a technical level, the *problematique de base* of the arbitrability of rights involving public interest relates to the nature of the arbitrator's mandate as a limited delegation of power. Constrained by the *privity* inherent in the source of his jurisdiction, an arbitrator has authority to dictate legal effects *inter partes* and not *vis-à-vis* third parties. To the extent it would dictate effects with respect to third parties, the arbitrability of mixed/public rights would simply conflict with the contractual nature of arbitration.

3-11 While this approach to arbitrability is associated with the earlier days of the development of arbitration in the 20th century, the idea that certain areas of law are so sensitive that it is felt they should be applied exclusively by State courts has continued to haunt the definition of arbitrability. In the U.S., as late as mid-1970s, public policy continued to be an important factor in restricting arbitrability. The pro-arbitration policy advanced by the Federal Arbitration Act

[11] Only national courts can give effect to the true intention of the legislator. Justice Andrew Rogers, "Arbitrability", 1 *Asian Pac. L. Rev.* (1992) 1.

was often outweighed by conflicting federal policies giving courts exclusive jurisdiction over certain matters.[12]

3-12 With the development of arbitral practice in the last 25 years, the public policy exception has gradually eroded. Progressively, courts in the U.S. and Europe started to reduce the role of public policy in the definition of arbitrability,[13] and as a defence to enforcement under Art. V(2)(a) of the New York Convention (NYC). With that, the scope of arbitrable claims expanded in international matters; and legal systems have

> [become] more supportive of the parties' right to elect private dispute resolution [in lieu of courts], even where the public interest might appear to be compromised by the nature of the dispute.[14]

3-13 *Autonomy* arguments played a central role in justifying the arbitrability of disputes tainted with public interest. The simple faith in freedom of contract,[15] the principle of good faith which prohibits a party from seeking refuge in domestic limitations, to deny an arbitration clause, to which he has freely consented,[16] and the protection of the parties' legitimate expectations in having their agreements honoured, would gradually outweigh a systematic invocation of public policy.

3-14 Extension of the scope of arbitrability took place in two directions: beyond contract[17] and to mixed and public rights. Areas of law traditionally falling within the "*domaine réservé*" of the State have fallen one after the other in the scope of arbitrable claims, notwithstanding their potential inarbitrability in domestic settings. The evolution is particularly evident in the U.S. and Europe.[18]

12 "[W]here compelling the arbitration of disputes conflicts with other important federal policies, the courts have frequently refused to order arbitration" *Bache Halsey Stuart, Inc. v. French,* 425 F.Supp.1231, 1233 (D.C. Cir. 1977) These important federal policies included the maintenance of confidence in the securities market; the preservation of competition in the economy; the protection of weaker parties such as consumers or investors in securities claims.

13 Antoine Kirry, "Arbitrability: Current Trends in Europe", 12(4) *Arb. Int'l* (1996) 373-389.

14 Douglas Jones, *supra* note 4 at 121-149.

15 See Roscoe Pound, "Liberty of Contract", 18 *Yale LJ* 454 (1909).

16 Federal Court of Canada, *Pilotes du Saint-Laurent Central Inc v. Laurentian Pilotage Authority,* August,8, 2002, 246 FTR 161 (FCTD).

17 An arbitration agreement can be "in respect of a defined legal relationship, whether contractual or not." Article II (1), New York convention and Article 7(1), UNCITRAL ML. Tort claims and rights directly created by the law are, in principle, arbitrable in virtually all legal systems today. See for *ex.* Section 7(1) of the 1996 Indian Arbitration Act.

18 Antoine Kirry, *supra* note 13 at 373-389.

Expansive approaches to arbitrability are most evolved in common law jurisdictions, but the liberal trend is also clearly noticeable in many civil law States. It has accelerated, in recent years, to reach emerging jurisdictions, and in some cases, to ultimately extend to *domestic* arbitration, as is the case in the U.S.

3-15 The marginalisation of public policy, the growing trust in international arbitration and assimilation of arbitrators to judges[19] have allowed the domain of arbitration to extend to areas of economic activity involving significant public interest. These include antitrust, intellectual property,[20] consumer and securities disputes.[21] However, the arbitrability of mixed or public rights is not given. They may not be under the applicable law. Areas of special difficulties exist.

4. Uncertainties

4.1. Patents & Trademarks

3-16 Arbitrability of intellectual property disputes is problematic with respect to rights which confer a *monopoly* and require the intervention of the State to grant it, such as trademarks and patents. To allow the arbitration of questions of grant or validity of patents or trademarks challenges the contractual nature of arbitration, since a private arbitrator is not authorised to dictate legal effects *erga omnes.*[22] An award ruling on the ownership or validity of a monopoly right also usurps the power of the State in granting the monopoly.

3-17 For these reasons, legal systems excluded questions of grant or validity of monopoly rights from the domain of arbitration. National laws either prohibited the arbitration of these rights altogether, or accepted it in principle, but excluded arbitrability when the dispute affected the rights of third parties. In French law, the principle of arbitrability of disputes concerning patents and trademarks is

19 Serge Lazareff, "L'arbitre est-il un juge?" in *Mélanges en hommage à François Terré* (1999) 173.

20 The arbitrability of intellectual property disputes is well recognized in a large number of jurisdictions, notably the US, France, Italy, Switzerland, Germany, Japan, Canada. See Douglas Jones, *supra* note 4 at 121-149; William Grantham, The Arbitrability of International Intellectual Property Disputes, 14 *Berkeley J. Int'l L.* (1996) 173 for a more comprehensive list.

21 Securities claims are arbitrable in the U.S. since the mid-1970s. *Sherk v. Alberto-Culver* [30] 417 U.S. S Ct 506 (1974).

22 Christopher John Aeschlimann, "The Arbitrability of Patent Controversies", 44 *J. Pat. Off. Soc'y* (1962) 655, 662-663.

explicitly recognised,[23] but considerable controversy exists as to whether the *validity* of registered rights can be submitted to arbitration. In comparative law, the arbitrability of validity and title is very likely to be denied.[24]

3-18 On the contrary, copyrights,[25] and *contractual* disputes related to patents and trademarks (such as licensing) are arbitrable in most European jurisdictions[26] and the U.S. However, the validity or ownership of a patent or trademark often arises, as a preliminary question or as defence, in the context of disputes on infringement or transfer of licenses. In this case, "there is no legal obstacle that bars an arbitration tribunal to rule on the validity of a patent, as a preliminary matter."[27] But the conclusions of the award will operate solely *inter partes,* since only a national court with proper jurisdiction can invalidate a monopoly.[28] If the award rules the patent invalid for purposes of the contractual dispute, it would still remain in force until cancelled according to law.

3-19 Following this new approach of giving *inter partes* effect to decisions that are by nature *erga omnes*, parties can agree that the validity of a patent or a trademark could be made an issue in arbitration even if the arbitral award could not invalidate the trademark or patent itself. In the U.S., explicit legislation permits the arbitration of disputes "relating to patent validity or infringement,"[29] while at the same time, restricting the effect of the arbitral award. The award "shall be binding between the parties to the arbitration, but shall have no force or effect on any other person."[30]

3-20 German law reserved the question of the formal validity of patents to the exclusive jurisdiction of the Federal Patent Court (*Patentgericht*). After the reforms of 1998, questions of revocation and annulment of patents are in

23 Consecutively, Articles L. 716.4 and L. 615.17 of the Code de Propriété Intellectuelle (C.P.I).

24 See William Grantham, *supra* note 20 at 205 and 206.

25 See in the U.S.: *The Saturday Evening Post Co. v. Rumbleseat Press Inc*; 816 F. 2d 1191 (1987), and more generally, See Bruno Oppetit, "L'arbitrabilité des litiges de droit d'auteur et droits voisins", in *Arbitrage et propriété intellectuelle*, (Institut de Recherche en Propriété Intellectuelle Henri-Desbois, ed, 1994) at 124. Greater controversy exists however as to the arbitrability of *moral* rights.

26 Antoine Kirry, *supra* note 13 at 373-389.

27 Interim Award in Case No. 6097 (1989), ICC Bulletin, Oct. 1993, 79.

28 *Ibid.*, at 78.

29 35 U.S.C. § 294: "Voluntary Arbitration", (a). Effective November 2, 2002.

30 35 U.S.C. § 294 (c).

principle arbitrable.[31] Swiss law displays the most liberal position. Rights that are subject to registration (patents, trademarks, designs) are arbitrable. All aspects of patent rights can be arbitrated, even their validity and their removal from the registry.[32] Belgian law competes in liberalism. The patent law expressly permits the arbitrability of the ownership and validity of patents.[33] The arbitration of monopoly rights is increasingly accepted, even in reluctant jurisdictions.[34]

4.2. Antitrust, Bribery & Corruption

3-21 The arbitrability of antitrust claims or of allegations of bribery or corruption is uncertain in a number of jurisdictions. In these cases, the arbitrability question is framed as follows: Whether the arbitral tribunal can rule on allegations that the contract under which the arbitration is brought is *illegal* because it constitutes a violation of antitrust laws, has been procured by bribery or corruption, or has as its object the payment of bribes. While the shadows of restraint of trade or fraudulent activities would intuitively incline in favour of an outright exclusion of these matters from the scope of arbitration, the issue here is not really one of arbitrability.

3-22 First, arbitrability in these cases is confused with *separability.* The doctrine of separability, universally accepted, should allow a tribunal to rule on a contract whose legality is challenged. An arbitral tribunal should thus be able to rule on whether the contract is or is not in violation of antitrust laws. With the U.S. Supreme Court opening the way,[35] today international antitrust disputes are

[31] Kommission zur Neuordnung des Schiedsverfahrensrechts, Report published by the Federal Ministry of Justice (February 1994) at 92.

[32] M. Blessing, "Arbitrability of Intellectual Property Disputes" 12(2) *Arb. Int'l* (1996) at 200; and Robert Briner, "The Arbitrability of Intellectual Property Disputes with Particular Emphasis on the Situation in Switzerland" in *Worldwide Forum on the Arbitration of Intellectual Property Disputes* (1994) WIPO Publication No. 728(E) at 72.

[33] Loi sur les brevets d'invention (du 28 mars 1984) Art. 73 s. 6, Moniteur belge, Mar. 9, 1985, p. 2774. Referred to in William Grantham, *supra* note 20 at 201.

[34] An Israeli court held that there was no bar to arbitrating an infringement claim where invalidity of a patent or registered design was raised as a defence. *Golan Work of Art Ltd. v. Bercho Gold Jewellery Ltd.*, Tel Aviv District Court civil case 1524/93, cited in Vidal Pearlman, "Arbitration of IP in Israel", *Managing IP*, (March 1994) 23.

[35] *Mitsubishi Motors Corp v. Soler Chrysler-Plymouth, Inc.* U.S. S Ct 473 U.S. 614 (1985) Arguments against arbitrability, namely that antitrust regulation is "primarily aimed at the regulation of free trade and raises very clear issues of public interest", were deemed insufficient to stand in the face of a sweeping policy in favour of arbitration.

widely arbitrable, in jurisdictions as diverse as New Zealand,[36] France,[37] Italy and Switzerland.[38]

3-23 Similarly, an allegation of bribery or corruption in the procurement or performance of the contract should not in itself deprive the arbitral tribunal of jurisdiction.[39] While the operation of separability was dubious in cases where the main contract was not only invalid but *never existed,* recent case law allows tribunals to rule on illegality for bribery or fraud.[40] Once jurisdiction is asserted, the question is then one of *enforceability*. If bribery or corruption is proven, the tribunal will declare the contract unenforceable.

5. The Conceptual Leap towards Universal Arbitrability

5.1. "Claims Arbitrable Unless..."

3-24 While some authors have warned that an absolute freedom to arbitrate may undermine State sovereignty,[41] the evolution of legal systems to expand the definition of arbitrable claims did not slow down. On the contrary, the trend in favour of arbitrability has recently taken a new dimension, with the inception of what can be termed "universal arbitrability."[42] Put simply, this means that arbitrability today is rarely an issue. All international disputes of an economic nature are *prima facie* arbitrable in most jurisdictions, and it would be hard to find a dispute arising out of the operation of global commerce that is not.

36 *Attorney General of New Zealand v. Mobil Oil New Zealand Ltd* (NZ High Court) [1989] 2 NZLR 649.

37 CA Paris, *Aplix c. Velcro*, 14 October 1993, [1994] Rev. Arb. 164, Note Ch. Jarrosson.

38 Antoine Kirry, *supra* note 13 at 373-389.

39 Kosheri & Leboulanger, "L'arbitrage face a la Corruption et aux Trafics d'influence", 3 *Rev. Arb.* (1984).

40 In a very recent decision, an English Court of Appeals decided that there is no reason why the arbitrators should not have jurisdiction to decide whether the contract was procured by bribery. The vitiating effect of bribery on the whole contract did not affect the arbitration clause, unless there was some extra element, which meant that the arbitration clause itself has to be tainted with the vice in question. *Fiona Trust & Holding Corporation & others v. Yuri Privalov & ors* [2007] EWCA Civ 20 Lovells International Arbitration E-Bulletin, January 2007.

41 K.H. Schwab, "Wandlung der Schiedsgerichtsbarkeit" in *Festschrift für W. Henkel* (1995) n. 10, at 814.

42 The term is used in a 1996 editorial of a special issue of arbitration international on arbitrability. 12(2) *Arb. Int'l* (1996) at iii-x.

Commentators have deemed the expansive trend of such a magnitude that it witnesses of the "ultimate doctrinal ascendancy of arbitration."[43]

3-25 The public policy test imposed the *individual* examination of the conformity of each subject matter to public policy and complex reflections on conflicting policy goals. Different areas of law were opened, one-by-one, to arbitrability. The disentanglement of arbitrability and public policy has opened the way for the formulation of *general* and more liberal criteria for the definition of arbitrability; and ultimately for a conceptual leap in the classical regulation of the question. The international policy in favour of arbitration has also contributed to the *simplification* of decisions on arbitrability. In doubt, arbitrability prevails over inarbitrability.

3-26 On the level of legal technique, universal arbitrability is implemented by national laws in one of two ways: Either all matters are considered, *a priori*, arbitrable, unless particular disputes are reserved to exclusive court jurisdiction. Alternatively, arbitrable claims are defined very broadly to encompass all disputes involving an economic or a financial interest. Accordingly, legal rights would be arbitrable by default, unless they fall outside a general criteria set by the law, or are specifically excluded from the scope of arbitrability. Both approaches are popular. While the first is found in U.S., Canadian, and to some extent French law, the second approach characterises Swiss and German Laws.

3-27 Arbitrators, more than courts, are likely to reason on arbitrability in simple and *global* terms. In doubt, arbitrators usually tend to assert jurisdiction, on the basis that in so doing, they are giving effect to the parties' intention to arbitrate.[44] Arguably, the duty of arbitrators to render an enforceable award would not limit the arbitrator's freedom to arbitrate what the parties have submitted to them, since this duty only exists to the extent that the parties have not waived it.[45] Nevertheless, in popular viewpoints, international arbitrators, by virtue of their growing *public* mission, are bound to raise arbitrability issues *ex officio*.[46]

[43] Douglas Jones, *supra* note 4 at 121-149.

[44] In this sense Craig, Park & Paulsson, *supra* note 2 at 60.

[45] Julian Lew, Loukas Mistelis and Stefan Kröll, *Comparative International Commercial Arbitration*, (Kluwer 2003) at 187-221, no. 9-96.

[46] *Ibid.*

5.2. Presumption of Arbitrability

(a) U.S. Law:

3-28 Over the last three decades, the U.S. Supreme Court has pioneered the international expansion of arbitrability to areas of economic activity heavily impregnated with public interest.[47] More, U.S. courts have provided a much-needed conceptual frame for universal arbitrability.

3-29 First, U.S. courts, with their explicit sensibility to international commerce, have supplied a fundamental policy *rationale* for the expansion of arbitrability in international matters. The court decisions which allowed the arbitrability of international securities and antitrust claims were invariably driven by basic reflections on the needs of international commerce; and in addition to the special reasons which founded arbitrability in the particular case, they typically contained arguments of a general nature which supported the parties' freedom to arbitrate *per se.* The "sensitivity to the need of the international commercial system for predictability in the resolution of disputes,"[48] or to avoid damage to "the fabric of international commerce and trade"[49] "require that we enforce the parties' agreement, even assuming that a contrary result would be forthcoming in a domestic context."[50] These explicit references to the jurisdictional needs of international commerce found echoes in other common law jurisdictions. In justifying the arbitrability of international antitrust claims, the New Zealand High Court has ruled that the importance of international trade and "adherence to international comity"[51] overrides national public interest.

3-30 Second, the U.S. is a model of a legal system, which solves arbitrability issues by reference to general principles governing arbitration in general. They include the treatment of arbitration agreements as ordinary contracts[52] (and thus

47 The trend often attributed to *Mitsubishi,* has begun a decade earlier, in cases like *Sherk v. Alberto-Culver* [30] 417 U.S. S Ct 506 (1974). (Claims under the securities Act are arbitrable in international settings). Reisman, Craig and Paulsson, *International Commercial Arbitration,* (Foundation Press 1997) at 309.

48 *Mitsubishi,* 73 U.S. 614 (1985).

49 *Sherk v. Alberto-Culver* [30] 417 U.S. S Ct 506 (1974).

50 *First Options v. Kaplan,* 115 U.S. S Ct. 1920 (1995).

51 *Attorney General of New Zealand v. Mobil Oil New Zealand Ltd.* [1989] 2 NZLR 668.

52 "Arbitration agreements are to be treated like other contracts, subject to the policy favoring arbitration." "If there are deviations from such standard contract doctrine, they should be in the

its parties benefit from the same measure of freedom of contract generally available for parties to other contracts); the federal policy in favour of arbitration; and its main expression: the general idea that doubt should be interpreted in favour of arbitral jurisdiction.[53] In *Moses*, the Supreme Court has articulated a general principle of interpretation of doubt in favour of arbitrability that is well-established today. "Any doubts concerning the scope of arbitral issues should be resolved in favor of arbitration."[54] The result is the domain of arbitrable claims is exceptionally large and "US courts will enforce almost all agreements to arbitrate disputes, regardless of the genesis of the claims."[55]

3-31 This general presumption of arbitrability has inspired solutions to arbitrability problems in other common law jurisdictions as well. While U.K., Australian and Canadian laws are silent on the arbitrability of securities claims, commentators tend to interpret silence in favour of arbitration.[56] The reasoning is: if nothing in the legal system expressly prohibits a specific right from being submitted to arbitration, then this right should be arbitrable, *a priori.*

(b) French Law: Autonomous Arbitration Agreements

3-32 The French notion of *arbitrabilité*, originally based on criteria of public policy,[57] constituted a major impediment to the development of arbitration. Art. 2060-1 was particularly ill-adapted to international arbitration.[58] To overcome this hurdle (which continued to exist after the reforms of 1981) and formulate a more liberal criteria that is suitable to international settings, has required serious judicial groundwork.

---

direction of arbitrability." I. MacNeil, R. Speidel & T. Stipanowich, Federal Arbitration Law: Agreements, Awards and Remedies Under the Federal Arbitration Act, (1994) § 18.7.1.1.

53 "A reviewing court examining whether arbitrators exceeded their powers must resolve all doubts in favor of arbitration." *Apache Bohai Corp. LDC v. Texaco China BV* F.3d, 2007 WL 587233, CA 5 (Tex.), 2007. Feb 27, 2007; *Brook v. Peak Intern.*, Ltd. 294 F.3d 668, CA 5 (Tex.), 2002; *Action Indus., Inc. v. U.S. Fid. & Guar. Co.,* 358 F.3d 337, 343 (5th Cir. 2004).

54 *Moses H. Cone Memorial Hospital v. Mercury Construction Corp.*, U.S. S Ct 460 U.S. 1 at 24 (1983).

55 J.T. McLaughlin, "Arbitrability: Current Trends in the United States", 12(2) *Arb. Int'l* (1996) 113.

56 J. Kerr, "Arbitrability of Securities Law Claims in Common Law Nations", 12(2) *Arb. Int'l* (1996) 171-178.

57 Article 2060-1 of the *Code Civil* (law reform of July 5th, 1972): "matières qui intéressent l'ordre public."

58 J-B. Racine, *L'Arbitrage Commercial International et l'ordre Public* (LGDJ 1999) 34.

3-33 The definition of arbitrability by reference to public policy has, at times, been interpreted restrictively. Courts would exclude arbitration every time the dispute involves the application of legislation, which relates to public policy.[59] This restrictive view has been heavily criticised, and ultimately abandoned in case law, for being particularly damaging to the expansion of arbitration.[60] Beginning in the 1950s, French courts have simply ignored the legislative text; and explicitly ruled out the restrictive association of public policy and arbitrability. "The arbitrability of a dispute is not excluded by the mere fact that rules pertaining to public policy are applicable to the disputed rapport."[61] The *jurisprudence* that followed has largely emptied Art. 2060 of its substance, and left it *lettre morte.*[62]

3-34 French courts did not only dissociate arbitrability from public policy, but have also gradually associated it with a more international and less restrictive notion. Indeed, French courts were the first to explicitly define arbitrability in international matters by reference to *international public policy.*[63] Non-arbitrable matters are those that are "of the closest interest to international public policy."[64] In subsequent case law, French courts developed the famous principle of *autonomy* of international arbitration agreements of all national law, which dictates that the validity of international arbitration agreements should be assessed solely

> within the limits of the mandatory norms of French law and international public policy, by reference to the common intention of the parties, without the need to refer to a national law.[65]

While the reference to the *lex fori* blurs the so-called autonomy of all national law, the evolution of *jurisprudence* left to inarbitrability only a *residual* place: personal status and criminal matters.

59 See Cass. Civ. 9 January, 1854, D.P. 1854, 1, 69 the dispute "*touchait a l'ordre public.*"; CA Paris, 9 February, 1954, D. 1954, at 192; CA Orleans, 15 May, 1961, Rev. Arb. (1961) 188 (the case involved an international arbitration). "le litige concerne l'ordre public et que le compromis est nul chaque fois que la solution de l'arbitrage suppose l'interprétation et l'application d'une règle d'ordre public".

60 P. Ancel, JCP, *Procédure Civile*, Fasc. 1024, 1986, n.11, p.5.

61 CA Paris 19 May 1993 (Arrêt *Labinel*) *Rev. Arb.* (1993) 645; See also in earlier decisions: CA Paris, 15 June 1956, Dalloz, 1957, at 587; CA Orleans, 15 February 1956 D. 1966, at 340.

62 J-B. Racine, *supra* note 58 at 29.

63 *Ibid.*, at 36.

64 CA Paris, 29 March, 1991, *Rev. Arb.* (1991) 478.

65 Arrêt *Dalico*, *Cass*, 1ere, 20 Décembre 1993, Rev. Arb. (1994) 116.

3-35 This general judicial liberalism in addressing arbitrability is particularly evident in international consumer disputes.[66] Essentially, international consumers are entirely assimilated to professional parties for the purpose of evaluating arbitrability. The Paris *Cour d'Appel* has ruled that *domestic* law prohibitions on arbitration agreements between merchants and non-merchants should *not* apply in the international context.[67] Similarly, international employment disputes are now arbitrable in France.[68]

(c) Swiss & German Laws: Economic Criteria of Arbitrability

3-36 Swiss law provides: "[a]ny dispute involving financial interests can be the subject matter of arbitration."[69] This is an extremely broad notion of arbitrability, perhaps unparalleled in the modern history of arbitration. All rights relating to "*property*", real or personal, tangible or intangible, are thus arbitrable. Only non-economic rights would fall beyond the reach of the parties' freedom to arbitrate. Arbitrability is truly "universal"; and international parties are given the autonomy to arbitrate virtually all disputes arising under the global economy.

3-37 Swiss law also totally rejects inarbitrability by reason of the public nature of the applicable rules. The Swiss Federal Tribunal has refused to consider the U.N. embargo on commercial activities with Iraq, which is effective in Switzerland, a bar to the arbitrability of a dispute arising under a contract for the sale of military equipment to Iraq.[70] The court thus did not exclude the possibility that a private tribunal could be brought to apply public international law.

3-38 German Law is based on the UNCITRAL Model Law, but is heavily influenced by Swiss law. In identifying arbitrable claims, it combined the two approaches, leading arguably to an even larger notion of arbitrability. Parties may

66 European law is increasingly favourable to arbitrating consumer disputes. See EU guidelines on the promotion of arbitration in consumer contexts, European Parliament Res. of 25 July 1994, EC Off. J. of 25th, July, 1994, n C 205/519; Rev. Arb. (1995) 355.

67 CA Paris, 7 December 1994; RTD com, 1995, at 401. Not only are consumer disputes arbitrable, but consumers are also subject to the very liberal French substantive norms on the extension of arbitration to non-signatories. Commentators have criticized this "*dangerous*" trend. Calais-Auloy (J.), Steinmetz (F.), *Droit de la consommation*, (6th ed, Dalloz , 2003).

68 CA Grenoble, 13 September 1993; Rev. Arb. (1994) 337. First French decision to hold that the "arbitration agreement included in an international individual employment agreement is valid."

69 Swiss Private International Law Act (PILA), Article 177(1).

70 *Fincantieri-Cantieri Navali Italiani S.p.A. et Oto Melara S.p.A. v. M. et Tribunal Arbitral,* ATF 118 II 353, 355 (June 23, 1992). Italian courts ruled this dispute was *not* arbitrable. (See Corte di Appello Genoa, 7 May 1994, 4 Rev. Arb. (1994) 505, XXI YBCA (1996) 594.

arbitrate "any claim involving an economic interest (*vermögensrechtlicher Anspruch*).[71] Arbitrable subject matter also includes "claims involving no economic interest", if they can be the object of settlement by the parties. The classic criterion is given a *residual* place in the sphere of non-economic rights, to transport these rights into the circle of arbitrability.

3-39 National laws which define the domain of arbitration with such *largesse* usually also explicitly reserve the case of claims excluded by specific legislation. This is the case of German law.

(d) Universal Arbitrability in Emerging and Third World Jurisdictions?

3-40 The trend towards liberating arbitration from local barriers transcends different degrees of arbitral development. A plethora of factors, including regulatory competition, legal borrowing and the needs to protect foreign investment and commerce have contributed to a gradual, yet deep, shift in third world voices on what is arbitrable and what is not. While local impediments to the arbitrability of certain types of disputes continue to exist in the third world, they are more reminiscences of past unpleasant arbitration experiences, than true reflections of present and potentially future attitudes. Many emerging jurisdictions have either borrowed or adopted very liberal approaches to arbitrability, or have considerably altered the way they protect what they deem "national interest" in a manner which does not conflict with their international commitment to arbitration.

(e) Canadian Law and the Arbitrability "Big-Bang"

3-41 In the matter of few years, Canada's traditional Anglo-Saxon distrust of arbitration[72] turned into a pronounced favourable policy.[73] Following Canada's adoption of the UNCITRAL Model Law (in 1986), the Canadian Supreme Court led an impressive enlargement of the scope of what parties can submit to arbitration.

[71] Code of Civil Procedure – as amended, Section § 1030.

[72] The domain of arbitrable claims was curtailed in a variety of ways and was sometimes *minimal*. For example, arbitration was refused when the sole question was the interpretation of the contract.

[73] See Cecil Branson describing this instant shift as a *"coup de foudre"*, "The Enforcement of International Commercial Arbitration Agreements In Canada", 16(1) *Arb. Int'l.*

3-42 The Court started by giving a restrictive interpretation to the concept of 'public interest', as a limitation to arbitrable claims.[74] It also prevented lower courts from reverting to narrow definitions of public policy.[75] In a famous 2003 decision, the court ruled that "parties to an arbitration agreement have virtually unfettered autonomy in identifying the disputes that may be the subject of the arbitration proceeding."[76] While the decision deals with the arbitrability of copyright disputes, the generality of the court's pronouncement suggests the inception of *une arbitrabilité de principe,* or a general presumption that claims which parties have chosen to arbitrate are arbitrable.[77]

3-43 Canadian law not only allows the parties to arbitrate virtually everything, but recent legislation also makes arbitration, not the courts, the *default* jurisdiction with respect to some disputes. The Quebec Professional Artists Act, Section 37 reads as follows

> In the absence of an express renunciation, every dispute arising from the interpretation of the contract shall be submitted to an arbitrator at the request of one of the parties.

In other words, unless parties to a professional artist's contract provide otherwise, the dispute is submitted to arbitration, not to judicial courts. Beyond a presumption of arbitrability, this is a presumption of consent to arbitration.

(f) Arbitration in International Administrative Contracts in the Arab World

3-44 In post-colonial Arab eyes (following deceiving arbitration experiences in government contracts relating to the exploration of natural resources) recourse of public entities to arbitration was not perceived to be in the public interest. As a result, Arab laws have widely prohibited arbitration in administrative or State contracts with foreign parties. However, and contrary to common misconception, this prohibition was not technically implemented by excluding the arbitrability of

[74] Under the Quebec code of civil procedure, issues of public interest cannot be referred to an arbitrator because the decision may be useful in the development of the law, and arbitral decisions are confidential. See *Pilotes du Saint-Laurent Central Inc v. Laurentian Pilotage Authority*, August, 8, 2002, 246 FTR 161 (FCTD) and 2003 FC 1470.

[75] *Éditions Chouette inc. v. Desputeaux*, 2003 SCC 17.

[76] *Éditions Chouette inc. v. Desputeaux*, 2003 SCC 17 (a very powerful statement in favour of the arbitrability in copyright disputes).

[77] Canada is known today to adopt one of the most liberal stances with regard to arbitrability. Richard Boivin and Nicola Mariani, "International Arbitration in Canada, *Highest Court Rules in Favor of Broad Interpretation of Arbitrability*", 20(5) *J. Int'l Arb.* (2003) 507–514.

these contracts, but by limiting[78] or totally depriving[79] State entities and public bodies from the legal *capacity* to enter into international arbitration agreements.[80] The same excluded subject matters, however, remained arbitrable in domestic settings or between private parties.

3-45 As entrenched as they were, these impediments to arbitrating administrative contracts in the Arab world are essentially history today. The State and public bodies can submit to arbitration, under Tunisian,[81] Algerian Law, and an express provision of Omani law.[82] In Egypt, to end uncertainty, the 1994 arbitration law was amended in 1997, to explicitly give public entities the capacity to arbitrate.[83] A 2002 legislative amendment in Lebanon[84] has reversed the well-established judicial exclusion of arbitration in administrative contracts.[85] A Saudi Regulation of 25 April 1983 (Article 3) removed the total restriction on the use of arbitration by government agencies. Arbitration may be stipulated with the approval of the president of the council of ministers.[86]

3-46 In all cases, the international effectiveness of domestic law limitations to the validity of State's consent to arbitrate, if any remain, has significantly decreased. A norm of *international public policy,*[87] found in a growing body of awards[88]

[78] In Iran, Art. 139 of the Constitution makes the referral to arbitration of public contracts with foreign parties, dependent, in every case, on the approval of the Council of Ministers and the Parliament.

[79] After *ARAMCO*, Saudi Arabia prohibited all public bodies to accept arbitration of international disputes. Decree No. 58 "constituted an impenetrable barrier to any arbitration in Saudi Arabia". Abudl Hamid El Ahdab, *Arbitration with the Arab Countries*, (2nd ed, 1999) 13.

[80] See generally Dhisadee Chamlongrasdr, "Tension in Domestic and International Law on Capacity to Enter into Arbitration Agreements: A Survey on Legal Restrictions", 16 *European Business Law Review* (2005) at 275-310.

[81] Law No. 13 of 7 March 1988 on representation before the courts for an implicit – though clear – recognition of this possibility; then an unequivocal recognition in article 21 of Law No. 89-9 of 1 February 1989 concerning participation in State undertakings.

[82] Art. 1 of Law of Arbitration in Civil and Commercial Disputes of 1 July 1997.

[83] Law No. 9/1997 (15 May 1997) added a paragraph to Article 1. See also Aboul-Enein, *International Handbook on Commercial Arbitration ICC* (n 67) vol I (Egypt) 3-4.

[84] Seven articles of the Lebanese New Code of Civil Procedure were amended by Law No. 440/2002 of 29 July 2002. N. Comair-Obeid, "The Impact and Consequences of Changes in Lebanese Arbitration Law" 14(1) *ICC Bulletin* (2003) 47.

[85] Conseil d'Etat libanais, 17 juillet 2001, Rev. Arb., 2001 - No. 4, at 868-870.

[86] However, in 1994, Saudi Arabia adhered to the New York Convention, but excluded oil-related disputes from the domain of its application.

[87] Dhisadee Chamlongrasdr, *supra* note 80 at 275-310.

[88] ICC award No. 3481 of 1986, 1986-1990 Collection al' ICC awards 263.

and court decisions,[89] prohibits a State from pleading its own law as an excuse to avoid the obligation to arbitrate it has undertaken. Swiss law explicitly provides that a State cannot invoke its internal law restrictions to arbitration, including not only issues of State capacity to arbitrate, but also defences to arbitrability.[90]

3-47 Today, Arab law approaches to arbitrability are rather positive. Arbitration is widely accepted in the area of the highest sensitivity: State contracts. International employment disputes are arbitrable under Saudi law.[91] Algerian and Tunisian laws formally recognize the concept of *ordre publique international.*[92]

5.3. Modern-day-Calvo-provisions[93]

3-48 Modern-day local barriers to arbitration in the Arab world, if any, are *different*. Legal systems rarely exclude arbitrability, even in areas involving predominant national interest. Instead, arbitration is permitted, but regulated in a way that is protective of the public interest in question. The Egyptian law on the transfer of technology (Embodied in the *Code de Commerce*) is a good example. Article 87[94] permits recourse to arbitration, but restricts freedom to arbitrate. The law mandates Egypt as the place of arbitration and Egyptian law as governing procedural and substantive law. The Supreme Constitutional Court (SCC) of Egypt has recently rejected, and rightly so, a constitutional challenge to the

89 In *Société Gatoil v. National Iranian Oil Company,* the court did not allow the National Iranian Oil Company to rely on the Iranian Constitution to invalidate the arbitration agreement it had entered into. CA Paris, 17 December 1990 (1993) Rev. Arb. 280.

90 PILA, Art. 177.2.

91 The Italian Supreme Court has refused to refer Italian parties to arbitration in an international employment contract, subject to Saudi Law, which, contrary to Italian law does not exclude arbitration of employment disputes. Albert Jan van den Berg, Consolidated Commentary on New York Convention, 1981, 223 Court Referral – Arbitrability.

92 Habib Malouche, "Recent Developments in Arbitration Law in Tunisia", 8(2) *J. Int'l Arb.* (1991) at 23-32.

93 The term is used here, *abstraction faite* of its historical or popular pejorative connotation.

94 "1. The Egyptian Courts shall have the jurisdiction to decide on the disputes arising from the technology transfer contract.... Agreement may be reached on settling the dispute amicably or via arbitration to be held in Egypt according to the provisions of the Egyptian Law.
2. In all cases, deciding the subject of the dispute shall be according to the provisions of the Egyptian Law, and any agreement to the contrary shall be null and void." 17(5) *J. Int'l Arb.* (2000) at 187

legislative provision.[95] While vaguely resembling old Calvo clauses, modern ones do not prohibit the principle of arbitration, but merely regulate its parameters.

6. The Changing Face of International Arbitration

3-49 A narrow scope of arbitrability was perhaps most fundamentally the natural emanation of a now old and outmoded perception of international arbitration as "*ouster*" of the natural jurisdiction of courts, if not a lesser competitor whose domain should be reduced to a minimum.[96] Similarly, the evolution towards universal arbitrability is the natural reflection of the universal development of arbitral justice, and its rising *cosmopolitan* spirit. Before, legal systems specified what subject matter *is* arbitrable. Today, with arbitration being the rule rather than the exception in international settings, legal system need to determine what disputes are *not* arbitrable.[97]

3-50 Universal arbitrability can be justified primarily by reference to the *institutional* progress of international arbitration: the simple yet fundamental observation that, over the last few decades, arbitration has become a *better* justice. For many contemporary thinkers, arbitration is the normal forum, if not the *juge naturel*[98] of global commerce. Today, international arbitration is a *sophisticated* justice that has "matured" to provide sufficient protection for weaker parties[99] or the public interest. International arbitrators are expected, if not required, to conform to a judge-like standard of conduct. The classic fear that arbitrators would under-enforce public laws is no longer tenable. International arbitrators routinely apply mandatory norms, foreign *lois de police* and may occasionally be brought to apply constitutional or international norms. They are

[95] Supreme Constitutional Court of Egypt, Case No. 253 for 2007, 15 April, 2007. Restrictions on freedom of contract (in this case, *post*-the initial free choice of arbitration) fall within the normal exercise of legislative power.

[96] Yves Fortier, "The Never-ending Struggle between Arbitrators and Judges in International Commercial Arbitration", in Briner, R. and K.-H. Bockstiegel (eds), *Law of International Business and Dispute Settlement in the 21st Century, Liber Amicorum* Karl-Heinz Bockstiegel, (2001) at 178.

[97] There must be a heavy presumption in favor of arbitrability. Bernard Hanotiau, "L'Arbitrabilité et la favor arbitrandum: un réexamen", 121 *Clunet* (1994) 899

[98] See Yves Derains, "Chroniques de Sentences Arbitrales", *Clunet* (1978) at 976 ; Hanotiau, "Problems Raised by Complex Arbitrations Involving Multiple Contracts—Parties—Issues", 18(3) *J. Int'l Arb.* (2001) 256.

[99] Securities claims are arbitrable in the U.S. since the mid-1970s. *Shearson/American Express v. McMahon*, 482 U.S. 220.

not insensitive to considerations of equity or efficacy, and may even apply moral norms.[100] Arbitrators are also equipped to deal with complex contracts or highly technical subject matter. The usual inclusion of commercial arbitration clauses in international State contracts relating to "investment," increasingly brings matters of national interest before private arbitrators. The expanding definition of "investment" under bilateral investment treaties to include contractual rights also contributes to this blurring of the line between the private and the public.

7. Future Perspectives

7.1. Subsidiarity

3-51 In the not too distant future, national laws would find vain the provision of definitions of what claims are arbitrable. The domain of international arbitration *vis-à-vis* that of national courts would simply be associated with the legal nature of the dispute and whether it relates to international commerce or involves its interests. That is to say that the allocation of jurisdictional competence between the two jurisdictional orders would be governed by a principle of *subsidiarity.* This principle would dictate, for the purpose of defining arbitrable claims, that national courts may assert exclusive jurisdiction in an international matter, only if arbitration is explicitly excluded by law. If the need for legislative reference to arbitrability would remain, it would take the form of *exclusionary* rules which keep non-patrimonial rights, mainly family and criminal law in the "*domaine réservé*" of State justice.

7.2 Merit-Review?

3-52 The emergence of universal arbitrability, as all-important evolutions, has come with uncertainties and unanswered questions. One of them is the idea expressed in the *Mitsubishi dicta* and developed in U.S. law under the name "second-look doctrine." In simple terms, arbitrability of public rights comes with a necessary price: the necessity of a parallel extension of "merits review" by courts to control the exercise of arbitral justice in its extended domain, and ensure the proper application of public laws or mandatory norms. A similar solution would cause arbitration to lose in finality and effectiveness what it has gained in universal application; and should not be considered.

[100] P. Mayer, "La règle morale dans l'arbitrage international", in *Etudes offertes à P. Bellet* (Litec, 1991).

7.3 Emergence of a Notion of "International Arbitrability"

3-53 Today, a well-established principle of the law of international arbitration dictates that international parties may agree to arbitrate matters which would be non-arbitrable under national laws. Whether conceptualized as a norm of national law, an "autonomous substantive rule of public policy,"[101] or a general principle of arbitration law, that this rule exists is beyond doubt. International practice has sanctified a notion of "international arbitrability" which is defined solely by reference to international public policy, or *l'ordre public véritablement international.*

8. CONCLUSION

3-54 In Bruno Oppetit's last reflections on the universal development of arbitration, "[a] concept usually loses in comprehension what it gains in extension. The concept of arbitration does not escape this rule of formal logic."[102] The significant broadening of arbitrability in international matters, and ultimately the transformation in the methods of its definition by the effect of the international policy in favour of arbitration, have announced a new phase in the life of the concept of arbitrability: the beginning of its end.[103] Arbitrability is a concept whose success has banalized and, to a large extent, emptied of significance. The "commerciality" reservation and the defence of inarbitrability as ground for non-enforcement under the New York Convention[104] have lost much of their role. With the gradual death of arbitrability, they would also fall in desuetude. The liberation of arbitrability from all references to local law, to favour the security of international contracts, has stripped arbitrability of its *essentiala* as a notion of national content, embodying political choices of a sovereign.

3-55 Scholarship on the subject is invited to explore the consequences of universal arbitrability and the extension of the concept. The new developments in the domain of arbitrability favour global and internationalist approaches to its study, rather than the examination of specific types of claims through the lens of local norms.

[101] Craig, Park & Paulsson, *supra* note 2 at 72

[102] Bruno Oppetit, *Théorie de L'Arbitrage*, (PUF 1998) 120.

[103] "The subject of arbitrability of disputes arising from international business transactions should – and hopefully will – become out of fashion in the not too distant future." Antoine Kirry, *supra* note 13 at 373-389.

[104] Consecutively Article I (3) and Article V-2-(a).

Laurence Shore[*]

CHAPTER 4

THE UNITED STATES' PERSPECTIVE ON "ARBITRABILITY"

1. INTRODUCTION

4-1 In accepting the assignment of presenting a paper on the current U.S. perspective on "arbitrability", I have entered into a tricky area of linguistics and arbitration law. The term "arbitrability" means something very different in the U.S. than it does in virtually any other mature arbitration jurisdiction. This has left me with a difficult initial decision – either (a) to consider what U.S. arbitration lawyers (and U.S. judges) mean when they argue about arbitrability, or (b) to avoid the American linguistic peculiarity and consider the European definition in the American context. I have opted for the former because in the house of international arbitration there are still many distinct rooms, and there may be some value in visiting the U.S. room and in understanding that a non-U.S. lawyer may be speaking past a U.S. lawyer if the discussion concerns the issue of arbitrability. Further, such a discussion with a U.S. lawyer will lead to consideration of the doctrines of separability and Kompetenz-Kompetenz, and should result in an appreciation of the complexities and uncertainties in U.S. law on arbitrability – as U.S. lawyers and judges use this term.

2. CLARIFYING THE TERM

4-2 "Arbitrability" is a far broader concept in the United States than in other countries. Internationally, arbitrability refers to whether specific classes of

[*] Partner and Head of International Arbitration Group, Gibson Dunn & Crutcher LLP, New York; Visiting Professor, School of International Arbitration, Centre for Commercial Law Studies, Queen Mary University of London.

L Mistelis & S Brekoulakis (eds), Arbitrability: International & Comparative Perspectives, 69-83

disputes are barred from arbitration either because of public policy or because they are outside the scope of the arbitration agreement.[1] In the context of international commercial arbitration, arbitrability thus generally refers to whether the specific claims raised are of a subject matter capable of settlement by arbitration, and are not subject to the exclusive jurisdiction of either party's national courts, the seat of arbitration's national courts, or the enforcement country's national courts. This inquiry is necessary to avoid encroaching upon the sovereignty of a country that would otherwise require certain classes of disputes—such as criminal or tax cases—to be resolved by its own national courts.

4-3 The U.S. also calls this arbitrability, and in this regard the U.S. courts have been very supportive of the arbitration process. The U.S. Supreme Court has noted that these "questions of arbitrability must be addressed with a healthy regard for the federal policy favoring arbitration."[2] But the term in the U.S. further includes the jurisdictional question that asks whether an arbitrator or a court should decide if a given dispute should be submitted to arbitration. The strong federal policy in the U.S. favouring arbitration has not traditionally applied to the initial determination of whether there is a valid agreement to arbitrate. Traditionally, U.S. courts have had the power to determine all questions of arbitrability before or after a dispute has been submitted to arbitration. These gateway questions of arbitrability include determining whether (1) there is a valid arbitration agreement; (2) the scope of the agreement covers the dispute in question; and (3) public policy would not otherwise bar submitting the dispute to arbitration. If all of these points are determined by the court in the affirmative, an arbitrator may decide the merits of the dispute. However, there has been some modernizing of this traditional gateway approach: relatively recent Supreme Court cases have shifted the ground, to an extent, toward permitting arbitrators to take the initial decisions on certain gateway questions.

4-4 These gateway questions are not absent in other countries, though different terminology is used and, for the most part, other countries have more readily entrusted the initial decisions on jurisdictional issues to arbitrators. This is not to say that U.S. courts have been unsupportive of arbitrators' authority. The

[1] See Julian Lew, Loukas Mistelis & Stefan Kröll, *Comparative International Commercial Arbitration* (Kluwer 2003), at 187: "Arbitrability involves the simple question of what type of issues can and cannot be submitted to arbitration."

[2] *Moses H. Cone Memorial Hosp. v. Mercury Construction Corp.*, 460 U.S. 1, 24-25 (1983).

doctrine of separability has long been recognised by the U.S. Supreme Court, providing that the arbitration clause in a contract exists independently from the rest of the contract, and that where a party challenges "the validity of the contract in general, as opposed to the arbitration clause in particular," an arbitrator—not the court—should decide the issue.[3] However, if the challenging party attacks the arbitration clause itself, the challenging party can seek court intervention to deem the arbitration clause invalid. The issue of whether the clause itself is being attacked in such a way as to justify a reference to the courts can be very complicated, and in this respect the U.S. loses some of its distinctiveness in the international arbitration world.

4-5 To be sure, some U.S. courts have issued judgments that render the separability doctrine somewhat vulnerable. For example, the U.S. Court of Appeals for the Fifth Circuit held that where a party challenges whether a contract (valid or not) ever existed, rather than the enforceability of a pre-existing contract, a court may decide this underlying issue without submitting the question to arbitration.[4] These types of challenges include allegations of forged signatures or lack of agency to bind a party. The Fifth Circuit acknowledged

> where parties have formed an agreement which contains an arbitration clause, any attempt to dissolve that agreement by having the entire agreement declared voidable or void is for the arbitrator. Only if the arbitration clause is attacked on an independent basis can the court decide the dispute; otherwise, general attacks on the agreement are for the arbitrator.[5]

4-6 However, the Fifth Circuit stated that the case before it, "[w]here the very existence of any agreement is disputed, it is for the courts to decide at the outset whether an agreement was reached, . . .".[6] The Fifth Circuit determined that to force a party to submit to arbitration on the other party's terms when there had never, in fact, been a contract would be wholly inequitable. The Circuit judges noted that the "base point to which the analysis inevitably returns is that the separability doctrine rests on the assumption that there is an underlying agreement," and a challenge to the very existence of that underlying agreement should not be for the arbitrator to decide.[7]

3 *Prima Paint Corp. v. Flood & Conklin Mfg. Co.*, 388 U.S. 395, 409 (1967).
4 *Will-Drill Resources, Inc. v. Samson Resources Co.*, 352 F.3d 211 (5th Cir. 2003).
5 *Ibid.*, at 218.
6 *Ibid.*
7 *Ibid.*

4-7 Although *Will-Drill* undoubtedly made a fine distinction between which types of claims are and are not separable, the doctrine of separability nonetheless remains in place in the U.S. In *Buckeye Checking, Inc. v. Cardegna*,[8] the U.S. Supreme Court upheld the separability doctrine and noted that the

> issue of the contract's validity is different from the issue of whether any agreement between the alleged obligor and obligee was ever concluded. Our opinion today addresses only the former, and does not speak to the issue decided in the cases cited by respondents . . . which hold that it is for courts to decide whether the alleged obligor ever signed the contract, whether the signor lacked authority to commit the alleged principal, and whether the signor lacked the mental capacity to assent.

At some stage, the U.S. Supreme Court may need to speak to the *Will-Drill* issue, and it can only be hoped that the U.S. will follow, for example, the position of the English courts on this issue.[9]

3. Jurisdiction

4-8 U.S. arbitrability analysis, then, addresses the question of "who should decide whether the parties agreed to arbitrate the merits of a dispute". Although the U.S. empowers arbitrators to rule on their own jurisdiction, courts may be called upon to address questions of arbitrability.

4-9 U.S. arbitrability disputes generally arise when a party compels a second party to submit to arbitration when the second party claims it is not bound to do so, or when a party brings suit against a second party in court in an apparent breach of an arbitration clause. While the U.S. grants the authority to arbitrators to rule on their own substantive jurisdiction, a party can call upon a court to decide whether a particular matter can be submitted to arbitration at any stage of the arbitral process. At that point, a court is empowered to either compel or enjoin arbitration. Part of the distinctiveness of the U.S. is that it provides for much readier access to judicial determinations.

8 546 U.S. 440, 444 (2006).

9 See the judgment of the House of Lords in *Premium Nafta Products v. Fili Shipping Co.*, [2007] 4 All ER 951, at paras 17-19, although there may be cases in which

> the ground upon which the main agreement is invalid is identical with the ground upon which the arbitration agreement is invalid, . . . the arbitration agreement can be invalidated only on a ground which relates to the arbitration agreement and is not merely a consequence of the invalidity of the main agreement.

3.1. Recent U.S. Supreme Court Jurisprudence Regarding Arbitrability

4-10 Over the last decade, the role of courts in deciding gateway questions of arbitrability has undergone a transformation. The question, "which gateway issues qualify as a question of arbitrability", has been at the centre of the U.S. Supreme Court's recent jurisprudence. In its past few decisions, the Court indicated a trend away from the clear distinction between gateway issues and merits-based issues. In *First Options of Chicago, Inc. v. Kaplan,*[10] the Court granted courts the authority to decide questions of arbitrability, but starting with *Howsam v. Dean Witter Reynolds, Inc.*,[11] the Supreme Court began parsing which gateway issues actually qualify as questions of arbitrability. Ultimately, these recent decisions have bolstered the federal policy in favour of arbitration.

(a) First Options and the Presumption that Courts Decide "Questions of Arbitrability"

4-11 In *First Options*, writing for a unanimous Court, Justice Breyer delineated the authority for deciding questions of arbitrability between arbitrators and courts.[12] There, a dispute arose between First Options and Kaplan over an unsatisfied payment of debt.[13] Kaplan claimed the dispute with First Options was not arbitrable, and that the arbitration agreement did not bind him because he did not sign the document where the arbitration agreement appeared.[14] Nonetheless, Kaplan filed his opposition to arbitration with the arbitrator instead of first raising his objections with a court.[15] The arbitrator ruled that arbitration was appropriate, and proceeded to rule against Kaplan on the merits.[16] Subsequently, Kaplan asked the federal district court to vacate the award, but instead, the court affirmed. On appeal, the Third Circuit Court of Appeals reversed in favour of Kaplan.[17]

4-12 The Supreme Court ruled that the question of who has the primary power to decide questions of arbitrability turns on whether the parties specifically contracted to have someone other than the courts decide it. In contrast to the

[10] 514 U.S. 938 (1995).
[11] 537 U.S. 79, 83 (2002).
[12] *First Options*, 514 U.S. at 938.
[13] *Ibid.* at 942.
[14] *Ibid.*
[15] *Ibid.*
[16] *Ibid.*
[17] *Ibid.*

presumption in favour of arbitration where there is ambiguity in the scope of a valid arbitration agreement,[18] the Court ruled that the opposite presumption should apply to the separate question of who the parties intended to decide whether an arbitration agreement ever existed. It further noted that whether the parties agreed to submit a question of arbitrability to an arbitrator is one of contract interpretation best left to the courts. Justice Breyer explained that "[C]ourts should not assume that parties agreed to arbitrate arbitrability unless there is "clea[r] and unmistakabl[e]" evidence that they did so.[19] Because arbitration is a matter of contract, mutual consent is a prerequisite to submitting questions to arbitration. It is fundamentally unfair to force an unwilling party "to arbitrate a matter they reasonably thought a judge not an arbitrator would decide".[20] Therefore, *First Options* established the propositions that contracting parties may elect to arbitrate questions of arbitrability (jurisdictional matters), and these agreements must be found on clear evidence.[21] However, in the absence of such intent, courts have the authority to decide questions of arbitrability.

(b) Howsam, Pacificare, and Green Tree: Defining the Gatekeeper Function

4-13 *Howsam* presented the issue of whether the National Association of Securities Dealers' (NASD) time-bar on filing claims constituted a gateway question of arbitrability for a court to decide, or whether it was a procedural dispute appropriate for an arbitrator.[22] During oral argument, the Court dissected the meaning of the term "arbitrability" to determine whether a gateway question—in this case, whether an arbitration forum's statute of limitations bars submitting a question to arbitration—necessarily qualifies as a question of arbitrability appropriate for a court. In particular, Justice Ginsburg asked the petitioner,

[18] See *Moses H. Cone*, 460 U.S. at 24-25.

> [A]ny doubts concerning the scope of arbitrable issues should be resolved in favor of arbitration.

[19] *First Options*, 514 U.S. at 944 (quoting *AT&T Technologies, Inc. v. Communications Workers*, 475 U.S. 643, 649 (1986)).

[20] 514 U.S. at 945.

[21] *Ibid.*

[22] 537 U.S. at 83.

> if it's a question of arbitrability, the courts decide it. If it's not a question of arbitrability, . . . then it's for the arbitrator. . . . What is the content of that label, arbitrable?[23]

4-14 Justice Breyer, writing for a unanimous Court,[24] noted the limited scope of what constitutes a question of arbitrability.[25] Addressing Justice Ginsburg's concern, he concluded that though "any potentially dispositive gateway question . . . [whose] answer will determine whether the underlying controversy will proceed to arbitration on the merits" linguistically would seem to qualify as a "question of arbitrability', the phrase has a narrower application, in line with the intent and expectations of the contracting parties.[26] In essence, a gateway issue is only a question of arbitrability if the parties would likely expect a court to decide it.

4-15 Justice Breyer further explored the reasoning behind the courts' hostility toward permitting arbitrators to decide questions of arbitrability, and in oral argument, noted that those concerns were not present in this case.

> What we're after is the parties' intent. In most places in the law, the law of arbitration is either neutral or sometimes favorable to arbitration. But there is one exception. The one exception is where the parties may or may not have agreed to arbitrate arbitrability. And there we, interestingly enough, use a presumption that's very hostile to finding the intent to have the arbitrators arbitrate arbitrability. Now, in terms of the reason for that hostility, how does that apply here? I would think, at first blush, it shouldn't apply at all. Why? Because we're talking about rules of an arbitration forum.[27]

4-16 Parties to an arbitration agreement would normally expect a forum-based decision maker to decide forum-specific procedural gateway matters. In the opinion, Breyer noted that the "narrow circumstances" where contracting parties would likely expect a court to decide a gateway matter were confined to the existence and scope of an arbitration agreement. But, "[w]here [the] parties would likely expect that an arbitrator would decide the gateway matter", such as where there is a "'procedural' question[] which grow[s] out of the dispute and

23 Tr. of Oral Argument at 9, 38, *Howsam*, 537 U.S. 79 (No. 01-800).
24 The Case was decided 8-0 with Justice O'Connor not taking part.
25 *Howsam*, 537 U.S. at 83.
26 *Ibid.*
27 Tr. of Oral Argument at 47, *Howsam*, 537 U.S. 79 (No. 01-800).

bear[s] on its final disposition," there is a presumption that the arbitrator—not a judge—decides these questions.[28] In this instance, the arbitrator's relative expertise with respect to its own procedures—the time-bar—lent support to the parties' expectation that the arbitrator would decide this gateway issue: "[T]he NASD's time limit rule [fell] within the class of gateway procedural disputes that [did] not present [a] question of arbitrability."[29] With the *Howsam* decision, then, the Court made its first distinction between questions of arbitrability and dispositive-on-the-merits gateway issues that do not qualify as questions of arbitrability.

4-17 In writing for another unanimous court in *Pacificare Health Sys., Inc. v. Book*, Justice Scalia further narrowed the category of what constitutes a question of arbitrability.[30] The case presented the question whether a remedial limitation in an arbitration agreement that potentially made meaningful relief impossible was a gateway issue that constituted a question of arbitrability appropriate for a court to decide. In the case, a group of physicians filed a RICO suit against certain managed health care organisations because they failed to reimburse the physicians for services the doctors provided to patients.[31] The health care organisations moved to compel arbitration in an effort to frustrate the physicians' claim.[32] The district court and circuit court denied the request to compel arbitration because the arbitration clauses would likely preclude the arbitrator from awarding any damages under RICO.

4-18 At the beginning of oral argument, the Supreme Court posited a hypothetical situation where the parties—instead of prohibiting punitive damages—prohibited treble damages by contract so as to constitute a prospective waiver of a contractual right under RICO. The Court then asked a series of questions that dissected when, if ever, a waiver of a statutory remedy could qualify as a gateway issue appropriate for a court. Justice Breyer essentially answered the court's question when he pronounced:

28 *Ibid.* at 84.

29 *Ibid.* at 86.

30 538 U.S. 401 (2003).

31 *Ibid.* at 402.

32 The arbitration clauses in the parties' agreements prohibited punitive damages, and successful RICO violations lead to the award of treble damages—often considered a form of punitive damages. As a result, if submitted to arbitration, there was a strong chance an arbitrator would rule there was no opportunity to be awarded meaningful relief. *Ibid.* at 403.

> if I have a contract which says, Jones and Smith agree to arbitrate all damage claims, but no damages shall ever be awarded, no matter what . . . that's pretty clear that the enforcement of that would invalidate that arbitration agreement because it can't be enforced. The person who should say that is the judge, because the judge says, look, you people don't have an arbitration contract. Now, why you'd leave that to the arbitrator – I guess you could, but I think that is a gateway matter that I think you'd have to be quadruple clear about that somebody wanted that point decided by an arbitrator.[33]

4-19 In contrast, when addressing the Respondent, the Court voiced concern with the possibility of frustrating the underlying purpose of arbitration—to have a quicker more cost-effective alternative to litigation—by requiring a time-consuming court proceeding aimed at speculating on how an arbitrator would decide on the arbitration forum's own rule. The Court seemed especially concerned that every limitation on statutory remedies in an arbitration agreement could be characterised as a public policy issue subject to a court's arbitrability analysis.

> [Y]ou want us to adopt a specific gateway rule when any arbitration agreement limits a statutory remedy . . . [where] . . . any limitation in an arbitration agreement of statutory remedy raises a question of public policy, a question of public policy is a gateway arbitrability question, and it always goes to court first. Is that a fair statement of your position?[34]

This concern ultimately led to Justice Scalia noting that

> *Vimar* instructs that we should not, on the basis of 'mere speculation' that an arbitrator might interpret these ambiguous agreements in a manner that causes their enforceability into doubt, take upon ourselves the authority to decide the antecedent question of how ambiguity is resolved.[35]

Justice Scalia continued that since the Court did not know how the arbitrator would rule on the remedial limitations, the questions of

[33] Tr. of Oral Argument at 10, *Pacificare*, 538 U.S. 401 (No. 02-215).

[34] Tr. of Oral Argument at 44, *Pacificare*, 538 U.S. 401 (No. 02-215).

[35] *Pacificare*, 538 U.S. at 406-07 (citing *Vimar Seguros y Reaseguros, S.A. v. M/V Sky Reefer*, 515 U.S. 528, 541 (1995) (holding foreign arbitration clauses in bills of lading not invalid under COGSA in all circumstances)).

> whether [the remedial limitations] render the parties' agreements unenforceable, and whether it is for courts or arbitrators to decide enforceability in the first instance are unusually abstract.[36]

In light of the ambiguity of whether treble damages were entirely punitive, and

> [the Court's] presumption in favour of arbitration, [the Court held] the preliminary question [of] whether the remedial limitations at issue . . . prohibit[ed] an award of RICO treble damages [wa]s not a question of arbitrability.[37]

Therefore, another gateway issue that could be dispositive on the merits—a potential waiver of a statutory remedy—was found not to be a question of arbitrability, and not a question initially for the courts to decide.

4-20 In *Green Tree Financial Corp. v. Bazzle*, in a 5-4 decision, Justice Breyer further expanded upon the arbitrator's power to determine gateway questions previously reserved to the courts.[38] *Green Tree* concerned a contract dispute between a commercial lender and a group of homeowners where each individual homeowner signed a contract containing a broad arbitration clause.[39] In an effort to capitalise on the broad contractual language, the homeowners formed two classes to fight the lenders. After the arbitrator ruled in favour of the class, the South Carolina Supreme Court consolidated the classes and ruled that the loan contracts permitted class arbitration. The Court granted *certiorari* to answer the question of whether the Federal Arbitration Act prevented the homeowners from getting certified as a class to collectively arbitrate where the arbitration agreement was silent as to whether class arbitration was permissible.[40]

4-21 Prior to *Green Tree*, there was a fairly broad presumption that

36 *Pacificare*, 538 U.S. at 407.

37 *Ibid.* at 407 n. 2.

38 539 U.S. 444 (2003).

39 *Green Tree*, 539 U.S. at 452. The arbitration clause in the contract read,

> All disputes . . . arising from or relating to this contract or the relationships which result . . . shall be resolved by binding arbitration by one arbitrator selected by [lender] with consent of you. *Ibid.* at 444.

40 *Green Tree*, 539 U.S. at 452.

> [f]or better or for worse, the Federal Arbitration Act d[id] not authorize forced consolidation of different arbitration proceedings, even if they present[ed] similar questions of law and fact.[41]

During oral argument, the Court seemed intent on examining why this was the case, and exploring whether permitting class arbitration would reduce the attractiveness of arbitration in general by making the process more onerous. Justice Breyer appeared determined to rebuff this contention by noting that permitting class arbitration would not by definition be hostile to arbitration.

> A State . . . could [not] possibly . . . interpret the word arbitration in a contract to contain all the bells and whistles of a court proceeding, because that would transform the arbitration into a court proceeding, and therefore they would have . . . not only . . . shown hostility to but destroyed the arbitration contract, but what about this one. Is this hostile to arbitration? I have no doubt that Green Tree wouldn't have agreed . . . had they known what was going to happen, and to that extent it is hostile to arbitration, but the consumers on the other side might have said, oh, we rather like it, in which case from their point of view it isn't hostile to arbitration, so sort of from one side it is, and from the other side it isn't, and how do we decide whether, overall, it is or it isn't?[42]

Though the plurality did not address the hostility question in its opinion, Justice Rehnquist's dissent focused a great deal on the potential for hostility. He noted that class certification was a question of arbitrability, and since the parties did not clearly and unmistakably contract to have an arbitrator decide this question, it amounted to coercion rather than consent to force Green Tree to arbitrate the matter.[43]

4-22 In contrast to the dissent, Justice Breyer's plurality noted that parties to an arbitration agreement do not generally submit every issue to an arbitrator.[44] Unless the contract clearly indicates otherwise, some issues—such as whether the parties have a valid arbitration agreement or whether the arbitration clause applies to a particular dispute—are reserved for judicial determination.[45] But,

[41] William Park, "The Arbitrability Dicta in First Options v. Kaplan: What Sort of Kompetenz-Kompetenz Has Crossed the Atlantic?", 11-10 *Mealey's IAR* (1996) 16.

[42] Tr. of Oral Argument at 44, *Green Tree*, 539 U.S. 444 (No. 02-215) [emphasis added].

[43] *Green Tree*, 538 U.S. at 458-59 (Rehnquist, C.J., dissenting).

[44] *Ibid.*

[45] *Ibid.*, at 452.

because the arbitration agreement was worded so broadly, the plurality chose to define these gateway issues narrowly.

> Unlike *First Options*, the question is not whether the parties wanted a judge or an arbitrator to decide whether they agreed to arbitrate the matter. . . . The relevant question here is what kind of arbitration proceeding the parties agreed to. That question does not concern a state statute or judicial procedures . . . . It concerns contract interpretation and arbitration procedures. Arbitrators are well situated to answer that question.[46]

In light of those considerations, and the sweeping language of the arbitration agreement, the plurality determined that the question of class certification for arbitration was a question for the arbitrator to decide.

4-23 The fifth vote for the plurality was Justice Stevens who concurred in the judgment. Steven's concurrence reasoned that the parties' agreements did not forbid class arbitration as a matter of law, and that remand was not required because the parties did not argue that the arbitrator, rather than the court, should have decided the appropriateness of class arbitration.[47] Though most circuits have followed the plurality's precedent,[48] at least one circuit has questioned the precedential value of the decision and whether there is in fact an overlap in reasoning between the plurality and Justice Steven's concurrence.[49] Regardless of the precedential value of the decision, *Green Tree* stands as the Court's most pro-arbitration ruling to date.

3.2. The Circuit Courts

4-24 As noted above, in *Will-Drill*, the Fifth Circuit addressed the question whether a court or an arbitrator should decide whether arbitration is appropriate

[46] *Ibid.* at 452-53 (internal citations omitted) (emphasis in original).

[47] *Ibid.* at 454-55 (Stevens, J. concurring).

[48] See, e.g., *Skirchak v. Dynamics Research Corp.,* 508 F.3d 49, 56 (1st Cir. 2007) (noting that *Green Tree* made clear the question of whether class arbitration is one of contract interpretation, not arbitrability); *Pedcor Mgmt. Co. Welfare Benefit Plan v. Nations Pers. of Tex., Inc.*, 343 F.3d 355, 359 (5th Cir. 2003) (finding the narrowest ground for decision in *Green Tree* was that the validity of class arbitration is to be decided by the arbitrator, absent evidence that the parties intended the court to resolve the issue).

[49] See *Employers Ins. Co. of Wausau v. Century Indem. Co.*, 443 F.3d 573, 579 (7th Cir. 2006) (declining to accept the Fifth Circuit's interpretation of *Green Tree*, and noting there was no overlap between Justice's Breyer's and Stevens' opinions).

where one party that signed a document containing an arbitration clause disputed whether the parties had ever reached any agreement.[50] The case involved an alleged contract to buy mineral leases between Samson Resources, an oil and gas company, and a group of land owners led by Will-Drill Resources. Samson claimed the signed Proposed Sale Agreement (PSA)—which contained the disputed arbitration clause[51]—was merely an offer to buy the mineral licenses from the land owners and never took effect because eight of the sellers indicated on the PSA backed out of the agreement.[52] Nevertheless, the magistrate and district court compelled arbitration under the Federal Arbitration Act,[53] invoking the doctrine of separability which provides that where a party attacks the enforceability of a contract to avoid compulsion to arbitration, "[the court] must presume that there is a valid contract and send any general attacks on the agreement to the arbitrator."[54]

4-25 As discussed above, on appeal, the Fifth Circuit distinguished attacks on the validity of a pre-existing agreement to which separability applies, from attacks on the very existence of an agreement, which requires resolution by the courts.[55] Where it is clear that a valid contract providing for disputes to be resolved by arbitration exists, arbitrators are well suited to rule on defences that attack the enforceability of the agreement, especially in light of the strong federal policy in favour of arbitration.[56] However, the Court held that parties cannot be forced to

[50] 353 F.3d at 211.

[51] The arbitration clause compelled arbitration in any "action dispute, claim or controversy of any kind now existing or hereafter arising between the parties in any way arising out of, pertaining to or in connection with" the PSA. *Ibid.* at 213.

[52] *Ibid.* at 213.

[53] Section 4 of the Federal Arbitration Act provides:

> A party aggrieved by the alleged failure, neglect, or refusal of another to arbitrate under a written agreement for arbitration may petition any United States district court . . . for an order directing that such arbitration proceed in the manner provided for in such agreement . . . . [U]pon being satisfied that the making of the agreement for arbitration or the failure to comply therewith is not in issue, the court shall make an order directing the parties to proceed to arbitration in accordance with the terms of the agreement. . . .

9 U.S.C. § 4 (2006); *Will-Drill*, 352 F.3d at 213 n. 2.

[54] *Will-Drill*, 352 F.3d at 214-15; see *Prima Paint*, 388 U.S. at 395 (establishing the autonomy of the arbitration clause when deciding a challenge to the validity of contract).

[55] *Will-Drill*, 352 F.3d at 218-19; see also *Mitsubishi*, 473 U.S. at 626 ("The first task of a court asked to compel arbitration of a dispute is to determine whether the parties agreed to arbitrate that dispute.")

[56] *Will-Drill*, 352 F.3d at 218 (citing *Prima Paint*, 388 U.S. at 395).

submit to arbitration if they have not agreed to do so.[57] The Fifth Circuit reasoned that if courts did not possess the power to decide the gateway issue of whether, in fact, there was a valid contract, courts would be faced with the same concerns as in *First Options* about coercing parties to arbitrate where they did not consent to do so. As a result, the Fifth Circuit verified that the question whether an enforceable contract with an arbitration agreement existed was a gateway issue that constituted a question of arbitrability for the courts to decide.[58]

4. CONCLUSION

4-26 The U.S. concept of "arbitrability" is a more expansive notion than the international conception. Internationally, "arbitrability" refers to whether specific classes of disputes are barred from arbitration because of the subject matter of the dispute or the language of the arbitration agreement.[59] However, in the U.S., arbitrability also includes the set of jurisdictional tensions between an arbitrator and the courts regarding who should be the initial decision-maker on issues such as the existence of an arbitration agreement. The recent U.S. Supreme Court cases indicate a shift toward granting arbitrators more autonomy in deciding their own jurisdiction to arbitrate disputes. However, both the Supreme Court and

57 *Volt Info. Sciences, Inc. v. Bd. of Trustees*, 489 U.S. 468, 478 (1989).

58 *Will-Drill*, 352 F.3d at 218. Other federal circuits have refused to order arbitration of disputes where one or more parties claim there never was a binding arbitration agreement, either because the contesting party was not an original party to the agreement, his signature was forged, or the person signing on the party's behalf was acting outside of his or her authority. See *Opals on Ice Lingerie v. Body Lines Inc.*, 320 F.3d 362 (2nd Cir. 2003) (declining to compel arbitration where signature was forged); *Sphere Drake Ins. Ltd. v. All Am. Ins. Co.*, 256 F.3d 587 (7th Cir. 2001) (refusing to order arbitration where a party contends its agent lacked authority to bind it to the arbitration agreement); *Sandvik AB v. Advent International Corp.*, 220 F.3d 99 (3rd Cir. 2000) (same); *Chastain v. Robinson-Humphrey Co.*, 957 F.2d 851 (11th Cir. 1992) (refusing to compel arbitration where one party did not sign the arbitration agreement and noting "*Prima Paint* has never been extended to require arbitrators to adjudicate a party's contention, supported by substantial evidence, that a contract *never existed at all.*"); *Three Valleys Mun. Water Dist. v. E.F. Huton & Co.*, 925 F.2d 1136 (9th Cir. 1991) (observing the holding of *Prima Paint* was "limited to challenges seeking to *avoid* or *rescind* a contract," and was inapplicable to "challenges going to the very existence of a contract that a party claims never to have agreed to."); *I.S. Joseph Co. v. Mich. Sugar Co.*, 803 F.2d 396 (8th Cir. 1986) (directing court rather than arbitrator to decide if purported assignee could enforce arbitration clause in a contract to which it was not an original party).

59 See, e.g., J. Paulsson, "Arbitrability, Still Through a Glass Darkly", in *Arbitration in the Next Decade* (ICC Bulletin, Special Supplement 1999), for a discussion of the issues raised by the international conception.

many Circuit Courts have attempted to strike a balance between the pro-arbitration federal policy of the FAA and the potential danger of coercing an unwilling party that never had agreed to arbitration to submit to arbitration. Though *Howsam*, *Pacificare*, and *Green Tree* have slightly modified the gatekeeper function of the courts, it remains in the courts' province to ensure that there is a valid arbitration agreement, the scope of the agreement covers the dispute in question, and that public policy would not otherwise bar submitting the question to arbitration. In this respect, the U.S. perspective, wholly apart from the distinctive arbitrability terminology, remains at odds with the approach of many (if not most) jurisdictions that seek to support international arbitration.

Domenico Di Pietro[*]

CHAPTER 5

GENERAL REMARKS ON ARBITRABILITY UNDER THE NEW YORK CONVENTION

1. Introduction

5-1 It is well known that the New York Convention on the Recognition and Enforcement of Arbitral Awards Rendered Abroad is one of the most successful International multilateral treaties. While it is not the scope of this paper to praise qualities and achievements of the Convention – which are well known to all and have been highlighted in recent publications and conferences on the occasion of the Convention's fiftieth anniversary – it must not be forgotten that the Convention has played a fundamental role in making arbitration the most popular means of dispute resolution in international trade.[1]

5-2 The New York Convention, despite its undeniable success, is not a perfect tool. Some aspects of the Convention have indeed been the objects of heated debate that does not seem to subsidise. There are indeed a number of issues relating to the very structure and the mechanics of the Convention that – surprisingly as one might suggest after fifty years – have not been thoroughly analysed and fully understood.

* Avvocato (Italy) and Solicitor (England and Wales). International Law and Arbitration Group, Chiomenti Studio Legale, Rome. The views contained in this article are the author's only and should not be attributed to Chiomenti Studio Legale. The author is grateful to Patricia Denise Labal for her help with this article.

1 Generally on the New York Convention see Emmanuel Gaillard & Domenico Di Pietro (eds), *Enforcement of Arbitration Agreements and International Arbitral Awards: The New York Convention in Practice*, (Cameron May, Ltd. 2008).

L Mistelis & S Brekoulakis (eds), Arbitrability: International & Comparative Perspectives, 85-98

5-3 One of the issues that have given rise to a considerable amount of interest, even though without being awarded the animosity of debate achieved by the issue relating to what constitutes an agreement in writing under the New York Convention, is the way the Convention deals with arbitrability. This article will attempt to identify and analyse the several issues connected to this problem. It will do so by first looking at the mechanics and the thread of the Convention in order to try clarifying how the Convention was meant to work, and secondly, by identifying the various "areas" of the Convention where the issue of arbitrability seems to emerge. At this stage, it must be clarified that despite the centrality of the issue, this article will not deal in depth with the issue of the law to be taken into account in order to establish arbitrability, as this task is entertained in another chapter of this volume. Reference to the topic of the applicable law shall, however, be touched upon for the sake of clarity. Finally, the article will attempt to analyse the interaction between the different provisions of the Convention dealing with arbitrability.

2. The New York Convention and its Device for Success

5-4 The Convention's objective of building an international legislative network for the recognition and enforcement of arbitral awards rendered abroad could only be achieved by attracting the highest possible number of Contracting States. In order to attain broad consensus, the draftsmen of the Convention had to devise a legal instrument which would facilitate international arbitration without clashing with the different fundamental legal principles of each Contracting State. Their task, therefore, was one of ensuring compatibility between furthering the objectives of international arbitration and protecting the public policies of the Contracting States. Such compatibility was achieved in the final draft of the Convention by performing what could be defined as a "balancing act". On one hand, the Convention imposes on the Contracting States a general obligation to enforce arbitration awards as well as arbitration clauses and agreements. On the other hand, it creates an exception to this obligation in circumstances where recognition and enforcement are incompatible with the fundamental principles of law at the place of enforcement.[2]

[2] An example of such a technique can be found at Article I (the Reservations), Article II (on arbitrability and substantial validity of the arbitration clause) and Article V. See on this subject Domenico Di Pietro, "Are the Principles of the New York Convention realised consistently?", in *Achieving Justice Through International Arbitration*, Report of the Society for Advanced Legal Studies (2004).

5-5 The adopted system is detectable by looking at the text of the main provisions of the Convention. The tension is indeed rather evident between the goal of establishing an arbitration-friendly, harmonising system and the concern that the Convention would allow most, if not all, legal systems to mould the application of the Convention to render it compatible with local rules and therefore suitable for ratification.

5-6 This system seems to be responsible for the perceived inconsistency in the application of the Convention. However at a closer analysis, it seems that, at least in the majority of cases, the issue is one of different degrees of application – which is allowed by the Convention itself – rather than one of inconsistency.[3] This is not to say that misapplication or misinterpretation of the Convention has never occurred in the past and it will never occur again in the future. Far from it. What is important to stress however is that:

- Most of the decisions that are pointed at as being inconsistent with the Convention are in fact the consequence of the above-mentioned structural device adopted in the Convention.
- The decisions that genuinely seem to misinterpret or misapply the Convention are a tiny percentage of the remarkable number of cases throughout thc world where the Convention is duly applied and abode by.

5-7 As it has been mentioned above, the system adopted by the drafters of the Convention, to make it appealing to the highest number of States, can be identified in the textual thread of the Convention's core provisions. Such provisions will be briefly identified and analysed in the following chapter.

3. Arbitrability in the Provisions of the New York Convention

5-8 Several provisions of the New York Convention address directly or indirectly the issue of arbitrability. More specifically the question is dealt with in Articles I, II, and V. Each of them is addressed in turn

[3] This view seems to be shared – at least to an extent – by other commentators. See for example Jan Paulsson, "Arbitrability, Still Through a Glass Darkly", in *Arbitration in the Next Decade* (ICC Bulletin, Special Supplement 1999) 95.

3.1. Article I(3)

5-9 The first of the New York Convention provisions dealing with arbitration, Article I(3) provides

> When signing, ratifying or acceding to this Convention, or notifying extension under article X hereof, any State may on the basis of reciprocity declare that it will apply the Convention to the recognition and enforcement of awards made only in the territory of another Contracting State. It may also declare that it will apply the Convention only to differences arising out of legal relationships, whether contractual or not, which are considered as commercial under the national law of the State making such declaration.

5-10 One of the two reservations available under Article I allowing Signatory States to limit their obligation to differences arising out of legal relationships that are considered as commercial, also known as the "commercial reservation",[4] is also indicative of the "arbitrability" thread contained in the Convention. The rationale behind such reservation is the belief that, without it, certain civil law countries that distinguish between commercial and non-commercial transactions would not have adhered to the Convention.

5-11 The "commercial reservation" is a tool clearly connected to arbitrability and to the right of Contracting States to benefit from the device adopted by the Convention. Additional evidence of this is the fact that the Convention did not attempt to define what is meant to be regarded as "commercial" under the Convention. Rather consistently with the aim of the provision, it leaves that definition to the law of each Contracting State. This feature is not exclusive to the New York Convention as it appeared in one of its predecessor instruments, the Protocol on Arbitration Clauses done in Geneva in 1923. The Protocol stated *inter alia* in Article 1 that:

> Each of the Contracting States recognises the validity of an agreement whether relating to existing or future differences between parties subject respectively to the jurisdiction of different Contracting States by which the parties to a contract agree to submit to arbitration all or any differences that may arise in connection with such contract relating to commercial matters or to any other matter capable of settlement by arbitration, whether or not

4 See *M. Pryles* "Reservations Available to Member States: The Reciprocal and Commercial Reservations", Chapter 6 in Gaillard & Di Pietro (eds), *supra* note 1.

> the arbitration is to take place in the country to whose jurisdiction none of the parties is subject.
>
> Each Contracting State reserves the right to limit the obligation mentioned above to contracts which are considered as commercial under its own law.

5-11 During the negotiation of the New York Convention some of the Contracting States made it clear that their acceptance of the draft was made conditional to the possibility of limiting the general obligation to recognise and enforce arbitration agreements only to agreements relating to relationships of a commercial nature.

5-12 The Lebanese delegation declared during the negotiation that it:

> Considers it necessary to maintain the reservation contained in Article I(2), to the effect that the Convention will apply only to the recognition and enforcement of arbitral awards made in the territory of another Contracting State and to disputes arising out of contracts which are considered as commercial under national law

5-13 Similarly in this regard the Mexican delegation explained that:

> The Mexican Government would be unable to accede this instrument without a proviso to the effect that it would be applied [...] only in respect of awards given under compromise (sic) which are regarded as commercial under Mexican law.

5-14 In this respect it is interesting to note that not all States that are often perceived – rightly or wrongly – as less arbitration-friendly have opted for the commercial reservation. Equally interesting is the fact that the courts of some of the members States that have adopted the commercial reservation seem prepared to construe the reservation rather narrowly. This is probably due to the fact that while a general cautious and perhaps defensive stance with regard to access of foreign judicial decisions is seen by many States as a necessary policy, in practice the application of the policy is loosened when it becomes clear to the judiciary that the foreign arbitral award does not conflict with the core principles of the jurisdiction. In other words, taking into account the international character of the transaction and the dispute that arose therefrom, it is concluded that the award should be recognised even though a strict application of the local rules might have resulted in a different conclusion.

5-15 An example of such an approach is a much-quoted case entertained by the Courts of India. The local High Court had held that the rendering of consultancy services by a company for promoting a related commercial deal should not be regarded – pursuant to Indian law – as a commercial transaction. The decision was reversed by the Supreme Court of India which held that:

> While construing the expression commercial, it has to be borne in mind that the aim of the Convention is to facilitate international trade by means of facilitating suitable alternative ways of settlement of international disputes and therefore any expression adopted in the Convention should receive, consistent with its literal and grammatical sense, a liberal construction. The expression commercial should therefore be construed broadly, having regard to the manifold activities which are an integral part of international trade nowadays.[5]

5-16 Needless to say that this approach is not common to all jurisdictions, and indeed it might not be common to all the courts within the same jurisdiction. In this regard, it is also interesting to mention the much quoted Tunisian case between a company and two architects that had been retained to draw up an urbanisation plan for a resort. The contract contained a clause referring all disputes to ICC arbitration in Paris. A dispute arose concerning payment of outstanding fees and an ICC arbitral tribunal rendered an award in favour of the architects. The architects sought enforcement of the award in Tunisia where the Court of Appeal confirmed the lower Court's decision and denied enforcement, finding that Tunisia had adopted the commercial reservation, and architectural and urbanisation works were not commercial under Tunisian law. The Supreme Court upheld the decision of the Court of Appeal as it considered that Tunisia had entered the commercial reservation. Since, in accordance with the relevant articles of the Tunisian Commercial Code, the contract signed by the parties in dispute was not commercial in nature, the arbitral award rendered in that dispute could not find enforcement in Tunisia.[6]

3.2. Article II

5-17 The next of the New York Convention provisions dealing with arbitration, Article II provides

[5] Supreme Court of India, 10 February 1994, *RM Investment & Trading Co. Pvt Limited* v. *Boeing Company*. Supreme Court Journal, 1994 vol. 1 at 657-664.

[6] Cour de Cassation [Supreme Court], 10 November 1993. *Société d'Investissement Kal* v. *Taieb Haddad and Hans Barett*, XXIII YBCA (1998) 770-773.

> (1) Each Contracting State shall recognize an agreement in writing under which the parties undertake to submit to arbitration all or any differences which have arisen or which may arise between them in respect of a defined legal relationship, whether contractual or not, concerning a subject matter capable of settlement by arbitration.
>
> (2) [...]
>
> (3) The court of a Contracting State, when sized of an action in a matter in respect of which the parties have made an agreement within the meaning of this article, shall, at the request of one of the parties, refer the parties to arbitration, unless it finds that the said agreement is null and void, inoperative or incapable of being performed.

5-18 The New York Convention imposes upon its Member States a general obligation to recognise arbitration agreements provided that they are intended to settle disputes that are arbitrable. This is a "*ratione materiae*" notion, which is normally referred to as "objective" arbitrability as it is independent of the quality of the parties or their will. It is distinguished from the so-called "*ratione personae*" or "subjective" arbitrability, which is concerned with the capacity of the parties to submit disputes to arbitration. Such exception to the general principle to recognise arbitration agreements is also reflected in the final paragraph of Article II of the New York Convention, dealing with the protection of arbitration agreements to be provided before state courts.

5-19 As is well known, Article II does not indicate which law should be taken into account in order to assess the arbitrability of a given dispute. Unlike Article II, Article V of the New York Convention – which deals with the grounds that make possible the denial of recognition and enforcement of arbitral awards rendered abroad – states *inter alia* in paragraph (1)(a), that recognition and enforcement of the award may be refused, at the request of the party against whom it is invoked, only if that party furnishes to the competent authority where the recognition and enforcement is sought, proof that the arbitration agreement was not valid under the law to which the parties have subjected it or, failing any indication thereon, under the law of the country where the award was made.

5-20 Given the absence of any express indication under Article II as to the law to be applied in order to ascertain arbitrability, and considering the solutions provided under Article V to deal with enforcement of arbitral awards, two main lines of interpretation are generally adopted by domestic courts to establish which law should be taken into account to assess arbitrability.

5-21 On one hand, it is believed by commentators, and it has been stated in a number of decisions, that the issue of arbitrability should be resolved in accordance with the *lex fori*, i.e. the law of the courts that have been seized with the question as to whether an arbitration agreement deals with a matter capable of being settled through arbitration. On the other hand, it is suggested (by other commentators and court decisions) that the issue of arbitrability should be settled through the application of the law applicable to the arbitration agreement.[7] In other words, the validity of the arbitration clause should be determined in all respects on the basis of the same law, whether the issue is one of arbitrability or whether it is an issue of validity of the parties' consent.

5-22 A point of view alternative to the one just mentioned submits that the analysis of the issue should start by looking at the peculiar nature of arbitral tribunals. More particularly, the idea is that arbitral tribunals should not be considered as organs of a particular legal order, and, therefore, they should determine arbitrability on the basis of a genuinely international policy rather than by looking at a set of legal provisions of a given domestic law.[8] Whilst this view is intellectually stimulating it may lead – where applied – to unwanted practical consequences in cases where the law of the place of arbitration contains a narrower concept of arbitrability than the "genuinely international public policy". In those cases, necessary measures of support from the courts of the place of arbitration may not be available and the award may be open to challenge.[9]

5-23 The majority of cases seem to follow the view that the issue of arbitrability should be settled with reference to the law in force at the place of arbitration, even though in some cases, arbitral tribunals have avoided to take a clear-cut position on the issue where it had been ascertained that the dispute would have been arbitrable under each of the laws that the transaction was connected to.[10]

5-24 An interesting approach, in this regard, was adopted by the U.S. District Court for the Eastern District of New York in *Meadows Indemnity v. Baccala &*

[7] See on the issue Homayoon Arfazadeh, "Arbitrability under the New York Convention; the Lex Fori Revisited", 17(1) *Arb. Int'l* (2001).

[8] Fouchard, Gaillard & Goldman, *on International Commercial Arbitration*, para 559 as quoted in Julian Lew, Loukas Mistelis & Stefan Kröll, *Comparative International Commercial Arbitration* (Kluwer 2003) at 9-29.

[9] *Ibid.*

[10] See, for example, ICC Case no. 6162, *Consultant v. Egyptian Local Authority*, XVII YBCA 153 (1992) and ICC Case no. 6149 XX YBCA 41 (1995) 144.

Shoop Insurance Services.[11] The Claimant commenced court proceedings in the U.S. despite an arbitration agreement alleging that the dispute in question was not arbitrable under the law of Guernsey, where it was incorporated and where an award would have to be enforced. In deciding whether to enforce the arbitration agreement under Article II of the New York Convention, the Court treated the provision of the Convention as a substantive rule providing for an autonomous concept of arbitrability. It observed that:

> Reference to the domestic laws of only one country, even the country where enforcement of an award will be sought, does not resolve whether a claim is "capable of settlement by arbitration under Article II(1) of the Convention.

According to the U.S. Court such determination:

> Must be made on an international scale, with reference to the laws of the countries party to the Convention.

5-25 It has however been observed that in the majority of cases, courts have determined the question of arbitrability according to their domestic law. This is normally done without any conflicts of law analysis, even though a number of decisions have been resolved by applying the provisions of Article V(2)(a) of the Convention.[12]

5-26 The issue at hand appears clearer under the provisions of the so-called European Arbitration Convention done in Geneva in 1961 (The Geneva Convention).

5-27 The Geneva Convention was signed, following the adoption of the New York Convention, to enact an instrument aimed at promoting the development of European trade by, as far as possible, removing certain difficulties that may impede the organisation and operation of international commercial arbitration in Europe. As regards the issue of arbitrability the Geneva Convention provides in Article VI(2) final paragraph that:

> The courts may also refuse recognition of the arbitration agreement if under the law of their country the dispute is not capable of settlement by arbitration.

Interestingly, Article VI(3) of the Geneva Convention also provides that:

[11] *Meadows Indemnity Co. Ltd. v. Baccala & Shoop Insurance Services, Inc.*, et al., 760 F. Supp. 1036 (EDNY 1991).

[12] Julian Lew, Loukas Mistelis & Stefan Kröll, *supra* note 7 at 9-13.

> Where either party to an arbitration agreement has initiated arbitration proceedings before any resort is had to a court, courts of Contracting States subsequently asked to deal with the same subject-matter between the same parties or with the question whether the arbitration agreement was non-existent or null and void or had lapsed, shall stay their ruling on the arbitrator's jurisdiction until the arbitral award is made, unless they have good and substantial reasons to the contrary.

5-28 It must be borne in mind that the scope of application of the Geneva Convention is obviously narrower than the scope of application of the New York Convention, as the former only applies to arbitration agreements concluded for the purpose of settling disputes arising from international trade between physical or legal persons having, when concluding the agreement, their habitual place of residence or their seat is in different Contracting States.

5-29 In summary, Article II(1) imposes on Contracting States a general obligation to enforce arbitration agreements, provided that they deal with a dispute that can be lawfully settled through arbitration. Any problematic issue in this respect is dealt by the domestic courts of the Contracting States in accordance with the provisions provided by the Convention under Article II(3), which can be regarded as the practical arrangement for the implementation of the system devised by the Convention for protection in favour and control over arbitration agreements.

5-30 Article II(3) indeed allows national courts of Contracting States to deny the stay of court proceedings in the presence of an arbitration agreement where the validity or the efficacy of such an agreement is affected by factual or legal circumstances. The language of Article II(3) has raised the question as to whether the three circumstances of invalidity indicated in the provision – i.e. null and void, inoperability and incapability of being performed – cover issues of arbitrability. The prevailing view is that in order to be forced to refer a dispute to arbitration, a court has to be dealing with a dispute capable of settlement in such a way. This requirement can be read within the lines of Article II(3) in the reference made to an agreement "within the meaning of this Article" as well as in the words "null and void" of its text.[13] Even though terminology may not bear great importance, it is possible to argue that lack of arbitrability may also be

[13] R. Doak Bishop, Wade M. Coriell & Marcelo Medina Campos, "*The null and void provision of the New York Convention*" in Gaillard & Di Pietro (eds), *supra* note 1 at 276.

considered as a ground leading to incapability of the arbitration being performed.[14]

5-31 It must be borne in mind in this respect, however, that as it has been often noted, the invalidity of the arbitration agreement should be accepted in manifest cases only.[15]

3.3. Article V(1)(a)

5-32 As it is well known, recognition and enforcement of the award may be refused by the enforcing Court (the "competent authority") if one of the grounds in Article V(1) is alleged and proven by the resisting party. Alternatively, enforcement of the award may be refused if the Court finds, on its own motion or on application by the resisting party, that one of the grounds indicated under Article V(2) is fulfilled. Thus, a Court cannot of its own motion inquire into whether the grounds in Article V(1) are fulfilled. These grounds are concerned with the arbitration agreement, the parties and the arbitration itself. The Court can accept and evaluate evidence as to these facts; however, it has no power to inquire itself. The burden of furnishing this evidence lies on the party attempting to resist enforcement.

5-33 This approach was adopted, as these are circumstances that affect the parties' rights and that do not clash against the core principles of the jurisdiction where recognition and enforcement are sought.

5-34 As far as arbitrability is concerned Article V(1)(a) provides that:

> Recognition and enforcement of the award may be refused, at the request of the party against whom it is invoked, only if that party furnishes to the competent authority where the recognition and enforcement is sought, proof that:
> (a) The parties to the agreement referred to in Article II were, under the law applicable to them, under some incapacity, or the said agreement is not valid under the law to which the parties have subjected it or, failing any indication thereon, under the law of the country where the award was made; or

[14] On the issue see Stefan Kroll, "*The Incapable of Being Performed Exception in article II(3) of the New York Convention*" in Gaillard & Di Pietro (eds), *supra* note 1.

[15] Albert Jan van den Berg, *The New York Arbitration Convention of 1958: Towards a Uniform Judicial Interpretation* (Kluwer 1981) at 155.

3.4. Article V(2)

5-35 Article V(2) provides

> Recognition and enforcement of an arbitral award may also be refused if the competent authority in the country where recognition and enforcement is sought finds that:
>
> (a) The subject matter of the difference is not capable of settlement by arbitration under the law of that country; or
>
> (b) The recognition or enforcement of the award would be contrary to the public policy of that country.

5-36 The situation is different under Article V(2), where the (law of the) enforcing country ("that country") is concerned. Here the Court can refuse recognition and enforcement of its own motion without any application by the parties.

5-37 Therefore, according to Article V(2) a court may refuse the recognition and enforcement of an arbitral award if the dispute is not arbitrable or if that recognition and enforcement is contrary to the forum's public policy.

5-38 On one hand, it must be emphasized that arbitrability is part of public policy even if Article V(2) separates in its text one from the other. On the other hand, it must be borne in mind that as a consequence of the continuous expansion of the scope of arbitrable matters, it has been observed that "arbitrability is the rule, inarbitrability is the exception".[16] Thus very few cases rendered under the Convention have led to the refusal of recognition or enforcement of an award on the basis of an alleged inarbitrability under Article V. A notable exception to the trend is the often quoted Belgian case of *Audi NSU* where the local courts refused the enforcement of an award rendered in Switzerland on the ground that the dispute which concerned the unilateral termination of an exclusive distributorship agreement submitted to a statute of 27 July 1961, was inarbitrable.[17]

5-39 A short reference should be made in this context to the issue as to the extent of the Court's control of compliance with public policy and arbitrability under Article V(2) of the New York Convention.

[16] Bernard Hanotiau & Oliver Caprasse, "Public Policy in International Commercial Arbitration" in Gaillard & Di Pietro (eds), *supra* note 1 at 819.

[17] Cass. Belgium, 28 June 1979, Pas. I, 1260, 1979 RCJB 332.

5-40 Some commentators advocate the adoption of the so-called "maximal judicial review". According to this approach, the control of the award must be total when public policy is at stake. As it has been suggested, "courts are the guardians of public policy, consequently, the courts control is obviously total".[18] This means that the degree of control by domestic courts encompasses the application of the law, the assessment of the facts and even the qualification given to those facts by the arbitral panel.

5-41 Other commentators seem to support the adoption of the opposite view, which is described as "minimal judicial review". According to this view, there should be very limited reconsideration of the merits of the case even in the presence of any grounds under Article V. Under this approach, various degrees of control have been advocated. They range from determining whether the applicable public policy norm has been taken into account by arbitrators to the very limited view according to which only obvious, effective and concrete violations should lead to denial of enforcement.[19]

4. Conclusion

5-42 As it was noted at the beginning of these short comments on the mechanics of the Convention with regard to arbitrability, the debate in this regard is likely to remain open and will most probably encounter further development as changes are happening fast in international trade, and more jurisdictions are likely to contribute their views on this issue through the decisions of their domestic courts.

5-43 The system – devised by the draftsmen of the Convention in order to create a system, which would on one hand impose a general obligation on Contracting States to recognise and enforce arbitration agreements and arbitral awards, but would on the other allow them to adjust the application of such general obligation to avoid any conflict with the core principles of their legal system – has proved extremely successful.

5-44 Each and every provision of the Convention, imposing a duty on the Contracting States and their domestic courts, either directly or indirectly, takes

[18] See Pierre Mayer, "La sentence contraire à l'ordre public au fond" 1994(4) *Rev. Arb.* 630-31.
[19] Hanotiau & Caprasse, *supra* note 15 at 805-818.

into account the situation where the fulfilment of such duty might be inappropriate.

5-45 This device, as it has been suggested at the beginning of these comments, achieved the remarkable results of persuading a considerable number of States to sign and ratify the Convention. It is, however, also responsible for that "feeling" of inconsistency that is sometimes perceived in the available jurisprudence of different Contracting States dealing with arbitration agreements and arbitral awards under the New York Convention. In fact, there seem to be no inconsistency, as what seem to be inconsistent decisions might just be the correct interpretation of the "custom-made" application allowed under the Convention. This is not to justify the handful of decisions that have been unfortunately rendered since the Convention came into force. There is no question that they must have been the result of ignorance and misconception – if not worse – of the core principles of the Convention. They are, however, a drop in the ocean of decisions rendered in very many different jurisdictions that have applied the Convention correctly, and – as a result – have not made the headlines of law reviews.

5-46 The fact that the Convention seems to allow – to a certain extent – different enforcement in different jurisdictions does not mean that any attempts to reach a commonly shared concept of arbitrability in international trade should be abandoned. Quite the contrary. As it has been the case for other similarly important issues affecting international trade law that have been the object of discussion over time and have finally developed in a principle of international trade, it is submitted that the same attempt should be made with respect to arbitrability. Domestic courts have already more than once expressed the view that the provisions of domestic law might be interpreted in a flexible manner when they are applied to international transaction. A general concept of arbitrability has started to develop and it may become generally accepted before long.

5-47 It is for this reason that any attempt aimed at understanding arbitrability better and at stimulating debate on the issue – such as the excellent publishing project tackled by the editors of this book – should be welcomed with great enthusiasm.

Stavros L. Brekoulakis[*]

CHAPTER 6

LAW APPLICABLE TO ARBITRABILITY: REVISITING THE REVISITED *LEX FORI*

1. INTRODUCTION

6-1 The question of what law applies to determine arbitrability is effectively related to the role and the interests that a State has in arbitration proceedings that take place within its territory. At a time when public policy was dominating the discussion on arbitrability, the argument that "*lex fori*"[1] should apply to determine arbitrability was based on sound territorial considerations: there would be a legitimate interest for a State to ensure that the subject matter of any arbitration proceedings taking place within its territory would comply with the public policy standards of that State, as these standards are reflected in its national laws. Thus, a State could forbid within its territory any arbitration whose subject matter was inarbitrable, i.e. at odds with the public policy of that particular State.

6-2 However, after a series of seminal national judgments in various jurisdictions holding that arbitrators are not excluded from deciding to apply national rules of public policy nature, it is safe to argue that the relevance of public policy to the

* LLB, LLM, PhD; Lecturer in International Dispute Resolution, Centre of Commercial Law Studies, Queen Mary, University London. I would like to thank Dr Stefan Kröll, in particular, for the very useful discussion we had on an earlier draft of this paper. Many of his comments have been incorporated here. My thanks are also extended to Mr Maarten Draye, Associate at Hanotiau & van den Berg, who critically read this paper.

1 It must be noted from the outset of the paper that the term "lex fori" is used when the issue is examined from the perspective of a national court, referring exactly to the national law of this jurisdiction. Whereas, the term "lex loci arbitri" is used when the issue is examined from the perspective of an arbitral tribunal, referring to the national law of the seat of the tribunal.

L Mistelis & S Brekoulakis (eds), Arbitrability: International & Comparative Perspectives, 99-119

discussion of arbitrability is now considered very limited.[2] As is discussed in detail in Chapter 2 above, the scope of inarbitrability is better determined by reference to the inherent characteristics of arbitration, such as its consensual nature, rather than public policy considerations.

6-3 However, despite the waning role of public policy, the prominence of *lex fori* as the most relevant law to determine arbitrability remains unquestionable, especially when the issue arises before a national court at the stage of enforcement. Here, the express mandate of the New York Convention (NYC) Art. V(2)(a) leaves very little space, if any at all, for a different view.

6-4 In fact, this provision has a wider effect than the scope of its application, endorsing the *lex fori* even when the issue of arbitrability would arise before a national court at other stages than the stage of enforcement. In particular, the *lex fori* plays also a predominant role when national courts review arbitrability at the stage of challenge, since the majority of national provisions on challenge mirror the NYC Art. V, and they, thus, make express reference to *lex fori*.[3] Similarly, national courts might also apply the *lex fori* when reviewing arbitrability at the stage of referral of a dispute, although here other views have been argued as well.[4]

6-5 Even arbitral tribunals usually take the *lex fori* into account when determining arbitrability. Although arbitral tribunals have no duty to apply the national law of the forum, it is accepted that the application of *lex fori* would be

[2] See the relevant cases in various jurisdictions: in the U.S., *Mitsubishi Motors Corp v. Soler Chrysler Plymouth Inc*, (with regard to anti-competition claims); in France, Court of Appeal (CA) Paris, 29 March 1991, *Ganz v. Nationale des Chemins de Fer Tunisiens (SNCFT)*, (1991) Rev. Arb. 478, (with regard to fraud allegations) – with note L. Idot; also CA Paris, 19 May 1993 *Labinal v. Mors*, (1993) Rev. Arb. 645, (with regard to anti-competition claims) – with note Jarrosson; in England, Court of Appeal, *Fiona Trust & Holding Corporation and Others v. Privalov and Others*, [2007] 2 Lloyd's Rep. 267 (with regard to fraud allegations) confirmed by the House of Lords, *Premium Nafta Products Limited (20th Defendant) and others v. Fili Shipping Company Limited (14th Claimant) and others*, [2007] UKHL 40; in Switzerland, Federal Tribunal, 23 June 1992, *Fincantieri- Cantieri Navali Italiiani and Oto Melara v. M and arbitration tribunal*, (1995) XX YBCA 766 (with regard to claims arising out of illegal activities); in the context of the European Union, ECJ, 1 June 1999, C- 126/97, *Eco Swiss China Time v. Benetton International*, [1999] ECR I 3055 (with regard to anti-competition claims).

[3] See, e.g., Model Law Art. 34(2)(b)(i): "the subject matter of the dispute is not capable of settlement by arbitration under the law of this State", i.e. the *lex fori*. See in more details 2.2 *infra*.

[4] See 2.1 *infra*.

the safest option for a tribunal, in order to insulate the award against a potential challenge which would eventually bring the issue before the national courts of the place of the arbitration, which in turn would be bound to apply the *lex fori*.[5]

6-6 The aim of this paper is to re-examine the scope of the application of national provisions on inarbitrability in general and the scope of the application of *lex fori* in particular, under the light of new theories on the rationale behind inarbitrability. In particular, this paper argues that the scope of national provisions on inarbitrability has been significantly reduced: it is no longer determined by public policy considerations, which would call for an extensive application of the *lex fori* on a territorial basis. Rather, it is determined by jurisdictional considerations, which call for the application of the *lex fori* only when the exclusive jurisdiction of the national courts of the *lex fori* is at stake.

2. Looking Again Into the Scope and the Relevance of the *Lex Fori*

6-7 The scope of inarbitrability is usually determined by national law in two different ways:

- First, by rules normally found in non-arbitration laws, which establish the exclusive jurisdiction of the national courts in relation to *specific* areas or subject matters. The typical example here is the EC Regulation 44/2001, Art. 22, providing that specific national courts of a Member State will have exclusive jurisdiction over disputes relating to the validity of the constitution, the nullity or the dissolution of companies (para. 2), or over disputes relating to the registration or validity of patents or trademarks or other similar rights (para. 4).[6]
- Second, by rules normally found in arbitration laws, which set out the scope of inarbitrability in *general* terms. A typical example of this drafting approach is the Swiss Private International Law Act (PILA) Art. 177(1), providing that "Any dispute involving property may be the subject-matter of an arbitration"

5 See 2.3 *infra*.

6 See also the Austrian Bankruptcy Code s. 43(5) KO and s. 111(1) and French Code de Commerce, Art. R662-3, providing for the exclusive jurisdiction of the Austrian and French national courts respectively over certain types of insolvency disputes. Similarly, the Belgian Law of 27 July 1961 on the Unilateral Termination of Exclusive Distributorship Agreements (M.B. 29.12.1961) provides that, from the moment the exclusive distributorship agreement is performed in Belgium, Belgian law applies and Belgian courts have exclusive jurisdiction, notwithstanding any contrary provision.

or the German ZPO s. 1030(1) providing that "Any claim involving an economic interest can be the subject of an arbitration agreement".

6-8 Eventually though, the essence of these two types of national provisions on arbitrability is the same. Despite the difference in the drafting style, both types of arbitrability laws are effectively conflict of jurisdiction rules, allocating jurisdiction between national courts and arbitral tribunals over specific types of disputes. In fact, their main purpose is to safeguard the exclusive jurisdiction of their national courts on specific types of disputes.

6-9 This purpose is more obvious in national provisions of the first type, such as EC Reg. 44/2001 Art. 22. This provision expressly identifies specific disputes (e.g. disputes relating to the registration or validity of patents) that can only be submitted to the national courts of a Member State. Thus, national courts are accorded exclusive jurisdiction, prohibiting arbitral tribunals to look into these disputes.

6-10 Exactly the same rationale underpins arbitrability provisions of the second type. Indeed, provisions, such as the Swiss PILA Art. 177, define which disputes are arbitrable, i.e. "any dispute involving property", leaving all other disputes to the jurisdiction of national courts. In effect, the purpose of this provision is to ensure that any dispute not involving property can be determined by the national courts of Switzerland exclusively.

6-11 Thus, ultimately both types of national provisions aim to delineate the area of exclusive jurisdiction of their national courts. From this viewpoint, the differences between a provision such as the EC Reg. 44/2001 Art. 22 and a provision such as the German ZPO s. 1030 lie in

- first, their scope: the latter is wider than the former; and
- second, their drafting technique: the latter define which disputes are arbitrable (positive arbitrability norms), whereas the former eventually define which disputes are inarbitrable (negative arbitrability norms).

6-12 However, both types of provisions are in essence conflict of jurisdiction rules, which allocate exclusive jurisdiction to their national courts with regard to specific types of disputes. Thus, the aim of these provisions is to safeguard the exclusive jurisdiction of their national courts over specific disputes, *rather than to ban arbitration in general.*

6-13 Indeed, state laws on arbitrability do not suggest that a particular type of dispute is *altogether prohibited from being arbitrated within the territory of a particular state*. Rather they suggest that a specific dispute cannot be submitted to a tribunal because the state courts of a particular country have the exclusive jurisdiction to hear the specific dispute on the basis of the factual circumstances surrounding the dispute.

6-14 The following sections re-examine the scope of the application of *lex fori* at different stages:
- First, when the issue of arbitrability arises before national courts at a pre-award (i.e. referral) stage
- Second, when the issue of arbitrability arises before national courts at the stage of annulment proceedings
- Third, when the issue of arbitrability arises before national courts at the stage of enforcement proceedings
- Finally, when the issue of arbitrability arises before a tribunal

2.1 When Arbitrability Arises Before National Courts at a Pre-Award Stage

6-15 The issue of arbitrability might come up at the referral stage before a national court, which might be either the national court of one of the parties or the national court of the seat of the arbitration. Although different views have been argued here,[7] the prevailing one seems to be that the national court reviewing an arbitration agreement should apply the *lex fori* to determine

[7] It has been argued, for example, that national courts should by analogy apply New York Convention (NYC) Art. V(1)(a) (providing for the application of law of the place "where the award *was* made") and thus apply the law of the place where the award *shall* be made (see, A. van den Berg, *The New York Arbitration Convention: Towards a Uniform Judicial Interpretation* (Kluwer 1981) 126; see also CA Paris, 4 December 2002, *American Bureau of Shipping v. Copropriétéé Maritime Jules Vernes*, 4 Rev. Arb. 1286 (2003)); this view refers to the case where the national court deciding on the case is the national law of one of the parties, rather than the national law of the seat of the arbitration, in which case the *lex fori* would apply. It has also been argued that arbitrability should be determined by the law applicable to the validity of the arbitration agreement (see here the decision of the Cour d'appel Brussels, 4 October 1985, *Company M v. M SA,* XIV YBCA 618 (1989)). Another view argues that the issue of arbitrability should be decided without reference to any domestic law, through the application of an international rule of substantive law (*Meadows Indemnity v. Baccala & Shoop Insurance Services*, 760 F Supp 1036, XVII YBCA 686 (1992) (EDNY 1991)). On all these views, see in detail, B. Hanotiau, "What Law Governs the Issue of Arbitrability?", 12(4) *Arb. Int'l* (1996) 391 et seq and P. Bernardini, "The Problem of Arbitrability in General", in *Enforcement of Arbitration Agreements and International Arbitral Awards: The New Convention in Practice*, E. Gaillard & D. Di Pietro (eds), (Cameron May 2008) 503 et seq.

whether the pending dispute is arbitrable or not.[8] This view is only partially correct: the *lex fori* will be relevant only to the extent that the jurisdiction of the national courts before which the dispute is referred (the national courts of referral) will be relevant for the specific dispute at hand.

6-16 In other words, the *lex fori* will apply only when there is a jurisdictional conflict between an arbitral tribunal and the national courts of referral. As was already mentioned, the legislative purpose of a state provision on arbitrability is to apply when there is a jurisdictional conflict between an arbitral tribunal and the courts of that state and allocate exclusive jurisdiction to the latter with regard to specific disputes.

6-17 However, this sort of jurisdictional conflict will occur only if the national courts of referral have in the first place exclusive jurisdiction over the specific dispute pending before the tribunal. This, in turn, will depend on whether the dispute at hand had any territorial link with the country of the national courts of referral.

6-18 To explain further: normally, national courts assume jurisdiction over a specific dispute on a territorial basis, namely whenever the pending dispute has a territorial link with the particular country of these national courts. Thus, if pending has no territorial connection with the national courts of referral, the national law of the courts of referral (*lex fori*) will be irrelevant to the matter of arbitrability. The national courts of referral would still have no jurisdiction over the pending dispute, even if an arbitration agreement covering the dispute did not

[8] Julian Lew, Loukas Mistelis & Stefan Kröll, *Comparative International Commercial Arbitration*, (Kluwer 2003) para 9-13: "However, in the majority of cases courts have determined the question of arbitrability at the pre-award stage according to their own national law" and para 9-18

> ...the better view is that the law applicable to the question of arbitrability in court proceedings should be governed by the provisions of the law of the national court which determines the case.

The same view is taken by H. Arfazadeh, "Arbitrability under the New York Convention: The *Lex Fori* Revisited", 17 *Arb. Int'l* (2001) 76 et seq; H. Arfazadeh, *Ordre Public Et Arbitrage International À L'épreuve De La Mondialisation*, (2006) 95 et seq. See additionally, European Convention Art. VI(2) "The courts may also refuse recognition of the arbitration agreement if *under the law of their country* the dispute is not capable of settlement by arbitration"; *Cf* also Court of Appeal of Genoa, 7 May 1994, *Fincantieri–Cantieri Navali Italiani SpA and Oto Melara SpA v. Ministry of Defence, Armament and Supply Directorate of Iraq, Republic of Iraq*, XXI YBCA 594 (1996).

exist. Thus, there would be no possible conflict of jurisdiction between the national courts of referral and an arbitral tribunal. Therefore, the national law of the courts of referral (*lex fori*), whose main objective is to safeguard the exclusive jurisdiction *of its national courts* over specific disputes, would have no *locus standi* to apply to determine the issue of arbitrability.

6-19 The above will apply even if the national court of referral is the national courts of the seat of the arbitration, rather than the national courts of one of the parties.[9] The fact that the arbitration takes place within the territory of a particular country does not mean that the national courts of that country have jurisdiction *over the pending dispute*, which *has been exclusively submitted to arbitration.* The jurisdiction of the national courts of the seat is limited to *disputes in relation to the arbitration proceedings* taking place in the seat.[10] Thus, for the national courts of the seat to apply their *lex fori*, the pending dispute needs to have an independent territorial connection with the seat. The fact that the arbitration takes place there will not be enough.

6-20 To illustrate, let us take the following scenario: a patent licence agreement between a U.S. and a Japanese party includes an arbitration clause providing for arbitration in Germany. A dispute arises out of the patent licence agreement, which was in fact concluded in the U.S. and performed in Japan. In general, the dispute has no other link with Germany or indeed Europe, apart from the fact that arbitration was agreed to take place in Germany. Prior to the constitution of the arbitral tribunal, one of the parties, by virtue of German ZPO s. 1032(2), resorts to the German courts (national courts of the seat), arguing that the dispute is directly relevant to the registration and validity of the patent, and thus not arbitrable.[11]

6-21 In this scenario, there is no reason for the German courts to apply their *lex fori* (ZPO s. 1030 or EC Regulation 44/2001 Art. 22(4)) to determine whether the dispute is arbitrable or not. There is no scope for the German *lex fori* to apply here. It is not within the scope of the German *lex fori* to altogether prohibit the arbitration within German territory of any claim not involving an economic

[9] See for example, EAA s. 32.

[10] However, their role is to supervise or assist the arbitral proceedings taking place in their territory. See for example, Model Law Art. 5-6, or the EAA 1996 s. 1(c).

[11] See about the arbitrability of these type of disputes in Germany Trittman/Hanefeld in K.-H. Böckstiegel, S. Kröll & P. Nacimiento (eds), *Arbitration in Germany – The Model Law in Practice* (Wolters Kluwer 2007) s. 1030, para 15-16.

interest or any claim touching on the validity of patents. As explained above, public policy does not underpin arbitrability laws. Rather, the real meaning of the *lex fori* on arbitrability (in this example, the ZPO s. 1030 or EC Regulation 44/2001 Art. 22(4)) is to preserve the exclusive jurisdiction of its national courts (in this example, the German courts): i.e. to ensure that the German courts will finally determine any claim that

- first, does not involve an economic interest or touches on the validity of the patents, and
- second *would fall under the jurisdiction of the German courts* if it were not for the arbitration agreement.

6-22 However, in this case the exclusive jurisdiction of the German national courts would not be at stake. In fact it would not be relevant at all, since the German courts would have no jurisdiction over the actual dispute, even if there were no arbitration agreement. The fact that the arbitration has its seat in Germany simply confers jurisdiction to the German courts over the arbitration proceedings (e.g. ZPO s. 1032) rather than over the dispute on the merits. Therefore, there would be no jurisdictional conflict between the arbitral tribunal, taking place in Germany, and the German courts. Consequently, there would be no reason for the German courts to apply their *lex fori* (ZPO s. 1030 or EC Regulation 44/2001 Art. 22(4)) to safeguard the jurisdiction of the German national courts. Here, the dispute does not disturb the jurisdictional system set out by the German jurisdictional rules. In fact, from the viewpoint of the German courts, the particular dispute will be *jurisdictionally neutral*, and thus fall out of the scope of their *lex fori* altogether.

6-23 In our scenario, there might be a jurisdictional conflict between the arbitral tribunal in Germany and the national courts of a different country (probably the national courts of the U.S. or Japan, or a third country, that would have a territorial link with the pending dispute at hand; for example, the country where the main contact was concluded). However, it is arguable whether in such a case the German courts should intervene to resolve this jurisdictional conflict, and safeguard the exclusive jurisdiction of the national courts of another country. The jurisdictional rules of a third country have no extraterritorial power over the German courts. Only in exceptional cases a national law provides that its national courts have a duty to safeguard the exclusive jurisdiction of the national courts of another country. This, for example, is set out in the UNCITRAL Model Law on Cross-Border Insolvency, which is also pertinent to arbitrability. This Model law provides in Article 20 that upon recognition of insolvency proceeding before the courts of a foreign country the commencement or continuation of individual actions or proceedings before the national courts of the Model Law country concerning the debtor's assets, rights, obligations or liabilities must be stayed. As is generally accepted, the term "Individual actions or proceedings" in Article 20 therein includes arbitration proceedings.[12] Therefore, if the issue of arbitrability is referred to the national courts of a country that has adopted the above Model Law, that national courts will have the duty to apply this law (*lex fori*) and prohibit any arbitration proceedings taking place within its territory, on the basis that insolvency proceedings have commenced before the national courts of a foreign country. Otherwise, the exclusive jurisdiction of the latter would be violated, which is exactly what the Model Law Cross-Border Insolvency aims to avoid. But, unless such an express provision exists in the national law of the courts of referral (*lex fori*), its national courts will have no duty to protect the exclusive jurisdiction of the national courts of foreign country.

6-24 Still, the crucial question remains: if the national law of the place of referral (*lex fori*) is irrelevant for the determination of the arbitrability matter, which law should the German courts, in our example, apply to determine arbitrability? The answer here is that, in such a case, the German courts should not attempt to determine arbitrability at all. Since their exclusive jurisdiction is not at stake, they should refer the determination of the arbitrability issue to the tribunal. They should have no jurisdictional interest in the arbitrability matter whatsoever. True, the German courts have a duty to assist the arbitration, which takes place in their territory.[13] However, in this case, it is arguable whether they are in a position to assist at all. Arbitrability here is an issue of jurisdictional conflict between the arbitral tribunal and the national courts of another country, and therefore, it is an issue effectively related to the *enforceability* of the award: if the tribunal proceeded with the merits of a dispute, which fall under the exclusive jurisdiction of the national courts of a particular country, the ensuing award will most likely not be enforceable in this country. However, this is a risk, which the tribunal is in a much better position to assess than the national courts of the seat. Therefore, here, the national courts should refrain from determining the issue of arbitrability altogether and refer the parties back to the tribunal.

6-25 To conclude, the national law of the place of referral (*lex fori*) will be relevant whenever there is a conflict of jurisdiction between the national courts of the place of referral and the tribunal. Only then should the national courts of

[12] See Guide to Enactment of the UNCITRAL Model Law on Cross-Border Insolvency, para 145.

[13] German ZPO s. 1032.

referral apply their national law (*lex fori*) to safeguard their exclusive jurisdiction over the particular dispute. However, if there is no jurisdictional conflict between the national courts of the place of referral and the tribunal, the national law of the place of referral (*lex fori*) will be irrelevant, and these national courts should arguably refrain from determining the arbitrability of the dispute. Instead, they should refer the parties to the arbitral tribunal. Here, arbitrability is a matter that relates to the enforceability of the award, which is a determination that the arbitral tribunal is in a better position to make.

2.2 When the Award is Challenged Before the National Courts of the Seat

6-26 When faced with an annulment action against the award on grounds of inarbitrability, the national courts of the seat will invariably apply their national law (*lex fori*). This is mainly because the majority of national provisions on challenge include a provision that mirrors the NYC Art. V(2)(a), which expressly refers to the national law of the seat. The typical example here is the Model Law Art. 34(2)(b)(i), providing that "the subject matter of the dispute is not capable of settlement by arbitration under the law of this State", i.e. the *lex fori* of the national courts before which the award is challenged, which will effectively be the national courts of the seat.

6-27 Nevertheless, the national law of the seat will not always be relevant to the determination of the arbitrability issue. A similar approach to the one under section 2.1. of this paper should also be taken when arbitrability arises at the stage of award annulment proceedings. In particular, the national courts should examine whether the resolution of the dispute by the arbitral tribunal violated any jurisdictional rule of the seat (i.e. the *lex fori*), granting exclusive jurisdiction to the national courts of the seat over the dispute which was actually determined by the tribunal.

6-28 The answer to this question depends on whether the national courts of the seat had jurisdiction on the specific dispute in the first place; this in turn will depend on whether the dispute had any territorial link with the seat. If the answer to this question is negative, the national courts of the seat should refuse to set the award aside. In such as case, the national law of the seat on arbitrability will not have been violated. In fact, the national law of the seat will not come into play at all.

6-29 To illustrate by reference to the above scenario: if the tribunal sitting in Germany decided to proceed with the merits of the dispute, the ensuing award should not be annulled by the German courts. On the basis of the above factual scenario, the German courts do not have jurisdiction over the particular dispute, since the dispute has no connection with Germany.[14] Therefore, the determination of the dispute by the tribunal would not violate the German *lex fori*. As was explained, the scope of the *lex fori* (in this case ZPO s. 1030) is to preserve the exclusive jurisdiction of its national courts, in this case the German courts, rather than to ensure that no arbitration touching on the validity of a patent would take place within German territory. Therefore, there should be no reason for the German courts to apply the *lex fori* and set the award aside.

2.3 Arbitrability Control by National Courts at the Place of Enforcement

6-30 Here, the view that the enforcement court is bound to apply their *lex fori* seems undisputable.[15] This is mainly due to the express wording of NYC Art. V(2)(a), providing that "The subject matter of the difference is not capable of settlement by arbitration under the law of that country." In principle, this view should not be challenged. The *lex fori* will be the sole point of reference for the enforcement courts to determine whether the award has violated any rule on inarbitrability.

6-31 However, it is questionable whether the *lex fori* will always be relevant for the determination of inarbitrability even at the enforcement stage. The enforcement courts should not engage in an examination of whether *the type of the dispute* determined by the tribunal was in general arbitrable in accordance with the notion of arbitrability determined by the *lex fori*. What is crucial for the enforcement courts is to examine whether the award, by determining a specific dispute, did *actually violate* the exclusive jurisdiction of the national courts of the place of enforcement.

6-32 Accordingly, the enforcement courts should examine whether the tribunal assumed jurisdiction over *a particular dispute*, notwithstanding the existence of a mandatory provision of the *lex fori* (i.e. the law of the enforcement courts) granting exclusive jurisdiction to the enforcement courts *over the same dispute*. Thus, the determination of whether the award is enforceable, must be made in the

[14] Apart from the fact that the arbitration took place in Germany, which however would not be enough to grant jurisdiction to the German courts over the merits of the dispute.

[15] See P. Bernardini, *supra* note 7, at 516.

light of the dispute *actually determined* by the tribunal, rather than on the basis of the general arbitrability views prevailing in the place of the enforcement.

6-33 From this viewpoint, the *lex fori* will be relevant to the determination of enforceability only if the enforcement courts have originally had jurisdiction over the dispute actually determined by the tribunal. That will depend on whether the specific dispute had any jurisdictional link with the enforcement state in the first place, apart from the fact that the award is sought to be enforced there. Otherwise, the *lex fori* will be irrelevant for the determination of inarbitrability, and the award should pass through the enforceability check on this ground.

6-34 If the dispute had no territorial link with the enforcement state, the enforcement courts would never have jurisdiction over the dispute. Accordingly, no national rule of the enforcement state aiming to safeguard the exclusive jurisdiction of the enforcement courts (i.e. *lex fori* on inarbitrability) would have ever been violated. The jurisdictional regime of the enforcement state, set out by the *lex fori* on inarbitrability, will remain intact, and, thus, there will be no reason for the enforcement courts to resist the enforceability of the award.

6-35 For example, suppose that a tribunal in Switzerland decided on a dispute in connection with a patent registered with the Italian Patent Office. If one of the parties sought to enforce the award in Italy, the Italian courts will most likely resist the enforcement on the basis that the award violated the *lex fori*,[16] granting Italian courts the exclusive jurisdiction over the specific dispute. Since the relevant patent was registered with the Italian patent authority, the Italian national courts would have exclusive jurisdiction over the particular dispute relating to the patent. The tribunal by assuming jurisdiction over this dispute violated the Italian *lex fori* and, therefore, the Italian courts would rightfully rely on the *lex fori* to resist the enforcement of the award in Italy.

6-36 However, if the dispute related to a patent registered, for example, in Japan, there would be no reason for the Italian courts to resist the enforcement of the award on the basis that this type of disputes "cannot be disposed by the parties" in Italy, in general. This would not be the purpose of the Italian Code of Civil Procedure Art. 806. Rather, its purpose is to allocate jurisdiction between arbitral tribunals and Italian courts, and in addition to preserve the exclusive jurisdiction of Italian courts on specific disputes. If the Italian courts never had jurisdiction

[16] Italian Code of Civil Procedure Art. 806 or EC Reg. 44/2001 Art. 22(4).

on a particular dispute, which the award determined, there would be no reason for the Italian courts to apply the *lex fori* and refuse the enforcement of the award.

2.4 When the Dispute is Before an Arbitral Tribunal

6-37 Strictly speaking an arbitral tribunal has no *lex fori*. However, traditionally the national law of the seat of the arbitration (i.e. *lex loci arbitri*) always played a significant role in the determination of arbitrability by the tribunal. This is for two reasons: first, the law of the seat is expressly referred to in the NYC.[17] Second and most importantly, the arbitrators tend to apply the law of the seat when deciding the arbitrability in order to avoid their award being annulled by the national courts of the seat.[18]

6-38 However, in accordance with what has been argued so far, the arbitrators should take the *lex loci arbitri* into account only when the pending dispute has a territorial connection with the seat of the arbitration. In particular, the tribunal should begin its analysis on the arbitrability by identifying the conflicting jurisdictions. The tribunal should answer the following questions:

- Is there any arbitrability rule of the national law of the seat, granting its national courts exclusive jurisdiction over a *type of dispute*, such as the one pending before the tribunal?
- If in the affirmative, is this national provision applicable to *the specific dispute pending* before the tribunal?

6-39 It is likely that the *lex loci arbitri* provides for the exclusive jurisdiction of its national courts over particular types of disputes, such as insolvency disputes, or disputes that the parties cannot be disposed of. However, the tribunal would be bound to apply this provision, only if the pending dispute had a territorial connection with the seat of the arbitration. Otherwise, no issue with regard to the jurisdiction of the national courts of the seat would arise at all, and therefore the *lex loci arbitri* on arbitrability (as a jurisdictional conflict of law rule) would not be relevant to the specific dispute.[19] There would be no potential conflict between the jurisdiction of the tribunal and the national courts of the seat, and,

17 Art. V(1)(a); Geneva Convention also makes reference to the *lex loci arbitri*, Art.IX(1)(a).
18 See P. Bernardini, *supra* note 7, at 513.
19 Even if this rule has a mandatory character in general, say EAA s. 2-4 or Model Law Art. 1

thus, the *lex loci arbitri* on inarbitrability would have no *locus standi* to apply and prevent the tribunal from assuming jurisdiction over the specific dispute.

6-40 Conversely, if the pending dispute had a territorial link with the seat of the arbitration, this link might trigger the exclusive jurisdiction of the national courts of the seat. In this case, the *lex loci arbitri* will be relevant, and the tribunal will have to take it into account to determine arbitrability.

6-41 Let us illustrate by reference to the same factual scenario above on a dispute related to the validity of a patent: if the tribunal had its seat in Germany but the pending dispute had no connection with Germany, there would be no basis for the tribunal to take the relevant *lex loci arbitri* on arbitrability[20] into account. From a jurisdictional point of view, the *lex loci arbitri* on inarbitrability would be irrelevant for the resolution of the pending dispute. The German courts would never have had jurisdiction over the dispute pending before the tribunal. Therefore, there would be no jurisdictional conflict between the German courts and the tribunal, and thus there would be no scope for the *lex loci arbitri* on arbitrability to apply.

6-42 By the same token, the tribunal should not be concerned that the award might be annulled by the national courts of the seat. As explained above,[21] there would be no basis for the national courts to set the award aside, as no national rule on arbitrability would have been violated.

6-43 Now, provided that the *lex loci arbitri* is not relevant, the following crucial questions would still remain open for the tribunal: against which standards should the tribunal determine the arbitrability of the pending dispute? Which rules should the tribunal seek guidance from to decide whether it has jurisdiction over the pending dispute?

6-44 The law applicable to the merits will not be relevant, as the issue of arbitrability is a matter of jurisdiction rather than substance. Thus, tribunals should avoid determining the arbitrability of the pending dispute by reference to the applicable substantive law. Similarly, the law applicable to the validity of the

[20] German ZPO s. 1032 and EC Reg. 44/2001 Art. 22(4).
[21] See *supra* 2.2.

arbitration agreement will not be relevant, as arbitrability is not a matter related to the validity of an arbitration agreement.[22]

6-45 The dispute pending before the tribunal will probably have a territorial connection with a country other than the seat of the arbitration. This territorial connection might well trigger the exclusive jurisdiction of the national courts of *that country*. In other words, there might be a jurisdictional conflict between the tribunal and the national courts of a country other than the seat, and there might be an arbitrability provision of this country granting its national courts exclusive jurisdiction over the dispute pending before the tribunal. However, it is questionable whether the tribunal is bound by this national rule. In fact, this issue relates to the pervasive debate on whether a tribunal should be bound by mandatory rules of a country other than that of the seat.[23]

6-46 In the above example where the tribunal sits in Germany, it is likely that the dispute has a jurisdictional link with the U.S. or Japan, whose arbitrability law will grant their national courts exclusive jurisdiction over the specific dispute. *Prima facie*, there will be no legal basis for the tribunal sitting in Germany to decline jurisdiction over the pending dispute, on the basis that the dispute will be inarbitrable in Japan or the U.S. The mandatory jurisdictional rules of Japan or the U.S. have no extra-territorial power over a tribunal sitting in a different country. Thus, there will be no obligation for the tribunal to apply these rules.

6-47 Eventually, the tribunal should determine arbitrability on the basis of the inherent or practical limitations of arbitration as a dispute resolution mechanism.[24] The crucial arbitrability question for the tribunal should be whether an arbitral award is able to successfully dispose of the dispute. If the answer to this question is in the affirmative, the dispute should be considered arbitrable by the tribunal.

6-48 For example, if the pending dispute related to the ownership of a patent is registered with the Swiss Patent Office,[25] the arbitrator should declare the

[22] S. Brekoulakis, Chapter 2 "On Arbitrability: Persisting Misconceptions And New Areas Of Concern", above.

[23] See, in more detail here various authors discussing the issue, in 18 (1-2) *Am. Rev. Int'l Arb.* (2007) and in particular at 51-155.

[24] *Cf* S. Brekoulakis, Chapter 2 "On Arbitrability: Persisting Misconceptions And New Areas Of Concern", above.

[25] As is known, the Swiss Patent Office accepts the award as a valid reason to amend the registry.

dispute arbitrable, even if the tribunal sits in a country that does not generally accept the arbitrability of this type of dispute. In such a case, the Swiss Patent Office would accept the arbitral award to amend its registry, and thus the dispute will be successfully resolved.

6-49 However, if the pending dispute relates to the ownership of a patent, which is registered with a national patent authority that does not accept arbitral awards as a valid legal reason for the amendment of its record, the tribunal should declare the dispute inarbitrable, even if the arbitration takes place in a country that accepts arbitrability of such type of disputes, for example Switzerland. In this case, only a national court could successfully resolve the dispute over ownership of the patent; thus, the dispute will in effect be inarbitrable.

3. A Brief Look Into Relevant Case Law

6-50 Before concluding, let us examine two recent cases (an arbitral award and a national judgement) looking into the issue of applicable law on arbitrability.

6-51 In first case, an arbitral tribunal sitting in Helsinki, Finland, applied the law of the seat to determine whether it had jurisdiction when the respondent in liquidation argued that the dispute was, in accordance with its national law, inarbitrable.[26]

6-52 More specifically, the respondent, a Latvian bank which was declared insolvent and put into liquidation, employed the claimant, a Swedish law firm, to represent it with respect to litigation before Stockholm Courts. The retainer agreement, signed after the respondent was put into liquidation, contained an arbitration clause providing for arbitration under the expedited arbitration rules of the arbitration institute of the Stockholm Chamber of Commerce (SCC). When the claimant commenced arbitration proceedings for unpaid legal fees, the Latvian bank objected to the jurisdiction of the tribunal on the basis that the dispute was inarbitrable, since under Latvian Law Latvian state courts had exclusive jurisdiction over any dispute involving the Latvian insolvent bank.[27]

[26] Final Award in 2006 in SCC Arbitration O53/2005, published in 1 Stockholm Int'l Arb. Rev. (2007) 211 et seq., with note C. Wallgren, H. Lindegaard & P. Franke, at 226 and E. Runesson, at 235.

[27] S. 487 of the Latvian Civil Procedure Law provides:

> Any civil dispute may be referred for resolution to an arbitration court with the exception of a dispute: 1) the adjudication of which may affect the rights and interests protected by

6-53 The tribunal, in a majority decision, held that the issue of arbitrability should be determined in accordance with Finnish law, on the basis of two arguments: first, by reference to the doctrine of separability the tribunal noted that the law applicable to the merits, in this case Swedish law, should not automatically be applicable to determine the arbitrability of the dispute. Therefore, since the tribunal was unable to infer any implied intention of the parties with regard to the law applicable to determine the arbitration agreement, the "law at the place of arbitration appears to be a viable and transparent fink for the determination of the law applicable to the arbitration agreement."[28] Second, the tribunal referred to NYC Art. V(2) and the Finnish Arbitration Act s. 40(1) providing that

> An award shall be null and void to the extent that the arbitral tribunal has in the award decided an issue not capable of settlement by arbitration under Finnish law.

Thus, the tribunal jumped to the conclusion that "in arbitrations conducted in Finland the arbitrators should be guided by Finish law when determining whether or not the dispute is arbitrable."[29]

6-54 Both arguments of the tribunal are questionable. First, as was showed in Chapter 2,[30] the matter of arbitrability is not related to the validity of an arbitration agreement. Accordingly, it does not follow that the law applicable to the determine arbitrability should be the law applicable to determine the validity of an arbitration agreement. Second, the tribunal's reading of Finnish Arbitration Act s. 40(1) is not correct. In accordance with what was argued above, the relevant section of the Finish Arbitration Act does not aim to prohibit tribunals sitting within Finnish territory from deciding arbitrability differently from what is the meaning of arbitrability in Finland. Arbitrability is not considered a matter of public policy any more. Rather, the aim of the Finnish Arbitration Act is not to allow a tribunal to decide on a specific dispute which falls under the exclusive jurisdiction of Finnish courts. However, in view of the factual scenario of the case, the Finnish courts have no jurisdiction over the particular dispute anyway, as the dispute has no jurisdictional link with Finland. Neither party was Finnish;

---

the law of a person who is not a party to the arbitration agreement; [...] 8) regarding rights and obligations of the persons who have been declared insolvent before the arbitration award is passed.

28 *Ibid.* para 46.

29 *Ibid.* para 47.

30 *Cf* S. Brekoulakis, Chapter 2 "On Arbitrability: Persisting Misconceptions And New Areas Of Concern", Section 2 above.

the conclusion and performance of the contract, including the arbitration agreement, did not take place in Finland. It seems very unlikely that the Finnish courts could have assumed jurisdiction, had there not been an arbitration agreement. The fact that the arbitration takes place in Finland does not alter the above conclusion: apart from the fact that Helsinki was determined by the SCC rather than by the parties, Finnish courts would only have jurisdiction to assist the arbitration proceedings, rather than to determine the merits of the disputes.

6-55 Thus, there was no risk that the exclusive jurisdiction of the Finnish courts would be circumvented, and therefore there was no *locus standi* for the Finnish law to apply and determine arbitrability. In fact, Finnish law was largely irrelevant to the arbitrability issue here.

6-56 Instead, the tribunal should have looked into the inherent limitations of arbitration and the factual circumstances of the case to determine arbitrability on the basis of whether an arbitral award would be able to effectively resolve the specific dispute, in which one of the parties was put into liquidation. More specifically, the tribunal should have examined whether the particular claim would be inextricably linked with any collective insolvent proceedings already pending before a national court. In such a case, the resolution of the dispute by the tribunal might affect the allocation of the limited funds to the several creditors in accordance with the security that each of the creditors had originally obtained. As was explained above,[31] arbitration has inherent limitations to accommodate this type of collective proceedings, and the claim should be considered inarbitrable. The resolution of this dispute could more efficiently be achieved by collective litigation proceedings where all the relevant parties may be brought before the same court. By contrast, if the tribunal found that the particular claim against the insolvent Latvian bank did not affect any collective insolvency proceedings, the dispute should be considered arbitrable.

6-57 In the second case, *Syska & Elektrim SA v. Vivendi & Others*,[32] Elektrim, a Polish company, entered into an agreement with Vivendi containing an agreement to arbitrate in London. After Vivendi commenced arbitration proceedings against Elektrim, the latter was declared insolvent. The question was whether the Polish Bankruptcy and Reorganisation Law, the application of which

[31] *Ibid.* Section 1.
[32] *Syska & Elektrim SA v. Vivendi & Others* [2008] EWHC 2155 (Comm).

would annul the arbitration agreement, was relevant to determine the arbitrability of the dispute.[33]

6-58 The Tribunal, by a majority, rejected Elektrim's objections to the Tribunal's jurisdiction. Elektrim sought to set the award aside by English courts. The English court looked into *the lex fori*, and in particular into the European Council Regulation (EC) No. 1346/2000 on Insolvency Proceedings, which forms part of English Law. Article 4 of the Insolvency Regulation (EC No 1346/2000) provides that the law of the country where the insolvency proceedings are started (in this case Poland) will determine among others

> 2(e) the effects of the insolvency proceedings on current contracts to which the debtor is a party; (f) the effects of the insolvency proceedings on proceedings brought by individual creditors, with the exception of lawsuits pending,

while Article 15 provides that

> the effects of insolvency proceedings on a lawsuit pending concerning an asset or a right of which the debtor has been divested shall be governed solely by the law of the Member State in which the lawsuit is pending.

Thus, under the Regulation, the matter boiled down as to whether the term "lawsuit" in Article 15 would include an arbitration claim, in which case the law of England would be applicable.

6-59 Clarke J saw no reason why the term "lawsuit" should not include arbitration claims, particularly as other regulations, when they intend to exclude arbitration, do so expressly.[34] Here, the question of whether Clarke J correctly applied Art. 4 and 15 of EC Regulation, which lead to the English law is not the main question. In fact, it is questionable whether the term "lawsuit" in the above EC Regulation should include an arbitration claim. This is especially so, if the term is read in its proper context: "law of the Member State in which the lawsuit is pending". Arbitration proceedings have no forum, and therefore the phrase "law of the Member State in which the lawsuit is pending" makes no sense in

[33] Polish Bankruptcy and Reorganisation Law, Art. 142:

> Any arbitration clause concluded by the bankrupt shall lose its legal effect as at the date bankruptcy is declared and any pending arbitration proceedings shall be discontinued.

[34] The Judge here referred to Article 1(2)(d) of EC Regulation No. 44/2001; Article 1(2)(d) of the Rome Convention on the Law Applicable to Contractual Obligations.

arbitration. There is no obvious analogy between "the Member State in which the lawsuit is pending" and "the state in which arbitration takes place". Nevertheless, the crucial issue here is the fact that Clarke J applied the *lex fori*, namely the EC regulation on Insolvency Proceedings, to determine the arbitrability issue in the first place. In view of the factual circumstances of the particular case, the application of the EC Regulation must be considered the right approach.

6-60 The purpose of the EC Regulation is, *inter alia*, to determine the effects of insolvency proceedings on other contracts or other proceedings to which the debtor is party. Therefore, provided that the wide interpretation to include arbitration given by Clark J is correct, the Regulation is also legislation closely relevant to arbitrability. The Regulation is relevant to the question of whether national courts of any Member State will have exclusive jurisdiction to determine a claim involving an insolvent party.

6-61 Moreover, the dispute largely falls within the scope of the territorial application of the regulation, since first, both parties were European based companies,[35] and second the original commercial activity between the claimant and the respondent took place in Poland.[36] Therefore, here the *lex fori*, i.e. the EC Regulation on Insolvency Proceedings, was relevant to the dispute, and the English courts rightly applied it to determine the effect of insolvency proceedings on arbitration. It is, of course, another issue, which goes beyond the scope of this paper, whether Clarke J correctly applied the conflict of laws provisions of the Regulation, deciding that English law rather than Polish law would eventually determine the issue.

4. Conclusion

6-62 As the relevance of public policy in the arbitrability discussion has been considerably waned in the last decades, the significance of the *lex fori* as the law applicable to arbitrability makes less and less sense. The aim of the paper was to re-examine the scope of application of the lex fori by looking into the rationale and the scope of application of national laws on arbitrability in general.

[35] Elekrim was a Polish company, whereas Vivendi is a French based company operating through other European subsidiaries.

[36] They entered into an agreement by which Vivendi was intended to acquire an interest in a Polish mobile telephone company in which Elektrim owned a substantial shareholding.

6-63 As was shown, all national provisions on inarbitrability, irrespective of any difference in the drafting style, are effectively conflict of jurisdiction rules, allocating jurisdiction between national courts and arbitral tribunals over specific types of disputes. Their main purpose is to safeguard the exclusive jurisdiction of their national courts on specific types of disputes, *rather than to ban arbitration in general.* State laws on arbitrability do not suggest that a particular type of dispute is *altogether prohibited from being arbitrated within the territory of a particular state*. Rather they suggest that a specific dispute cannot be submitted to a tribunal because the state courts of a particular country have the exclusive jurisdiction to hear the specific dispute on the basis of the factual circumstances surrounding the dispute.

6-64 From this jurisdictional point of view, the application of the *lex fori* to determine the arbitrability matter seems less justified. The *lex fori* will be relevant only to the extent that the exclusive jurisdiction of the national courts of the *lex fori* is at stake, which presupposes that the national courts have exclusive jurisdiction over the specific dispute pending before the tribunal. This, in turn, will depend on whether the dispute at hand has any territorial link with the country of the national courts, before which the issue of arbitrability arises.

6-65 This applies to all different stages where the issue of arbitrability may come up before national courts. If, for example, the arbitrability question arises before the courts of the seat at the stage of annulment proceedings, and neither the dispute nor any of the parties thereto have any jurisdictional connection with the seat of the arbitration, the *lex fori* will usually be irrelevant to determine arbitrability.

6-66 The same approach should be taken by an arbitral tribunal, which usually tends to apply the *lex loci arbitri*. There is no reason for a tribunal to take the law of the seat into account, unless the exclusive jurisdiction of the national courts of the seat is at stake, which would depend on whether the dispute pending before the tribunal has any jurisdictional link with the seat.

6-67 Issues related to applicable laws are by nature technical and complex matters. Eventually, the right answer to these issues depends on which viewpoint one would take. As the paper argued, a jurisdictional rather than a public policy viewpoint is more suitable for the purposes of international arbitration.

*Charalambos Pamboukis**

CHAPTER 7

ON ARBITRABILITY: THE ARBITRATOR AS A PROBLEM SOLVER

Thoughts About the Applicable Law on Arbitrability

1. Introduction

7-1 Arbitrability is a cornerstone issue in international arbitration and has probably become the most fashionable[1] subject in that field. One may even argue that it actually is the cornerstone of international arbitration in the sense that it ties up the opposing poles of party autonomy and the state's exclusive adjudicatory domain. In other words, it is the area of tension between these two poles representing the general and the individual interest.

1.1. The Concept and Function of Arbitrability: Limitation to the Power to Arbitrate

7-2 We can define arbitrability as the absence to contest the *rationae personae et materiae* to the power conferred to the arbitral tribunal (by the arbitration agreement) to resolve a dispute.[2] In fact arbitrability, along with the arbitration agreement, produces two effects (functions). One positive, which confers jurisdictional power to an arbitral tribunal, and one negative, which imposes a

* Charalambos P. Pamboukis is Associate Professor at the Athens University Law School and Attorney-at-law (Pamboukis, Maravelis, Nikolaidis Law firm). He has been appointed as arbitrator and acted as counsel in many international (ICC or ad hoc) arbitrations.

1 Ch. Jarosson, *Rev. Arb.* (1994) 170.

2 Compare to Poudret & Besson, *Droit comparé de l'arbitrage international* at 298,

> L'arbitrabilité (objective) désigne l'aptitude d'une cause à être soumise à l'arbitrage. Elle constitue une condition de validité de la convention d' arbitrage et donc de la compétence des arbitres.

The difference in the definition relies on the different perception of arbitrability as merely a choice of law problem or jurisdictional problem.

L Mistelis & S Brekoulakis (eds), Arbitrability: International & Comparative Perspectives, 121-142

duty upon state courts to accept and protect the jurisdictional power of an arbitral tribunal. And of course the last effect due to arbitrability relates to the admissibility of the arbitration agreement[3] by other legal orders.[4] In that sense someone can state arbitrability does not participate in the essence of the arbitration agreement – it is an external factor that limits the effectiveness of an arbitration agreement. Arbitrability belongs to a broader category of relevance rules,[5] which aim to recognise and give effect to external, foreign legal relations.[6]

7-3 That last function is, in the globalisation era, of tremendous importance. International law governance of private relations has become relative and complex, and it seems that only a *holistic* view can face contemporary complex problems.[7] Thus, in such a context, it is important to accept that the jurisdictional power of an arbitral tribunal must have a global effect and be respected by the national courts of all states.

7-4 Arbitrability in essence *limits* the power of an arbitral tribunal and the power of the parties as to what subject matter can be arbitrated.[8] In that sense, limitations can only arise from a state law aiming to protect its own general

[3] N. Coipel-Cordonnier, *Les conventions d'arbitrage et d'élection de for en droit international privé* (LGDJ 1999) nos 208 seq., p 220 seq.

[4] That is why the statement of Paul Lagarde ("Approche critique de la lex mercatoria", *Mél. B. Goldman*, no 37, p. 148) "...l'arbitrabilité du litige est une notion qui n'a de sens que par reference à un ordre juridique étatique" is profoundly correct in my opinion.

[5] It does not confer jurisdictional power, it recognises it. Concerning the relevance rules, see P. Mayer, "Le phénomène de coordination des ordres juridiques étatiques en droit privé, Cours général de droit international privé", *RCADI* t. 327 (2007) at 52, Ch. Pamboukis, "Droit international privé holistique : droit uniforme et droit international privé", *RCADI* t. 330 (2007) at 433.

[6] That is why I believe that the two issues of the validity of the arbitral agreement and arbitrability are two separate issues deserving distinct legal treatment. The validity of the arbitral agreement remains a choice of law or private international substantial rules problem, thus arbitrability is a jurisdictional problem.

[7] Ch. Pamboukis, *supra* note 5 at nos 27 seq., p. 56 seq.

[8] Redfern & Hunter, *International Commercial Arbitration* (4th ed, 2006) at 164. "Whether or not a particular type of dispute is "arbitrable" under a given law is in essence a matter of public policy for that law to determine", Compare to the 2nd ed at 137,

> The concept of arbitrability, properly so called, relates to *public policy limitations* upon arbitration as a method of settling disputes. Each State may decide, in accordance with its own economic and social policy which matters may be settled by arbitration and which may not.

social or economic interest.[9] The limitations may concern either persons (subjective arbitrability) or more properly, matters (objective arbitrability).[10] It is evident that these limitations are exclusively connected to a given state and mainly to its own specific general interest. They do not emanate from arbitration itself.

7-5 Consequently, speaking about arbitrability is naturally an exercise in analysing limitations on the power of the parties and arbitrators. One has to take into consideration that in the context of *international arbitration*, there are various sources of limitations: they may aim to protect the general interests of the State (e.g. taxation) or a collective social interest (e.g. categories of contractually weaker parties) or a fundamental ethical norm (e.g. bribery contracts). Schematically, we can describe three levels of sources of possible limitations:

- national/unilateral limitations emanating from State law,
- supranational limitations emanating from regional or international statutes, e.g., European law and
- transnational limitations emanating from a common core of public policy as perceived by an arbitrator (often called, following the suggestion of *Lalive,* truly international[11] public policy).

7-6 They can also be divided in two categories: first, *internal* limitations, coming from the applicable law[12] providing arbitrators with power to arbitrate/determine the dispute.[13] Problems that arise from this perspective relate to the *jurisdictional foundation* of the power to arbitrate[14] in accordance to the will of the parties submitting their dispute to arbitration.[15]

9 D. Hascher, "Les conditions d'arbitrabilité et la jurisprudence", in *Competition and Arbitration Law* (CCI 1992) at 151,

> Le caractère inarbitrable de certaines matières rend compte du lien étroit qui existe entre celles- ci et les *fondements de l'organisation économique et sociale* de l'État…

10 B. Hanotiau, "L'arbitrabilité et la *favor arbitrandum:* un réexamen", *Clunet* (1994) 899 seq.; B. Hanotiau, "What Law Governs the Issue of Arbitrability?", 12 *Arb. Int'l* (1996) 391 seq.

11 "Ordre public transnational (ou "réellement international") et arbitrage international" *Rev. Arb.* (1986) 329 seq.

12 If such law really exists, or as it seems to me being the most accurate analysis arbitral award been a floating norm (Ch. Pamboukis, *Lex Mercatoria as Applicable Law in International Contractual Arbitration* (1996) [in Greek]).

13 P. Mayer, "La règle morale dans l'arbitrage international" in V. Heuzé, *Études offertes à P. Bellet* (Litec 1991) 396.

14 The difference of angle, perception is perceivable if one compares the arbitral precedent (ICC 6379, YBCA (1992) 213; ICC 6162/1990, YBCA (1992) 154, 155; ICC 6474/1992, YBCA

7-7 Secondly, *external* limitations of various sources and even different mechanisms such as *lois de police*, international mandatory rules, which of course give rise to the question: which of these multiform and multipurpose mandatory rules are *relevant to the issue submitted to arbitration.* That type of problem is, in fact, a relevance problem concerning the admissibility by a state legal order of the effects of an arbitral award.

7-8 The problem must also be examined through the different stages in which they can be raised, either before an arbitral tribunal or before a state judge. In that respect, we should briefly underline some main differences among these *fora*.

1.2. Differences Between Arbitrators and State Judges

7-9 International arbitration is the jurisdictional expression of increasing individual freedom, the result, in part, of globalisation and the rise of the individual and non-state actors as factors in transnational activity. Therefore, the natural tendency of many international arbitrators is to resist any limitations not emanating from the parties themselves[16] attached to the sacrosanct principle of *pacta sunt servanda.*[17]

7-10 It is of great importance to repeat once again a qualitative difference between a *national* judge and an arbitrator. The latter has no *organic forum,*

(2000) 297 seq.,) and state case law (*Mitsubishi Motors Corporation v. Scherk* U.S. Supreme Court 417 U.S. 506, Court of First Instance Bologna, 18 July 1987, YBCA (1992) 534, *Shearson* U.S. Supreme Court 107 S Ct 2332 (1987). The arbitrators are trying to localise the applicable law, which is the foundation of the parties' will to arbitrate and ultimately their own jurisdictional basis. The state judges are directly examining their own law as they have to check the relevance, if the award would be given or not effects.

15 In fact through the applicable law if that law considers the dispute to be inarbitrable. Here of course there is, in fact, an antinomy which must be resolved by the arbitral tribunal relying on the competence–competence principle between the will of the parties to arbitrate and the limitation provided by the chosen applicable law to the arbitration agreement.

16 See Hanotiau, *supra* note 10 at 906 seq.; *Mitsubishi v. Soler* (U.S. Supreme Court, 2 July 1985, YB 1986, 555 seq.) based on the agreement of the parties to arbitrate in its result extending the arbitrability to antitrust disputes can also be constructed in that sense. In fact *Mitsubishi* had proposed a favourable arbitrability presumption (if there is no express legal prohibition every issue is arbitrable). It is indeed true that one of the recent trends is the declining relevance of public policy, see Kirry, "Arbitrability: Current Trends in Europe", *Arb. Int'l* (1996) 373 seq., and for the U.S.: McLaughlin, "Arbitrability: Current Trends in the United States", *Arb. Int'l* (1996) 113 seq., and for the Commonwealth: Rogers, "Arbitrability", 10 *Arb. Int'l* (1994) 263 seq.

17 In fact it is *that* principle from the point of view of international arbitration, which has been sometimes considered as of *truly international public order*.

meaning a prescriptive legal order in which he belongs and which is expressed by him, as the state judge. More precisely, an arbitrator derives his power from the will of the parties. The centre of the arbitrator's *jurisdiction* is to decide a dispute in accordance with the will, and the legitimate expectations of the parties. Every arbitral tribunal defines its jurisdictional mission in accordance primarily with the will of the parties, which technically constitutes its *ad hoc arbitral forum*. It is therefore essential to distinguish between the two possible *fora* before which the question of arbitrability can be raised. The cardinal point of *arbitral jurisdiction* is fairness in accordance with the will of the parties and the prerequisites of the case. An arbitrator is *a pragmatic problem solver*.[18] A state judge is *a social engineer* in the sense that he has to deal with a case within the boundaries of the general interest of society. The forum of arbitrator is *autonomous*, while the forum of the state judge is *heteronomous*.

7-11 The second main difference is that an arbitrator has no *imperium*, which is reserved, naturally to states. He is therefore inclined or expected by the parties to take into consideration different laws, which can adversely affect the enforceability of the award. In my opinion that type of consideration constitutes *external contingencies to arbitration norms perceived as floating norms*, logically unnecessary and often complicating erroneously the problem.

1.3. Is Arbitrability a Jurisdictional or a Conflict of Laws Problem?

7-12 In order to complete the consideration of parameters pertaining to the subject matter, one has to distinguish the problem of jurisdiction from the problem of applicable law. Usually the former refers to the power to decide, whereas the latter refers to how to decide. Often the thesis of application of the *lex fori*[19] disguises, and hides the more accurate analysis that arbitrability is a problem of lacking jurisdiction, meaning: from the scope of a national legal order, for certain matters or persons (objective and subjective arbitrability) the state *forum* has exclusive jurisdiction and thus does not recognize unilaterally jurisdiction to any other forum (arbitral or state). More often the problem of arbitrability is perceived as a choice of laws problem.[20] In that perspective, an

[18] M. Alberstein, *Pragmatism and Law, From Philosophy to Dispute Resolution* (Ashgate Dartmouth 2003).

[19] H. Arfazadeh, "Arbitrability under the New York Convention: the *Lex Fori* Revisited", *Arb. Int'l* (2001) 73.

[20] N. Coipel-Cordonnier, *supra* note 3 at 244 seq.; B. Hanotiau, *supra* note 10 at 391 seq., Lew, Mistelis & Kröll, *Comparative International Commercial Arbitration* (Kluwer 2003) at 196.

analysis of different possibilities is made in favour of one or another system. Lew, Mistelis, and Kröll[21] summarised the practice of arbitration tribunals to eight different approaches: 1) the national law of the parties or one of them, 2) the law applicable to the contract as such (*lex causae*), 3) the law of the seat of the arbitral tribunal (*lex arbitri*), 4) the law of the country whose ordinary courts would be competent to handle the dispute in absence of arbitration clause, 5) the law of the country in which is more likely that enforcement of the award will have to be sought, 6) the law governing the arbitration clause, 7) a combination of law and the *tronc commun* approach (common and fundamental principles of law) and 8) common and fundamental principles of law, applying thus a denationalised approach.

7-13 The latter approach to treat arbitrability as a choice of law problem is not satisfactory. Mainly because it is confusing the problem of jurisdiction with the problem of choice of law through the notion of arbitrability. Confusion is often made between arbitrability, *ordre public*, *lois de police* and especially the validity of the arbitration agreement. The aim, thus, of this paper is to show that the title focusing on the applicable law is erroneous. In fact, arbitrability is proposed to be perceived as a jurisdictional problem, more precisely, as a relevance problem and not a choice of law problem.

7-14 If that view is admitted, the practical effect would be at the arbitration level to treat arbitrability as a founding jurisdictional problem, and thus only the arbitral tribunal should be proper to decide that issue in accordance with the principle of Kompetenz–Kompetenz. One important implication emanating from the principle of equality among a state and an arbitral jurisdictional order is that a preliminary point of jurisdiction cannot be brought before a state court.

7-15 At the level of the state judge, the arbitrability issue, in that thesis, becomes a relevance problem, which has to be decided only in conformity to the *forum executionis*. The problem is no longer what law governs arbitrability. That aspect is absorbed by the award. The problem is then whether we will accept or not the effects on the arbitral award.[22]

[21] *Ibid.*, 196.

[22] On these methodological aspects see S. Bollée, *Les méthodes du droit international privé à l'épreuve des sentences arbitrales* (Economica 2004) *passim*.

7-16 It seems that two fundamental mistakes have often disoriented the problem: an imprecise and broad notion of arbitrability which has not been elucidated in a clear way, and has been confused with other notions and mechanisms is also often made. The second refers to the very nature of the method, because, often the arbitrability problem is seen as a conflict of laws problem and not as a conflict of jurisdictions problem. We will further discuss these two aspects.

2. The Notion of Arbitrability (What is Arbitrability)

2.1. Distinction Between Arbitrability and Validity of an Arbitration Agreement

7-17 The validity of an arbitration agreement belongs to the private and regulation sphere while arbitrability belongs to the public/mandatory sphere. The validity of an arbitration agreement poses problems of choice of law while arbitrability, as a jurisdictional problem, is governed by the *lex fori*. Thus, even a valid arbitration agreement can pose a problem of arbitrability of a dispute. The arbitrability is closely related to the appropriate *forum* and thus it is relative by its own nature. Definitively, arbitrability as a jurisdictional problem is a "public" law problem of posing limits to private power closely related to the forum, while validity is a private problem related to parties (qualities).[23]

2.2. Distinction from Other Important Notions

(a) Distinction from International Public Policy

7-18 International public policy is an exception mechanism that normally belongs to the conflict of laws method. International public policy is also a ground for refusal of the recognition or setting aside of the arbitral award. Thus, the mechanism of international public policy expresses fundamental principles of a *given state's legal order.* Often, we distinguish between internal public policy (applied thus to domestic arbitrations) and international public policy (applied to

[23] See on the analysis of jurisdiction and its relation as a private or public issue, P. Mayer, "Droit international privé et droit international public sous l'angle de la notion de competence", *Revcrit dip* (1979) at 1, 349, 537; P. de Vareilles de Sommières, *La compétence international de l'État en matière de droit privé – Droit international public et droit international privé* (LGDJ 1997) *passim.*

international arbitrations).[24] It is then disputed if a truly international public order exists, as Professor Lalive claimed, independently of any given legal order, *in vacuum*.[25] Arbitrability deals with the power to arbitrate, not as protection mechanism of the forum. It intervenes at the jurisdictional level, at the very beginning not at the end. It refers to the power of the arbitrators, not to the award changing rights and obligations of the parties. Clearly there is a notional and methodological difference.

(b) Distinction from the Lois de Police

7-19 Here of course the answer is easy. As it is not a choice of law problem the *lois de police* can intervene at two stages: the arbitrators could take into consideration foreign *lois de police* if the parties expected them to do so, and a state judge could refuse the recognition and enforcement of an award which did not take into consideration the *lois de police* of the *forum executionis*.[26] But in any case, that does not affect, the power of the arbitral tribunal to decide the case (if they can decide), but rather *how* the case has to be decided.

2.3 Arbitrability Seen as a Jurisdictional Problem – Distinction Between Internal and International Jurisdictional Exclusive Rules

7-20 All the above distinctions become evident if arbitrability is seen as a *jurisdictional problem* (even exclusive jurisdiction) as it deals with the power to arbitrate. From the point of view of the arbitral tribunal, the problem is to what extent should an arbitrator respect the rules on exclusive jurisdiction of another legal order.

7-21 In that respect, one has to distinguish between internal and international exclusive jurisdictional rules. Not all jurisdictional rules – as for the public policy rules – aim to embrace international disputes. So, generally speaking, one has to

[24] See among others, K-H., Böckstiegel, "Public Policy and Arbitration", in *Comparative Arbitration Practice and public policy*, ICCA Congress, Series 3 at 177 seq.

[25] *Supra* note 11.

[26] Seraglini, *Lois de police et justice arbitrale internationale* (Dalloz 2001) 178 seq.; Arfazadeh, *Ordre public et arbitrage international à l'épreuve de la mondialisation* (LGDJ 2006) 82-83, Mayer, "L'autonomie de l'arbitre international dans l'appréciation de sa propre competence", *RCADI* t. 217 (1989) 326, Radicati di Brozolo, "Mondialisation, juridiction, arbitrage : vers des règles d'application semi-nécessaire?", *Rev.crit dip* (2003) 146 seq., Bucher, *Le nouvel arbitrage inernational en Suisse* (Helbing & Lichtenhalhn 1988) 41 seq.

examine if the purpose of the jurisdictional rule in question is to embrace international disputes as well, or whether it is reserved only to domestic disputes.

3. ARBITRABILITY AND APPLICABLE LAW (HOW ARBITRABILITY HAS TO BE DECIDED)

3.1. Is Arbitrability a Conflict of Laws Problem?

7-22 Often the problem of arbitrability is analysed as a conflict problem indistinctive of the procedure and the authority. Thus, national courts have contemplated mainly the *lex fori,* the *lex contractus,* the *lex arbitri* or the *lex executionis*.[27]

7-23 That palette of choice of law possibilities gives rise to inconsistency of court decisions as *Jan Paulsson* showed,[28] especially regarding the application of the New York Convention.

7-24 It has recently been correctly pointed out,[29] by *Arfazadeh,* that at least at the stage of enforcement of the award the non-arbitrability issue has been regarded erroneously as a problem of conflict of laws instead of as a problem of conflict of jurisdiction. Some Courts followed that approach[30] and others can be construed in that sense.[31]

7-25 The jurisdictionally correct approach lays down the foundation of the application of the *lex fori*, which in fact, excludes the multilateral conflict of laws approach.

7-26 An accurate answer cannot be given without distinguishing the authority and the procedure in which the problem of arbitrability arises. As arbitrability

[27] B. Hanotiau, *supra* note 10 at 391, B. Hanotiau, "L'arbitrabilité et le favor arbitrandum: un réexamen", *Clunet* (1994) 899; Marc Blessing, "The Law Applicable to the Arbitration Clause and Arbitrability, in 40 Years of Application of New York Convention", *ICCA* (1999) 168.

[28] Jan Paulsson, "Arbitrability, Still Through a Glass Darkly", in *Arbitration in the Next Decade* (ICC Bulletin, Special Supplement 1999) at 95.

[29] H. Arfazadeh, "Arbitrability under the New York Convention: the Lex Fori Revisited", 17 *Arb. Int'l* (2001) 73.

[30] Swiss Federal Supreme Court, *Fincantieri*, ATF 118 II 353; Paris CA, 16 February 1989, *Almira*, Rev. Arb. (1989) 711.

[31] U.S. Supreme Court, *Mitsubishi*, 437 U.S. 614 (1986); Arfazadeh, *supra* note 29 at 77.

deals in fact with the mandatory domain, the difference between a state judge and an arbitrator is important when determining what is or is not permitted. If one accepts that a judge needs not only to decide a case but also to protect the coherence of its own legal order, comprising of rules defending the general interest, and the arbitrator does not need *a priori* to protect any kind of general interest, we understand that an arbitrator will be reluctant not to arbitrate a matter. An arbitrator will assume jurisdiction unless reasons exist relating to their own concept of justice, i.e. the protecting of the general interest of a legal order and thus refusing the expressed will of the parties to arbitrate their dispute. Thus, the arbitration agreement is for the arbitrator a clear indication, if not a presumption, that the parties wish to arbitrate the referred differently.[32] What is important for the arbitrator is not to check if the subject matter is arbitrable, but if the parties have agreed to submit it to arbitration. By contrast, for the judge, it is important first to check if the arbitrator had the jurisdictional power to decide the case.[33] Arbitrability deals with jurisdictional power. Therefore, what is prohibited is defined unilaterally by the law of the forum (a sort of jurisdictional mandatory rule), except for bilateral or multilateral international conventions. There is no space for a choice of law problem: the judge necessarily will apply its own law.

3.2. The Relativity of the Answer According to the Stage and Nature of the Procedure in which the Problem is Raised

7-27 The second variable parameter is the stage and the nature of the procedure. Indeed the problem of arbitrability can be raised either before an arbitral panel, before a state court during a declaratory pre-arbitral procedure, as a ground of annulment, or as a ground to refuse the recognition of the arbitral award.

7-28 If the argument of arbitrability is raised before the arbitral tribunal it is associated to the power to arbitrate. That practically means that the arbitral tribunal should consider it in accordance to its arbitral mission which constitutes the prime source of its jurisdictional power.[34]

32 Paulsson, *supra* note 28 at 103; Washington Court of Appeals, 27 July 1988, *Kamaya Co Ltd et al. v. American Property Consultants Ltd*, YBCA (1999) 836.

33 We will not deal with the question who should determine arbitrability, the arbitrator or the judge which relates to the Kompetenz-Kompetenz doctrines. See Alfaro & Guimarey, "Who Should Determine Arbitrability? Arbitration in a Changing Economic and Politics Environment", *Arb. Int'l* (1996) 415.

34 See *infra*.

7-29 If the argument is raised before the state judge, it is more often proposed to be seen as a relevance problem, meaning, in practice, whether or not the legal order of the state judge would recognize and enforce (in the future if an arbitral award is not yet rendered or presently if it has already been published) the arbitral award. But it is important to underline that arbitrability is not properly a problem of applicable law to the validity of the arbitral agreement.

7-30 As it has been explained above, arbitrability should be distinguished from the validity of the arbitration agreement. Arbitrability deals merely with the extent of jurisdictional power. One legal order may not tolerate that a certain matter can be either arbitrated or decided by another jurisdictional organ, other than its own. Before a state judge, all that can be decided in the pre-arbitral stage is that the matter is not arbitrable according to the law of the forum and that, therefore, the arbitral tribunal lacks jurisdiction: the sanction is that the forum will not recognise the award. In fact, that does not invalidate the arbitration agreement – the decision of the judge will be irrelevant to another jurisdiction – but it is decided pre-emptively if the award will or will not be recognised in that forum.

3.3. Arbitrability and Arbitrator Seen as a Problem Solver

7-31 Here we have to deal with the mission of the arbitral tribunal. What is the source of its power and what are its functions and limits. From that point of view, one may distinguish *ad hoc* arbitration from institutional arbitration. The reason is mainly that the source of the primary power in the first case is only the will of the parties; thus, in the *ad hoc* the limitation of the institutional framework is also chosen by the parties.

7-32 If the correct jurisdictional approach is adopted, no problem of applicability arises at the arbitral tribunal level, as the arbitrators have to decide in accordance with the will of the parties at hand and as they have no limitations emanating from the arbitral forum. Is that broad freedom unlimited? Should an arbitral tribunal be able to decide *any* matter because only the parties have submitted it to the panel? Are there no limitations to the power of the arbitrators? These questions cannot be answered without an analysis of the arbitral *forum*, or in more appropriate terms, without an analysis of its arbitral jurisdictional mission. In other words the arbitral tribunal should decide the point of arbitrability in accordance to its own jurisdictional framework. Indeed the arbitral tribunal – as opposed to a state judge – is not subject to the authority of a state. It is thus important for the tribunal to establish its own jurisdiction in the first stage. And that is happening, actually, when the arbitral tribunal decides on important preliminary issues (what are the issues to be decided, what is the procedural applicable law,[35] what is the applicable law in the merits etc). The authority of a tribunal is thus defined in accordance with some criteria, which are different than those defining the authority of a state judge. What should these criteria be? Mainly and in brief: (a) the legitimate expectations of the parties and (b) the efficiency of its forthcoming arbitral award, meaning the broader possibility to be largely recognized.[36]

7-33 This analysis relies on the distinction made by H.L.A Hart:[37] among norms conferring power and norms regulating behaviour, the power conferred upon arbitrators is a *power norm*, giving the power, thus, to produce other norms. Therefore an arbitral tribunal[38] will have the freedom not only to arbitrate but also to determine its *ad hoc* jurisdictional frame. Of course, parties can limit that power by also choosing the *way* of deciding (for instance in accordance to a particular law). That means that the arbitrators have the freedom to construct their own jurisdictional framework almost freely.[39] In doing so, arbitrators have to take into account the will of the parties, and also their legitimate expectations. They can also construct independently or by reference to a state law, the law of the seat of the arbitration. That also means that arbitrators have a *forum* – not necessarily a state forum – constituted on the basis of the will of the parties, and *broader* than that of expressed will, as it has to take into account the legitimate expectations of the parties, in particular that the award will be enforceable.

7-34 Does that mean that the arbitrators are *absolutely free* to arbitrate any dispute submitted to them by the parties, only and simply because the parties wish so? The answer must be negative. It is true that international arbitration operates largely in a non-state space. But that does not that mean that arbitrators are without constraints. These constraints (legitimate expectations of the parties and international efficiency of its award) are rather internal and subjective, but still remains constraints.

[35] See on that Petrochilos, *Procedural Law in International Arbitration* (Oxford University Press 2004) *passim*.

[36] I have proposed that analysis in more length some years ago, see Ch. Pamboukis, *supra* note 12, 179 seq.

[37] H.L.A. Hart, *The Concept of Law* (Bruxelles 1976) at 103 seq [in French].

[38] P. Mayer, *supra* note 26 at 319 seq.

[39] Ch. Pamboukis, *supra* note 12 at 172-173.

7-35 How then should the problem of arbitrability be decided from an arbitrator's perspective? Is it a choice of law problem? Certainly not, as all state laws stand on an equal footing from arbitrator's perspective, and it is thus impossible to find criteria in order to give application to one of them. The answer is that arbitrators have to decide in accordance with their jurisdictional mission. Consequently they have to avoid rendering an award which may be unenforceable. In this sense, arbitrators also have to follow a "*lex fori*" approach and not a conflict of laws approach.

7-36 Thus, the *reasonable* expectations of the parties constitute the foundations of an arbitral forum. In this context it is safe to assume that the parties could never reasonably expect for a tribunal to grant an arbitral award that cannot be enforced. Therefore, arbitrators should *take into consideration* (not properly apply) different jurisdictions, which would not accept arbitrator's jurisdiction. This can be made in regard to the facts of the case and by an exercise of comparative law. There are indeed some areas, which are generally admitted to be non- arbitrable.[40]

7-37 From a comparative law perspective, a common core or at least a general guidance is offered as to which matters are generally admitted as arbitrable.[41] Some national laws refer to broad notions such as "disputes involving economic interest"[42] or "disputes involving property"[43] or "rights of which he has full disposition".[44] Arbitrators, being normally pragmatic and cosmopolitan problem

[40] In a similar direction, Fouchard, Gaillard & Goldman, *On International Commercial Arbitration,* para 559 even if the thesis of a genuine international public policy is not defendable because international arbitration evolutes in a non-state space and constitutes a "droit individual". There is no expression of general interest in that space, and there are no mandatory rules or limitations. It is the space of *pacta sunt servanda.*

[41] Lew, Mistellis & Kröll, *supra* note 20 at 194. These authors are distinguishing between two main approaches of national laws. The first one relies on substantive criteria and the second relies on the parties' power to dispose freely their rights. The second approach requires a conflict of law analysis according to the authors. In my opinion it requires, in fact, a comparative analysis as it is not possible to make a choice of law; all laws being in an equal footing and having no criteria to proceed to a such analysis from the point of view of the arbitral forum.

[42] Germany, ZPO section 1030(1).

[43] Art. 177, Swiss Private International Law.

[44] Art. 2059, French Civil Procedure Code. A similar approach is the one of Belgian law: Art. 1676 Civil Procedure Law and of Italian law: Art. 806 of Civil Procedure Law. See for a comparative study on the recent trends in U.S., Switzerland and Germany, Baron & Liniger, "A Second Look at Arbitrability", *Arb. Int'l* (2003) 27 seq.

solvers, have to follow this general guidance, and not necessarily apply one of these national laws.

7-38 Following that analysis we should then also distinguish between internal and external constraints from the point of view of the arbitrator. As to the former, in fact, internal constraints emanate mainly from the will of the parties and from fairness and moral duty of the arbitrator.

7-39 As to the latter, we should discuss certain cases covered under Lalive's truly international public policy, comprising of, for instance, bribery contract disputes.

7-40 Sometimes it has been decided that consultancy contracts relating to public procurement are not arbitrable.[45] It is today correctly admitted, after the famous Lagergen award,[46] that the immoral undercover relation does not neutralise the arbitrator's power to arbitrate and to decide the nullity or the annulment of the contract under the applicable law.[47] Hence it is not a problem of arbitrability.

7-41 An arbitrator is bound only by the will of the parties. That will is to arbitrate the submitted dispute (or at least to have the dispute removed from the jurisdiction of national courts) and constitutes the real theoretical foundation of a *favor abitrandum*.[48] In that approach, no conflict of laws problem arises except for a possible construction of the will of the parties to that regard in case it is not clear. It is a pure substantive approach.

7-42 If one adds to the criterion of the will of the parties the respect for their legitimate expectations, an arbitrator may opt for or choose a broader approach. He might include to his jurisdictional mission the legitimate expectation of the parties, also understood as the maximisation of possibilities for the forthcoming award to be respected and enforced in different jurisdictions. It is a pragmatic interest of the high legal efficacy of his award. Logically, this view is external, as it does not participate inherently to the jurisdictional power of the arbitral

[45] Tribunal de Commerce Brussels, 20 September 1999, *Matermaco*, XXV YBCA (2000), 675.

[46] Wetter, "Issues of Corruption before the International Tribunals: The Authentic Text and True Meaning of Judge Gunnar Lagergren's 1963 Award in ICC Case no 1110", *Arb. Int'l* (1994) 277.

[47] London CA, *Westacre v. Jugoimport* [2000] QB 288; a contract between a drug traffickers, see Bortolotti, "International Agency Agreements and ICC Arbitration", *ICC Bulletin* (2001) 54 seq.

[48] Which in accordance to Hanotiau is confirmed by the historic evolution, ("L'arbitrabilité et la favor arbitrandum: un réexamen", *Clunet* (1994) 899 seq.).

tribunal. Sometimes the arbitral panel will even embark on a rather difficult exercise to identify the various possible places of enforcement (*forum executionis*). However, this is normally an unnecessary exercise, in my opinion. The arbitral award will be a floating norm that can potentially be enforced by various jurisdictions in the context of an interconnected and complex world.[49]

7-43 Often a different view is taken which relies on the applicable law analysis. That view is not accurate. An arbitrator is facing a peculiar problem: what should the applicable law be, and in accordance with which criteria should it be determined? He will embark on an adventure with no evidently satisfactory result. This is explainable because the conflict of laws approach is wrong, as there is no indication from the point of view of the arbitral forum which state law is better suited to answer this problem. Often indication is not given about the likely places where the award will be enforced or whether the award could be challenged. An arbitrator should answer this problem referring to its own *forum*,[50] in other words accomplishing its own jurisdictional mission, in accordance to the jurisdictional approach.

7-44 In the majority of cases, arbitral tribunals determine the arbitrability of a dispute on the basis of the law of the place of arbitration regarded as the arbitral *lex fori*.[51] In other words, the arbitrator, instead of constructing its own arbitral forum, may choose the *forum* of the seat of the arbitration (*lex loci arbitri*). There are reasons favouring this approach: being in conformity to the law of its seat gives the tribunal a clear overall procedural legal reference and avoids the risk that the award might be set aside.[52] Of course that option gives rise to some problems. In some cases, the determination of the seat of arbitration, absence a choice by the parties, is disputed and remains an issue for the arbitrators to decide.

[49] See Ch. Pamboukis, "La renaissance- metamorphose de la méthode de reconnaissance", *Rev. Crit. Dip.* (2008) 513 seq.

[50] This is the appropriate term. We used previously, the word frame, in order to show, in a more explanatory way, the relationship among arbitrator and arbitral forum.

[51] ICC 6162 YBCA (1996) 153, ICC 4604 YBCA (1985) 975.

[52] Dr Mann defended that view by saying that an arbitration cannot exist outside a particular state legal order, "Lex facit arbitrum", in Martinus Nijhoff, *Liber amicorum for Martin Domke*, (1967) 157 seq. Even if we do not agree to that basic thesis of Dr Mann, the possibility of the arbitrator to choose as *its own lex fori* the law of the seat of the arbitration remains a coherent possibility. According to some legislation, such as Article 177 of the Swiss PILA arbitrability has to be decided in accordance with the law of the seat.

7-45 If the arbitrator opts for a choice of law approach (not including the *lex fori* approach) he will face serious difficulties in electing the proper law. The possibilities are as follows:

- *Lex loci executionis*: unforeseeable and thus irrelevant as that place is or could be anywhere. The probable place of enforcement is at the arbitral stage (not the post arbitral stage) uncertain and often there are more than one.[53] Furthermore at the arbitral phase (before an award is rendered) often there are no objective clouds on where the parties could reasonably enforce the forthcoming award and therefore the arbitral tribunal cannot rely on the basis of legitimate expectation of the parties.
- *Lex arbitri*: arguably the law applicable to an arbitration agreement, it is the source of power of the arbitrator. According to that view the arbitral tribunal will decide the issue of arbitrability by application of the law that governs the arbitration agreement, irrespective of the principle of separability (severability), being, often, the law that governs the main contract. But why should we necessarily submit the will of the parties to a national legal order? The will of the parties can also be viewed as a substantial direct norm, independent of a national legal order.[54] In other terms, why should a tribunal allow a national law to prevail over the will of the parties (perhaps in breach of the doctrine *pacta sunt servanda*)? There is no logical foundation in admitting that the parties located their relationship in a system which will not give effect to their will.[55]
- *Lex contractus – lex causae*: only to the extent that the law applicable to an arbitration agreement has not been determined.
- *Lex mercatoria* (combination of the above): no *lex mercatoria* is conceivable as the arbitrator is not a social engineer. The *lex mercatoria* approach supposes a legal order in which the arbitrator belongs, which is totally artificial and probably adds nothing practically.[56]

[53] Lew, Mistelis & Kröll, *supra* note 20 at 198, who also notes why (arbitral) tribunals have been reluctant to deny jurisdiction on the basis that the dispute is not arbitrable under the law of the possible place of enforcement. ICC 2476 Clunet (1977) 937; ICC 4604 YBCA (1985) 973.

[54] Craig, Park & Paulsson, *International Chamber of Commerce Arbitration* (2nd ed) 81.

[55] Derains, "Détermination de la lex contractus", in *L'apport de la jurisprudence arbitrale* (ICC 1986) 28.

[56] See in that respect Ch. Pamboukis, "La lex mercatoria reconsiderée", in *Mélanges Paul Lagarde*, (Dalloz 2005) 635 seq.

– Substantive approach: what deems fair and appropriate to the arbitral tribunal without considering the applicable law analysis.[57]

3.4. Arbitrability and the State Judge Seen as Social Engineer

7-46 The application of the *lex fori* is a natural application by a judge, as it expresses unilaterally its own international mandatory jurisdictional rules. The inconvenience of that approach is the lack of uniformity, but that is a given problem because states' interests and understanding on the general interest may diverge.

7-47 A state judge is bound to apply its own law on jurisdiction, at least at the stage of recognition or annulment.[58] The *lex fori* is the only possible solution.

(a) Recognition and Enforcement-Annulment

7-48 It is reasonable to consider that arbitrators and state judges should be treated on an equal footing regarding their jurisdictional function. In international jurisdiction, a delimitation of powers to decide has to be made. Delimitation in that field is unilateral, meaning that every legal system – and in that sense only national law systems can be conceived as such – determines the matters reserved for a (national) jurisdictional monopoly; such determination is made following national criteria and/or international conventions. That determination comprises of, of course, the international arbitrator as well. We have thus to distinguish the situation of state law from the one of uniform law.

i. State Law

7-49 First of all, the notion of mandatory rules is conceivable only in relation to a system of law in which the jurisdictional authority belongs. This obviously is the case of a state judge.

7-50 The matter of what should be considered mandatory jurisdiction rules, excluding jurisdiction of arbitrators (and foreign state judges), has been discussed

[57] The same stands for the Tronc Commun analysis, R. Sammartano, *International Arbitration Law* (Kluwer 2001) 274 seq.

[58] Park, "The Arbitrability Dicta in First Options v. Kaplan: What sort of Kompetenz-Kompetenz Has Crossed the Atlantic?" *Arb. Int'l* (1996) 139, 140.

by *Arfazadeh*.[59] That author makes a distinction between two categories of mandatory jurisdictional rules, but he reaches a false conclusion. The first one is the category of "pure" mandatory jurisdictional rules from which no derogation from the will of the parties is admitted. More often that category is called more properly: exclusive jurisdiction rules. Undoubtedly for disputes which fall into that category (for example Art. 22 of the Brussels I Regulation) a jurisdictional monopoly of a given state is clearly established, and thus, the *forum executionis* will not recognise an arbitral award if it violated its own exclusive jurisdiction rule.

7-51 Is the judge of the *forum executionis* also obliged to refuse recognition if the award violated the exclusive jurisdictional rule of a third state? The answer should be positive if the *forum executionis* is tied up by an international obligation (convention, EC law). In any case, that will be decided in accordance with the unilateral exclusive jurisdiction rules of the *forum executionis*.

7-52 Coming now to the second category: the *quasi* mandatory jurisdictional rules, which afford special jurisdictional protection of the weaker party, usually the consumer, the worker, the insurer. *Arfazadeh* is of the opinion that arbitrability should not be restricted because there is no valid reason to adopt a more cautious attitude towards international arbitrators than to foreign judges.

7-53 That position does not take into account the following considerations: the protection of the weaker party in the contractual field is a manifestation of a general social interest. The judge of the *forum executionis* will have to preserve the aim of the aforesaid general interest of its own legal system. Therefore, no general rule can be drawn, and the general idea is that the *forum executionis* will decide what the limits of arbitrability are in accordance with its own criteria. Technically speaking, either the rule will be considered as an exclusive or as a concurrent jurisdictional basis. In the last case the parties probably have the power to submit their dispute to arbitration since the state legal system does not impose a jurisdictional monopoly. The argument of equality does not stand because the arbitration agreement is mainly considered as instituting an exclusive jurisdiction in favour of the arbitrator. Thus, the main limitation should be drawn by the legal system of the *forum executionis* on the basis of the limitation of party autonomy, and for the reason of jurisdictional protection of the weaker party,

[59] Park, "Arbitrability under the New York Convention", *Arb. Int'l* (1996) 77 seq.; Arfazadeh, *supra* note 26 at 84 seq.

which serves some general social interest.[60] In my opinion this situation falls under the protection of the weaker party or at least a party requiring special protection. Referring their dispute to arbitration would normally disfavour them, at least because of the cost associated with arbitration.[61]

7-54 We can reach the conclusion and suggest that the exclusive jurisdictional area will emerge by a comparative exercise and somehow it will be mainly uniform in the future, either by unilateral convergence or by progressive unification by Convention.

7-55 The third category is jurisdictional monopoly: exclusive jurisdiction rules are not the only ground to refuse the recognition of an award pursuant the *forum executionis*. If a *lois de police* of the forum had not been taken into account or a procedural international public policy rule, or more rarely, a substantial public policy rule has been manifestly disregarded, this could provide grounds for refusing recognition. The category here is the violation of the mandatory substantial rules of the forum, or violation of general principles. One has, in that respect, to note that these grounds do not constitute, properly speaking, an inarbitrability[62] ground, they are not comprised in the arbitrability notion as has been explained above. The result is almost the same, except for the important practical consequence that these grounds of refusal cannot be evoked under the New York Convention in the pre-arbitral stage, and are evoked only in the recognition or during the annulment procedure, meaning the post-arbitral stage.

[60] Meaning, in fact, that a "weaker party" is the one who normally has not the same bargaining power, which is important also in the field of jurisdiction, especially in the case that the "weak" party looses the right to see his case decided by his natural judge.

[61] These considerations are in principle valid concerning the control by the state judge of an arbitral award regarding, especially, the *lois de police* of the forum – limiting from the forums point of view the jurisdictional power of the arbitral tribunal – as now is generally admitted, see P. Mayer, "L'étendue du contrôle, par le juge étatique, de la conformité des sentences arbitrales aux lois de police", in *Mél, Gaudemet Tallon* (Dalloz 2008) 459 seq.

[62] See Arfazadeh (*supra* note 26 at 83 notes 221 and 222) who considers that the "…impératif de police n'est plus une entrave à la compétence de l'arbitre international". Although the lois *de police* does not in fact interfere at the jurisdictional level, it is a ground (under the broader concept of international public order) for refusal of the recognition of the arbitral award. This is not true if used as a ground of jurisdictional refusal. That means, in fact, that the *lois de police* of the *forum executionis* does not indeed challenge arbitrability, but constitutes, nevertheless, a ground of refusal of the arbitral award.

ii. Uniform Law

7-56 Two main figures should be briefly examined: NYC Art. II and the UNCITRAL Model Law.

7-57 *New York Convention*: The main problem in that area arises from the *construction of Art. II(1) of the NYC*. Under the NYC a specific problem of construction of Art. II and Art. V has been debated. Article II states that arbitration agreements have to be recognised so that courts have to deny jurisdiction, unless the dispute is not capable of settlement by arbitration (paras 1 and 3 combined). According to which law the dispute has to be arbitrable, however, is not expressly provided for and it has given rise to a number of divergent views in national court practices.

7-58 Two main approaches have been suggested. According to the first one, the same law should resolve the issue of arbitrability whether Article II or V is applied.[63] Since Article V expressly refers to the law of the forum, it is that law which prevails. Needless to say that in accordance with the jurisdictional approach, the application of the *lex fori* constitutes the only conceivable solution.[64]

7-59 According to the second view,[65] a distinction should be drawn depending on whether the issue of arbitrability is raised at the level of validity of the arbitration agreement, in which case arbitrability should be determined in accordance with the law of autonomy, or in the context of the recognition or enforcement of the award. In my opinion validity has nothing to do with arbitrability. We may have a valid arbitration agreement, which refers to arbitration a non-arbitrable dispute.

63 Italian Supreme Court, 27 avril 1979, *Rivista di Diritto Internazionale Privato e Processuale*, (1979) 565, Hanotiau, *supra* note 10 at 400 seq.

64 Arfazadeh, *supra* note 26 at 80, states that nothing in Article II of the Convention indicates that arbitrability per se is subject to any law other than the *lex fori* and that all decisions can be construed as simply permitting arbitrability under the *lex fori*.

65 Hanotiau, L'arbitrabilité et la favor arbitrandum: un réexamen, *Clunet* (1994) 920 seq., who distinguishes arbitrability as a jurisdictional exception made before the arbitral tribunal and considered as a condition to the validity of the arbitration agreement and as ground of refusal of the recognition of the arbitral award. The Court of Appeal of Brussels in its decision of 4 October 1985 YBCA (1989) 619 accepted that view. *Contra* Nuyts, note, *RDCB* (1993) 1118 seq. who does not see why one should treat arbitrability on a different conflict of laws approach depending on the stage of arbitration, and Partch, "L'arbitrabilité des litiges dans la Convention de New York", *Actualité de droit* (1992) 1261 seq., Coipel-Cordonnier, *supra* note 3 at 249 seq.

7-60 *UNCITRAL Model Law*: The lack of arbitrability constitutes, in accordance with Article 34(2) of UNCITRAL Model Law, a specific reason for annulment besides public policy, always to be assessed pursuant the law of the place of arbitration.

(b) Pre-arbitral State Control

7-61 Here comes the problem of construction of Article II NYC. According to Article II(3) a court should recognise the parties' agreement to refer to arbitration any disputesd relating to a subject matter capable of settlement by arbitration as seen in Article II(1). The construction of that article plays, in practice, a role only if a party refers to a state court, either in order to obtain a declaratory decision deciding that the arbitration agreement is null and void or if a court is seized of an action on the merits of the dispute and, of course, incidentally the same question arises.

7-62 It is therefore important first to define what that article allows the judge to determine and control, and second to establish the law to be applied to determine the issue of arbitrability. As far as the second question is concerned, it is clear that it should be decided only in accordance with the *lex fori:* a judge would not normally apply a different law. The true meaning of Article II is that the arbitration agreement should be enforced unless the dispute falls into the scope of an exclusive basis of jurisdiction of the forum.

7-63 The controlling jurisdiction is the one of the *forum* whether the judge is enforcing an arbitration agreement under Article II or an arbitration award under Article V.[66] That reading of the Convention provides internal consistency. Of course, the consequence would not be to proclaim the nullity of the arbitration clause. The state judge has no such power. Simply the arbitration agreement would not produce any effect regarding the power of the state judge to decide in accordance to its forum jurisdictional rules.

4. Concluding Remarks

7-64 We therefore can conclude by supporting the following proposals: First, an arbitral award is a floating norm which can be given effect by several

[66] Van den Berg, *The New York Arbitration Convention of 1958* (Kluwer 1981) 152 and 153; Arfazadeh, *supra* note 26 at 85.

jurisdictions. Thus, arbitrability, as a jurisdictional issue at the arbitral phase, should be decided in conformity to the jurisdictional mission of the arbitral tribunal, based mainly to the legitimate expectations of the parties. That also explains the *favor arbitrandum*.

7-65 Second, arbitrability at the post arbitral phase should be seen more properly as a relevant, jurisdictional issue in a globally interconnected legal reality. Thus the limits always derive from the imperative jurisdictional rules of the *forum* in which recognition of the arbitral jurisdictional power or arbitral award is sought.

7-66 Any uncertainty that may arise out of the above proposals, mainly due to the fact that they depend on different approaches taken by several jurisdictions as to what issues are of mandatory or public policy nature, will remain. However, it is hoped that eventually they will fade, as the different jurisdictions will increasingly become more harmonised.

PART II

SUBSTANTIVE RULES ON ARBITRABILITY

Thomas E. Carbonneau[*]

CHAPTER 8

LIBERAL RULES OF ARBITRABILITY AND THE AUTONOMY OF LABOR ARBITRATION IN THE UNITED STATES

1. INTRODUCTION

8-1 Arbitrability establishes the respective domains of law and arbitral adjudication. It is the essential dividing line between public and private justice.[1] Courts exercise a general public authority to adjudicate, while arbitrators rule pursuant to the parties' contract and act to resolve claims that arise in the parties' transaction. Disputes are inarbitrable as a result of the subject matter of the claim or because of deficiencies in the contractual agreement to arbitrate.[2] In U.S. law, subject-matter inarbitrability has waned considerably as an impediment to arbitration. Moreover, courts generally construe the defence of contract inarbitrability to favour the recourse to arbitration. In its remaking of American arbitration law, the U.S. Supreme Court has developed its own doctrinal thinking on arbitrability. The Court's originality, tied like all of its other rulings to accomplishing the objectives of the underlying policy on arbitration, resulted in a

* Orlando Distinguished Professor of Law, Penn State University and Faculty Director of the Institute of Arbitration Law and Practice.

1 See generally T. Carbonneau, *The Law and Practice of Arbitration* (2nd ed, 2007) 23-26. See also John Beechey, "Arbitrability of Anti-Trust Competition Law Issues—Common Law", 12 *Arb. Int'l* (1996) 179; Bernard Hanotiau, "L'arbitrabilité", 296 *Recueil des Cours* (2002); Charles Jarrosson, "La notion d'arbitrabilité", 1 *Rev. Brasileira Arb.* (2003) 173.

2 See Patrice Level, "L'arbitrabilité", *Rev. Arb.* (1992) 213. See also Michelle St. Germain, "The Arbitrability of Arbitrability", *J. Disp. Res.* (2005) 523.

L Mistelis & S Brekoulakis (eds), Arbitrability: International & Comparative Perspectives, 143-163

sui generis terminology that reduces the role of arbitrability in the U.S. legal regulation of arbitration.[3]

2. The General Rules on Arbitrability in U.S. Law

8-2 From a general perspective, arbitrability under U.S. law is no different than arbitrability in other national laws of arbitration – at least, among like-minded States that endorse and participate in the international consensus on arbitration.[4] It is recognised as a basic element in the law's governance of the contractual recourse to arbitration. A more penetrating analysis, however, reveals that the concept has a special function and meaning in U.S. law. American arbitration law is not a civil law edifice. The governing statute is truncated; it is not a comprehensive regulatory enactment on arbitration. It lacks significant doctrinal content; it is neither rigorous nor systematic. In some respects, it has failed to develop the intellectual discipline and cohesion characteristic of significant legislative frameworks.[5]

8-3 To a substantial degree, the U.S. law of arbitration resembles the French law of arbitration prior to the promulgation of the French decrees on arbitration[6] at the beginning of the 1980s. In a word, U.S. arbitration law is opportunistic in character.[7] It has been forged on an episodic basis as decisional necessity

3 See, e.g., *Mitsubishi Motors Corp. v. Soler Chrysler-Plymouth, Inc.*, 473 U.S. 614 (1985); *Rodriguez de Quijas v. Shearson/American Express, Inc.*, 490 U.S. 477 (1989). See also Steven C. Bennett, "The Developing American Approach to Arbitrability", 58 *Disp. Res. J.* (2003) 8. On *Mitsubishi*, see Ronald E.M. Goodman, "Arbitrability and Antitrust: Mitsubishi Motor Corp. v. Soler Chrysler-Plymouth, Inc.", 23 *Columbia J. Transnat'l L.* (1986) 655; Lisa Sopata, "Mitsubishi Motor Corp. v. Soler Chrysler-Plymouth, Inc.: International Arbitration and Antitrust Claims", 7 *NW. J. Int'l L. & Bus.* (1986) 595.

4 See, e.g., Thomas Carbonneau, "The Ballad of Transborder Arbitration", 56 *Miami L. Rev.* (2002) 773.

5 See generally Patrick Glenn, *Legal Traditions of the World: Sustainable Diversity in Law* (2nd ed, 2005); Stehan Frommel (ed), *Conflicting Legal Cultures in Commercial Arbitration: Old Issues and New Trends* (1999); Christian Borris, "Common Law and Civil Law: Fundamental Differences and Their Impact on Arbitration", 60 *Arb.* (1994) 78.

6 See Thomas Carbonneau, "The Reform of the French Procedural Law on Arbitration: An Analytical Commentary on the Decree of May 14, 1980", 4 *Hastings Int'l & Comp. L. Rev.* (1981) 273; Yves Derains, "France: National Report", 6 *YBCA* (1981) and 7 *YBCA* (1982) 35; Philippe Fouchard, "L'arbitrage international après le Décret du 12 mai 1981", 109 *Clunet* (1982) 374. See also Jean Robert, *L'Arbitrage-Droit Interne, Droit International Prive* (6th ed, 1993).

7 See, e.g., Thomas Carbonneau, "The Story of American Law", 2 *J. Am. Arb.* (2003) 299.

required. Judicial pronouncements were intended to fill a gap that opened suddenly, to supply a new segment of doctrine that had just become essential to the law-in-the-making (*de lege ferenda*) enterprise. Arbitrability in U.S. law was born of the pragmatic disposition of the common law methodology; its form, content, and definition arose from a converging, albeit chaotic, patchwork of cases.[8]

8-4 The governing American statute on arbitration, the U.S. Arbitration Act or the Federal Arbitration Act (FAA),[9] originated as a special interest bill providing for the limited validity of arbitration agreements in specialised commercial matters.[10] In writing the statutory provisions, the proponents of the law were careful to preserve legal procedural safeguards and to restrict the scope of arbitration to specific circumstances.[11] Over the course of nearly four decades of decisional law, the U.S. Supreme Court revamped the content of the FAA and converted it into a more comprehensive, albeit improvised, set of rules on arbitration.[12] In its contemporary form, the FAA is not only a tribute to the genius of the common law, but also a textbook example of judicial legislation.

8-5 Despite its narrow focus and restrictive origins, the FAA contains the most unequivocal statement of subject-matter inarbitrability in U.S. arbitration law. FAA § 1 incorporates the celebrated "employment contract exclusion,"[13] which renders the FAA and its validation of arbitration inapplicable in employment contracts. The statutory policy of legitimating arbitration agreements as contracts and enforcing arbitral awards does not govern these relationships and transactions. The reason for the prohibition presumably was due to the specific employment laws that existed at the time of the FAA's enactment, as well as the

8 See, e.g., Thomas Carbonneau, "American and Other National Variations on the Theme of International Commercial Arbitration", 18 *Ga. J. Int'l & Comp. L.* (1988) 143. See generally Ian R. MacNeil, *American Arbitration Law: Reformation, Nationalization, Internationalization* (1992).

9 See generally Ian R. MacNeil, Richard E. Speidel, & Thomas J. Stepanowich, *Federal Arbitration Law: Agreements, Awards, and Remedies Under the Federal Arbitration Act* (1994); William W. Park, "Saving the FAA", 19 *Mealey's IAR* (2004) 27; William W. Park, "Determining the Arbitrator's Jurisdiction: Timing and Finality in American Law", 8 *Nev. L. Rev.* (2007) 135.

10 See, e.g., Carbonneau, *supra* note 1, ch. 4.

11 *Ibid.*

12 *Ibid.*

13 *Ibid.* at 84-99.

perception that inequity attended the parties' disparity of position in the employment relationship.[14] In effect, the latter made effective legal consent to arbitration impossible. Confirming the favourable-to-arbitration rulings of the lower federal courts, the U.S. Supreme Court, however, minimised the impact of the employment contract exclusion,[15] holding that it applied only to the contracts of a limited group of interstate transportation workers. Nonetheless, the "employment contract exclusion" as a symbol of the inequity of disparate-party arbitration continues to foment debate and disagreement among courts and legislators. The discord is not expressed in terms of subject-matter inarbitrability (as analysis would require), but rather as a matter of contract fairness and enforceability (contract inarbitrability). In effect, the application of arbitration in circumstances of inequality between the parties exemplifies the divisions surrounding the arbitrability of basic rights and the mandatory imposition of the obligation to arbitrate.[16]

8-6 In its case law, the U.S. Supreme Court first confronted the doctrine of subject-matter inarbitrability in transborder litigation[17] and later in domestic cases involving the submission of securities disputes to arbitration.[18] The Court concluded that the FAA permitted the arbitration of regulatory law disputes because it contained no express limitation of the jurisdictional scope of

14 See Matthew W. Finkin, """"Workers' Contracts" Under the United States Arbitration Act: An Essay in Historical Clarification", 17 *Berkeley J. Emp. & Lab. L.* (1996) 282, cited in *Pryner v. Tractor Supply Co.* and *Sobierajski v. Thoesen Tractor & Equipment Co.*, 109 F.3d 354 (7th Cir.), *cert. denied* 522 U.S. 912 (1987).

15 See *Circuit City Stores v. Adams*, 532 U.S. 105 (2001) (holding that the employment contract exclusion only applies to the employment contracts of transportation workers directly involved in the interstate transport of goods).

16 See, e.g., *Cole v. Burns International Security Services*, 105 F.3d 1465 (D.C. Cir. 1996); *Shankle v. B-G Maintenance Management of Colorado, Inc.*, 163 F.3d 1230 (10th Cir. 1999); *Armendariz v. Foundation Health Psychcare Services, Inc.*, 6 P.3d 669 (CA 2000); *Bradford v. Rockwell Semiconductor Systems, Inc.*, 238 F.3d 549 (4th Cir. 2001); *Blair v. Scott Specialty Gases*, 283 F.3d 595 (3d Cir. 2002); *Leodori v. CIGNA Corp.*, 814 A.2d 1098 (2003). See also *Green Tree Financial Corp.-Ala. v. Randolph*, 531 U.S. 79 (2000).

17 See *Mitsubishi Motors Corp. v. Soler Chrysler-Plymouth, Inc.*, 473 U.S. 614 (1985). For commentary and debate on the case, see Thomas Carbonneau, "The Exuberant Pathway to Quixotic Internationalism: Assessing the Folly of Mitsubishi", 19 *Vand. J. Transnat'l L.* (1986) 265; Andreas Lowenfeld, "The Mitsubishi Case: Another View", 2 *Arb. Int'l* (1986) 178; Hans Smit, "Mitsubishi: It Is Not What It Seems to Be", 4 *J. Int'l Arb.* (1987) 7.

18 See *Shearson/American Express, Inc. v. McMahon*, 482 U.S. 220 (1987); *Rodriguez de Quijas v. Shearson/American Express, Inc.*, 490 U.S. 477 (1989). See also C.E. Fletcher, *Arbitrating Securities Disputes* (1990).

arbitration in terms of these claims.[19] Of course, the FAA did not expressly prohibit the submission of criminal law disputes to arbitration either and few, if any, commentators would conclude that such disputes are arbitrable as a result. Be that as it may, statutory claims could be submitted to arbitrators as a matter of law. In so holding, the Court did not focus upon subject-matter arbitrability or the public policy considerations that it encompasses. Rather, the Court articulated a number of makeshift doctrines that allowed it to avoid a direct confrontation of the central public law question. These doctrines sustained the central theme of permissive submission to arbitration that statutory claims fell within the arbitrator's domain. They included the following propositions: Arbitration was a "mere form of trial" that had no impact upon the substantive character of the rights at issue.[20] Statutory non-waiver provisions were intended to protect substantive rights guaranteed by the statute, not the procedural provisions that regulated contests involving those rights.[21] In any event, arbitration was the equal of the judicial trial as a means of adjudication, fully capable of serving as a process for adjudicating statutory controversies.[22] In effect, the court elaborated its own conception of arbitration that allowed it to answer obliquely, but effectively, the public policy dilemmas associated with the submission of public law claims to private arbitral adjudication.

8-7 These statements of doctrine coincided (somewhat fortuitously) with the concept of contractual freedom. The parties had bargained for arbitration and they were entitled to the benefits of their bargain.[23] In effect, the parties had the right to have all their disputes heard by arbitrators. The intent of the contracting parties was manifest and should be enforced at law. In reality, the rulings were imperative because they promoted the Court's policy in regard to the management of adjudicatory resources and its objective of creating greater access to effective adjudicatory procedures in American society. Only an express congressional declaration that the area was "off-limits" to arbitration could

19 *Ibid.* See also M. Scott Donahey, "From The Bremen to Mitsubishi (and Beyond): International Arbitration Adrift in U.S. Waters", 7 *Am. Rev. Int'l Arb.* (1996) 149.

20 See sources cited in *supra* notes 17 and 18.

21 *Ibid.*

22 *Ibid.*

23 *Ibid.*

prevent arbitral recourse.[24] The Court, however, never found any statutory language limpid enough to thwart the reference to arbitration.

8-8 Except for insurance disputes (owing to the language of the governing statute)[25] and some tort matters in a few states,[26] – and, possibly, employment relationships in a few other jurisdictions[27] – subject-matter inarbitrability is a negligible part of U.S. arbitration law. The Court's determination that statutory disputes were arbitrable basically extinguished the concept as a rule of substantive law. Only issues of contract inarbitrability had continuing analytical significance. Contract arbitrability focuses upon the agreement to arbitrate as opposed to the provisions of enacted legislation. It asks whether a contract of arbitration exists; if so, whether it is an enforceable contract; and, then, whether it covers the submitted dispute. In some national laws, contract inarbitrability can also arise from a failure of the arbitral tribunal or administrator to follow the stipulations in the parties' arbitration agreement.[28]

8-9 Because of the early date of its enactment and its special interest character, the FAA does not recognise the *Kompetenz-Kompetenz* doctrine, authorising arbitrators to rule on jurisdictional challenges.[29] In the U.S. law, therefore, issues of contract inarbitrability are generally decided by courts. FAA § 3, the relevant statutory provision, (and, to a lesser extent, FAA § 4) provides that a federal

24 *Ibid.* See also Christine L. Davitz, "U.S. Supreme Court Subordinates Enforcement of Regulatory Statutes to Enforcement of Arbitration Agreements: From The Bremen's License to the Sky Reefer's Edict", 30 *Vand. J. Transnat'l L.* (1997) 59.

25 The McCarran-Ferguson Act, 15 U.S.C. § 1012. The statute provides:

> No Act of Congress shall be construed to invalidate, impair, or supersede any law enacted by any state for the purpose of regulating the business of insurance . . . unless such Act specifically relates to the business of insurance.

15 U.S.C. § 1012(b).

26 See, e.g., *Episcopal Diocese v. Prudential Securities* (Fla. CA April 7, 2006); *Seifer v. U.S. Home Corporation*, 750 So.2d 633 (Fla. 1999). But see *Community State Bank v. Strong*, 2007 WL 1225343 (11th Cir. 2007). See also David E. Zukher, "The Role of Arbitration in Resolving Medical Malpractice Disputes: Will a Well-Drafted Arbitration Agreement Help the Medicine Go Down?", 49 *Syracuse L. Rev.* (1998) 135; *Henry v. Gonzalez*, 18 S.W.3d 684 (Tx. App. 2000) (arbitrability of legal malpractice claims).

27 See, e.g., *Walker v. Ryan's Family Steak Houses, Inc.*, 400 F.3d 370 (6th Cir. 2005); *Leodori v. CIGNA Corp.*, 814 A.2d 1098 (2003).

28 See UK Arbitration Act 1996 s. 30(1)(c).

29 See Carbonneau, *supra* note 1, at 189-193.

district court decides whether an arbitration agreement exists and is an enforceable contract.[30] *First Options of Chicago, Inc. v. Kaplan*[31] was the first case to address the *Kompetenz-Kompetenz* void in U.S. law by focusing upon the "who decides?" question. Writing for a majority of the U.S. Supreme Court, Justice Breyer asserted that the enforcement of an arbitration agreement posed a serious preliminary question that directly implicated the availability of important legal rights.[32] Justice Breyer never referred to the governing provision of the FAA. He did maintain nonetheless that threshold jurisdictional issues should be decided by courts because they exercised public adjudicatory authority and were a disinterested party. As a consequence, courts decide whether an alleged arbitration agreement existed and was enforceable.[33] Justice Breyer then invoked the contract freedom idea and concluded that the contracting parties could invest the arbitrators with the power to hear and decide front-end jurisdictional challenges.[34] This contractual integration of *Kompetenz-Kompetenz* had the effect – at least, potentially – of pushing the courts to the outer periphery of the arbitration process, thereby conferring even greater autonomy upon the process. Arbitrators would decide basic jurisdictional questions initially and perhaps conclusively – given the realities of judicial supervision.

30 See sources cited in *supra* note 9.

31 514 U.S. 938 (1995). On *Kaplan*, see Dulic, "First Options of Chicago, Inc. v. Kaplan and the Kompetenz-Kompetenz Principle", 2 *Pepperdine Disp. Res. L.J.* (2002) 77; Rau, "The Arbitrability Question Itself", 10 *Am. Rev. Int'l Arb.* (1999) 287; Park, "The Arbitrability Dicta in First Options v. Kaplan: What Sort of Kompetenz-Kompetenz Has Crossed the Atlantic", 12 *Arb. Int'l* (1996) 137.
A large number of cases have followed the ruling in *First Options.* See, *e.g.*, *Marie v. Allied Home Mortgage Corp.*, 402 F.3d 1 (1st Cir. Mass. 2005); *Alliance Bernstein Investment Research & Management, Inc. v. Schaffran*, 445 F.3d 121 (2d Cir. N.Y. 2006); *China Minmetals Import & Export Co., Ltd. v. Chi Mei Corp.*, 334 F. 3d 274 (3d Cir. N.J. 2003); *Rock-Term Co. v. United Paperworkers International Union*, 184 F.3d 330 (4th Cir. Va. 1999); *Williams v. CIGNA Financial Advisors Inc.*, 197 F.3d 752 (5th Cir. Tx. 1999); *Dantz v. Apple American Group, LLC*, 123 Fed. Appx. 702 (6th Cir. Ohio 2005); *Employers Insurance Co. v. Century Indemnity Co.*, 443 F.3d 573 (7th Cir. Wis. 2006); *Liberty Mutual Insurance Co. v. Mandaree Public School District # 36*, 503 F. 3d 709 (8th Cir. N.D. 2007); *Theis Research, Inc. v. Brown & Bain*, 400 F.3d 659 (9th Cir. Cal. 2005); *Hardin v. First Cash Financial Services.*, 465 F.3d 470 (10th Cir. Okla. 2006); *Gianelli Money Purchase Plan & Trust v. ADM Investor Services*, 146 F. 3d 1309 (11th Cir. Fla. 1998).

32 514 U.S. 938 (1995).

33 *Ibid.*

34 *Ibid.*

8-10 The *First Options* addendum was another illustration of judicial creativity in arbitration. It also demonstrated that the U.S. Supreme Court was willing to be "activist" in the area and to arrogate to itself categorical legislative authority. In effect, judicial construction compelled a modest statutory framework to dictate a rule of absolute arbitral autonomy. The judicial mission was limited to rectifying rare instances of flagrant arbitral injustice. In effect, arbitrators (with party permission) controlled and conducted the arbitral process, making it an independent and functional adjudicatory mechanism.

8-11 *First Options* was followed by two landmark cases that also addressed the contract arbitrability or "who decides?" question. Both decisions widened the jurisdictional range and sovereignty of the arbitrator. *Howsam*[35] and *Bazzle*[36] established, in keeping with the language of the ill-conceived Revised Uniform Arbitration Act (RUAA),[37] that arbitrators had the authority, as a matter of law, to

35 *Howsam v. Dean Witter Reynolds*, 537 U.S. 79 (2002). The ruling in *Howsam* has been followed in subsequent case law. See, e.g., *Skirchak v. Dynamics Research Corp.*, 508 F. 3d 49 (1st Cir. Mass. 2007); *Mulvancy Mechanical, Inc. v. Sheet Metal Workers International Association, Local 38*, 351 F. 3d 43 (2d Cir. N.Y. 2003); *Gay v. CreditInform*, 511 F. 3d 369 (3d Cir. Pa. 2007); *Dockser v. Schwartzberg*, 433 F.3d 421 (4th Cir. Md. 2006); *Smith v. Dean Witter Reynolds, Inc.*, 102 Fed. Appx. 940 (6th Cir. Ky. 2004); *Pro Tech Industries v. URS Corp.*, 377 F. 3d 868 (8th Cir. Mo. 2004); *Oil, Chemical & Atomic Workers International Union Local 5-391 v. Conoco, Inc.*, 64 Fed. Appx. 178 (10th Cir. Okla. 2003); *Sheet Metal Workers' International Local 15, AFL-CIO v. Law Fabrication, LLC*, 237 Fed. Appx. 543 (11th Cir. Fla. 2007).

36 *Green Tree Financial Corp. v. Bazzle*, 539 U.S. 444 (2003). See John J. Barcelo, "Who Decides the Arbitrators' Jurisdiction? Separability and Competence-Competence in International Perspective", 36 *Vand. J. Transnat'l L.* (2003) 1115; William W. Park, "Determining Arbitral Jurisdiction: Allocation of Tasks Between Courts and Arbitrators", 8 *Am. Rev. Int'l Arb.* (1997) 133.
Despite its plurality standing, most lower federal courts adhere to the ruling in *Bazzle*. See, e.g., *Richard C. Young & Co. v. Leventhal*, 389 F. 3d 1 (1st Cir. Mass. 2004); *Certain Underwriters at Lloyd's of London v. Westchester Fire Insurance Co.*, 489 F.3d 580 (3d Cir. N.J. 2007); *Pedcor Management Co. Welfare Benefit Plan v. Nations Personnel Of Texas Inc.*, 343 F.3d 355 (5th Cir. Tex. 2003); *Dealer Computer Services v. Champion Ford*, 2008 U.S. Dist. LEXIS 5061 (E.D. Mich. 2008); *Gone To The Beach, LLC v. Choicepoint Services*, 514 F. Supp. 2d 1048 (W. D. Tenn. 2007); *County Concrete Corp. v. Burns & Russell Co. of Baltimore City, Inc.*, 2005 U.S. Dist. LEXIS 17913 (W. D. Wis. 2005); *Schreiner v. Credit Advisors, Inc.*, 2007 U.S. Dist. LEXIS 74014 (D, Neb. 2007); *Johnson v. Gruma Corp.*, 123 Fed Appx. 786 (9th Cir. Cal. 2005); *Anders v. Hometown Mortgage Services*, 346 F. 3d 1024 (11th Cir. Ala. 2003).

37 The proposed statute is a uniform arbitration law for states and was intended to modernize its 1956 predecessor. The latter was highly successful legislation, whereas its successor is a rather dismissal approximation. It is poorly drafted and badly organized; it also fails to address some emerging issues in the law. See Thomas Carbonneau, *Cases and Materials on Arbitration Law*

decide so-called gateway issues. In the absence of a *First Options* jurisdictional provision, the judicial role was limited to ascertaining whether an arbitration agreement could be materially identified. Once it concluded that the parties had entered into some sort of arbitration contract, the court's front-end supervisory authority ended and the arbitrator decided all other issues, including (for example) whether the arbitral clause provided for class action arbitration or was rendered ineffective because of a statute of limitations violation or extended its effects to non-contracting parties.[38] The circumscribed judicial role in the law of vacatur confirmed the minimalist function of courts.[39] *Vimar*[40] and *PacifiCare*[41] reinforced the non-interventionist position with a ripeness requirement that precluded the emergence of an "anticipatory vacatur" action.

8-12 A small group of courts, however, resisted their perfunctory role and disfavoured broad arbitrability. They did so by giving a rigorous interpretation to the controlling state law of contract and declaring that the arbitration agreement in question was an unenforceable contract because it was unconscionable.[42] Such holdings, in effect, stood as an implicit ruling that the subject matter of the

---

and Practice (4th ed, 2007) 88-120. See also Thomas Carbonneau, "A Critique of the Uniform Arbitration Act (2000)", Part One, 11-12 *WAMR* (2000) 326; Part Two, 12-4 *WAMR* (2001) 94; Matthew E. Brown, "The Revised Uniform Arbitration Act", 18 *Ohio St. J. Disp. Res.* (2002) 237. See generally Joseph L. Franco, "Casually Defining the Clear and Unmistakable: A Re-evaluation of First Options in Light of Recent Court Decisions", 10 *Lewis & Clark L. Rev.* (2206) 443.

38 See *Bazzle supra* note 36.

39 On FAA § 10, see Carbonneau, *supra* note 1, at 124, 359.

40 *Vimar Seguros y Reasaguros v. M/V Sky Reefer*, 515 U.S. 528 (1995). See, e.g., Elizabeth A. Clark, "Foreign Arbitration Clauses and Foreign Forum Selections Clauses in Bills of Lading Governed by COGSA: Vimar Seguros Y Reaseguros, S.A. v. M/V Sky Reefer", 1996 *BYU L. Rev.* (1996) 483; Stuart C. Gauffreau, "Foreign Arbitration Clauses in Maritime Bills of Lading: The Supreme Court's Decision in Vimar Seguros Y Reaseguros v. M/V Sky Reefer", 21 *NC J. Int'l L. & Com. Reg.* (1996) 395; C. Christine Fahrenback, "Vimar Seguros Y Reaseguros v. M/V Sky Reefer: A Change in Course: COGSA Does Not Validate Foreign Arbitration Clauses in Maritime Bill of Lading", 29 *Akron L. Rev.* (1996) 371; Kimberly D. Gilbert, "Conflicts of Law: Validating Foreign Arbitration Clause in Maritime Bill of Lading", 29 *Suffolk U. L. Rev.* (1995) 265; Cherie L. Lacour, "The Enforceability of Foreign Arbitration Clauses Under the Carriage of Goods by Sea Act After Vimar Seguros Y Reaseguros, S.A. v. M/V Sky Reefer", 4 *Tulsa J. Comp. & Int'l L.* (1996) 127; Brandon L. Milhorn, "Vimar Seguros Y Reaseguros v. M/V Sky Reefer: Arbitration Clauses in Bills of Lading Under the Carriage of Goods by Sea Act", 20 *Cornell Int'l L.J.* (1997) 173; and Mark S. Rubin, "The Validity of Foreign Arbitration Clauses in Bills of Lading Governed by COGSA: Vimar Seguros Y Reaseguors, S.A. v. M/V Sky Reefer", 19 *Tul. Mar. L.J.* (1995) 499.

41 *PacifiCare Health Systems, Inc. v. Book*, 538 U.S. 401 (2003).

42 See, e.g., *Nagrampa v. MailCoups, Inc.*, 469 F.3d 1257 (9th Cir. 2006).

parties' dispute was inarbitrable.[43] An unsympathetic court could then use unconscionability to express its conviction that the rights at issue or the legislation involved should not be submitted to private justice mechanisms. These rulings were especially common in cases involving disparate-party arbitrations (consumer transactions and non-union employment relationships).[44] They amounted to subject-matter inarbitrability determinations by ricochet. In the wake of *Bazzle,*[45] however, courts may no longer retain the jurisdiction to decide unconscionability issues. The latter determination may now belong more properly to the arbitrator. Once a contract of arbitration is identified, the arbitrator decides all other matters. In any event, the arbitrator would have pre-emptive jurisdiction to rule in a situation subject to a *First Options* provision.[46]

8-13 In the end, there is substantial confusion among U.S. courts as to what arbitrability actually means. Traditional demarcations have not been made in the case law patchwork. The concept and the analysis are unclear and confused. Moreover, subject-matter inarbitrability is essentially ignored and unknown, subsumed in the decisional law rule of statutory arbitrability. Many courts have difficulty distinguishing between "gateway" issues and threshold jurisdictional matters. Finally, *First Options*[47] adds another twist to the doctrinal meanderings – this time, relating to contract inarbitrability by allowing contract choice to dictate the rule of law on jurisdictional matters. The applicable rules are scattered; they are often impenetrable and resistant to clear interpretation and application. Despite the architectural and substantive imperfections, the gravamen of these rulings is unmistakable – to foster the quickest, most frequent and effective recourse to arbitration.

3. The Specific Example of Labour Arbitration

8-14 Labour arbitration is a self-standing form of arbitration in the U.S. Its procedures are elaborate and well-settled. Labour arbitration is not governed by the FAA, but rather by Section 301 of the Labor Management Relations Act of 1947.

43 *Ibid.*

44 See Carbonneau, *supra* note 37, at 408.

45 See *supra* note 36.

46 See *supra* note 31

47 *Ibid.*

> The Supreme Court has interpreted section '301 as a congressional mandate to the federal courts to fashion a body of federal common law to be used to address disputes arising out of labor contracts.'[48]

8-15 Notwithstanding their specialised origin and scope, court rulings on labour arbitration have served as the foundation of U.S. arbitration law. The *Steelworkers Trilogy*[49] are the foundational labour arbitration cases. These landmark decisions address the arbitrability of labour disputes and the enforcement of labour arbitration awards. They also establish that arbitration is the principal adjudicatory mechanism for resolving disputes that arise from collective bargaining agreements between labour unions and corporate management. Arbitration has been instrumental in shaping U.S. labour-management relations by providing an effective means for implementing the provisions of collective bargaining agreements. The U.S. Supreme Court provided the following appraisal of the basic principles of the judicial doctrine on labour arbitration:

> The principles necessary to decide this case are not new. They were set out by this Court over 25 years ago in a series of cases known as the *Steelworkers Trilogy*. . . . These precepts have served the industrial relations community well, and have led to continued reliance on arbitration, rather than strikes or lockouts, as the preferred method of resolving disputes arising during the term of a collective-bargaining agreement. We see no reason either to question their continuing validity, or to eviscerate their meaning by creating an exception to their general applicability.
>
> The first principle gleaned from the *Trilogy* is that "arbitration is a matter of contract and a party cannot be required to submit to arbitration any dispute which he has not agreed so to submit." . . . This axiom recognizes the fact that arbitrators derive their authority to resolve disputes only because the parties have agreed in advance to submit such grievances to arbitration. . . .
>
> The second rule, which follows inexorably from the first, is that the question of arbitrability – whether a collective-bargaining agreement creates a duty for the parties to arbitrate the particular grievance – is undeniably an issue for judicial determination. Unless the parties clearly and unmistakably

48 *Allis-Chalmers Corp. v. Lueck*, 471 U.S. 202, 209 (1985).

49 *United Steelworkers of America v. American Manufacturing Co.*, 363 U.S. 564, 80 S Ct 1343, 4 L. Ed. 2d 1403 (1960); *United Steelworkers of America v. Warrior & Gulf Navigation Co.*, 363 U.S. 574, 80 S Ct 1347, 4 L. Ed. 2d 1409 (1960); *United Steelworkers of America v. Enterprise Wheel & Car Corp.*, 363 U.S. 593, 80 S Ct 1358, 4 L. Ed. 2d 1424 (1960).

provide otherwise, the question of whether the parties agreed to arbitrate is to be decided by the court, not the arbitrator. . . .

[. . .]

The third principle derived from our prior cases is that, in deciding whether the parties have agreed to submit a particular grievance to arbitration, a court is not to rule on the potential merits of the underlying claims. Whether "arguable" or not, indeed even if it appears to the court to be frivolous, the union's claim that the employer has violated the collective-bargaining agreement is to be decided, not by the court asked to order arbitration, but as the parties have agreed, by the arbitrator. "The courts, therefore, have no business weighing the merits of the grievance, considering whether there is equity in a particular claim, or determining whether there is particular language in the written instrument which will support the claim. The agreement is to submit all grievances to arbitration, not merely those which the court will deem meritorious." . . .

Finally, it has been established that where the contract contains an arbitration clause, there is a presumption of arbitrability in the sense that "[a]n order to arbitrate the particular grievance should not be denied unless it may be said with positive assurance that the arbitration clause is not susceptible of an interpretation that covers the asserted dispute. Doubts should be resolved in favor of coverage." . . . Such a presumption is particularly applicable where the clause is as broad as the one employed in this case, which provides for arbitration of "any differences arising with respect to the interpretation of this contract or the performance of any obligation hereunder. . . . " In such cases, "[i]n the absence of any express provision excluding a particular grievance from arbitration, we think only the most forceful evidence of a purpose to exclude the claim from arbitration can prevail." . . .

This presumption of arbitrability for labor disputes recognizes the greater institutional competence of arbitrators in interpreting collective-bargaining agreements, "furthers the national labor policy of peaceful resolution of labor disputes and thus best accords with the parties' presumed objectives in pursuing collective bargaining." . . . The willingness of parties to enter into agreements that provide for arbitration of specified disputes would be "drastically reduced," however, if a labor arbitrator had the "power to determine his own jurisdiction. . . ." . . . Were this the applicable rule, an arbitrator would not be constrained to resolve only those disputes that the parties have agreed in advance to settle by arbitration, but, instead, would be empowered "to impose obligations outside the contract limited only by his

> understanding and conscience." . . . This result undercuts the longstanding federal policy of promoting industrial harmony through the use of collective-bargaining agreements, and is antithetical to the function of a collective-bargaining agreement as setting out the rights and duties of the parties.[50]

8-16 The thousands of collective bargaining agreements that are active nationwide in the U.S. generate a multitude of alleged violations on a daily basis. Resolving such disputes through court proceedings would overwhelm the judicial process and require courts to acquire specialised knowledge of an inordinate number of individual workplaces. The system of labour arbitration provides a corps of professional labour arbitrators who not only dispose of the disputes in an efficient and orderly manner, but also elaborate and apply a type of *stare decisis* of labour disputes.[51]

8-17 The *Steelworkers Trilogy* emphasised the importance of grievance arbitration to the stability of the workplace: "[T]he grievance machinery under a collective bargaining agreement is at the very heart of the system of industrial self-government".[52] The U.S. Supreme Court also underscored the need to maintain the autonomy of the arbitration agreement and the supremacy of the arbitrator's jurisdiction. The federal courts, therefore, have a very modest gatekeeping function: "the judicial inquiry under § 301 [is] . . . strictly confined to . . . whether the reluctant party . . . agree[d] to arbitrate . . . ".[53] The courts can only screen claims on the basis of whether they are covered by the contract. The courts' triage function cannot be accomplished on the basis of or lead to an assessment of the merits of the claim. Once deemed to be within the ambit of the parties' arbitration agreement, disputes fall within the sovereign decisional domain of the arbitrator.

50 *AT&T Technologies, Inc. v. Communications Workers of America*, 475 U.S. 643, 648-51, 106 S Ct 1415, 1419-1420, 89 L. Ed. 2d 648 (1986) (citations omitted).

51 See Timothy J. Heinsz, "Grieve It Again: Stare Decisis, Res Judicata and Collateral Estoppel in Labor Arbitration", 38 *BC L. Rev.* (1997) 275, 277

> Some views have become so embedded in labor arbitration that, although not technically binding precedents, arbitrators almost universally apply these principles.

52 *United Steelworkers of America v. Warrior & Gulf Navigation Co.*, 363 U.S. 574, 581 (1960).

53 *Ibid.* at 582.

8-18 The task of the labour arbitrator is to fashion solutions to specific workplace disputes that exceed the generalities of the collective bargaining agreement. Such disputes generally require a sense of the *modus vivendi* of the workplace: "The grievance procedure is, in other words, a part of the continuous collective bargaining process".[54] The labour arbitrator can refer to the "industrial common law – the practices of the industry and the shop"[55] to decide disputes. In addition to the agreed-upon labour contract, the arbitrator's determination reflects the common practices of the workplace and takes the impact of the decision upon the parties and their relationship into account – elements which generally are beyond the courts' capabilities.

8-19 Subject-matter inarbitrability has ostensibly a more pronounced role in labour arbitration than in FAA arbitration. Since the *Steelworkers' Trilogy*,[56] the U.S. Supreme Court has been a staunch supporter of labour arbitration. Even Justice Douglas took a holiday from his steadfast opposition to arbitration and supported the recourse to arbitration for disputes in the unionised workplace.[57] Support also comes from the other side of the ideological judicial divide. Some conservative pro-arbitration courts have expressed a distrust of labour unions. A number of their judicial opinions maintain that the union's collective or corporate interest does not necessarily coincide with the union member's individual interest.[58] Therefore, a union cannot agree in a collective bargaining agreement to submit civil liberty or other statutory matters affecting the personal rights of its members to arbitration. The submission of these rights of citizenship must be confirmed by the individual beneficiaries of the rights.[59] Otherwise, the submission is unenforceable. Succinctly stated, the rule of statutory arbitrability

54 *Ibid.* at 581.

55 *Ibid.* at 581-82.

56 See *supra* note 48.

57 See *American Manufacturing Co.*, 363 U.S. 564 (1960); *Warrior & Gulf Navigation Co.*, 363 U.S. 574 (1960).

58 See, e.g., *Pryner v. Tractor Supply Co.* and *Sobierajski v. Thoesen Tractor & Equipment Co.*, 109 F.3d 354 (7th Cir.), *cert. denied* 522 U.S. 912 (1987).

59 See *Wright v. Universal Maritime Service Corp.*, 525 U.S. 70 (1998). As the book containing this chapter was on the way to the presses, the U.S. Supreme Court granted *certiorari* and heard oral arguments (December 1, 2008) in *14 Penn Plaza LLC v. Pyett*, 129 S Ct 1223 (2008). The case involves the arbitrability of statutory rights in CBA arbitration and addresses, or could address, the tension between *Alexander v. Gardner-Denver*, 415 U.S. 36 (1974) and *Gilmer v. Interstate/Johnson Lane Corp.*, 500 U.S. 20 (1991). One suspects that the eventual opinion might reverse *Gardner-Denver*.

in labour arbitration depends upon individual acquiescence because of the union's intermediating function. The practical implementation of this legal principle, however, can be readily achieved through formulary means. The rule of statutory inarbitrability, therefore, is largely rhetorical and symbolic in character.

8-20 There is also greater reverence in labour arbitration for the integrity of law. The collective bargaining agreement creates this reverence because it serves as the constitution or civil code of the workplace.[60] Labour arbitrators cannot denature the collective covenant or despoil its spirit by integrating their own personal views of industrial justice into their decisions. They must remain faithful to the "essence" of the agreement, the protocol that governs workplace relationships.[61] Arbitrator fealty to the agreed-upon governing law is assessed by the courts under three common law grounds that can lead to the nullification of the award: 1) manifest disregard of the law, 2) irrational determinations, or 3) violations of a statutorily-imposed public policy.[62] These grounds for vacatur do not establish a rule of subject-matter inarbitrability *per se*, but rather emphasise that the product of the negotiations between key institutional actors (the company and the union) is the true source of substantive governance. Arbitrator decisional discretion cannot tread upon the supremacy of this "legislated" rule of law.

8-21 In reality, the courts have developed an exceedingly lax standard for protecting the substantive law in labour arbitration litigation.[63] Arbitrators need only ostensibly embed their rulings in the provisions of the collective bargaining agreement in order to avoid the judicial nullification of their rulings. Public policy violations can only be established if the public policy provision is an explicit and dominant provision in an enacted statute.[64] In general, large, fluid public policy objections to arbitral rulings are unavailing. In fact, judicial protection of the rule of law in labour arbitration takes a secondary position to the autonomous and independent operation of the arbitral process. There is a basic parallelism between the legal regulation of labour and FAA arbitration, despite their different statutory source.

[60] See *supra* note 48.
[61] See Carbonneau, *supra* note 37, at 531-555, 574-603.
[62] *Ibid.*
[63] *Ibid.*
[64] *Ibid.*

8-22 The basic rules pertaining to arbitrability in labour arbitration can be summarised in a few salient principles. The effect of these principles is to address and resolve matters that are classically attributed in other national laws on arbitration to contract inarbitrability and *Kompetenz-Kompetenz*. As stated earlier, there is little, if any, recognition of subject-matter inarbitrability in labour or other forms of arbitration litigation in the U.S. Merely having an arbitral clause in a collective bargaining agreement creates a presumption of contract arbitrability.[65] Moreover, when the clause states a broad obligation to arbitrate, the strength of the presumption is enhanced to a nearly irrebuttable status.[66] Accordingly, any dispute that arises between the parties is likely to be resolved in arbitration. Disputes are adjudged inarbitrable only when convincing evidence is presented that the parties intended to exclude the particular dispute from the general submission to arbitration.[67]

8-23 According to the landmark ruling in *John Wiley & Sons, Inc. v. Livingston*,[68] courts determine only questions of substantive arbitrability (whether the parties agreed to arbitration and, if so, whether that agreement reaches the dispute in question),[69] while arbitrators rule on matters of procedural arbitrability:

65 See *United Steelworkers of America v. Retirement Income Plan for Hourly-Rated Employees of ASARCO, Inc.*, 512 F.3d 555 (9th Cir. 2008). But see *Duthie v. Matria Healthcare, Inc.*, 2008 WL 482364 (N.D. Ill.) (stating that a court was not required to grasp at straws in construing the contract just to blindly vindicate the broad public policy that supports the arbitration of disputes).

66 See *E.I. Dupont De Nemours and Co. v. Ampthill Rayon Workers, Inc.*, 516 F. Supp. 2d 588 (E.D. Va. 2007); *S. Strauss, Inc. v. United Food and Commercial Workers Union, Local 342*, 503 F. Supp. 2d 567 (EDNY 2007).

67 See *E.I. Dupont De Nemours and Co. v. Ampthill Rayon Workers, Inc.*, 516 F. Supp. 2d 588 (E.D. Va. 2007); *Steris Corp. v. International Union, United Automobile, Aerospace and Agriculture Implement Workers of America, Local No. 832*, 489 F. Supp. 2d 501 (W.D. Pa. 2007).

68 376 U.S. 543, 556-558 (1964).

69 See *Vera v. Saks and Company*, 335 F. 3d 109 (2003); *International Brotherhood of Electrical Workers, Local Union No. 545 v. Hope Electrical Corp.*, 380 F. 3d 1084 (2004) (employer did not participate in the arbitration or object to it or try to prevent it; instead, the employer waited until the arbitration had concluded and the arbitrators had rendered their award to file a timely motion to vacate the award; in the vacatur action, the employer objected to the arbitrators' jurisdiction; the court confined its ruling to the specific facts of the case and held that a waiver had not taken place and that the employer could challenge the arbitrators' substantive jurisdiction in the vacatur action).

> 'Arbitration is a matter of contract and a party cannot be required to submit to arbitration any dispute which he has not agreed so to submit.' . . . It is the duty of the court to use general contract law principles to determine whether the parties agreed to arbitrate disputes and to ascertain and implement the reasonable expectations of the parties. . . . Agreements to be [sic] arbitrate must be 'consciously made.'[70]
>
> 'The genesis of arbitral authority is the contract, and the arbitrators are permitted to decide only those issues that lie within the contractual mandate.'[71]

8-24 In *John Wiley & Sons*, the U.S. Supreme Court held that an issue involving whether a dispute was time-barred under the workplace contract fell within the arbitrator's jurisdictional range.[72] Whether separate arbitrations should be consolidated is a matter of procedural arbitrability for the arbitrator.[73] Whether the arbitration provision in a labour contract applies to non-signatory parties is also for the arbitrator to decide.[74] Courts, however, determine whether there has been a waiver of the right to arbitrate because of "inconsistent activity in another

70 *MI Installers and Furniture Service, Inc. v. New York City District Council of Carpenters Pension Fund*, 476 F. Supp. 2d 387 (SDNY 2007) (citing *AT&T Technologies Inc.*, 475 U.S. 643 (1986) (the case involved an action by an employer for declaratory and injunctive relief to bar non-signatory benefits funds from pursuing arbitration against the employer for delinquent payments that were owed allegedly under the collective bargaining agreement; the court ruled that the labour contract generally gives rise to a presumption of [contract] arbitrability, that the presumption can apply to benefits disputes, but it does not extend to third-party beneficiaries of the collective agreement; the court determined that the labour contract did not evidence any intent to arbitrate the implicated disputes; it enjoined the funds from initiating arbitration).

71 *Davis v. Chevy Chase Financial Ltd.*, 667 F. 2d 160, 165 (D.C. Cir. 1984).

72 See also *E.I. Dupont De Nemour and Co. v. Ampthill Rayon Workers, Inc.*, 516 F. Supp. 2d 588 (E.D. Va. 2007).

73 See *Shaw's Supermarkets, Inc. v. United Food and Commercial Workers Union, Local 791*, 321 F. 3d 251 (1st Cir. 2003) (arbitrator would decide whether similar grievances arising under three separate labour agreements could be consolidated; each grievance was individually arbitrable under the relevant governing labour contract; the question was one of procedural arbitrability; moreover, there was no evidence in the contracts that the parties did not want disputes consolidated); *Employers Insurance Co. of Wausau v. Century Indemnity Co.*, 443 F.3d 573 (7th Cir. 2006).

74 See *Road Sprinkler Fitters Local Union No. 669, U.A., AFL-CIO v. Cosco Fire Protection, Inc.*, 363 F. Supp. 2d 1220 (C.D. Cal. 2005) (court concluded it had jurisdiction to compel arbitration between union and both signatory and non-signatory parties; the arbitrator would decide whether the arbitral clause in the labour contract applied to non-signatory parties; the arbitrator has exclusive jurisdiction to interpret the contract).

litigation forum".[75] Courts also rule upon claims of fraud that could directly affect the validity of the arbitral clause.[76] Questions of the unconscionability of the arbitration agreement are resolved by the courts, whereas claims that the general contract is unconscionable are for the arbitrator.[77] Finally, matters relating to the *res judicata* effect of prior arbitral rulings are to be assessed and resolved by the arbitrator.[78] The basic distinction between the role of courts and the arbitrator is operative unless the parties provide otherwise in their agreement;[79] parties who enter into a *First Options*-type of provision on the matter are bound by the arbitrator's decision on arbitrability.[80] Any doubts as to the resolution of arbitrability issues are to be decided in favour of arbitration.[81]

75 See *Marie v. Allied Home Mortgage Corp.*, 402 F. 3d 1 (1st Cir. 2005).

76 See *Duthie v. Matria Healthcare, Inc.*, 2008 WL 482364 (N.D. Ill.).

77 See *Herrington v. Wells Fargo Bank, N.A.*, 374 B.R 133 (Bankruptcy, E.D. Pa. 2007).

78 See *Steris Corp. v. International Union, United Automobile, Aerospace and Agriculture Implement Workers of America, Local 832*, 489 F. Supp. 2d 501 (W.D. Pa. 2007).

79 See *AT&T Technologies, Inc. v. Communication Workers*, 475 U.S. 643 (1986).

80 See *Vail-Ballou Press, Inc. v. Graphic Communications International Union/International Brotherhood of Teamsters, Local 898-M*, 480 F.Supp. 2d 569 (NDNY 2007).

81 See *Walsh v. WOR Radio*, 2008 WL 240993 (SDNY) (in an action for wrongful termination, the court compelled arbitration on the basis of an allegation that the employer had orally extended the contract containing the arbitration agreement; doubts as to arbitrability are to be resolved in favour of arbitration). See also *Armco Employees Independent Federation v. AK Steel Corp.*, 252 F. 3d 854 (6th Cir. 2001) (if the labour contract provides for the arbitration of a claim, meaning that there is contract arbitrability, the possible procedural bars to arbitration are to be decided by the arbitrator; although courts rule on matters of so-called substantive arbitrability, a clause in the labour contract that provides for the arbitration of a specific disputes is controlling and deprives courts of jurisdiction to hear the designated dispute); *General Warehousemen and Helpers Union Local 767 v. Albertson's Distribution, Inc.*, 331 F. 3d 485 (5th Cir. 2003) (questions relating to the timeliness of claims [so-called procedural arbitrability] or the contract's scope of application are for the arbitrator; an opposite conclusion could only apply if the parties unmistakably expressed an explicit contrary intent); *Local Union No. 898 of the International Brotherhood of Electrical Workers, AFL-CIO v. XL Electric, Inc.*, 380 F. 3d 868 (5th Cir. 2004) (court concluded that case involved an issue of substantive arbitrability because the circumstances pointed to the expiry of the parties' agreement to arbitrate; if no agreement existed, the employer could not be compelled to arbitrate disputes); *United Steel Workers of America, AFL-CIO-CLC v. Saint Gobain Ceramics & Plastics, Inc.*, 505 F. 3d 417 (6th Cir. 2007); *R.J. Corman Derailment Services, LLC v. International Union of Operating Engineers, Local Union 150, AFL-CIO*, 422 F. 3d 522 (7th Cir. 2005); *Ehleiter v. Grapetree Shores, Inc.*, 482 F. 3d 207 (3d Cir. 2007); *Crown Cork & Seal Co., Inc. v. International Association of Machinists and Aerospace Workers*, 501 F. 3d 912 (8th Cir. 2007); *Conax Florida Corp. v. Astrium Ltd.*, 499 F. Supp. 2d 1287 (M.D. Fla. 2007); *Defazio v. Expetec Corp.*, 2006 WL 162327 (D.R.I.) (not rep. in F. Supp. 2d); *S. Strauss, Inc. v. United Food and Commercial Workers Union, Local 342*, 503 F. Supp. 2d 567 (EDNY 2007); *Howard University v.*

4. CONCLUSIONS

8-25 Arbitrability may represent the law of a by-gone era in which legal rules played a significant role in the regulation of arbitration and arbitration had a specialised scope of application. Arbitration was an exceptional remedy to be used in special circumstances. The modern law of arbitration responds to a different assessment of the role and function of arbitration. Arbitration is being integrated into a society that has evolved and been transformed. The practical exigencies of contemporary life demand the secularisation of justice and dispute resolution. Bloated populations and enhanced expectations place enormous pressures on limited resources. The blasphemies of the past have become today's accepted wisdom. For example, gambling is no longer a vice, but a legitimate source of state revenue. Likewise, adjudication is no longer the exclusive province of the judiciary. The unavoidable and growing confidence in arbitration has resulted in transferring much of civil litigation to arbitrators. In this setting, partial proceedings, segregating regulatory from contract disputes, were unlikely to provide an operationally viable rule of law. Therefore, the concept of subject-matter inarbitrability or the rule of statutory inarbitrability had to be reconsidered and reversed. The courts retain a role in policing access to arbitration by determining matters of contract arbitrability, but – even there – arbitrators have been given increased authority by the U.S. Supreme Court.

8-26 For the last several decades, the U.S. Supreme Court has been the guardian of the U.S. law of arbitration. It has systematically made the institution of arbitration impervious to judicial interference. That practice accounts for the special and rather opaque definition of arbitrability in U.S. law. The Court has been vigilant in making adjustments to the law to prevent arbitration from becoming dysfunctional and ineffective – a narcissistic companion to judicial litigation. It has established a list of necessary democratic priorities, placing utmost importance upon citizen access to workable adjudicatory resources.

8-27 The California courts, both at the state and federal level, have spearheaded a movement in the opposite direction.[82] The latter is founded upon ideological suppositions that emphasise the importance of liberal contract formation. The relevant judicial opinions demonstrate a reflexive embracing of an ideology that prevailed at an anterior stage of society that has been superseded by events and

---

Metropolitan Campus Police Officer's Union, 519 F. Supp. 2d 27 (D.C. Cir. 2007) (university voluntarily participated in the arbitration and failed to object to the arbitrability of the claim; it, therefore, waived its right to seek judicial relief).

82 See Thomas E. Carbonneau, *Employment Arbitration* (2nd ed, 2006) 137-230.

emerging social needs. It is no longer sufficient, in the name of fairness, to condemn citizens to an unworkable, inefficient, costly, and inaccessible public process of adjudication—even if it may be theoretically sound and compelling to do so. That it is a public process supported by public revenues does not account for or excuse its staggering failings that render its protection of legal rights largely ritualistic.

8-28 The "fairness" of the contract for arbitration and the means by which a legal obligation to arbitrate is imposed are not critically important issues or even disadvantages in the contemporary U.S. law of arbitration. The true danger to the U.S. law of arbitration and its aggressive advocacy for arbitration comes from the recent change in congressional power configurations and the concomitant likelihood of enacting legislation antagonistic to arbitration. Wide-scale arbitrability and arbitrator determination of arbitrability issues could become "things of the past". The ideological shift to the left has given greater credibility to efforts to disparage the use of arbitration especially in circumstances of consumer transactions and non-union employment relationships. Legislation[83]

[83] The introduction of these bills represents the latest and most serious attempt to place restrictions on the arbitral process by modifying the FAA. Prior efforts (for example, the Civil Procedures Protection Act) were generally unsuccessful or, like the Bono Law in 2002, limited in application. The proposed legislation is aimed at restricting the application of, if not eliminating, mandatory arbitration in consumer transactions and employment relationships. Its supporters essentially want to outlaw arbitration agreements in these circumstances. They also object to the construction and application of civil rights legislation by private arbitrators. One of the bills even prevents arbitrators, as a matter of law, from addressing contract inarbitrability issues when they are authorised by the contract to rule on jurisdictional challenges, while the other bill introduces various procedures to make mandatory arbitration fairer to the weaker party. In effect, the latter judicialises arbitration and makes it more rigorous and dysfunctional than a judicial proceeding on the matter.

It is difficult to understand the necessity of either approach. In many respects, the solutions are far too radical and are likely to be counterproductive, if not destructive of implicated interests. The proposed legislation will reverse a judicial doctrine that has been in-the-making for forty years and endorsed by all sides of the Court. The bills embody opposition that is ideological in character—at least in one case. In the other case, the intended legislation reflects the local peculiarities and idiosyncrasies of state law and practice in arbitration. While the Court has laboured for decades to maintain citizen access to functional adjudication, the legislation, in effect, seeks to advance sectarian positions and interests. It ignores the larger considerations of the public welfare and only pretends to be the standard bearer of the weak and downtrodden. The proposals are wrong-headed and advance the law in the wrong direction.

See Arbitration Fairness Act of 2007, s. 1782 (110th Congress, 1st Session) (July 12, 2007); Fair Arbitration Act of 2007, s. 1135 (110th Congress, 1st Session) (April 17, 2007). See also "'Arbitracide': The Story of Anti-Arbitration Sentiment in the U.S. Congress", *Am. Rev. Int'l Arb.* (2009) (forthcoming).

has been proposed that would invalidate arbitration agreements in disparate-party situations and eliminate the *Kompetenz-Kompetenz* power of arbitrators. It would also restrict the rule of statutory arbitrability in these circumstances. If arbitration were resorted to, it would be substantially judicialised.

8-29 This politically concocted version of arbitrability defines inarbitrability on the basis of a narrow and impractical sense of contract fairness. The sense of fairness stems from the political rhetoric of class warfare. It ignores the true needs of the parties and the necessities of the legal system, as well as the virtue of pragmatic accommodation. It corrects a situation in which real abuse has yet to be established. The legislative effort is misguided, unfair, counterproductive, and ill-conceived. It does, however, hit the judicial doctrine on arbitration where it is most theoretically vulnerable: the unilateral imposition of adhesionary agreements to arbitrate upon unsophisticated, average people by an economically superior party. In some respects, this weakness has some of the overreaching flavour of the subprime mortgage loan fiasco. In order to address the problem, the new, but still lunatic revolutionary hordes profess faith in the defunct mythology that surrounds the beleaguered judicial process. They gain reassurance from its traditions and view it as a cure for all social ills and diseases. Through its policy on arbitration, the Court has been a much more astute protector of citizen rights than either disabled courts or dated politicians who, draped in the vestments of artificial piety, mouth the falsehoods of failed utopian beatitudes. A true course of action has never flowed from the trite platitudes of ideology. For the arbitration bar and American society, the recent legislative proposals represent an unfortunate turn of events and an ill-conceived redefinition of arbitrability.

Christoph Liebscher[*]

CHAPTER 9

INSOLVENCY AND ARBITRABILITY

1. Introduction

9-1 Insolvency and arbitration are both legal procedures, but of a very different type and nature. They have distinct purposes and underlying policies, and dissimilar objectives and principles; *inter alia*, the following distinctions can be observed:[1] insolvency proceedings are proceedings for the collection and distribution of the assets of a debtor in financial difficulties for the benefit of all creditors involved or proceedings providing for reorganization and rehabilitation of the debtor's business in such situation. Arbitration is a method of resolving disputes between – normally only two – parties solely based on those parties' autonomy and privity, even though such authority is of course subject to the even superior authority of the legislator to empower parties to agree on such "private settlement mechanisms" in the first place.[2]

9-2 By way of example, in Austria the following claims may be brought during insolvency and bankruptcy proceedings:

- Challenge of creditors' claims on behalf of the estate initiated by the trustee in insolvency proceedings and disputes concerning the acknowledgement of contested claims;
- Secured claims and preferred claims;
- Unsecured claims, including claims regarding the costs of the insolvency proceeding, administrative expenses of the estate (which include the administration and maintenance of the estate); taxes, social insurance

* Dr. Christoph Liebscher M.B.A (Insead), FCIArb. The author is senior partner of Wolf Theiss and Head of the Arbitration Department.

1 V. Lazić, *Insolvency Proceedings and Commercial Arbitration* (1998) at 2.

2 S. Riegler in Riegler et al, *Arbitration Law of Austria: Practice and Procedure* (2007) at 706.

contributions and employees' claims (dismissal pay, vacation compensation);
- Asset claims arising through the bankruptcy proceedings itself;
- Claims resulting from behaviour in violation of duty by the trustees, the administrators, the board of creditors or the experts;
- Claims resulting from rescission or termination of a contract due to special statutory rights of the trustee (e.g., employment contract, lease contract); and
- Claims not regarding the estate (e.g., matrimony and parentage claims).

9-3 Each claim which may arise in the course of bankruptcy proceedings must be dealt with separately regarding its arbitrability.[3]

9-4 Unlike arbitration, insolvency proceedings do not generally have the characteristics of adversarial proceedings. They are normally not meant to be a dispute settlement mechanism, although the laws on insolvency do contain provisions for solving outstanding disputes concerning the bankruptcy estate, often through summary proceedings.

9-5 The jurisdiction of an arbitrator can be established only by a valid agreement of the parties, whereas the jurisdiction of the courts in insolvency proceedings is determined by legislation. Arbitration is a "private" or "extra-judicial" method of resolving disputes, whilst insolvency proceedings, as such, are judicial proceedings in the national courts.

9-6 Certain subject matters are regarded as so important in some countries that, according to the legislator's or the court's opinion, their resolution can only be entrusted to the regular court system. Thus, these subject matters may not be settled by arbitration *viz*. they are not "arbitrable".[4]

9-7 That "pure" bankruptcy issues (i.e., bankruptcy proceedings as such) are not arbitrable is almost undisputed in the literature, and it is sometimes regarded as a question of no practical importance; or as F. Mantilla-Serrano has concluded in his survey about the examination of ICC arbitral awards in the years 1989 – 1994: "The arbitrators were never requested to rule upon issues directly

3 *Ibid.* at 714.
4 C. Liebscher, *The Healthy Award* (2003) at 168.

concerning the insolvency proceedings (i.e. 'core issues')."[5] This may certainly be true in most jurisdictions with regard to issues like the nomination of the trustee, the commencement of insolvency proceedings, the reorganisation of the business, orders opening and closing the bankruptcy proceedings, and other measures of conduct and surveillance, as well as appropriate criminal offences, particularly in corporate insolvency.[6]

9-8 The real problem, however, is to determine the exact list or actual scope of 'core' issues, which would serve as a line of jurisdictional delimitation, and accordingly, would serve as a factor of determination as to the scope of non-arbitrable matters. In other words, to state that under the prevailing view, non-arbitrable issues are those that are 'core' bankruptcy issues is very much true, but it gives no answer *in concreto* which those issues are.[7] Another question that also arises is whether a matter usually regarded as capable of settlement by arbitration becomes a non-arbitrable one after the opening of bankruptcy proceedings. Furthermore, when and how do provisions of insolvency law limit the domain of (or exclude) arbitration (which is then a question of arbitrability)?

9-9 There is no uniform and universal answer to these and similar questions, which would be valid for all legal systems. What appears to be virtually impossible is to determine the actual scope of arbitrable matters and to indicate with certainty in which type of dispute

> the interest of third parties or society in general are so heavily implicated [. . .] that the state feels the need to intervene and limit the adjudication of such cases to the municipal court.[8]

9-10 The aforementioned issues will be addressed with regard to the jurisdictions of Austria, England, France, Germany, the Netherlands, and Switzerland.

5 F. Mantilla-Serrano, "International Arbitration and Insolvency Proceedings", *Arb. Int'l* (1995) 69.

6 Lazić, *supra* note 1 at 154.

7 *Ibid.* at 156 *et seq.*

8 A. Samuel, *Jurisdictional Problems in International Commercial Arbitration* (1989) 125.

2. JURISDICTIONS

2.1. Austria

9-11 Pursuant section 582 para 1 Austrian Procedural Law

> Any claim involving an economic interest that lies within the jurisdiction of the courts of law can be subject of an arbitration agreement. An arbitration agreement concerning claims not involving an economic interest shall have legal effect to the extent that the parties are entitled to conclude a settlement on the subject-matter in dispute.

9-12 The fact that one of the parties is subject to bankruptcy proceedings is not in itself sufficient to render a dispute non-arbitrable *per se*.[9] Therefore, every claim which may arise in the course of bankruptcy proceedings has to be dealt with separately regarding its entitlement to being settled.

9-13 The following types of claims may be considered:

- Claims for the separation of property from the estate, i.e., secured claims and preferred claims
- Asset claims arising through the bankruptcy proceedings itself
- Unsecured claims
- Challenge of creditors' claims on behalf of the estate
- Acknowledgement of contested claims
- Any regular claims of the estate.

9-14 With the commencement of bankruptcy proceedings, a debtor no longer has legal capacity to conclude arbitration agreements with respect to disputes concerning the bankruptcy estate (sections 1 and 3 Austrian Bankruptcy Code [KO]). Such arbitration agreements are invalid, since only the trustee may validly conclude such agreements.[10] However, prior arbitration agreements remain valid.[11]

[9] Fouchard, Gaillard & Goldmann, *International Commercial Arbitration* (1999), paras 355 *et seq*.

[10] Riegler, *supra* note 2 at 713.

[11] OGH 17.4.1996 RdW 1997, 135.

9-15 With regard to the arbitrability of claims for the separation of property from the estate, i.e., secured claims and preferred claims and claims against and on behalf of the estate (excluding challenge claims), the situation is not any different than with other claims, which may arise outside the bankruptcy proceedings. Also during the bankruptcy proceedings there is no doubt that the trustee and the creditor or debtor of the estate may settle their respective claims, which – by the way – is constant practice. In addition, no public policy considerations require these claims to be handled exclusively by state courts; therefore these claims are arbitrable.[12]

9-16 Challenge claims on behalf of the estate, according to sections 27 et seq KO, accrue after the beginning of the bankruptcy proceeding. Therefore, hardly any constellation is imaginable in which a prior arbitration agreement with regard to these claims is concluded. The challenge claim is to the disposition of the trustee, whereas the profit amounts to the estate and not to a single creditor.[13] However, this claim can also be fulfilled by the debtor even before such claim is filed, and it can also be settled. Therefore, the prevailing opinion in Austrian judiciary and legal writing is that such claims are also arbitrable.[14]

9-17 The matter is not that straightforward with regard to the acknowledgement of contested claims, as the subject of such a claim is not (only) a claim for payment, but rather the determination of the validity or existence of the claim. It also has to be stressed that a creditor, whose claim was found to be valid, is also entitled to vote with regard to a possible composition. Of course, in this regard the standing of third parties is also concerned (i.e., the other creditors in the bankruptcy proceedings). Nevertheless, the question still remains the same, namely whether such claim is subject to a settlement. In this regard, the case is not different to the other possible claims already mentioned. However, it has to be observed that all persons who are affected by such a settlement (i.e., the trustee and all the creditors) would have to agree to refer this matter to arbitration, which will not happen very frequently. Under this condition, the prevailing opinion in Austria is that contested claims are also arbitrable.[15]

9-18 Although challenge claims and claims against the estate can be settled, one question still has to be addressed, namely whether the exclusive jurisdiction of

[12] S. Riegler, *Schiedsverfahren und Konkurs*, Univ. Diss. (2004) at 63 *et seq.*
[13] OGH 5.6.2007, 10 Ob 29/07y at 58.
[14] A. Konecny, ÖBA 1987, 311, cf. OGH 11.11.1999, RdW 2000/26.
[15] *Supra* note 12 at 66 *et seq.*

the bankruptcy court with regard to these claims – as stipulated in section 43 para 5 KO and section 111 para 1 KO – hinders their arbitrability. Analysis of the aforementioned provisions of the Bankruptcy Code reveals that these provisions only address the question of jurisdiction within the different courts in the Austrian court system, and do not deal with the delimitation of state courts versus arbitral tribunals. Therefore, the exclusive jurisdiction of the bankruptcy courts for challenge claims and claims against the estate does not prevent these claims from also being arbitrable.[16]

9-19 To conclude, the prevailing opinion in Austria is that all disputes related to bankruptcy proceedings are arbitrable, including claims for the separation of property from the estate, i.e., secured claims and preferred claims as well as claims against and on behalf of the estate, including challenge of creditors' claims and acknowledgement of contested claims.

2.2. England

9-20 Objective arbitrability is not a concept which is part and parcel of English arbitration law.[17] Therefore, the relationship between insolvency proceedings and bankruptcy do not seem be considered under this angle. Under English law disputes calling for remedies that may affect the rights of third parties such as bankruptcy or a winding up order may well raise issues of arbitrability.[18]

9-21 As a matter of law, insolvency does not affect the ability of a party to proceed with arbitration – though it may expose a party to, for example, orders for the provision of security or security for costs. However, if a company is wound up according to the English companies' legislation, then the decision as to whether or not to proceed with the arbitration at all lies with the liquidator.[19]

9-22 The Arbitration Act 1996 introduced a specific procedure into the Insolvency Act 1986. According to section 349A Insolvency Act 1986, an arbitration agreement prior to bankruptcy will not be respected without the trustees' consent. Where the trustee has decided not to adopt the arbitration agreement prior to bankruptcy, arbitral proceedings may nevertheless be brought

[16] *Supra* note 12 at 68 *et seq.*
[17] M. Mustill & S. Boyd, *Commercial Arbitration* (2001) at 72.
[18] K. Maxwell in F.-B. Weigand, *Practitioner's Handbook on International Arbitration* (2002) at 600.
[19] *Supra* note 18 at 617.

to resolve a dispute. Therefore, an application to the English High Court must be made in order to obtain the courts' permission. As a precondition for the application, either the creditors' committee or the bankrupt party's counterparty to the arbitration agreement has to state its consent, according to section 349A para 3 Insolvency Act 1986. It is then open to the court to consider the circumstances of the case and decide whether the dispute in question ought to be referred to arbitration.[20]

9-23 An insolvent claimant can pursue a claim by way of arbitration. However, in the context of corporate insolvency, the office-holder appointed in the insolvency proceedings will be the agent of the company and will be the person who has the right to pursue arbitration in the insolvent claimant's name.[21]

9-24 If the liquidator does not bring arbitration proceedings, an applicant may file an application to the court under section 130 para 2 of the Insolvency Act 1986. Under section 130 para 2, the court has a broad and wide discretion to do what is right and fair in the circumstances.[22] In the case of *Re Atlantic Computer Systems Plc*[23] the court set out in detail the principles which apply in deciding whether to grant permission:

- The person seeking permission to bring proceedings must make a case;
- If granting permission to an owner of land or goods to exercise proprietary rights, it is unlikely to impede the achievement of the purpose of the administration, permission should normally be granted;
- In other cases the court will carry out a balancing exercise, weighing the legitimate interest of the applicant against those of the companies or creditors;
- In carrying out the balancing exercise, weight should be given to those applying to enforce proprietary rights since an administration should not be conducted for the benefit of unsecured creditors at the expense of those with proprietary interests;
- If permission is not granted, the court may apply conditions such as giving directions to the administrator;

20 G. Burn & E. Grupp, "Insolvency and Arbitration in English Law", *Int'l ALR* (2005) 124 *et seq.*
21 *Supra* note 20 at 127 *et seq.*
22 *Supra* note 20 at 128.
23 *Re Atlantic Computer Systems Plc* [1992] CH. 505; [1990] B.C.C. 859.

- The court on a permission application will generally not seek to adjudicate upon the dispute over the existence, validity or nature of a security unless the issues raises a short point of law which can be determined conveniently.[24]

9-25 As regards existing arbitral proceedings, the courts' permission must be obtained, once a compulsory winding-up order has been made.

9-26 Usually an administrative receiver and an administrator can initiate or defend any proceedings in the company's name and on its behalf, according to schedule 1 para 5 of the Insolvency Act 1986. A creditor could commence arbitration proceedings until an administration order has been made in respect of a company. The creditor has to obtain the administrator's permission through the court (schedule B1, paras 42 and 43 of the Insolvency Act 1986).[25]

2.3. France

9-27 Article 2060 of the French Civil Code (CC) provides that

> [o]ne may not enter into arbitration agreements in matters of status and capacity of the persons, in those relating to divorce and judicial separation or on controversies concerning public bodies and institutions and more generally in all matters in which public policy is concerned.

Those matters remain reserved for adjudication in state courts.

9-28 It has to be observed that domestic provisions, such as sections 2059 et seq. CC, do not apply in international arbitration where only international public policy can set a limit to arbitrability.[26] In an international arbitration, the Paris Court of Appeal held that a dispute concerning the rights of the parties in case of the bankruptcy of one of them is arbitrable.[27]

9-29 In domestic arbitration the following may be observed: the provisions on exclusive jurisdiction may limit an arbitrators' jurisdiction; however, only those which are part of public policy.[28]

[24] Burn & Grupp, *supra* note 20 at 129.
[25] *Ibid.*
[26] CA Paris 29 March 1991, *Ganz v. SNCFT*, 3 *Rev. Arb.* 478 (1991) with note by L. Idot.
[27] CA Paris 20 September 1995, *Matra Hachette v. Reteitalia*, 1 *Rev. Arb.* 87 (1996) with note by D. Cohen.
[28] P. Ancel, "Arbitrage et Procédures collectives", 3 *Rev. Arb.* 256 (1983).

9-30 The court before which the insolvency procedure has been brought has jurisdiction to hear and determine everything that concerns those proceedings. The purpose of this provision is the centralisation of all matters in one proceeding, before one court.[29]

9-31 A question arises as to whether the exclusive jurisdiction of commercial courts exclude any other jurisdiction, thus also that of arbitrators, implying non-arbitrability of bankruptcy issues.

9-32 According to Vesna Lazić,

> [t]he prevailing view in French literature seems to be that it is not appropriate to consider generally exclusive jurisdiction as a formula for determining arbitrability, but only when it is a rule pertaining to public policy.[30]

9-33 In the case of insolvency, the exclusive jurisdiction of commercial courts may not be an absolute bar to arbitrability.

9-34 In accordance with article L.642-24 of the Code de Commerce (which replaces the previous article 158 of the Loi du 25 janvier 1985), the liquidator may conclude an arbitration agreement and may compromise with respect to all disputes that concern creditors, including those relating to immoveables, provided that the authorisation of the court and the debtor has been heard or duly given notice. If article R662-3 was to be understood as an absolute exclusion of arbitration, the express provisions on conditions for the liquidator (or administrator or the debtor) to conclude arbitration agreements after the opening of the insolvency proceedings would have no meaning.

9-35 In addition, although the wording used in the then article 174 or the current article R662-3 implies a broad jurisdiction for commercial courts in insolvency matters, French case law has developed a restrictive interpretation of this provision. In accordance with this interpretation, the competence of the commercial courts extends only to issues originating from insolvency proceedings[31] or matters which have their source in the application of the provisions of insolvency law, or where the insolvency law affects the resolution

[29] P. Ancel, "Arbitrage et Procédures collectives après la loi du 25 janvier 1985" 2 *Rev. Arb.* 127 (1987).

[30] See Lazić, *supra* note 1 at 161 with further references.

[31] Cass. Com., 4 February 1986, 4 *Rev. Arb.* 718 (1988) (summary).

of the dispute.[32] The provision on jurisdiction is also liberally construed so as to exclude claims against the debtor based on retention of the title clause from the competence of the commercial court.[33]

9-36 It has even been argued that arbitration agreements may be concluded with respect to pure bankruptcy issues in the context of bankruptcy proceedings.[34] This opinion finds support in the express provisions on the possibility to agree on arbitration. In accordance with these provisions, the entering into an agreement is always subject to authorisation of the public authority. Obviously, the opinion of those authors is based on the requirement that the authorisation and/or approval would serve as a "corrective", and therefore those issues should also be considered to be arbitrable.[35]

2.4. Germany

9-37 Under the former German law of arbitration, the concept of arbitrability was linked with the power of the parties to settle their dispute. If the parties lacked the power to dispose of their dispute on their own, they could not defer that task to an arbitral tribunal.

9-38 Under the new section 1030 para 1 German Civil Procedure Law (ZPO), the requirement that the parties possess settlement authority is limited to claims for a non-pecuniary interest. In contrast, all actions for money or other assets are arbitrable *per se.*[36] The only matters which are not arbitrable are those where the prevailing interest of the state denied the parties the right to dispose of certain matters. In support of this possible restriction to arbitrability, the German Federal Supreme Court, in the judgment of a shareholder's suit, expressed the view that there may be limits on arbitrability in pecuniary matters.[37]

9-39 In general, the insolvency of a party does not in itself affect the arbitral proceedings. The arbitrability of issues arising in bankruptcy does not seem to be controversial in the German literature.[38] The arbitration agreement remains

[32] Cass. Com., 19 May 1987 1 *Rev. Arb.* 144 (1988) with note by P. Ancel.
[33] *Ibid.* at 142, with note by P. Ancel.
[34] J. Robert & T. Carbonneau, *The French Law of Arbitration* (1983) I: 1-9 and I: 1-10.
[35] *Ibid.*
[36] G. Wagner in F.-B. Weigand, *Practitioner's Handbook on International Arbitration* (2002) at 701.
[37] BGH 29.3.1996, BGHZ 132, 278, 289 seq.
[38] Lazić, *supra* note 1 at 163.

binding, and the insolvency of one party neither prevents the initiation of the arbitral proceedings nor the termination of existing proceedings, unless the parties agree otherwise.[39] Thus, the trustee is bound by the arbitration agreement and has to take up the proceedings wherever they stand.[40] The bankruptcy courts are only competent to decide on some core issues of bankruptcy, whereas the usual rules on jurisdiction remain preserved to a great extent.[41] Therefore, a great number of disputes arising in bankruptcy are to be decided outside the bankruptcy courts.[42] It has to be mentioned that the criterion of exclusive jurisdiction of national courts is not accepted in German literature as a decisive determination of arbitrability of the disputes.[43]

9-40 Proceedings in front of a state court are stayed in the case of the bankruptcy of one of the parties pursuant section 240 ZPO until either the trustee takes up the court proceedings or the insolvency proceedings are terminated.[44] According to the prevailing case law, insolvency proceedings do not interrupt arbitral proceedings, since section 240 ZPO is only applicable to state court proceedings.[45] However, the arbitral tribunal has to take care that the trustee has sufficient time to prepare further proceedings.[46] The trustee is only barred from relying on an arbitration agreement in proceedings before the state court if the court finds the arbitration agreement is incapable of being performed. The German Federal Supreme Court held that if the insolvent party lacks the necessary funds to participate in the arbitral proceedings, the arbitration agreement becomes inoperable.[47]

9-41 In summary, all disputes related to bankruptcy proceedings are arbitrable, including: proceedings relating to claims on behalf of the estate, to the separation of property from the estate, i.e., secured claims, preferred claims, as well as to

[39] K.-H. Böckstiegel, S. Kröll & P. Nacimiento in K.-H. Böckstiegel, S. Kröll & P. Nacimiento (eds), *Arbitration in Germany – The Model Law in Practice* (2007) at 61, and K. Sachs & T. Lörcher at 295; J.-P. Lachmann, *Handbuch für die Schiedsgerichtsbarkeit* (2008) at 144.

[40] BGH 19.7.2004, SchiedsVZ 2004, 259 (260); Böckstiegel, Kröll & Nacimiento, *supra* note 39 at 61; Lachmann, *supra* note 39 at 144.

[41] Lazić, *supra* note 1 at 163 *et seq.*

[42] *Ibid.* at 164.

[43] T. Jestaedt, *Schiedsverfahren und Konkurs* (1985) at 64.

[44] Lachmann, *supra* note 39 at 519; Böckstiegel, Kröll & Nacimiento, *supra* note 39 at 61.

[45] OLG Köln, SchiedsVZ 2008, 152; OLG Dresden, SchiedsVZ 2005, 159; Lachmann, *supra* note 39 at 519.

[46] Böckstiegel, Kröll & Nacimiento, *supra* note 39 at 61.

[47] BGH 14.9.2000 in DIS, Financial Capacity of the Parties (2004) appendix.

proceedings to establish contested claims.[48] In any insolvency of a party after the award has been rendered, the state court is not prevented from declaring the award enforceable. Insolvency proceedings avoid execution, but not any preceding act such as the declaration of enforceability.[49]

2.5. Switzerland

9-42 Article 177 section 1 Swiss Private International Law Act (SPIL) deals with arbitrability. It states that any dispute involving an economic interest may be the subject matter of arbitration. Since article 177 section 1 SPIL is broadly understood, the only bar to arbitrability is public policy within the meaning of article 190 section 2 e SPIL.[50]

9-43 Public policy considerations regarding bankruptcy proceedings are, in particular, the equal treatment of the creditors, the exclusive and the mandatory jurisdiction of the bankruptcy judges, and the stay of certain legal remedies against debtors. Thus, basically arbitration and bankruptcy are of heterogeneous natures. Arbitration is based on party autonomy and privacy. In contrast, bankruptcy proceeds from official and collective considerations. For that reason – not only pursuant Swiss law – bankruptcy proceedings itself are beyond the reach of any arbitrator.[51]

9-44 Nevertheless, in general, civil and commercial disputes can be settled by arbitration, although one of the parties is or went bankrupt.[52] Article 178 section 2 SPIL determines which persons are bound by an arbitration agreement. Accordingly, the arbitration agreement will be valid if it conforms either to the law chosen by the parties, the law governing the subject-matter of the dispute or Swiss law.[53] Under Swiss law, bankruptcy does not void an arbitration clause, if the parties did not exclude arbitration explicitly in their arbitration clause in case one of them becomes insolvent.[54] Thus, despite a party's insolvency, the

[48] Jestaedt, *supra* note 43 at 58 *et seq.*
[49] *Supra* note 39.
[50] Z. Abdulla in G. Kaufmann-Kohler & B. Stucki, *International Arbitration in Switzerland* (2004) at 22.
[51] L. Lévy, "Insolvency in Arbitration (Swiss Law)", *Int'l ALR* (2005) 23.
[52] W. Wenger in S. Berti, *International Arbitration in Switzerland* (2000) at 355; B. Berger and F. Kellerhals, *Internationale und interne Schiedsgerichtsbarkeit in der Schweiz* (2006) at 178; L. Lévy, *supra* note 51 at 23.
[53] Abdulla, *supra* note 50 at 22.
[54] Lévy, *supra* note 51 at 26, 27.

arbitration agreement remains valid and binding for the trustee and the debtor itself.[55]

9-45 However, arbitrators, who are appointed in an arbitration in which one party is insolvent, have jurisdiction but will have to take the existence of the bankruptcy proceedings into consideration in respect of public policy regulations.[56]

9-46 If a party becomes bankrupt in the course of an arbitration, the SPIL does not include any provision regarding a suspension of the arbitral proceedings. However, a stay of the proceedings might be mandatory due to public policy, equal treatment of the parties or the parties' right to be heard.[57]

9-47 One of the mandatory clauses[58] in the Swiss bankruptcy law (Bankruptcy Law) reads:

> Save for urgency cases, civil proceedings, to which the bankrupt debtor is a party and which have some influence on the state of the estate, are stayed. Such proceedings may be resumed, in case of ordinary liquidation, only ten days after the second assembly of the creditors [. . .].

9-48 The main purpose of article 207 Bankruptcy Law is to give the trustee the necessary time to review the files of the debtor and to acquire a global overview of the debtor's assets and liabilities.[59]

9-49 In conclusion, Swiss bankruptcy law does not void any agreement to arbitrate.[60] This applies to procedures where the estate in bankruptcy is either claimant or respondent, and independent of whether the arbitration proceedings have already been instituted at the time of the opening of the bankruptcy or not.[61]

55 Wenger, *supra* note 52 at 355; Berger & Kellerhals, *supra* note 52 at 178; Lévy, *supra* note 51 at 27.
56 Lévy, *supra* note 51 at 30.
57 *Ibid.*
58 Article 207 Bankruptcy Law.
59 Mantilla-Serrano, *supra* note 5 at 56 refers to a case between an Italian claimant and a Swiss defendant in bankruptcy, in which the arbitrators, sitting in Geneva and applying Swiss law to the merits, decided to suspend the arbitration upon joint request of the parties in accordance with Article 207 Bankruptcy Law. *Cf* L. Lévy, *supra* note 51 at 31.
60 T. Rüede & R. Hadenfeldt, *Schweizerisches Schiedsgerichtsrecht* (1993) at 81.
61 Wenger, *supra* note 52 at 355; Berger & Kellerhals, *supra* note 52 at 178.

3. Conclusions

9-50 Which public policy considerations would require non-arbitrability of insolvency matters? None.

9-51 However, for practical reasons, pure insolvency procedures, i.e., the insolvency procedure itself, will not be subject to arbitration due to the great number of involved persons and the contractual basis of arbitration.

9-52 Hypothetically speaking, where all the relevant parties agreed to conclude an arbitration agreement, the goal of insolvency law would be sufficiently protected as the core elements of insolvency law pertain to public policy.[62]

[62] See e.g., OLG Köln, SchiedsVZ 2008, 152.

William W. Park[*]

CHAPTER 10

ARBITRABILITY AND TAX

"The art of taxation consists in so plucking the goose as to obtain the largest amount of feathers with the smallest amount of hissing."[1]

1. Introduction

10-1 Assertions that tax matters remain "non-arbitrable" bring to mind the story of an elderly farmer who met his pastor while walking by the village church one Sunday. The clergyman asked the farmer if he believed in infant baptism. Being a sceptic, but hoping to avoid a theological controversy that might delay supper, the old man replied, "Believe in it? Reverend, I've seen it done!"

10-2 Arguments do exist to suggest that disputes about fiscal measures should remain beyond the reach of private adjudicators.[2] Taxation directly implicates

[*] Professor of Law, Boston University. General Editor, Arbitration International.

[1] Attributed to Jean-Baptiste Colbert, finance minister to Louis XIV of France. The original reads, "L'imposition est l'art de plumer une oie pour obtenir le maximum de plumes avec le minimum de cris."

[2] See Thomas Carbonneau & Andrew Sheldrick, "Tax Liability and Inarbitrability in International Commercial Arbitration", 1 *J. Trans'l Law & Policy* 23 (1992) 38: "[T]he resolution of statutory claims involving tax issues is unsuitable for arbitration." See generally, Bernard Hanotiau, *L'Arbitrabilité* (2003) in *Recueil des cours* (2002), *Académie de Droit International de la Haye* at 171–180; Pascal Ancel, "Arbitrage et ordre public fiscal", *Rev. Arb.* (2001) 269; Matthieu de Boisseson, *Le Droit français de l'arbitrage* (1990) Section 33 at 37; Ibrahim Fadallah, *L'ordre public dans les sentences arbitrales*, *Recueil des cours* (2002), *Académie de Droit International de la Haye*, 369 (1994) paras 54–56, at 410–411; Philippe Fouchard, Emmanuel Gaillard & Berthold Goldman, *International Commercial Arbitration* (English Language edition, E. Gaillard & J. Savage eds., 1999), at 348 & 359 (Sections 579, n. 478, & 589–1). For a survey of ICC arbitrations touching on tax matters, see Luca Melchionna, "Tax Disputes and International

L Mistelis & S Brekoulakis (eds), Arbitrability: International & Comparative Perspectives, 179-205

the fund-raising by which modern political collectivities operate. Thus it would not be odd for national courts to seek a monopoly on litigation touching such a vital sovereign prerogative.

10-3 In practice, however, arbitration of tax-related disputes proves very much a reality despite the doctrinal objections. The scholarly debate notwithstanding, arbitrators routinely address problems of taxation in the context of ordinary commercial contracts as well as claims by foreign investors brought against host states.[3]

10-4 The amenability of tax disputes to arbitration remains highly fact-intensive, however. Although no hard-and-fast rule prohibits all tax arbitration *per se*, many arbitration claims related to fiscal matters will (and should) fail. In some instances the claim may not be ripe for adjudication, perhaps because the government has not yet ruled on the amount of tax (if any) payable. In other cases, the relevant investment treaty or arbitration clause may remove certain types of tax controversies from the arbitrators' adjudicatory power.[4]

10-5 This essay begins by comparing the various contexts in which fiscal matter may be subject to arbitration, exploring why the nature of tax measures affects the universe of questions that arbitrators could normally be expected to address. Discussion then turns to a case study of the increasingly critical area of investment protection treaties. In this connection, the modest aim of the paper lies in suggesting an analytic starting point for distinguishing legitimate from illegitimate taxes.

Commercial Arbitration", 74 *Diritto e Pratica Tributaria Internazionale* (2003) 769. See also Luca Melchionna, "Arbitrability of Tax Disputes", IBA Section on Business Law, Arbitration and ADR Committee Newsletter 21 (May 2004).

3 Academic debate on the arbitrability of tax measures brings to mind the comment from one professor to another in a law school faculty workshop: "Perhaps your ideas do work in practice. But will they work in theory?"

4 Distinctions are sometimes made between arbitral jurisdiction (*compétence*) and the "admissibility" (*recevabilité*) of a claim. When claims are barred for reasons such as ripeness, they are said to be not admissible (*recevable*). While otherwise subject to an arbitrator's jurisdiction, the pre-conditions for their proper consideration have not been met. By contrast, a treaty prohibition on arbitration of particular tax claims could constitute a bar to the legitimate authority of an arbitrator even to consider such matters.

2. Three Faces of Tax Arbitration

10-6 Distinctions should be drawn among three broad categories of fiscal arbitration: (i) tax controversies arising from business relationships; (ii) overlapping tax on the same transaction by two or more countries; and (iii) disputes implicating tax issues between a foreign investor and the host state. This last category of tax arbitration remains the most controversial, and thus forms the focus of this paper. For the sake of conceptual clarity, however, let us begin with a brief comparison of these three varieties of tax disputes.

2.1. Business Relationships

10-7 With respect to the first category (business relationships), several different scenarios arise.[5] In the wake of a corporate acquisition, there might be questions on whether the buyer or the seller should bear taxes due for previously accrued tax liabilities. Or, an allegation might be made that the seller misrepresented corporate tax liabilities, either by reason of accounting irregularities or in hiding investigations by local revenue authorities. There might be issues about which party gets the benefits and/or burdens of credits and liabilities under a "tax allocation agreement" concluded pursuant to a corporate spin-off. In some instances, disputes among joint venture partners might arise with respect to whether one partner was authorised to make payments to a foreign country on behalf of another. Last but not least, taxpayers have been known to sue their advisers when advice about a tax shelter proves unfounded and leads to liability.[6]

2.2 Income Tax Treaties

10-8 Country-to-country arbitration under income tax treaties provides a second fertile ground for fiscal arbitration. Recently, the process received endorsement

[5] For examples of domestic and international tax arbitration, see *Ace Ltd. v. Cigna Corp.*, 2001 WL 767015; ICC Awards No. 6515 & 6516, in *Collection of Arbitral Awards/Recueil des sentences arbitrales de la CCI*, Volume IV (1996–2000) (Jean-Jacques Arnaldez, ed.) at 241. For tax arbitration within the U.S., see I.R.S. Ann. 2000–4 and 2002–60.

[6] *Reddan v. KPMG*, 457 F. 3d 1054 (9th Cir. 2006) (tax shelter sponsor held bound to arbitrate on the basis of an arbitration clause in brokerage contract related to the tax shelter transaction); *Vassaluzzo v. Ernst & Young*, 2007 WL 2076471 (Mass. Super. Ct. 2007); *Vassaluzzo v. Ernst & Young and Sidley Austin* (Mass. Super. Ct, C.A. No. 06-4215, 2007) (malpractice action for advice on an unsuccessful tax shelter, arbitration clause in engagement letter found to cover some but not all transactions).

[endorsed] by international organisations such as the OECD (Organisation for Economic Cooperation and Development) and the ICC (International Chamber of Commerce), as well as several national fiscal authorities, including Austria, Belgium, Canada, Germany and the U.S..[7] Such tax treaty arbitration meets the needs of multinational corporate groups seeking symmetrical treatment of income inclusions and deductions in different countries.

10-9 For example, a royalty payment might be made by a French subsidiary to its American parent. As between the French and American tax authorities, different views might exist on the correct amount of royalty. The varying applications of national anti-avoidance measures, intended to prevent abusive "transfer pricing", might result in income to the American parent without an equal deduction to the French subsidiary.

10-10 Although not double taxation in a *juridical* sense (given the separate corporate personalities of parent and subsidiary), such situations do present *economic* double taxation. The same income is taxed twice, to the extent that an inclusion in the American company's taxable profits has not been offset by a corresponding deduction in France. The multinational's position would be that of a stakeholder, willing to pay tax to either the U.S. or to France, but not to both countries. Tax treaty arbitration provides one hope for fiscal symmetry, thereby reducing the fiscal barriers to cross-border trade and investment.

2.3 Investment Disputes

10-11 Finally, arbitration of tax disputes occurs in the context of relationships between foreign investors and host states. On rare occasions, a government

7 William W. Park & David R. Tillinghast, *Income Tax Treaty Arbitration* (2004); Marcus Desax & Marc Veit, "Arbitration of Tax Treaty Disputes: The OECD Proposal", 23 *Arb. Int'l* (2007) 405; Organization for Economic Cooperation and Development (OECD); *Improving the Resolution of Tax Treaty Disputes* (OECD Committee on Fiscal Affairs, 30 January 2007); Mario Züger, *Arbitration Under Tax Treaties* (2001); Zvi D. Altman, *Dispute Resolution under Tax Treaties* (2005); Draft Bilateral Convention Article, Doc. No. 180/455 Rev. (10 September 2001) (Draft Proposal by ICC Commission on Taxation); Robert Couzin, "Arbitration in Tax Treaties",29 *Tax Planning International Review* (March 2002) 12; Sed Crest, "A New Way to Resolve International Tax Disputes", *International Tax Review* at 24, May 2005 (Interview with Tjaco van de Houte, Secretary General of Permanent Court of Arbitration). For a more doubtful view of tax treaty arbitration, see Michael J. McIntyre, "Comments on the OECD Proposal for Secret and Mandatory Arbitration of International Tax Disputes", 9 *Florida Tax Review* (2006) 622.

may agree on an *ad hoc* basis to arbitrate disputes over the quantum of a foreign investor's tax liability.[8]

10-12 Much more common, however, are treaty-based claims by investors alleging that the host state imposed tax in a discriminatory or arbitrary manner, or used tax as a vehicle for expropriation without compensation.[9] Such tax-related investment disputes remain qualitatively different from the commercial or tax treaty context. In an investment dispute, the very legitimacy of the tax is put into question.

10-13 The controversy does not concern shifting normal fiscal burdens between a buyer and a seller, or the tax authorities in the parent's home state as opposed to the subsidiary's country of incorporation. Rather, an assertion might be made that the governmental payment is not really a tax at all, but rather a disguised attempt at confiscation. To this type of controversy we now turn our attention.

3. The Nature of Tax Measures

3.1. Fire, Passion and Taxes

10-14 Like fire and passion, taxation can bring ruin as well as blessing. Justice Oliver Wendell Holmes rightly observed that taxes provide the wherewithal for public benefits we associate with civilised life. In one of his famous dissents he observed, "Taxes are what we pay for civilized society."[10]

[8] See Jean-Pierre LeGall, "Fiscalité et arbitrage", 1994 *Rev. Arb.* 3 (noting at 24–25 several international tax arbitrations); Emmanuel Gaillard, "Tax Disputes between States and Foreign Investors", *NYLJ* (April 1997) at 3.

[9] See generally, Thomas Wälde & Abba Kolo, "Investor-State Tax Disputes: The Interface Between Treaty-Based International Investment Protection and Fiscal Sovereignty", 35 *Intertax* (August/September 2007) 424; Richard Happ, "Beilegung von Steuerstreitigkeiten zwischen Investoren und ausländischen Staaten durch Schiedsgerichte", *IStR* (2006) at 649-654.

[10] The line comes from a dissent while a Justice on the U.S. Supreme Court, in the case *Compañia General de Tabaco de Filipinas v Collector of Internal Revenue*, 275 U.S. 87, at 100 (1927). The catchphrase was later taken by President Franklin D. Roosevelt, who said that taxes were "the dues that we pay for the privileges of membership in an organized society." Address in Worcester, Massachusetts, 21 October 1936. See Volume 5, Public Papers and Addresses of Franklin D. Roosevelt (Samuel I. Rosenman, ed, 1938) 522-523.

10-15 Fiscal measures also have a darker side, sometimes serving as a vehicle for indirect asset confiscation. As the oft-cited paraphrase of another American Supreme Court Justice suggests, "The power to tax is the power to destroy."[11]

10-16 This special potential for abuse reflects itself in the fiscal provisions of most investment treaties, which set forth intricate rules to assist in the fact-intensive *triage* between normal and abnormal taxes. Some tax measures give rise to claims for expropriation or discrimination, while others do not. As we shall see, line-drawing resists facile analysis, in large measure because taxation by its nature constitutes an involuntary seizure of property that resembles expropriation in even the best circumstances.

3.2. Tax as Taking

10-17 No consensus exists on why tax measures should receive special attention in investment treaties. Raising revenue does constitute a core activity of all political collectivities. However, the same can be said of many other government functions (such as administration of justice or environmental protection) that regularly give rise to claims by foreign investors. For example, an effective judiciary remains vital to any concept of sovereignty. [12] Nevertheless, court proceedings have long been a fruitful source of state

[11] *McCulloch v Maryland*, 17 U.S. (4 Wheat) 316, 327 (1819). A federally chartered bank had established branches in various states, one of which was Maryland. When that state imposed a tax on bank operations, the cashier of the Baltimore branch (one James McCulloch) refused to pay. The opinion by Chief Justice Marshall, upholding the power of Congress to create a national bank and ruling the Maryland tax unconstitutional, contained the following language: "An unlimited power to tax involves, necessarily, a power to destroy; because there is a limit beyond which no institution and no property can bear taxation."

[12] We remember that Absalom's revolt against his father King David all started with his claim that the king was unable to put in place an effective adjudicatory mechanism. The Bible recounts that Absalom would stand on the roadside and shout to those with pending litigation: "Your claims are good and right; but there is no one deputed by the king to hear you. If only I were judge in the land! Then all who had a suit or cause might come to me [for] justice." II Samuel 15 2–4. See generally Max Weber, *The Protestant Ethic and the Spirit of Capitalism* (ed. and trans. P. Baehr & Gordon Wells, 2002), Appendix II, *Collected Essays in the Sociology of Religion*, at 365 ("Modern rational capitalism requires…calculable law and administration conducted according to formal rules, without which no rational private economic business with standing capital…is possible."). See also Max Weber, *General Economic History*, trans. F. Knight (1966) at 277.

responsibility under both customary international law[13] and modern investment treaties.[14]

10-18 Any explanation for the treaty carve-outs given to tax measures remains tentative, and unlikely to give complete satisfaction. However, one rationale may prove more right than wrong. The best account for taxation's special status probably lies in the very nature of taxation. As mentioned earlier, tax constitutes a form of confiscation, thus opening the way to investor arguments (however misconceived) that an actionable taking of property has occurred. Money leaves private hands and enters government coffers without any necessary *quid pro quo*. In particular, taxes lend themselves to characterisation as a form of indirect or "creeping" confiscation, which might in principle give rise to claims under investment treaty provisions related to expropriation and discrimination.[15]

10-19 Unlike charitable contributions or purchases of goods and services, wealth transfer through taxation remains involuntary. Taxpayers have no option to say, "Sorry, we'll just skip this year's contribution." The only escape lies in ceasing the activity that otherwise triggers the tax.[16]

[13] See J. L. Brierly, *The Law of Nations* (1963) at 286–287, noting different views on what constitutes *déni de justice*. A narrow interpretation contends that denial of justice exists only when foreigners have been refused access to courts. The broader view includes substandard judicial acts such as corruption, dishonesty, and unwarranted delay. The term is sometimes misapplied to national court disregard of international law. In his study *Denial of Justice in International Law* (2005), Jan Paulsson rightly suggests abandonment of the term "substantive" denial of justice to describe such violations of the law of nations. See also A. W. Freeman, *The International Responsibility of States for Denial of Justice* (1938); Ian Brownlie, *Principles of Public International Law* (6th ed, 2003) at 506–508.

[14] See e.g., *Mondev International Ltd. v. United States of America*, ICSID case no. ARB (AF)/99/2; Award of 11 October 2002 published in 42 ILM. 85 (2003); *Loewen Group, Inc. v. U.S.A.*, ICSID case no. ARB (AF)/98/3, Final Award 26 June 2003, 42 ILM 811 (2003).

[15] For a South American view on tax as indirect expropriation, see Marco Chavez, "La expropiacion indirecta y el Capitulo 10 del TLC suscrito por el Peru con Estados Unidos de Norteamerica", 4 *Revista Peruana de Arbitraje* (2007, Ed. Magna, Lima) 367.

[16] From the perspective of a government (democracy and dictatorship alike), taxation can be compared to payment for benefits such as roads, schools and diplomatic protection. They need not involve either discrimination or a design to damage the underlying business activity. Like any analogy, the comparison is far from perfect. Analytic problems arise when one examines the relationship between the tax and the service. Although fiscal jurisdiction assumes some taxpayer contact with the state, the benefit received is rarely calibrated to the fee paid. In towns where real estate taxes finance public education, wealthy but childless homeowners pay more toward schools than modestly housed residents with large broods.

10-20 In attempting to distinguish legitimate revenue measures from *de facto* confiscation through taxation, one is reminded of the line by U.S. Supreme Court Justice Potter Stewart reversing a movie theatre's obscenity conviction. Admitting an inability to define "hard core" pornography, Stewart added, "But I know it when I see it."[17] British judges sometimes apply a similar (but less risqué) characterisation test. In deciding that a floating crane was not a "ship or vessel" for purposes of insurance policy, Lord Justice Scrutton referred to the gentleman who "could not define an elephant but knew what it was when he saw one."[18]

10-21 Like elephants and obscenity, the contours of legitimate taxation leave many fuzzy edges that frustrate rigorous discussion. Although telling them apart is not always easy, differences do exist between what might be called "normal" and "abusive" taxes. The former aims to fund government. The latter are crafted to force abandonment of a business enterprise by ruining its economic value, or to provide an investor's competitors with a beneficial fiscal framework that permits more favourable competition.

10-22 As discussed below, various treaty-based limitations come into play when an investor contends that an allegedly abusive tax violates some provision of an investment convention or free trade agreement. The relevant distinctions go far beyond technical matters such as depreciation methods and timing of rebates, and touch on the very notion of revenue-raising legitimacy.[19]

[17] See *Jacobellis v. Ohio*, 378 U.S. 184 (1964) at 197 (concurring opinion), examining when erotic expression falls outside the limits of constitutionally protected speech. The object of inquiry was a Louis Malle film *Les Amants* about a woman in an unhappy marriage. See also Paul Gewirtz, "On "I Know It When I See It"", 105 *Yale LJ* (1996) 1023.

[18] See *Merchants Marine Insurance Co. Ltd. v. North of England Protecting & Indemnity Association*, [1926] 26 Lloyd's Rep. 201, at 203; 32 Com. Cas. 165, at 172. In the Charente River near Rochefort, a steamship had collided with the crane. If the crane was a "ship or vessel" then the insurance company apparently paid three-fourths of the damages; otherwise the damage was paid by the North of England Protecting & Indemnity Association. See also *O'Callaghan v. Elliot* [1966] 1 Q.B. 601 (a Denning decision that attributes the saying to Balfour); and *Cole Brothers Ltd. v. Phillips* [1981] STC 671, 55 Tax Cases 188. The statement is attributed to Balcombe in the article "Land Contracts: An Evolving Policy", *JBL* 39 (Jan. 1996) 46.

[19] See discussion in Section V, *infra*.

3.3. The Silesian Claims

10-23 Tax-related claims have not always benefited from investment protection regimes. In the early 20th century, an arbitral tribunal took the view that fiscal measures by their nature did not constitute expropriation. Under this now-discredited doctrine, investors had no general recourse to arbitration for relief from abusive taxation.

10-24 The origins of the case, *Kügele v. Polish State*,[20] lie in a part of Central Europe called Upper Silesia, now found in the southeast corner of Poland.[21] Following the First World War, the ethnically Polish portion had become an autonomous region, while the largely German-speaking areas remained in Germany. Following uprisings among the Polish-speakers, part of Upper Silesia was awarded to Poland pursuant to a Geneva Convention brokered by the League of Nations.[22]

10-25 To address claims by Germans for expropriation, the treaty established what seems to be the first modern European investment protection regime, giving investors a direct cause of action against the host country.[23] The Arbitral

[20] *Kügele v. Polish State*, 5 February 1932. English language summary as Case No. 34, *Annual Digest of Public International Law Cases* (Hersch Lauterpacht, ed., 1931/1932). The terms of the relevant treaty are reproduced in Case No. 33 of that volume of the *Annual Digest*.

[21] The adjective "Upper" remains somewhat of an irony, since the region appears in the lower right corner (the southeast) of most maps of Poland, near its borders with the Czech Republic and Slovakia. Apparently labelled for its location between the "upper" parts of two rivers (the Oder and the Vistula) flowing down from the Silesian highlands, the region was alternatively under the control of Poland, Bohemia, Austria, Prussia, and Germany. Rich in agriculture and coal, the area included towns such as Chorzow, Katowice and Bytom (Beutem).

[22] Geneva Convention of 15 May 1922, Poland and Germany.

[23] The 1922 treaty (apparently concluded only in French) can be found as an Annex in Georges Kaeckenbeeck, *The International Experiment of Upper Silesia: A Study in the Working of the Upper Silesia Settlement 1922-1937* (Oxford, 1942). Kaeckenbeeck served as President of the Arbitral Tribunal from 1922 through 1937. See also Georges S. Kaeckenbeeck, "Essential Human Rights", 243 *Annals of the American Academy of Political and Social Science* (Jan., 1946) 129-133. North America had experimented with a prototype of investment arbitration in 1794, when the so-called "Jay Treaty" (named for its American negotiator John Jay) gave British creditors the right to arbitrate claims of alleged despoliation by American citizens and residents. See Treaty of Amity, Commerce and Navigation, London, 19 November 1794, U.S.–U.K., 8 Stat. 116. Under Article 6, damages for British creditors were to be determined by five Commissioners, two appointed by the British and two by the U.S.. The fifth was to be chosen unanimously by the others, in default of which selection would be by lot from between candidates proposed by each side. See generally Barton Legum, "Federalism, NAFTA Chapter Eleven and the Jay Treaty of 1794", 18 *ICSID News* (Spring 2001).

Tribunal of Upper Silesia (officially "*Tribunal Arbitral de la Haute Silésie*") provided an avenue for vindication of investor rights independent of either local courts or the diplomatic protection of the investor's home state.

10-26 Under the label "license fees" (which today might be called excise taxes), Poland had imposed an allegedly confiscatory levy on a brewery owned by an ethnic German, which according to the owner was forced to cease business because of the tax. Claiming that the tax was tantamount to expropriation, the German proprietor filed a claim for compensation.

10-27 In a 1932 decision, the Arbitral Tribunal rejected the claim on the basis that taxation by definition cannot give rise to expropriation. According to the Tribunal, the imposition of a tax implies the existence of a business, which in turn presupposes that the enterprise has not been confiscated. An arbitral tribunal chaired by the eminent Belgian Professor, Georges Kaeckenbeeck, reasoned as follows:

> The increase of the tax cannot be regarded as a taking away or impairment of the right to engage in a trade, for such taxation presupposes the engaging in the trade. […] The trader may feel compelled to close his business because of the new tax. But this does not mean that he has lost the right to engage in the trade. For had he paid the tax, he would be entitled to go on with his business.[24]

10-28 Today, such reasoning would be difficult to imagine. As discussed in the following section, barriers to tax arbitration still exist. However, none of them rest on the view that fiscal measures somehow must be deemed non-arbitrable.

4. Investment Treaty Arbitration

4.1. The Matryoshka: Rules within Rules

10-29 The current network of investment and free trade agreements was adopted to enhance economic cooperation and cross-border capital flows through a two-part regime: (i) substantive investor protections against discrimination,

[24] Case No. 34, *Annual Digest of Public International Law Cases* (Hersch Lauterpacht, ed., 1931/1932), at 69, summarizing with excerpts from *Schiedsgericht für Oberschlesian*, Volume III, No. 1, at 24 (1932).

confiscation and other unfair governmental measures, and (ii) a relatively neutral dispute resolution mechanism in the event of disagreement on how those protections should operate.[25]

10-30 The cornerstone of most investment treaties lies in a prohibition of uncompensated expropriation of foreign-owned property, whether such expropriation is direct or indirect.[26] However, the treatment of tax measures related to expropriation remains far from simple, and brings to mind the Russian nested doll, or *matryoshka*. One carved figure opens to reveal another, which in turn unlocks to yield yet more diminutive figurines. Treaty-based investor protection schemes contain fiscal provisions that unfold with exceptions to the exceptions.

10-31 In one significant way, however, interpreting investment treaties differs from opening a *matryoshka* in one significant way. While the doll releases smaller figures, treaty exceptions often reveal other exceptions that prove as capacious as the provision from which they derogate.

[25] See generally, William W. Park & Guillermo Aguilar Alvarez, "The New Face of Investment Arbitration", 28 *YJIL* (2003) 365. Not all would agree with this positive assessment of investment protection regimes, as witnessed by the recent denunciation of Bolivia's denunciation of its obligations under the ICSID Convention (effective in late 2007), followed by Nicaragua's threat to withdraw from that Convention, Venezuela's decision to withdraw from the World Bank and Ecuador's declaration of intent to abrogate its bilateral investment treaty with the U.S. and remove ICSID jurisdiction related to oil and mining. See Emmanuel Gaillard, "The Denunciation of the ICSID Convention", *NYLJ* (June 2007) 26. For a historical view of investment protection, see William W. Park, "Legal Issues in the Third World's Economic Development", 61 *BULR* 1321 (1981). For an intriguing perspective on the origins of the debate, see Eugene Staley, *War and the Private Investor* (1935).

[26] On indirect expropriation, see Michael Reisman & Robert Sloane, "Indirect Expropriation and Its Valuation in the BIT Generation", 2003 *BYIL* (2004) 115; Rachell Edsall, "Indirect Expropriation under NAFTA and DR-CAFTA: Potential Inconsistencies in the Treatment of State Public Welfare Regulations", 86 *BULR* (2006) 931; Burns H. Weston, ""Constructive Takings" under International Law: A Modest Foray into the Problem of "Creeping Expropriation"", 16 *Va. J. Int'l L.* (1975) 103. For an illustration of indirect expropriation, see *Case Concerning the Barcelona Traction, Light and Power Co, Ltd (Belgium v Spain) (2d Phase)*, 1970 ICJ 3, 9 ILM 227 (1970), where a Canadian company's profitable Spanish assets were taken through a bankruptcy proceeding allegedly orchestrated to reward a supporter of then-dictator General Francisco Franco. The bankruptcy resulted when Spanish authorities refused to permit transfer of foreign currency necessary to service Sterling bonds.

10-32 To illustrate, the Energy Charter Treaty ("ECT")[27] establishes a general rule on fiscal measures in Article 21: "Nothing in this Treaty shall create rights or impose obligations with respect to Taxation Measures of the Contracting Parties."[28] The same Article then enumerates provisions that *will* apply to tax measures: prohibitions against discrimination [29] and uncompensated expropriation,[30] for which investors may seek redress through arbitration.[31] The non-discrimination rule, however, excludes from its application both income and capital taxes, as well as tax collection measures. A carve-out for collection measures that "arbitrarily" restrict treaty benefits creates another exception from the exclusion, thus allowing claims based on some (but not all) collection practices.[32]

[27] Energy Charter Treaty, Lisbon, 17 December 1994, 2080 UNTS 95; 33 ILM 360 (1995). The ECT was intended to facilitate East-West cooperation between countries of the former Soviet Union (holders of large oil and gas resources) and western European countries with a strategic interest in diversifying their energy supplies. See generally, Thomas W. Walde, *The Energy Charter Treaty: an East-West Gateway for Investment and Trade* (London 1996); Julia Doré & Robert De Bauw, Robert, *The Energy Charter Treaty: Origins, Aims and Prospects* (1995); Clarisse Ribeiro (ed), *Investment Arbitration and the Energy Charter Treaty* (2006); Mirian Kene Omalu, *NAFTA and the Energy Charter Treaty* (1999). See also, Kaj Hobér, "The Energy Charter Treaty – Awards Rendered", 1 *Disp. Res. J.* (IBA, June 2007), Steivan Defilla, "Trade under the ECT and Accession to the WTO", 21 *Journal of Energy and Natural Resources Law* (2003) 428; Lawrence Herman, "NAFTA and the ECT: Divergent Approaches with a Core of Harmony", 15 *Journal of Energy and Natural Resources Law* (1997) 131.

[28] Other bilateral or multilateral investment regimes have analogous provisions. See e.g., NAFTA Article 2103(1); 2004 U.S. Model BIT, Article 21; U.S.-Ecuador BIT, Article 10; Canada-Ecuador BIT, Article 12. See Appendix for the text of these provisions.

[29] Article 21(3) says that Articles 10(2) and 10(7) "shall apply to Taxation Measures of the Contracting Parties other than those on income and on capital". These two subsections of Article 10 relate to non-discrimination and most-favoured-nation treatment. In turn, exceptions to the exception exist *inter alia* for tax collection mechanisms or provisions of economic integration organizations and income tax treaties in Article 21(7)(a)(ii). The carve-out for tax on income and on income leave some of the most significant categories of fiscal measures, including value added tax, import and export duties, and stamp taxes. Significantly, the ECT exclusion does not refer to Article 10(1), mandating "fair and equitable treatment".

[30] ECT Article 21(5) states "Article 13 shall apply to taxes". Article 13(1)(d) requires compensation to be accompanied by "the payment of prompt, adequate and effective compensation."

[31] ECT Article 26 permits arbitration under the rules of ICSID, UNCITRAL and the Stockholm Chamber of Commerce. For investors from countries that are not a party to the 1965 Washington Convention, the dispute may be subject to the rules of the ICSID Additional Facility.

[32] ECT Article 21.

10-33 Thus the interaction of investment treaties and tax measures often contains a level of complexity that makes discourse difficult, with multiple qualifiers for even simpler propositions. Other than insurance policies and revenue codes, few public documents present as many exegetical challenges.

10-34 As mentioned above, the ECT says that it does not create rights or impose obligations with respect to taxation measures,[33] but then makes an exception for non-discrimination and most-favoured-nation provisions, which *do* apply to tax measures.[34] But the exception applies only to measures other than income and capital taxes, which would seem to leave all other government imposts, such as value added tax, excise tax, stamp duties, import and export taxes.

10-35 Moreover, the rule that non-discrimination provisions apply to tax measures contains several exceptions that include, *inter alia*, tax collection mechanisms.[35] This exception to an exception contains its own additional exception, with respect to measures that "arbitrarily" discriminate against investors from the other contracting party. There are also exceptions for advantages accorded under regional economic integration organisations[36] and income tax treaties.[37] As to these items, one is sent back into the general rule that no rights are created or obligations imposed.

10-36 The ECT definition of "taxes" further complicates things by explicitly excluding customs duties.[38] If customs duties are *not* taxes, then the initial exclusion (creating no rights and imposing no duties with respect to tax measures) would not apply in the first place. So the otherwise applicable investor protections (including fair and equitable treatment) remain in force, notwithstanding that they were initially excluded with regard to tax measures.[39]

[33] ECT Article 21. At some places the ECT refers to "Taxation Measures" (Article 21, subsections 1 through 4), while at other places the treaty uses the term "taxes" (see Article 21(5) concerning expropriation rules under Article 13), without any explicit indication of why the different phraseology was chosen.

[34] ECT Articles 10(2) and 10(7).

[35] ECT Article 21(3)(b).

[36] ECT Article 21(3)(a).

[37] See ECT Article 21(3)(a), with its cross reference to Article 21(7)(a)(ii), which includes any international agreement "for the avoidance of double taxation."

[38] ECT Article 21(7)(d).

[39] Article 21(3) states explicitly that the non-discrimination and most-favoured-nation provisions of Article 10(2) and (7) will apply to taxation measures, but makes no mention of Article 10(1), the provision mandating "fair and equitable treatment" with a goal to "encourage and create stable, equitable, favourable and transparent conditions for investors".

10-37 As a general matter, most (but not all) conventions contain few provisions that permit tax claims to be brought with respect to denial of "fair and equitable" treatment. Taxes that seem unfair and inequitable remain subject to general exclusions for tax measures, and are thus non-arbitrable. The fear seems to be that notions of fairness and equity remain too malleable and chameleon-like to be useful, and could lend themselves to mischief, at least from the host state's perspective.

10-38 The exceptions make more sense when viewed in the light of specific national tax measures. To illustrate, NAFTA Article 2103(4) allows the non-discrimination provisions to apply to taxes "other than those on income or capital gains."[40] Why the carve-out? What is it about income taxes that might pose problems?

10-39 The answer is not hard to find when one looks at common features of income tax codes. Most national tax systems are full of provisions, which on their face, apply in a discriminatory fashion. Understandably, such discrimination often exists for reasons of administrative convenience, given the difficulty of overseas auditing and enforcement.

10-40 To illustrate, U.S. Internal Revenue Code Section 884 imposes tax on the "dividend equivalent amount" of profits earned by foreign (but not domestic) corporations. Sound reasons may exist for this tax, which tends to equalise the burden imposed on foreign entities operating through branches and those using corporate subsidiaries. Nevertheless, the measure is clearly discriminatory. Foreign companies are subjected to a tax not imposed on their domestic counterparts. Indeed, the American tax authorities have recognised that in appropriate instances relief may be available through non-discrimination provisions of double tax conventions.[41]

10-41 Or to take another case in point, most developed countries tax non-resident aliens and foreign corporations on their passive income (such as dividends and

[40] The provision goes on to include

> the taxable capital of corporations, taxes on estates, inheritances, gifts and generation skipping transfers and those taxes listed in paragraph 1 of Annex 2103(4), which designates certain excise taxes on insurance premiums.

[41] See Treasury Regulations § 1.884-1(g). See also Article 24 ("Non-Discrimination"), United States Model Income Tax Convention, 16 November 2006.

interest) based on "gross receipts" although citizens and residents, by contrast, pay tax on net income.[42] For example, the default rule in the U.S. remains a thirty per cent (30%) tax on gross amounts of dividends received by foreigners, and ten per cent (10%) on the gross realised by them on real estate dispositions.[43] By contrast, resident and citizens are taxed only on net gain, whether from securities or real estate.

4.2. The Competent Authority Filter

10-42 To distinguish normal and abusive taxes, many investment treaties require that claims of tax-related expropriation may be sent to arbitration only after the matter is first referred to the two competent fiscal authorities of the host and investor states.[44] For example, under NAFTA, the authorities are given six months to try to work things out, and together may veto any arbitration implicating tax measures. The veto (sometimes called a "filter") must be exercised *jointly* by both countries, which means that the investor loses the right to file an expropriation claim only if its own home state authorities have not been convinced to endorse the view that the tax is confiscatory.

10-43 The analogous ECT provision says only that the competent authorities shall "strive to resolve" the issues.[45] That treaty adds, however, that "under no circumstances" will arbitration be delayed because of involvement by the tax

[42] See, e.g., Reuven Avi-Yonah, "Globalization, Tax Competition and the Fiscal Crisis of the Welfare State", 113 *Harvard Law Review* (2000) 1573; Michael J. Graetz, *Foundations of International Income Taxation* (2003), Chapter 7.

[43] See e.g., I.R.C. § 871 & 881 on dividends and other passive income. When applicable, most treaties reduce this gross amount to more reasonable proportions. See OECD Model Income Tax Convention, Articles 10 (dividends), 11 (interest) and 12 (royalties). With respect to real estate dispositions I.R.C § 1445 impose a tax on gross amount realized, which can in some instances be adjusted if the taxpayer reaches an agreement with the government. Unlike passive income, however, real estate dispositions do not benefit from treaty-based tax benefits. See FIRPTA "Treaty Override" in P.L. 96-499 (1980) § 1125.

[44] ETC Article 21(5) provides,

> The Investor or the Contracting Party alleging expropriation shall refer the issue of whether the tax is an expropriation or whether the tax is discriminatory to the relevant Competent Tax Authority.

NAFTA Article 2103(6) contains a slight variant in its language:

> The investor shall refer the issue of whether the measure is not an expropriation for a determination to the appropriate competent authorities set out in Annex 2103.6 at the time that it gives notice under Article 1119 (Notice of Intent to Submit a Claim to Arbitration).

[45] ECT Article 21(5)(b)(ii).

authorities beyond a six-month period following referral by the investor or host state. Thus the governmental "meet and confer" process takes on the nature of a conciliation stage of sorts, followed by binding arbitration under the dispute resolution provisions of Article 26. The competent authorities (at least those of the investor's state) can be expected to balk at arbitration only if the relevant measures are intended to operate *de facto* as takings rather than legitimate revenue gathering.

5. A TALE OF TWO CASES: *OCCIDENTAL* AND *ENCANA*

10-44 In his intricate novel *A Tale of Two Cities*, Charles Dickens addresses themes related to love, justice and sacrifice during the French Revolution. A dissolute and habitually drunk English barrister voluntarily mounts the guillotine in Paris to save his romantic rival, a French aristocrat wrongly condemned for crimes committed by his cruel uncle. In so doing, the drunkard finds redemption through a noble act far better than he had imagined himself capable.

10-45 Tax arbitration has none of the passion of the Dickens novel. However, it does present stark contrasts of a different kind. Slight drafting differences from one treaty to another yield dramatically different levels of investor protection.

10-46 Perhaps the most striking illustration can be found in the different treatment of Ecuador's refusal to refund value added tax for purchases made by two foreign oil companies, one American and the other Canadian. The *Occidental*[46] and *Encana* [47] decisions were rendered slightly more than eighteen (18) months apart, in July 2004 and February 2006, respectively. Each addressed an oil company's entitlement to value added tax (VAT) refunds on goods and services in Ecuador.[48] Each related to a "participation contract" for oil and gas exploration, whereby the foreign company bore all risk and expenses in return for a share in the production at the contract area. Each contract calculated the amount due the company as percentages of the oil extracted based on similar factors.

[46] *Occidental Exploration and Production Company v. Ecuador*, 1 July 2004. Charles Brower, Francisco Orrego Vicuña & Patrick Barrera Sweeney. UNCITRAL arbitration, with LCIA serving as Registrar. Susan Franck, Note in 99 *Am. J. Int'l L.* (2005) 675.

[47] *Encana v. Republic of Ecuador*, 6 February 2006. James Crawford and Christopher Thomas in the majority, with Horacio Grigera Naón issuing a Partial Dissenting Opinion on expropriation, reprinted 45 ILM 895 (2006) with comment by Devashish Krishan. UNCITRAL arbitration, with LCIA serving as Registrar.

[48] Taxes were imposed on local purchases and services, as well as imports of goods.

10-47 Here the similarities end. In *Occidental* (which arose under Ecuador's BIT with the U.S.) the investor won a refund. In *Encana* (brought under Ecuador's BIT with Canada) the investor lost. The cases underscore the significance of subtle treaty wording, as we shall see in the following discussion.[49]

5.1. Occidental

(a) The Award

10-48 The dispute between Occidental and Ecuador arose under the 1993 Bilateral Investment Treaty between the U.S. and Ecuador, with respect whether Occidental was entitled to obtain VAT refunds on payments made for goods and services purchased in connection with the production and export of oil under the parties' Participation Contract. Initially, Ecuador had refunded the VAT, but later changed position. Occidental alleged that the actions of the Ecuadorian revenue service amounted to breaches of Article II of the BIT which prohibits discrimination and mandates "fair and equitable" treatment.

10-49 The contractual aspect of the *Occidental* dispute implicated the question of whether or not the formula for determining the oil company's participation (referred to as "Factor X"[50]) implicitly took into account VAT reimbursement.

[49] *Occidental* and *Encana* are only two among a number of investment cases that implicate tax measures. See e.g., *Marvin Roy Feldman Karpa v. United Mexican States*, ICSID case no ARB(AF)/99/1; *Award and Dissenting Opinion of December 16, 2002,* published in 42 ILM 625 (2003), finding Mexico liability for discriminatory tax under NAFTA, which in Section 2803(4) says that non-discrimination provisions of Article 1102 shall apply to tax measures. It is reported that the tax filter was in fact applied in this case, allowing two of the three expropriation claims to pass through. See also *Enron Corporation and Ponderosa Assets, L.P. v. The Argentine Republic*, ICSID case no. ARB/01/3; Decision on Jurisdiction of January 14, 2004, published in stamp duty issue was settled between the parties. See also *El Paso Energy International Company v. Argentine Republic*, ICSID case no. ARB/03/15; Decision on Jurisdiction of April 27, 2006; and *Duke Energy International Peru Investments No. 1, Ltd. v. Peru*, ICSID case no. ARB/03/28; Decision on Jurisdiction of February 1, 2006. One of the most well-known cases brought under the ECT to date (Yukos/Menatap) involves taxation. See *Hulley Enterprises Limited* (Cyprus) v. *Russian Federation* (PCA case no. AA 226), *Yukos Universal Limited* (Isle of Man) v. *Russian Federation* (PCA case no. AA 227); *Veteran Petroleum Limited* (Cyprus) v. *Russian Federation* (PCA case no. AA 228).

[50] The terms of "Factor X" contained in Participation Contract Article 8.1 (whose subheading was titled "Calculating Contractor Participation") apparently contain no references to cost elements or value added taxes, but simply allocate production volumes between Ecuador and Occidental,

In other words, did the contract fix the oil company's revenue (calculated according to Factor X) at a level higher than it would have been otherwise, so that the company would make enough money to offset the payment of value added tax? Was the revenue participation a "back door" form of VAT reimbursement?

10-50 The arbitral tribunal answered that question in the negative, and found that Ecuador's denial of VAT refunds breached the treaty's non-discrimination provision and its duty of "fair and equitable" treatment. Consequently, Ecuador was ordered to reimburse the VAT in an amount of $71 million plus interest.

10-51 To get to this point, however, the tribunal had to decide a preliminary jurisdictional matter related to Article 10(2) of the US-Ecuador BIT, which applies the treaty to tax matters but only with respect to several limited provisions. One was expropriation.[51] However, the tribunal found no evidence of direct or indirect expropriation, and held that claim inadmissible.[52]

10-52 Another portion of Article 10(2) said that the treaty would apply to tax matters with respect to "the observance and enforcement of terms of an investment agreement or authorization."[53] The arbitrators found that the Participation Contract between the host state and the investor was just such an investment agreement, and the Factor X dispute related to that agreement. Consequently, the tribunal confirmed its jurisdiction.[54]

10-53 An additional consideration was found in the introductory provision in Article 10(1) which stated that with respect to its tax policies, each country should "strive to accord fairness and equity" in the treatment of investments by the other's nationals. Finding that this provision was "not devoid of legal significance" the arbitrators determined that its obligations were not dissimilar to the duties of "fair and equitable" treatment in treaty Article II.[55] The tribunal read this language as imposing an obligation of fairness and equity with respect

with the state participation in subheading 8.5 calculated simply as the difference between the number 100 and Occidental's participation percentage.

51 Article 10(2)(a).

52 Occidental Award of 1 July 2004, at para 92.

53 Article 10(2)(c). This provision contained its own exception for claims subject to dispute settlement procedures in a double tax treaty, or when such settlement provisions do not resolve the matter in a reasonable time. A third prong of that article (Article 10(2)(b) applied the BIT to tax matters with respect to "transfers".

54 Occidental Award of 1 July 2004, at para 7.

55 Occidental Award of 1 July 2004, at para 70.

to the three categories of matters contained in Article 10, including observance of an investment agreement.

10-54 Ultimately, the arbitrators found that the failure to refund the VAT was due not to any deliberate action, but from the arbitrariness of what they called "an overall rather incoherent tax structure".[56] Consequently, Ecuador was held to have breached its obligations to guarantee both national treatment and "fair and equitable" treatment under Article II of the treaty.

10-55 This did not end the story, however. Ecuador challenged the award in London (the arbitral seat) under the English Arbitration Act, alleging that the arbitrators exceeded their powers by considering the VAT matter. As discussed below, the English courts supported both the arbitrators' power in the particular case to consider tax matters and the judiciary's general exercise of supervisory jurisdiction over investment arbitration.

(b) The English Court Action

10-56 The 1996 English Arbitration Act contains at least two provisions permitting courts to address what might be called excess of authority (*excès de pouvoir*) in the broad sense. The first permits challenge as to the "substantive jurisdiction" of the award.[57] The second allows challenge for "serious irregularity" which is defined to include a tribunal "exceeding its powers" in some way not covered by the provision on substantive jurisdiction, but which causes "substantial injustice".[58]

10-57 Ecuador attacked the award in favour of Occidental on both grounds. Each was rejected.[59] Following some of the same lines of argument as the arbitral tribunal, the court determined that the dispute indeed fell within the terms of Article 10(2)(c) of the treaty as it related to observance and enforcement of an investment agreement. The Participation Agreement was such an agreement, and the dispute over the meaning of "Factor X" clearly related to that agreement.

56 Occidental Award of 1 July 2004, at para 200.
57 1996 Arbitration Act, § 67 (1).
58 1996 Arbitration Act, § 68 (2)(b).
59 *Republic of Ecuador v. Occidental Exploration and Production Company* (OEPC), [2006] 1 Lloyd's Rep. 773, [2006] EWHC 345, 2006 WL 690585 (QBD (Comm Ct), decided 2 March 2006).

10-58 Although the investor's claim was based on the treaty rather than a particular investment agreement, this did not prevent the tribunal from possessing jurisdiction by virtue of the treaty provisions related to observance of investment agreements.[60] The decision was upheld by the Court of Appeal in a carefully reasoned opinion that looked to the Vienna Convention on the Law of Treaties to provide guidance in the construction of the bilateral investment treaty between Ecuador and the U.S..[61]

10-59 Prior to addressing the jurisdictional challenge, the High Court also had to examine whether the challenge was "non-justiciable" because it pertained to a treaty between two sovereigns.[62] Although acknowledging that the treaty obligations derived from public international law, the court noted that the performance of treaty-derived rights (i.e., the arbitration itself) had been made subject to the municipal law of England, permitting English courts to hear challenge to an award.[63]

10-60 It is important to keep in mind that the decision on "justiciability" does not affect arbitrability either way. The award addressing the VAT questions would have remained valid even if the court had found that the BIT questions were *not* justiciable. What would have changed was not the result of the arbitration, but simply the judicial power to look at claims of excess of arbitral jurisdiction under the English Arbitration Act.

60 *Ibid.*, para 113.

61 *Republic of Ecuador v. Occidental Exploration & Production Company*, [2007] EWCA Civ 656 (4 July 2007). Article 31 of the Vienna Convention takes into account factors such as the object and purpose of the treaty, while Article 32 refers to "supplementary means of interpretation" such as preparatory work and circumstances of conclusion.

62 Apparently the challenge to justiciability was brought with respect to the challenge under Section 67 of the 1996 Arbitration Act, but not the challenge under Section 68.

63 See decision of Justice Aikens in *Republic of Ecuador v. Occidental Exploration and Production Company* (OEPC) [2005] 2 Lloyd's Rep 240, [2005] EWHC 774 (Comm. Ct.), 2005 WL 1104120 (29 April 2005), upheld by the Court of Appeal on 9 September 2005, [2005] EWCA Civ 111.

5.2. Encana

(a) The Majority Award

10-61 The relevant jurisdictional limits relevant to *Encana* can be found in Article 12 of the Canada-Ecuador BIT, which diverges from the analogous provisions of the US-Ecuador BIT in both form and substance.[64] The opening subsection of Article 12 of the Canadian treaty states that "[e]xcept as set out in this Article, nothing in this Agreement shall apply to taxation measures." The treaty begins with a negative [is there a word missing here? "definition" or "approach" or "wording" possibly?] but quickly proceeds to exceptions (including rules for expropriation[65] and breach of specific contracts with the central government[66]) as to which claims may be brought with respect to tax measures.

10-62 By contrast, the American convention begins with an affirmation that "the treaty shall apply to matters of taxation" but only with respect to certain delineated measures that establish protective hedges around the general rule.

10-63 Most significant, however, was the absence of any Canadian equivalent to Article 10(1) in the U.S. treaty, which states that the host state will "strive to accord fairness and equity in the treatment of investment of nationals and companies of the other Party." The Canada treaty did contain a provision stating that the expropriation provisions (requiring prompt, adequate and effective compensation pursuant to Article 8) would apply to taxation measures.[67] Otherwise, the only tax-related right given to the investor derived from fiscal measures that resulted in the breach of an agreement with the host state "central government authorities" in which event the measures would be considered a claim for treaty violation.

[64] In addition, Article 13(3)(c) of the Canada-Ecuador BIT provides that an investor may submit a matter to arbitration only "if the matters involves taxation, the conditions specified in paragraph 5 of Article 12 have been fulfilled." Article 12(5) states that the tax authorities of the contracting states will be given six months to reach a joint determination that a fiscal measure does not contravene an investment agreement with the central government or does not constitute an expropriation.

[65] Canada-Ecuador BIT, Article 8.

[66] Canada-Ecuador BIT, Article13(3).

[67] The "tax filter" is applicable to expropriation claims, giving the two fiscal authorities a six-month window to impose a joint veto by determining that a tax measure does not constitute an expropriation. See Canada-Ecuador BIT, Article12(4).

10-64 Under the facts of the case, the majority of the tribunal found that failure to provide a VAT refund did not constitute a breach of any agreement between the oil company and the government of Ecuador. Moreover, no evidence persuaded the tribunal majority that the failure to give a rebate constituted a *de facto* expropriation.[68] Unlike the arbitrators in *Occidental*, the *Encana* tribunal was not able to rely on any provision concerning fair and equitable treatment in fiscal matters.[69]

(b) The Dissent: Expropriating Investment Returns

10-65 A partial dissent in *Encana* disagreed with the majority's view of the benefits accorded under the investment treaty. According to the highly fact-specific dissent, the Ecuadorian Tax Court and the Ecuadorian Congress interpreted the relevant portions of the national tax statute in a fashion that discriminated against the oil and gas sectors of the economy and resulted in deprivation of property in violation of Article 8 of the investment treaty.

10-66 The dissent raised an interesting distinction between investment returns as contrasted with the investment itself, looking to the fruit rather than the tree. While admitting that the Ecuador's behaviour did not give rise to indirect expropriation of the investment itself, the dissent noted that the revenue seemed to have been "negatively affected" and in essence expropriated.

6. Abusive Taxes

6.1. Treating Like Taxpayers in Like Manner

10-67 Given the ubiquity and the diversity of modern tax systems, the passage of time can be expected to generate a rich tapestry of cases that address the interaction of investment treaties and fiscal measures. Any laundry list of issues to watch would likely be led by the *quaere*, "What makes tax abusive?"

[68] As noted below, the dissent found that an expropriation had in fact occurred "to the extent that [investment] returns have been negatively affected as a consequence of the denial of VAT refunds."

[69] Article 10(1) of the U.S.-Ecuador treaty had required the host state to "strive to accord fairness and equity in the treatment of investment of nationals and companies of the other Party."

10-68 The lion's share of *bona fide* investor claims can be expected to rely on some element of abuse or arbitrariness by the fiscal authorities. A particular tax measure will be said to violate host state duties to the investor (whether phrased as expropriation, discrimination or unfair treatment) in function of how other similarly situated taxpayers were treated.

10-69 In today's world, few fiscal measures reveal themselves as confiscatory on their face. Tax laws do not normally aim at only one taxpayer or impose foreigners at rates of 100% on profits or asset value. Greater sophistication is usually shown in the fiscal measures that render business operation futile or property ownership untenable. For example, gross revenue might be taxed without adequate deduction for cost of goods sold or reasonable business expenses. Or, long-term capitalisation might be required for items whose useful life spanned much shorter accounting periods.[70]

10-70 In this context, one might return to the quotation of Justice Holmes that served as epigraph to this essay: taxes are what we pay for civilized society.[71] The statement appeared in a case decided at a time when the Philippine islands were an American colony. A local tax had been levied on fire insurance premiums paid by a Spanish tobacco company to English and French insurers.

10-71 The majority opinion by Chief Justice Taft held the taxes to be invalid. "[A]s a state may not deprive a person of his liberty without due process of law," reasoned Taft, "it may not compel any one within its jurisdiction to pay tribute to it for contracts or money paid to secure the benefit of contracts made and to be performed outside of the state."[72]

10-72 Justice Holmes disagreed in a dissent that bears closer scrutiny. "It is true," wrote Holmes, "that every exaction of money for an act is a discouragement to the extent of the payment required."[73] He continued, however, by noting that "there may be a difficulty in deciding whether an imposition is a tax or a

[70] In theory, any expense can be capitalised if the accounting interval is short enough. A lunch could be capitalised if one hour were taken as the relevant period. In most tax administration today, an annual cycle would be considered normal.

[71] *Compañía General de Tabaco de Filipinas v Collector of Internal Revenue*, 275 U.S. 87, at 100 (1927).

[72] 275 U.S. 87, at 95.

[73] It was in this context that Holmes characterized taxes as "what we pay for civilized society, including the chance to insure."

penalty." While noting that the intent to prohibit activity may be plainly expressed, Holmes concluded that sometimes a tax may be "shown to be a penalty by its excess in amount over the tax in similar cases."[74]

10-73 This last expression, the "excess in amount over the tax in similar cases," lies at the heart of distinctions between normal and abusive taxes. The test looks not only to the way the fiscal legislation is drafted, but also to the fashion in which the measures are implemented, comparing how taxpayers are treated when in similar circumstances. While not likely to address all situations of abusive taxation, the "similar cases" test serves as a useful starting point for identifying taxes intended to expropriate assets rather than raise revenue.

10-74 For example, taxes imposed only on people of a particular religion or race would normally be suspect, even if levied at very low rates. However, the same tax (or one at a much higher rate) would pass muster if all creeds and colours were required to pay equally.75

10-75 Not every discriminatory tax will lack legitimacy, however. For administrative convenience, most countries impose special fiscal burdens on non-resident aliens and foreign corporations. As mentioned earlier, these include tax on gross receipts (rather than net income) for investment returns such as dividends, interest and royalties received by non-resident aliens, as well as taxes on the gross amount received from real property gains and taxes on branches of foreign corporations that are not imposed on domestic entities.[76]

[74] *Ibid.*, at 100-101. With respect to the specific tax at issue Holmes continues,

> But here an act was done in the Islands that was intended by the plaintiff to be and was an essential step towards the insurance, and, if that is not enough, the government of the Islands was protecting the property at the very moment in respect of which it levied the tax.

[75] See generally, Richard Epstein, *Takings* (1985), at chapter 18 (pages 283-305). Professor Epstein distinguishes various forms of taxation (such as special assessments, progressive income taxes and estate/gift taxation), with particular attention to proposals for the so-called "flat tax" discussed in the U.S. from time to time.

[76] On the branch profits tax, see U.S. International Revenue Code § 884, which is so patently aimed at foreigners that it can trigger application of anti-discrimination prohibitions of income tax treaties.

6.2. Analogies from Non-Fiscal Contexts

10-76 Determining when tax constitutes expropriation for treaty purposes may in some instances be furthered by reference to the intellectual and legal tools that address related questions in other contexts. For example, governmental measures that impair an investor's enjoyment of property have given rise to host state liability under the Energy Charter Treaty.[77]

10-77 In the U.S. "takings" have been found to occur when government regulations have substantial negative economic effect on private interests.[78] Although the taxing power is commonly understood to lie outside the scope of the Fifth Amendment taking clause,[79] the law of regulatory takings might, nevertheless, provide elements of an analytic framework to explore what makes fiscal measures abusive.

10-78 When American courts address the matter of regulatory takings, they ask what governmental actions might be the functional equivalent of a traditional government ouster of owners from their property.[80] A taking occurs if governmental regulation goes too far. The tricky part of the exercise is to determine how far is "too far".

77 For a non-tax analogy under the ECT Treaty, see *Nykomb Synergetics Technology Holding AB v. Latvia* (Stockholm Chamber of Commerce, 16 December 2003), discussed in Kaj Hobér, *Energy Investment Arbitration in Eastern Europe* (2007) at chapter 5. With the alleged complicity from the central government, the Latvian national electricity grid had refused to pay a Swedish company the tariff provided in a contract for construction of co-generation facilities producing electric power from natural gas. Finding discrimination (based on higher multipliers applied to another company) the tribunal also raised the prospect that the investor suffered "impairment" in its use and enjoyment of the property through unreasonable or discriminatory measures contrary to treaty Article 10.

78 For example, United States Constitution Article V provides that "private property [shall not] be taken for public use without just compensation".

79 In *Penn Central Transportation Company v. City of New York*, 438 U.S. 104, the U.S. Supreme Court observed

> that government may execute laws or programs that adversely affect recognized economic values. Exercises of the taxing power are one obvious example

at 124. See also Abraham Bell & Gideon Parchomovsky, "Taking Reassessed", 87 *Va. L. Rev.* (2001) 277 at 284, suggesting that "when the government 'takes' through taxes, or reduces value by exercise of its police powers, it need not compensate."

80 *Lingle v. Chevron U.S.A. Inc.*, 544 U.S. 528 (2005).

10-79 Few "bright line" rules exist in this connection. However, the U.S. Supreme Court has identified several factors of particular significance, including economic impact of a regulation on the owner; the extent to which a regulation interferes with investment related expectations; and the character of the government action.[81] Moreover, legitimate takings must be for public use, a notion now defined (rightly or wrongly) so broadly as to include almost any taking that is "rationally related to a conceivable public purpose"[82]

7. CONCLUSION

10-80 The arbitrability of tax disputes presents itself with particular acuity in the hierarchy of rules contained in investment treaties, which attempt to balance competing interests of the foreign investor and the host state. Allowing routine tax measures to be translated into relief under an investment convention might open the door for misuse of the treaty's investor protection regime. However, there can be little justification to deny investors all direct recourse against the host state when discrimination has been dressed in fiscal garb.

10-81 In considering the interaction between taxation and investment protection regimes, one may be forgiven for recalling the line attributed to Jean-Baptiste Colbert, proposing that the art of taxation consists in "so plucking the goose as to obtain the largest amount of feathers with the smallest amount of hissing."[83]

[81] *Penn Central Transportation Company v. City of New York* 438 U.S. 104 (1978). Pursuant to New York City's Landmarks Preservation Law had designated the Grand Central Terminal (owned by the Penn Central) as a landmark, thus interfering with Penn Central's plan to have a lessee construct a multi-storey office building over the Terminal. Penn Central argued that its property had been taken without just compensation. The court held that a taking did *not* occur in this case. Even though the owner had been denied the right to exploit the airspace, the law did not prevent him from realizing a reasonable rate of return on the investment.

[82] *Kelo v. City of New London*, 545 U.S. 469 (2005), where a Connecticut municipality approved a development plan intended to revitalize an economically distressed portion of the city. Some of the property needed for the project was to be acquired through the use of eminent domain. Part of the expropriated property was to be transferred to the pharmaceutical Company Pfizer to build a research facility. A split court held that "economic development takings" remain constitutional.

[83] In 17th century France, of course, taxation implicated a tangle of *ad hoc* mechanisms to finance royal life style, rather than a systematic instrument of economic or social policy. See André Meurrisse, *Histoire de l'impôt* (1978) at 83-90, recounting more than a century of tax escapades ultimately contributing to the French revolution of 1789. Nevertheless, many aspects of taxation continue from one century to another, including the perennial need for more money in wartime. Shortly after Colbert's death in the late 17th century, French aggression in the German Palatine created a need for more creative revenue-raising measures, and also triggered a half-century of

Among the constants in taxation through the ages, few have been more persistent than the need to distinguish taxes "*à la Colbert*" (looking simply to seize the most money with the least fuss) from the more legitimate form of revenue-raising that enables or shapes desirable social and economic behaviour.[84] Drawing that line in concrete cross-border investment disputes will challenge arbitrators for years to come.

armed conflict against the so-called Grand Alliance, a prototype European Union, minus France of course.

84 For an in-depth treatment of conduct-shaping taxation, see Xavier Oberson, *Les Taxes d'Orientation* (1991).

Alexis Mourre[*]

CHAPTER 11

ARBITRATION AND CRIMINAL LAW: JURISDICTION, ARBITRABILITY AND DUTIES OF THE ARBITRAL TRIBUNAL

1. INTRODUCTION

11-1 Arbitration and criminal law appear to live on two distant planets, and their paths do not seem to ever have to cross each other. Arbitration is based upon private autonomy, and its purpose is to adjudicate private disputes. Criminal law endeavours to restrict private autonomy for the sake of the general interest. Criminal law is at the core of the State's mandatory laws, while arbitration is autonomous from states. Yet, because criminal law rules might have an impact on both the arbitral proceedings and the solution of the dispute, these two disciplines have more points of connection than could be suspected from the outset.

11-2 The international business legal environment is nowadays characterised by a double trend. On one side, globalisation and the creation of a true world marketplace have sidelined national states and undermined their traditional role as the ultimate source of legality. In countries like France or Germany, ever since the time of Napoleon III and Bismarck, well before the Welfare State was invented, the State was perceived as having unlimited resources and unrestricted

[*] Founding Partner of "*Castaldi Mourre & Partners*", Paris, France. Member of the Paris Bar as well as of the London Law Society (Foreign Lawyer).
This article is an extension of the presentation made by the author at the Hellenic Arbitration Initiative colloquium on Arbitrability held in Athens, 23 September 2005. This paper was first published in 22 (1) *Arb. Int'l* (2006) 95. This article does not deal with issues of procedural fraud and arbitrators' corruption, nor does it address the general topic of challenges against awards for contradiction with public policy. In respect to procedural fraud, see S. Gee, "The Autonomy of Arbitrators, and Fraud Unravels All", *Arb. Int'l* (2006) 337.

L Mistelis & S Brekoulakis (eds), Arbitrability: International & Comparative Perspectives, 207-239

power. This is no longer true in today's economy. Transnational law has become a reality. Arbitration, the autonomy of which from national jurisdictions is more and more widely recognised, has emerged as the normal way to settle international business disputes. With the growing flow of state contracts, state arbitrations and investment arbitrations, states have become subject to international liability, just like private parties.

11-3 On the other side, however, mandatory rules tend to proliferate, particularly in the field of economic and business law. The causes of this trend are various. In Europe, the tendency to over-regulate is one of them. Of no less relevance, the growing penalisation of business law is another. A recent French statute provides a good example of such tendency. On 2 August 2005, the French Parliament adopted rules whose purpose of which is to regulate the relationship between product manufacturers and distributors.[1] Such rules provide that any sales relation between suppliers of consumer goods and distribution chains has to be based upon a written contract compliant to certain precise conditions of validity.[2] Non-compliance with such conditions is a criminal offence, which may be punished by a fine.[3] One might wonder why such sanctions are needed. Surely, civil liability, or maybe antitrust rules, would have been sufficient to prevent abusive behaviour. Yet, French law-makers felt that private mechanisms of regulation were not sufficient, and that criminal sanctions were necessary to ensure the correct application of the rule. Endless examples of that kind could be given, in the fields of company law,[4] commercial law,[5] financial law,[6] etc. In fact, most of the time, penalising business behaviour does not result in making law enforcement more effective. However, in a world in which legislators often have

---

1 Act of 2 August 2005 No. 882.

2 Article L. 441-7, paragraph 1, of the French Commercial Code, as amended by Act of 2 August 2005, No. 882.

3 Fines up to 75,000 € (article L. 441-7, II, of the French Commercial Code, as amended by Act of 2 August 2005, No. 882).

4 According to Article L. 245-3 of the French Commercial code Commercial Code, the directors of a company can be punished by imprisonment up to six months and a fine of 6,000 € if the company does not comply with regulations applicable to preferred shares. Article L. 245-9 of the same code provides for fines up to 9,000 € in case of a violation of regulations applicable to the issuance of bonds, etc… Such fines have a criminal nature and are pronounced by criminal courts.

5 For example: Article L. 122-2 of the French Commercial Code punishes by an up to six months imprisonment and a 3,750 € fine a foreigner who enters into a commercial profession without having obtained an administrative permit to that effect. Article L. 442-2 of the French Commercial Code provides that the fact of reselling a product or service at loss may be punished by a fine of up to 75,000 €.

6 Articles L. 571-1 and seq. of the French Monetary and Financial Code.

a sense of impotence, criminal law tends to become the ultimate medicine to impose rules where it is feared that the voice of the law would otherwise not be heard.

11-4 So, quite paradoxically, the state crisis comes along with increased state restrictions to party autonomy. Arbitration stands in the midst of that contradiction, because on the one side it is a private and truly international way of solving disputes, but on the other it exercises a function which is still perceived to be part of state monopoly, i.e., justice. Arbitrators are not judges of the State, but they are allowed to perform the same activity as state judges. How should they then react when a criminal law rule is applicable? How should they behave when faced with an illicit behaviour? With a criminal inquiry? What should they do if they suspect that a fraud has been committed by one of the parties? That a contract has been signed because of influence peddling? What should they do if they suspect that a claim hides a money laundering operation? Finally, how should they react if criminal law is used to disrupt the arbitration?

11-5 The answer to these questions should not be one of confrontation. In many jurisdictions, where the State's role is still pervasive, international arbitrators are too often perceived as the servants of selfish individual interests, and hence, as a potential instrument for fraud. Such a perception entails a tight control of arbitrators by local courts, in particular when mandatory rules have to be applied. Ultimately, arbitrators tend to be perceived as part of each jurisdiction's national judicial structure, and their duties assimilated to those of national judges. Defiance towards the arbitrators' capability to take the general interest into account leads to the discussion of the well established and widely recognised principle of arbitrability of disputes involving public policy issues, and to jeopardise the main advantage that parties seek in adopting arbitration, i.e., the finality of the award.

11-6 We believe, on the contrary, that international arbitrators are perfectly suited to take the general interests of the forum into due consideration. This is also true regarding criminal law, because, as we shall see, the rules which aim at fighting illicit behaviours in international trade are becoming increasingly international, and international arbitrators have a natural vocation to take them into consideration. The answer to the question of ethics in international arbitration does not therefore lie in the integration of arbitral tribunals into each state's own jurisdictional system, which would in fact kill the specificity of arbitration and destroy its advantages both for the parties and for international trade, but in a balanced and reasonable cooperation between States and international arbitral justice. Arbitrators are naturally sensitive to the need for morality in international business. States should, on their side, acknowledge the autonomy of arbitration and the difference between arbitrators and judges. In a nutshell, there is no contradiction between the autonomy of arbitration and the need to fight crime in international trade: this is because arbitrators are the natural judges of international trade, and they are the natural guardians of ethics and good morals in international commerce. They may even be better placed than national judges to combat international fraud.

11-7 Criminal law has long been perceived as raising an issue of jurisdiction of the Arbitral Tribunal. This is no longer true (**2**). Arbitrators, however, may still face difficult questions when dealing with allegations of fraud (**3**), and need to find the proper balance between the private nature of their mission (**4**) and the necessary protection of ethics and good morals in international trade (**5**).

2. Issues of Jurisdiction and Arbitrability

2.1. Severability Set Aside?

11-8 The first issue to which an arbitrator may be confronted when faced with an allegation of fraud or illegality is whether, in spite of the principle of severability of the arbitration agreement,[7] said fraud voids the contract in its entirety, including the arbitration agreement. In his famous award in the ICC case 1110 of 1963,[8] Judge Lagergren seemed to answer that question in the affirmative:

> …under French law the arbitrators are not merely prevented from entertaining cases reserved for the ordinary courts, but they will also, in a general manner, like the courts, not lend their aid to enforce contracts based on grave offence to *bono mores*, whether committed in France or abroad. In view of these considerations and with regard to the nature of the adventure in which the parties to this dispute have engaged, French law cannot admit this case to be settled by arbitration, regardless of whether the adventure was located in France or elsewhere.

---

7 On that principle, see *inter alia* P. Mayer, "The Limits of Severability of the Arbitration Clause", 9 *ICCA Congress Series* 261.

8 3 *Arb. Int'l* (1994) 282, and the article of J.G Wetter, "The Authentic Text and True Meaning of Judge Gunner Lagergren's 1963 Award in ICC case No. 1110", *Arb. Int'l* (1994) 227.

Such *dictum* was generally understood as setting a principle of the non-arbitrability of fraud allegations.[9] However, it is arguable that what Judge Lagergren really decided was not, in fact, that allegations of fraud would not be arbitrable in the sense that the arbitration agreement would not be valid and the issue reserved to the jurisdictions of the State, but that such allegations are not capable to be submitted to *any* judge, be it an arbitrator or a state judge, because fraud makes the contract inexistent in the eyes of the law. In other words, the claims would be inadmissible in the merits, rather than non-arbitrable.[10] In this regard, it should be noted that the Lagergren award went deep into substantive issues in order to determine that the contract was tainted by fraud. If that interpretation of the Lagergren award is correct, unlike a situation of non-arbitrability, the parties should also have been barred from presenting the same claims before a state court. Besides, the idea that fraud renders any claim based on an illicit contract inadmissible (rather than non-arbitrable) is not an isolated position in arbitral case law.[11] The consequences of the qualification of the decision as one of inadmissibility rather than non-arbitrability are of course important as far as recourses against the award are concerned. As a matter of fact, arbitral tribunal's decisions on arbitrability are likely to be controlled in case of an action to set aside the award, which is not the case for a decision on admissibility.

---

9 A. Sayed, *Corruption in International Trade and Commercial Arbitration*, (Kluwer 2004) at 65 seq.; amongst the vast literature on corruption and fraud in international arbitration, see also *Arbitration, Money Laundering, Corruption and Fraud* (ICC Publishing 2003); "Bribery of Foreign Public Officials in International Business Transactions", *International Business Law Journal*, Special Issue (Jan 1999).

10 In French law, the qualification would be that of an *irrecevabilité de fond* rather that one of *inarbitrabilité*. For a study of the difference between inadmissibility and lack of jurisdiction, see G. Block, *Les fins de non-recevoir en procédure civile* (Bruylant 2002). Block defines the inadmissibility as a defence which prevents a judge who has jurisdiction from deciding the merits. For an award having dismissed an allegation of non-arbitrability based on fraud, see the ICC Award 6401, 7(1) Mealey's IAR (1992). See also, on the difference between jurisdiction and admissibility, J. Paulsson, "Jurisdiction and admissibility", in *Global Reflections on International Law, Commerce and Dispute Resolution, Liber Amicorum in honour of Robert Briner* (ICC Publishing 2005) at 601.

11 See e.g., ICC Award 3913:

> the agreement [...] is based on an illicit consideration, and [...] it is for this reason null and void, and therefore it renders the parties ill-founded to claim its enforcement or compensation for damages resulting from its non-enforcement, and even the taking into account, or, as the case may be, the restitution of the funds paid or any advance payments made as part of its performance

1 Collection of ICC Awards 498; Clunet 920 (1984). Only the inadmissibility of the claim can explain that, in case of nullity, a party would be barred from claiming the restitution of amounts paid in compliance with a voided contract.

11-9 The impact of fraud on the validity of the arbitration agreement has been dealt with in the *Westacre* dispute.[12] When reviewing the ICC award having ordered the principal to pay the fees due to the consultant, and faced with the argument made by the principal that the contract's purpose was bribery, the English Court had to address an argument of Westacre, according to which, by seeking the enforcement of the award, it was not enforcing an allegedly illegal contract, but the separate arbitration agreement. The Court, in order to deal with that issue, made a distinction based on the degree of illegality involved:

> it would therefore seem in principle that if the underlying contract were illegal and void at common law the question whether an arbitration agreement ancillary to it was also impeached by the illegality would have to be answered by reference to the policy of the Court in relation to the particular nature of the illegality involved. […] No doubt, if it were proved that the underlying contract was, in spite of all outward appearances, one involving drug trafficking, the alleged offensiveness of the transaction would be such as to outweigh any countervailing consideration. Where, however, the degree of offensiveness is far down the scale as in the present case, I see no reason why the balance of policy should be against enforcement.[13]

The decision has been confirmed by the Court of Appeal,[14] and departs from the earlier *Soleimany* decision.[15] According to the court's reasoning in *Westacre*, the arbitrability of the dispute would depend on a subjective assessment of the degree of illegality involved. But in order to decide whether the fraud is more or less up or down in the scale of illegality, the arbitrator necessarily needs to have jurisdiction to assess the merits, which implies a valid arbitration agreement.[16] It is therefore preferable to apply the principle of severability strictly, and to adopt

---

12 [1998] 2 Lloyd's Rep. 111. See also: A. Sheppard, "Case Comment: Westacre Investments Inc. v. Jugoimport-Spdr Holding Co. Ltd [1998] 3 W.L.R.", *Int'l ALR* (1998) 54; S. Wade, "Westacre v. Soleimany: What policy? Which public?" *Int'l ALR* (1999) 97.

13 [1998] 2 Lloyd's Rep. 111.

14 CA, Civil Division, *Westacre v. Jugoimport* [1999] 3 All ER 864.

15 *Soleimany v. Soleimany* [1998] 3 W.L.R. 811. English courts also held that an arbitration agreement in a gaming contract would be void: *Harbour Assurance Co (UK) v. Kansa General International* [1993] QB 701, quoted by S. Gee, *supra* note 1 at 339.

16 See, in a case in which corruption was alleged, the ICC Awards No. 6474, YBCA 279 (2000), and No. 8891, Clunet 1076 (2000).

an approach according to which claims based on fraud, although they may not be admissible, and, hence, not decided on the merits, are nevertheless arbitrable.[17]

11-10 Such was the solution adopted by the House of Lords in *Fiona Trust*.[18] The House of Lords recognised that arbitrators are fully able to determine their own jurisdiction, regardless of the basis on which the arbitration is challenged. The case was concerned with an agreement which had allegedly been induced by bribery. The appellants alleged that the contract could therefore be rescinded, and that this included the arbitration agreement providing for arbitration in London. The Lords recognised that not even an allegation of bribery can undermine the arbitration agreement, and that arbitral tribunals are as able as national courts to determine whether there was bribery and what the effect of that bribery is on the main contract.[19]

11-11 In a 4 October 2006 award,[20] an ICSID tribunal held that the claims of an investor who had paid a bribe to the president of the host country were inadmissible. After having said that "the tribunal is aware of the fact that, on the occasion of visits to heads of state, gifts are often exchanged as a matter of protocol". Yet,

> under [the] circumstances, [...] the tribunal has no doubt that the concealed payments [...] could not be considered as a personal donation for public purposes. Those payments were made not only to obtain an audience with president Moi (as submitted by the Claimant), but above all to obtain during that audience the agreement of the president on the contemplated investment. The tribunal considers that those payments must be regarded as a bribe.

The tribunal followed by holding that:

---

17 In *Commercial Union v. Lines*, the U.S. Second Circuit seemed to admit that, unless the arbitration agreement itself was obtained by fraud, illegality does not deprive the tribunal of its jurisdiction: 378 F.3d 204 (2d Cir. 2004), quoted by S. Gee, *supra* note 1 at 340.

18 *Premium Nafta Products Limited (20th Defendant) and others v. Fili Shipping Company Limited (14th Claimant) and others* [2007] UKHL 40.

19 The House of Lords upheld a decision by the Court of appeal overturning a High court decision ([2006] EWCH 2583), where Justice Morison had said:

> it is not simply the fact that the matrix contract has been rescinded: it is the basis on which that has been done. I fail to see how one can distinguish between the unenforceability of the matrix contract without necessarily impugning the validity of the arbitration clauses.

20 Case ARB/00/07, *World Duty Free v. Republic of Kenya* (Andrew Rogers, V.V. Veeder, arbitrators, G. Guillaume, chair).

> bribery or influence peddling, as well as both active and passive corruption, are sanctioned by criminal law in most, if not all, countries [...]. In order to render more effective this general condemnation, a number of international conventions were concluded during the last decade [...]. In concluding these conventions, states have shown their common will to fight corruption, not only through national legislation, [...] but also through international cooperation. In doing so, states not only reached a new stage in the fight against corruption, but also solidly confirmed their prior condemnation of it [...].

After having made references to state court and to arbitral case law, including the Lagergren award, the tribunal concluded that:

> bribery is contrary to the international public policy of most, if not all, states or, to use another formula, to transnational public policy. Thus, claims based on contracts of corruption or on contracts obtained by corruption cannot be upheld by this arbitral tribunal.

The decision therefore confirms that an allegation of corruption does not void the arbitration agreement. The consequence is rather one of inadmissibility.

11-12 As to the consequences of the avoidance of the contract of the arbitral tribunal's jurisdiction, which jurisdiction was based on an arbitration agreement included in the investment contract, the tribunal noted that:

> no evidence was adduced or argument submitted by either of the parties to the effect that the bribe specifically procured Article 9 of the agreement, containing the parties' agreement to arbitration under the ICSID convention. Accordingly, in accordance with well-established legal principles under English and Kenyan law, the tribunal operates under the assumption that the parties' arbitration agreement remained subsisting valid and effective for the purpose of this proceeding and award.

11-13 The same conclusion should be reached in treaty-based arbitrations. The case would be that the investment contract giving rise to a BIT or ICSID arbitration has been obtained by corrupting the representative of the State or of a public entity.[21] In such cases, the alleged corruption cannot affect the validity of

---

[21] See B. Cremades, "Corruption and Investment Arbitration", in *Global Reflections on International Law, Commerce and Dispute Resolution, Liber Amicorum in honour of Robert Briner* (ICC Publishing 2005), and the cases cited in 213-224.

the Treaty upon which the consent to arbitrate is based, and the consequence will again be inadmissibility of the investor's claims.[22]

11-14 The allegation may also be made that the signature of the BIT agreement itself was obtained by corrupting a representative of the State. The State would then submit that there is no consent to arbitrate, based on Article 50 of the Vienna Convention.[23] In such hypothesis, the jurisdiction to assess the purported corruption would not lie upon the investment tribunal, but upon a state to state arbitration pursuant to Articles 65 and 66 of the Vienna Convention. Meanwhile, the investment arbitration would presumably have to be stayed. Such situation, to our knowledge, never occurred and is probably theoretical.

2.2. The Power of Arbitral Tribunals to Take Criminal Law Rules into Consideration

11-15 From the arbitrator's point of view, a criminal law rule is no more and no less than a mandatory rule. It is, to use a French expression, a "*loi de police*" which institutes a particular non-derogatory prescription or prohibition. The particularity of said rule lies in that the policy it promotes is deemed to be so important to the forum that its infringement is criminally punished, either by way of fines or by imprisonment. The arbitrator has obviously no power to apply such rules in the same way as a criminal judge would, but he can take them into consideration provided they have a reasonable title to be applied to the dispute. Thus, in broad terms, the problem could simply be presented as a question of arbitrability of mandatory provisions of law.

---

22 See B. Cremades, *Ibid.* 214:

> the corrupt investor will be estopped from claiming the benefit of the substantive rights in the BIT. This view is supported by the doctrine of "clean hands" or ex injuria jus non oritur in public international law.

This situation implies, in our view, that the claim is not capable to be judged in the substance. But, in order to assess whether the allegation of corruption is grounded, the arbitrators need to proceed to a detailed instruction of the facts, which imply that the allegedly corrupt investor's offer to arbitrate has been validly accepted. The issue is therefore one of admissibility rather than jurisdiction (*contra*, Cremades, *Ibid.* 215).

23 Article 50 of the Vienna Convention on the Law of Treaties provides that:

> If the expression of a State's consent to be bound by a treaty has been procured through the corruption of its representative directly or indirectly by another negotiating State, the State may invoke such corruption as invalidating its consent to be bound by the treaty.

11-16 We shall not dwell on this question, as it could drive us way out of the boundaries of this presentation. It suffices to say that the arbitrability of rules of public policy is now widely recognised. Depending on jurisdictions, a dispute is deemed to be arbitrable either when the subject matter of the arbitration concerns rights the parties may dispose of (France,[24] Belgium,[25] Italy,[26] Spain,[27] Denmark[28]), or rights or assets of a patrimonial nature (Switzerland,[29] Germany[30]). Beyond these differences, in most jurisdictions, unless there is a special provision to the contrary (such might be the case, for example, when the law applicable to a public tender provides for the exclusive jurisdiction of local courts in case of disputes related to the tender), the existence of a mandatory provision does not make the dispute non-arbitrable. It should be acknowledged, though, that in a small number of countries hostile to arbitration, an allegation of illegality is still perceived to be a cause of non-arbitrability of the dispute.[31]

11-17 The *Labinal* 1993 judgment of the Paris Court of appeal[32] is a good example of the liberal approach adopted in most jurisdictions in respect to the arbitrability of rules of public policy. The dispute related to a joint-venture agreement in which, in spite of the arbitration clause included in the joint-venture, one of the parties sued the others before French municipal courts by arguing that the conclusion of a confidentiality agreement between two of them amounted to an abuse of dominant position contrary to Article of the 82 EC Treaty. The Court of appeal upheld the challenge to the Paris court's jurisdiction by stating that

> the arbitrability of a dispute is not excluded by the sole fact that rules of public policy are applicable to the dispute", and concluded that arbitrators "have the power to draw the civil consequences of an illicit behaviour under the profile of rules of public policy which can be directly applicable to the legal relationship at hand.

On the basis of the same reasoning, an arbitrator has the power to draw the civil consequences of a rule of criminal law on a business dispute. Such consequence

---

[24] Articles 2059 and 2060 of the French Civil Code.

[25] Article 1676 of the Belgian *Code Judiciaire.*

[26] Article 806 of the Italian *Codice di Procedura Civile.*

[27] Article 2 of the Arbitration Act 60/2003 of 23 December 2003.

[28] Act No. 181 of 24 May 1972 on Arbitration, Article 7-4.

[29] Swiss Federal Statute on Private International Law, Article 177.

[30] German Code of Civil Procedure, § 1025 ZPO.

[31] See, for example Pakistan: Pakistani Supreme Court, *Hubco vs. Wapda,* 15(7) Mealey's IAR (2000), cited by Sayed, *supra* note 9 at 71.

[32] Paris, 19 May 1993, *Labinal v. Mors,* Rev. Arb. 645 (1993), with the note of Ch. Jarrosson.

will most of the time be the nullity of the contract.[33] The basis for declaring the contract null and void may be public policy.[34] It can also be that the fraud committed by a party, such as the bribery of an official of the State, is treated as a misrepresentation having vitiated the consent of the other party.[35]

11-18 When the basis for nullity is submitted to be that of contradiction with *bono mores*, the arbitrator will be faced with the issue of whether the party responsible for the fraud should be entitled to invoke the nullity of the contract, in order for example, to claim restitution of the bribe. The principle *nemo auditur propriam turpitudinem allegans*[36] should lead to a negative answer. As rightly held by the arbitral tribunal in *World Duty Free*:

> there may be legal consequences following the avoidance of the agreement, although *restitutio in integrum* cannot include the return of the bribe to claimant.[37]

Applying that principle leads one to consider that the claim is inadmissible (see above). Arguably, though, applying this could lead to the unpleasant result of allowing the fraud to remain undiscovered. Nevertheless, overriding considerations of good faith and procedural loyalty should prevail.

11-19 Avoidance of the contract for fraud will normally give the aggrieved party right to claim for damages or restitutions,[38] while any outstanding amount due under the voided contract will not be collectable. Here again, however, allowing the party having committed fraud to recover amounts paid pursuant to a voided contract could be considered as immoral. Hence, such party is frequently denied that right, on the basis of the old latin principle *in pari causa turpitudinis cessat repetitio.*[39] Arbitral awards have frequently applied such principle of non-recovery.[40] In cases of corruption, the nullity of a consultancy or of an agency agreement may then lead to the unpleasant result of the company which

---

33 ICC 3916/82, Clunet 930 (1984); and the first award in the *Hilmarton* case ICC 5622/88, Rev. Arb. 327 (1993), YBCA 105 (1994).

34 See, for example, Article 6 of the French Civil Code or Article 20 of the Swiss *Code des Obligations.*

35 UNIDROIT Principles, Art. 3.8.

36 On the principle, see Roland & Boyer, *Adages du droit français* (Litec 1999) at 483.

37 In so deciding, the tribunal referred to *LogiRose v. Southend Limited Football Club* [1988] 1 W.L.R. 1256.

38 UNIDROIT Principles, Art. 3.17, 3.18.

39 On the principle, see Roland & Boyer, *supra* note 36 at 335.

40 See the ICC Awards 3913, 1 Collection of Arbitral Awards 497; 5622, YBCA 122 (1994); 5943, 4 Clunet 1014 (1996); 6248, YBCA 124 (1994).

instigated corruption to benefit from the fraud without having to pay the agreed price.[41] But it is not necessarily the case. In fact, the purpose of the corruption agreement generally consists in the award of a contract whose counterpart – generally a state or a public entity – may well sue for damages on the basis of the fact that the price was artificially inflated, or ask for its annulment on the basis that the corruption constitutes fraudulent misrepresentation.

3. Arbitrating Issues of Criminal Law

3.1. Issues of Evidence

11-20 From a procedural point of view, arbitrators will frequently be confronted to the issue of the level of evidence required to establish a fraud.

11-21 First of all, there may be an issue as to whether it should be established that both parties had a fraudulent intent. There is indeed case law requiring that both parties had knowledge of the illegality and had the common intention of committing the fraud.[42] This is a stringent requirement, which may render such proof impossible. In agency or consultancy agreements, it is arguably sufficient to prove that the intermediary had the intention to commit corruption.[43]

11-22 Another issue is that of the quality of the evidence. Should a mere suspicion suffice? For example, it might appear, during the proceedings, that the respondent's defence to the claim is surprisingly weak. Should that be taken as an indication that the arbitration is simulated? The arbitral tribunal might be surprised to discover that, in an apparently large case, only very little evidence of works performed is produced. Should that be considered as an indication that the contract was entered into with the purpose of paying bribes? The arbitrators might realise that a state official is also a shareholder or an officer of a private investor, etc. In such situations, there would be no conclusive evidence of a fraud or of a corruption. Should the arbitrators then void the contract on the basis of a mere suspicion?

---

41 See for example the ICC Award 8891 (*supra* note 16), in which the Arbitral Tribunal qualified this result as "*unpleasant*", but ruled that it would be even more unsatisfactory to validate an illicit corruption agreement.

42 ICC Award 4145, 2 Collection of ICC Arbitral Awards 53; ICC Award 7047, ASA Bulletin 301 (1995).

43 See the Award in *Lunik v. Soliman*, ASA Bulletin 210 (1998), quoted by Sayed, *supra* note 9 at 114.

11-23 On this issue, reference can be made to an award rendered in a case where a party had submitted that the contract was null and void because the Indonesian officials who signed it were corrupt. The allegation was rejected because "there is a presumption in favour of the validity of contracts" and "a finding of illegality or other invalidity must not be made lightly, but must be supported by clear and convincing proof".[44] Several ICC awards[45] have adopted the same solution, and rejected allegations of criminal offences such as bribery because of the insufficient evidence brought thereof. The principle so affirmed is healthy. As stated above, an arbitrator is not an investigator or a criminal judge. If the evidence of a criminal offence has not been clearly brought, he cannot void the parties' agreement on the sole basis of suspicion.[46]

11-24 The suggestion has been made, though, that in cases in which corruption is suspected, the burden of proof could be shifted to the party suspected of corruption,[47] who would then have to bring evidence of the absence of corruption. Such a reversal of the burden of proof does not seem to be acceptable or compatible with the right to a fair trial.[48] In some cases, however, arbitral tribunals seem to have accepted to shift the burden of proof. For example, in the ICC Award 6497[49] where an allegation of bribery was at stake, the tribunal held that

> the alleging party may bring some relevant evidence for its allegations, without these elements being really conclusive. In such cases, the arbitral

---

44 YBCA 13 (2000).

45 ICC Award 4145, Clunet 985 (1985), YBCA (1987); ICC Award 5622, 3 Collection of ICC Awards 220, YBCA 105 (1994); ICC Award 6286, YBCA 141 (1994); ICC Award 6401, 7(1) Mealey's IAR (Jan. 1992). In the latter case, the Arbitral Tribunal held that "the party having the burden of persuasion must establish the facts on which it relies by a "preponderance of evidence". In other words, it must have the "superior weight of evidence" and establish that its version of the facts "is more likely true than not true" (quoted by Sayed, *supra* note 9 at 104). See also the ICC Award 8891, Clunet 1076 (2000), where the arbitral tribunal required serious indices to establish bribery.

46 The Swiss Federal Tribunal has refused to set aside an award which had found that allegations of corruption had not been proven: SFT, 2 September 1993, *National Power vs. Westinghouse*, ASA Bulletin 244 (1994).

47 Such suggestion has for example been made by K. Mills, *Corruption and Other Illegality in the Formation and Performance of Contracts and in the Conduct of Arbitration Relating Thereto*, ICCA Congress Series (No. 11): International Commercial Arbitration: Important Contemporary Questions (Kluwer 2003) at 295.

48 On the principle that a party has the burden of proving its allegations as a principle of transnational law, see J. Ortscheidt, *La reparation du dommage dans l'arbitrage commercial international* (Dalloz 2001) at 26-28.

49 YBCA 71 (1999).

> tribunal may exceptionally request the other party to bring some counter-evidence, if such task is possible and not too burdensome. If the other party does not bring such counter-evidence, the arbitral tribunal may conclude that the facts alleged are proven (Article 8 of the Swiss Civil code). However, such change in the burden of proof is only to be made in special circumstances and for very good reasons.

But it could be submitted that what the tribunal really did in this case is to draw adverse inferences of the refusal of a party to cooperate fully to the procedure rather than to really shift the burden of proof.[50]

11-25 That the alleging party has the burden of evidence does not mean, though, that the arbitral tribunal should not be free in its assessment of the value of the evidence of an alleged fraud. As stated above, refusal by a party to loyally cooperate to the proceedings can be used by the arbitral tribunal as a presumption. Likewise, the absence of any proof of the performance of the services for which the intermediary pretends to be paid,[51] the unusually short period of time between the appointment of an intermediary and the procurement of a contract,[52] or the unusual amount of an intermediary's remuneration[53] may – if established with sufficient certainty – be used as presumptive evidence.[54] In all cases, the alleging party should be required to meet a reasonable standard of proof and, even if the respondent does not cooperate, an allegation of bribery or corruption should be rejected if such standard was not met.[55]

3.2. Direct Application by Arbitral Tribunals of Sanctions of a Mixed Nature

11-26 In certain cases, arbitral tribunals will not limit themselves to take a rule of criminal law into consideration in order to draw the civil consequences thereof,

---

[50] For another case in which the tribunal held that the refusal of a consultant to provide information about the nature of his intervention was an indication that the contract had the purpose of bribing public officials, see the ICC Award 3916, 1 Collection of ICC Arbitral Awards 507.

[51] ICC Award 8113, cited by Sayed, *supra* note 9 at 149.

[52] Like in the ICC case 3916, 1 Collection of ICC Arbitral Awards 507.

[53] ICC Award 6497, YBCA 73 (1999); ICC Award 8891, Clunet 1076 (2000).

[54] On the issue of presumptive evidence of corruption, see Sayed, *supra* note 9 at 125-157; A. El-Koshery & Ph. Leboulanger, "L'arbitre face à la corruption et aux trafics d'influence", *Rev. Arb.* (1984) 3 ; M. Sherer, "Circumstancial Evidence in Corruption Cases Before International Arbitral Tribunals", 2 *Int'l ALR* (2002) 29; J. Rosell & H. Prager, "Illicit Commissions and International Arbitration: the Question of Proof", *Arb. Int'l* (1999) 329.

[55] For cases in which the arbitral tribunal rejected an allegation of corruption or bribery, see ICC Award 6497, YBCA 71 (1999); ICC Award 9333, 4 ASA Bulletin 757 (2001).

but they will make a direct application of it. This might be the case for sanctions of a mixed nature, such as punitive or treble damages. In American law, treble damages play the role of a civil sanction in case of the violation of certain statutes to which the forum attaches a general interest, such as the Sherman Act or the civil section of the RICO (*Racketeer Influenced Corrupt Organisations Act*). Punitive damages are meant to sanction fraud, oppressive or wilful misconduct. Unlike treble damages, punitive damages are not limited in their amount, and can be applied in absence of a particular statutory provision. As such sanctions do not only play a compensatory role, but also have a punitive function, the question arises of whether an arbitrator should be allowed to award them.

11-27 With respect to treble damages, the U.S. Supreme Court ruled, in *Mitsubishi*[56], that, notwithstanding their policy function, they are of a civil nature. This solution applies to antitrust treble damages,[57] as well as to the treble damages provided by the RICO Statute.[58] American jurisdictions have therefore repeatedly held that claims concerning treble damages are arbitrable. Reference can be made in this respect to the U.S. Supreme Court's 1987 ruling in *Willis v. Shearson/American Express Inc.*,[59] and to the 1990 *Kerr Mc Gee vs. Triumph Tankers* Second Circuit decision.[60] The Supreme Court also held, in *Pacificare Health Systems vs. Book*,[61] that arbitrators have jurisdiction to determine whether they have jurisdiction to grant treble damages. The case involved a controversy between doctors and managed health care organisations, where the claimant doctors claimed treble damages based on the RICO Statute, while the respondents objected that the arbitration agreement explicitly denied the right to punitive damages, which in their view also applied to treble damages. The Court held that such issue of construction of the arbitration agreement was for the arbitrators to decide.

11-28 The problem is, however, to determine the conditions under which an arbitrator might apply such a sanction. The easiest answer to that question would be to refer to the applicable law. If the parties submitted their contract to U.S. law, or if the arbitrator finds that, in the absence of a choice of law, U.S. law is

---

56 *Mitsubishi Motors Corp. v. Soler Chrysler-Plymouth Inc.*, 473 U.S. 614 (1985).

57 Antitrust treble damages are designed in part to punish past violations and also serve to deter future violations and compensate victims.

58 The RICO treble damages provision, 18 U.S.C. 1864(c).

59 569 F. Supp. 821 (M.D.N.C. 1983).

60 YBCA 150 (1993).

61 538 U.S. 401 (2003).

applicable, then treble damages may be applied. The particular nature of such damages, however, makes the answer slightly more complex. For example, in an ICC case in which Brazilian law applied,[62] the arbitrators seemed not to exclude the application of the treble damages provided by U.S. law, because: "the main purpose of the RICO law is to protect the economy and the society of U.S. against the adverse effects of organised racket". The Tribunal however refused to apply the RICO Act because "the alleged fraud mainly took place outside the United States." The Tribunal also noted that the alleged fraud produced its effects outside the U.S.. It would thus appear from that decision that the application of treble damages does not depend on the law applicable to the contract (as determined by the parties' choice of law or by the arbitral tribunal), but from the effects of the parties' conduct within the territory which the criminal rule aims at protecting. The method on the basis of which treble damages can be applied would therefore be similar to the one which commands the taking into consideration of antitrust rules. Another example of that approach is the ICC arbitral award 8385 of 1995,[63] in which, although the law chosen by the parties was that of the State of New York (which includes the RICO Act), it was held by the arbitral tribunal that such choice could not be meant to include the RICO Act, because of its exceptional character, peculiar to the American tradition. The RICO Act was therefore treated as if it were a mandatory law extraneous to the law chosen by the parties, and its application rejected on the basis that, in the case at hand, the contract did not present sufficient links with the territory of the U.S.

11-29 That method is, however, dangerous. In fact, a claim for exemplary damages cannot be treated in the same manner as the taking of consideration of a mandatory rule having the purpose of protecting the public interest. The first has a private nature, even if it has the function of a penalty and of a deterrent, while the second directly touches upon public interest. Here again, a parallel with competition law can be made. In European competition law, Article 81 of the EC Treaty provides for the nullity of a contract affecting trade between European Member States. This rule applies independently of any choice of law. Yet, the civil consequences of such nullity are left to the *lex contractus*.[64] Likewise, the so-called "effects theory" has no reason to govern the allocation of damages to a party, as such allocation does not constitute such a powerful and legitimate

---

[62] ICC Award 6320, Clunet 986 (1995).

[63] ICC Award 8385, Clunet 1061 (1997).

[64] ECJ, *Manfredi*, C-295/04/C-298/04; ECJ, *VAG France v. Magne*, 10/86. With limitations, though. For example, Community law does not allow a State to exclude damages as a remedy on the basis of the principle *nemo auditor,* ECJ, 20 September 2001, *Courage v. Crehan,* C-453/99.

interest of the State as to justify the extra-territorial application of its laws. It is even more so that treble damages might obviously be plainly contrary to the legitimate expectation of parties having submitted their contract to the law of a country which ignores them. As the sole arbitrator rightly felt in the ICC case 8385,[65] treble damages are a sanction peculiar to the American tradition, which application can be discussed in an international context.

11-30 As a consequence, exemplary damages should be applied in arbitration only if permitted by the law chosen by the parties. However, it should also be seen whether they are materially applicable to the dispute. This might not be the case when they are provided by a statute, such as the RICO, which applies to torts. It is however generally admitted that, when the arbitration agreement refers to all disputes in relation with the contract, its application encompasses claims based on torts and having a close link with its performance. In the ICC case 6320,[66] the arbitral tribunal noted that the limitation of liability clause included in the contract referred to both contractual and non-contractual liability, and therefore held that non-contractual liability was contemplated by the arbitration agreement.[67]

11-31 Punitive damages are a civil sanction of quasi-criminal nature,[68] which used to be considered as reserved to domestic Courts. According to the New York court's ruling in *Garrity vs. Lyle Stuart*[69]:

> punitive damages is a sanction reserved to the State, a public policy of such magnitude as to call for judicial intrusion to prevent its contravention. Since enforcement of an award of punitive damages as a purely private remedy would violate strong public policy, an arbitrator's award which imposes punitive damages should be vacated… The freedom of contract does not embrace the freedom to punish, even by contract.

U.S. Federal Courts have, however, adopted a different view. In its *Willoughby Roofing* 1985 judgment,[70] the 3rd Circuit upheld an award of punitive damages on the basis of the following considerations:

---

65 Clunet 1061 (1997).

66 *Ibid.*

67 Ortscheidt, *supra* note 48 at 290-291.

68 On the arbitrability of punitive damages, see A. E. Farnsworth, "Punitive Damages in Arbitration", 1 *Arb. Int'l* (1991); Y. Derains, *Intérêts moratoires, dommages et intérêts compensatoires et dommages punitifs devant l'arbitre international*, in Mélanges Bellet (Litec 1991) at 101; J. Ortscheidt, *La réparation du dommage dans l'arbitrage commercial international* (Dalloz 2001) 281-327.

69 *Garrity v. Lyle Stuart, Inc.*, 40 N.Y.2d 354, 356, 353 N.E.2d 793, 794 (1976).

> arbitrators are better equipped than judges to determine what behaviour is unacceptable in a specific context, and to determine the amount needed to punish and deter the unacceptable behaviour… Denying arbitrators the power to award punitive damages would undermine the value and sufficiency of the arbitral process as a method of dispute resolution… Prohibiting arbitrators from awarding punitive damages would totally frustrate the public policies and purposes served by punitive damages.

The First Circuit has also ruled in favour of the arbitrability of punitive damages in its 1989 *Raytheon vs. Automated Business Systems* decision,[71] whereby it was judged that the power to award exemplary damages was not subject to a specific provision of the arbitration agreement, but to the parties not having expressly excluded it. Finally, the U.S. Supreme Court adopted the same position in its 1995 *Mastrobuono* decision.[72]

11-32 The power recognised by U.S. Courts to arbitrators to apply punitive damages illustrates how advanced the conception of arbitration is in the U.S.. Not only is the idea that arbitrators would not take public interest into account with the same care as State judges clearly repudiated, but it is also acknowledged that arbitrators are in fact better suited than State judges to determine if a behaviour is unacceptable to the forum in a certain context. Nevertheless, such power still needs to have been, in some way, granted to the arbitrators by the parties. The intention of the parties to that effect does not, however, need to have been manifested with an express reference to punitive damages. In *Mastrobuono*, the U.S. Supreme Court considered that the power of the arbitrators to award punitive damages depended on the construction of the arbitration agreement:

> The Court saw the arbitration clause, which provided that any controversy shall be settled by arbitration according to rules that gave the arbitrators authority to "award damages and other relief", as broad enough to allow for an award of punitive damages.

Arguably, this decision sets the principle that arbitrators may award punitive damages provided that the arbitration agreement does not exclude, explicitly or implicitly, such power.

---

70 *Willoughby Roofing v. Kajima International*, 776 F2d 269 (11th Cir. 1985), affirming 598 F. Supp. 353 (M.D. Ala. 1984).

71 *Raytheon v. Automated Business Systems*, 882 F.2d 6, 10 (1st Cir. 1989).

72 *Mastrobuono v. Shearson Lehman Hutton, Inc.* (94-18), 514 U.S. 52 (1995).

11-33 Still, *Mastrobuono* does not answer the question of whether the power to grant an award of punitive damages should depend on the provisions of the substantive law applicable to the contract in an international context[73]. For the reasons expressed above, we believe that the answer should, in principle, be in the affirmative. In fact, the arbitrators having no forum, there is no reason to refer to the rules of conflict of law of the seat of the arbitration to solve that problem. In addition, the rules applicable to the compensation of damages belong, in many jurisdictions, to substantive law rather than to procedure (although procedural rules, like class actions in the U.S., have a deep impact on the victim's ability to recover their losses). Finally, arbitrators should, in these matters, act with the greatest care in order not to deceive the parties' legitimate expectations. Such would certainly be the case if an arbitral tribunal were to surprise them by applying punitive damages when they have elected a law which disregards that kind of sanction. If the parties have chosen to apply to their contract a substantive law which ignores punitive damages, they should be deemed not to have granted such power to the arbitrators. In this regard, the ICSID award rendered in 1984 in *Letco vs. Liberia*[74] is interesting. The Arbitral Tribunal examined the applicable law of Liberia, and held that such law did not permit a civil judge to increase damages beyond the amount needed to compensate the loss of the injured party, unless in cases where *"the actions of the liable party are of a criminal character"*.[75] Likewise, a 1988 AAA award held that, according to the applicable law of the State of Columbia, "*punitive damages may be awarded when an insurer acts in bad faith in rejecting a claim*", but it finally rejected that claim because such bad faith did not appear in the case.[76] In these two cases, it seems that the arbitrators looked at the law applicable to the contract to determine whether the power to grant punitive damages was vested in them.

11-34 Yet, the law of the seat of the arbitration can play an excluding factor. As a matter of fact, an award of punitive damages might be considered as contrary to public policy in the country where the seat of the arbitration is located. As a consequence, even if the *lex contractus* allows punitive damages, an arbitral

---

73 In *Mastrobuono*, the contract was submitted to the law of the State of New York, which law does not allow arbitrators to award punitive damages. However, the reference made by the parties to said law was construed as applying to substantive issues, while the power to award punitive damages was viewed to be an issue of procedure submitted to the Federal Arbitration Act.

74 *Liberian Eastern Timber Corporation (LETCO) v. Liberia*, ICSID ARB/83/2.

75 In that particular case, the Tribunal rejected the claim for punitive damages because such criminal character was not established.

76 YBCA 73 (1989).

tribunal might refuse to grant them if such decision would put the validity of the award at risk at the place of the arbitration. For example, an arbitral tribunal sitting in Switzerland refused to award punitive damages in spite of the submission of the contract to a law allowing that sanction.[77] We are not aware of any court case in respect of a challenge of an award on such a ground, even though it seems that the Court of Basel accepted to enforce in Switzerland a judgment from a court of California having awarded punitive damages in application of English law.[78] However, there is case law in Germany,[79] England,[80] and Italy,[81] according to which the recognition of a U.S. judgment which has awarded punitive damages is contrary to public order and should be denied.

11-35 Still, the solution would not necessarily be the same for a foreign judgment and for an award. In most jurisdictions, the powers of the court to vacate an award are limited to the violation of the most fundamental principles,[82] and courts are not allowed to review the merits of the arbitrators' determination.[83] On the basis of the principle of finality of awards, it is arguable that the decision of an arbitral tribunal to award punitive damages should not be opened to review, insofar as the law chosen by the parties, or the parties' agreement itself, does not prohibit that kind of private sanction.

---

77 ICC 5946, YBCA 97 (1991), 3 Collection of ICC Awards 46.

78 Civil Court of Basel, 1 February 1989, quoted by A. Court de Fontmichel, "L'arbitre, le juge et les pratiques illicites du commerce international", *Panthéon Assas* 392 (2004), citing R.A. Brand, "Punitive Damages and the Recognition of Judgements", *NILR* (1996) 169.

79 Bundesgerichstof, 4 June 1992; Bundesverfassungsgericht, 7 December 1994.

80 QB Division, 28 Feb. 2003, *Lewis v. Eliades.*

81 Venice Court, 15 October 2001.

82 For a general overview, see A. Mourre, *Le libre arbitre, ou l'aveuglement de Zaleucus (variations sur l'arbitrage, l'ordre public et le droit de la concurrence)*, in Mélanges Knoepfler (Neuchâtel, Helbing & Lichtenhahn 2005) at 283.

83 See the House of Lords 30 June 2005 decision having overturned a Court of appeal decision which had set aside an award on the basis of excess of power because the arbitrators had awarded amounts in a different currency than that provided by the contract: *Lesotho Highlands development Authority v. Impregilo SpA, Cahiers de l'arbitrage* (2) 2005, Gaz. Pal. 294-295, in panorama de jurisprudence anglaise, 49; see also, in respect to that decision, A. Crivellaro: "All's well that ends well: London remains a suitable venue for international arbitration – but only thanks to the House of Lords", 22(4) *ICL Rev.* 480.

4. ARBITRATORS AS PRIVATE JUDGES…

4.1. The Duty of International Arbitrators to Take Rules of Criminal Law into Consideration

11-36 As stated above, arbitrators may take a rule of criminal law into consideration. But when should they do so? Here again, criminal law rules should not be treated differently than ordinary rules of public policy. In principle, if said rules are part of the *lex contractus*, the consequences therefrom – insofar as applicability to the circumstances of the case – should be drawn on the civil dispute. By submitting their contract to the laws of a particular country, the parties elected such laws in their entirety, including mandatory provisions of a criminal character. Still, arbitrators will frequently be confronted with the problem of whether they should raise such rules on their own motion. Under most arbitration rules[84] and arbitration laws,[85] arbitral tribunals certainly have the power to do so. But do they have that obligation? A judge has the duty to raise *ex officio* any applicable criminal rule which is part of his own national law.[86] The position of the international arbitrator is different, because he looks at the case from an international perspective. Being a private international judge, an arbitrator will not put on an equal footing local prohibitions and internationally recognised rules. This is not to say that he will necessarily disregard the first, but considerations of parties' equality and procedural fairness will make him less inclined to disrupt the arbitration proceedings by raising a local prohibition *ex officio* than if it were to ensure the application of a widely recognised principle.[87] The question is not specific to criminal law, and reference can simply be made to the abundant literature on the crucial problem of *ex officio* duties of the arbitral tribunal.[88] In short, the decision of an arbitral tribunal to raise a local prohibition *ex officio* will mainly depend on an assessment of the degree of illegality involved, and on the consequences that disregarding the rule at stake would likely have on the validity of the award.

---

[84] Most arbitration rules grant arbitrators the greatest discretion in the management of the proceedings: Articles 15(2) and 20(1) of the ICC Rules; Article 14.1 of the LCIA Rules; Article 16.1 of the AAA Rules; Articles 34(2), 35(1) and 36(b) of the ICSID Rules of arbitration.

[85] See D. Bensaude, "Les moyens relevés d'office par l'arbitre en arbitrage international", *Cahiers de l'arbitrage* (1) 2004, *Gaz. Pal.* 19-20 (May 2004) No. 141.

[86] Or to report the facts to the attorney general.

[87] For an award in which the Tribunal raised an issue of bribery on its own motion, see ICC Award 8891, Clunet 1076 (2000).

[88] See D. Bensaude, *supra* note 85.

11-37 What should the arbitrator do if the criminal rule at stake is not part of the *lex contractus*? The starting point of the reasoning is again that the arbitrator, unlike the judge, has no forum. Unlike the judge, all legal rules are extraneous to him. As a consequence, the only source of his obligation to apply the laws of a particular country is the will of the parties, as expressed in their contract. As a matter of principle, an arbitrator should therefore not apply to the dispute a law different from the one chosen by the parties. This is also true for criminal rules, under certain reservations that we will analyse hereinafter. For example, an arbitral tribunal has disregarded the U.S. Foreign Corrupt Practices Act in a case where Swiss law was applicable on the basis of the following reasoning:

> Even if one supposes that (i) the FCPA is a mandatory law and (ii) the arbitrator admits that such a law can be applied notwithstanding the choice of another substantive law, the powerful and legitimate interests of the United States in the application of this law must also be shown. Serious doubts can in this matter result from the fact that the FCPA does not primarily aim to protect the fundamental public policy of the United States, but rather has the purpose to restore confidence of the public in the integrity of American corporations whose reputation has been tarnished by a series of high profile corporate scandals."[89]

Likewise, in an arbitration submitted to the Geneva Chamber of Commerce rules, the tribunal disregarded Algerian regulations on the prohibition of intermediation, because Swiss law applied and said regulations are "*only part of the economic policy of the country*".[90]

11-38 Two exceptions, however, should be made to the principle according to which arbitral tribunals may not apply mandatory rules extraneous to the law chosen by the parties.

11-39 The first is when the criminal rule at stake is, notwithstanding the parties' choice of law, particularly relevant and it, thus, has a very strong title to be applied. For example, in the field of antitrust law, which is close in many respects to criminal law (in particular where hardcore cartels are involved), it is clear that the parties' choice of law cannot have the effect of avoiding the application of a rule which has a manifest interest in being applied. Hence, EU antitrust law will apply to a contract having the purpose of fixing prices within

---

89 ICC Award 9333, 4 ASA Bulletin 757 (2001).

90 ASA Bulletin 136 (1988). See also, in a case involving Algerian law, the second *Hilmarton* award, cited in Sayed, *supra* note 9 at 242.

the European territory, even though the parties have submitted it to the law of a non-EU country. The same reasoning would apply to a criminal law rule.

11-40 The second is where such rule is part of transnational or truly international public policy. This is the case, for example, of the prohibition of contracts made with the purpose of corrupting foreign officers or committing money laundering. We will address that question in more detail later on.

4.2. Consequences of the Private Nature of the Arbitrator's Mission when Confronted with a Criminal Offence

11-41 As a general rule, arbitrators should act with great caution when introducing in the arbitral debate elements which were not included in the parties' submissions. Although there is no doubt that arbitrators should be sensitive to states' legitimate interests, they should not turn themselves into investigators, policemen or prosecutors. As opposed to state judges, the primary role of an arbitrator is to enforce the contract, and not to defend public policy. It is submitted, as a consequence, that an arbitrator has no duty to investigate possible breaches of criminal law of which there is no evidence at all and which were not raised by the parties in their submissions. In this respect, Redfern and Hunter wrote in the third edition of their treatise that:

> … it is not the duty of an arbitral tribunal to assume an inquisitorial role and to search officiously for evidence of corruption where none is alleged.[91]

This does not mean, however, that an arbitral tribunal would be bound by a fraudulent agreement to exclude an aspect of illegality from the arbitration. If there are indications that the contract might be illegal, the arbitrators should raise the issue and ask the parties to provide explanations. This derives from the arbitrators' duty not to be accomplices to fraud, and also from their duty to make their best efforts to render an award enforceable at law. Yet, they should not self initiate an investigation on the basis of a mere belief or – even worse –, of hearsay or whistle-blowing. It is fair to say, however, that this issue remains to some degree one of uncertainty and concern to practitioners. It is interesting, for example, to note that the same authors as those quoted above wrote, in the fourth edition of their treatise, that:

> if an allegation of corruption is made in plain language in the course of the arbitration proceedings, the arbitral tribunal is clearly under a duty to

[91] Redfern & Hunter, *Law and Practice of International Commercial Arbitration* (3rd ed, Sweet & Maxwell 1999) at 3-28.

consider the allegation and to decide whether or not it is proved. It remains less clear, however, whether an arbitral tribunal has a duty to assume an inquisitorial role and to address the question of corruption on its own initiative, where none is alleged. Initiating its own investigation, and rendering a decision on the outcome of such a self-initiated investigation, might leave a tribunal open to charges of straying into territory that is ultra petita. Conversely, a failure to address the existence of such illegality may threaten the enforceability of the award, and thus may sit uncomfortably with the arbitral tribunal's duty under some modern rules of arbitration to use its best endeavours to ensure that the award is enforceable. Striking the right balance between these competing considerations may not be easy. At the time of the preparation of this edition, the extent of an arbitral tribunal's duty – if any – to probe matters of illegality of its own motion remains unclear.[92]

11-42 The approach according to which arbitrators should not be turned into investigators or prosecutors in absence of any evidence of an illegality leads to oppose strong resistance to any suggestion that an arbitrator should report possible violations of criminal law to the state authorities. For example, there is a French law rule according to which any judge who, in the course of judicial proceedings, learns about a violation of criminal law, must report such situation to the Attorney General.[93] Such rule, however, is explicitly directed to state judges, and therefore it does not apply to arbitrators. Nevertheless, there are views according to which the duty to report suspicions of criminal offences should also be applied to arbitral tribunals.[94] Even though such views are certainly isolated, they illustrate the dangers of a tendency to an excessive assimilation between judges and arbitrators.[95] Vesting upon arbitrators an obligation to report to a national authority or jurisdiction a suspicion of illegal

---

[92] Redfern & Hunter (with N. Blackaby and C. Partasides), *Law and Practice of International Commercial Arbitration* (4th ed, Sweet & Maxwell 2004) at 3-22.

[93] Article 40 of the Code of Criminal Proceedings provides:

> Every constituted authority, every public officer or civil servant who, in the performance of his duties, has gained knowledge of the existence of a felony or of a misdemeanour is obliged to notify forthwith the district prosecutor of the offence and to transmit to said prosecutor any relevant information, official reports or documents.

[94] A. Court de Fontmichel, *supra* note 78 at 351.

[95] For another illustration of the dangers of assimilating judges and arbitrators, see the debate on the UNCITRAL Project on *ex parte* interim measures, see Y. Derains, "L'arbitre et l'octroi de mesures provisoires ex parte", *Cahiers de l'arbitrage, Recueil, Vol. II, Ed. Gaz. Pal.* (2004) 74.

behaviour would be totally incompatible with the private nature of their mission and the trust the parties have in them. No arbitration could ever take place in a context of trust and mutual cooperation if the parties had the doubt that anything they say might be reported by an arbitrator to a public prosecutor, let alone tax authorities…

11-43 Likewise, it has been suggested that an arbitrator should report to the criminal authorities any doubt or suspicion he might have on the criminal origin of the funds at stake in the arbitration proceedings. This suggestion has been made, in particular, in respect to money laundering. The dangers of money laundering should certainly not be underestimated. According to an IMF survey, it would represent 2 to 5% of the world gross product.[96] Yet, the fight against this dangerous form of criminality should be respectful of fundamental liberties, amongst which is the right of access to justice, including the right to arbitral justice if the parties made that choice.[97] It has been suggested, however, that arbitrators could be bound to make a declaration of suspicion pursuant to EU Money Laundering. While Directive 91/308 referred only to banks, insurance companies and other financial institutions as being obliged to report suspicions, Directive 97/2001 and now Directive 2005/60[98] have included in that list auditors, external accountants, tax advisors, notaries and members of independent legal professions. In the latter case, the obligation to report is provided in respect to real estate transactions, asset management, activities related to trusts or companies, or activities performed on behalf of a client in the context of a financial or real estate transaction. In addition, the list of illegal behaviours for which there is an obligation to report a suspicion has been extended to include almost any violation of a criminal rule.

11-44 With respect to members of the Bar, there are limits to the obligation to report. As mentioned earlier, such obligation applies only when the activities of the lawyer relate to a financial or real estate transaction. Conversely, no such obligation exists when a lawyer is involved in activities related to litigation. Article L. 562-2-1 of the French Monetary and Financial Code includes an

[96] Cited by F. Baillet, "Blanchiment, l'état de la législation", *Gaz. Pal. 12-13* (Oct. 2005) at 2.

[97] For a decision acknowledging the right to arbitral justice as a fundamental right, see the French decision of the Supreme Court, Cass. Civ. 1ère 1 February 2005, *NIOC v. Israël*, *Cahiers de l'arbitrage*, (1) 2005, in Sommaires de Jurisprudence des Cours et Tribunaux, 34, Gaz. Pal. (2005) 117-118.

[98] The previous Directives 97/2001 and 91/308 have been abrogated and replaced by Directives 2005/60 and 2006/70 respectively adopted on 26 October 2005 and 1 August 2006.

express provision to that effect.[99] In the United Kingdom, the Court of Appeal ruled on 8 March 2005[100] that submitting lawyers to the Directive would be contrary to the European Convention on Human Rights. The case related to a real estate dispute, in which the claimant's solicitors, further to discovery, decided to report to the National Criminal Intelligence Service certain documents showing that the defendant had included the costs of works carried out in his personal property with his business accounts and VAT returns, even though they were unconnected with his business. Such disclosure clearly amounted to a breach of the privileged character of documents obtained through litigation disclosure. The Court rightly held, in respect to Section 328 of the Proceeds and Crime Act 2002, that

> legal proceedings are a State-provided mechanism for the resolution of issues according to the law. Everyone has the right to a fair and public trial in the determination of his/her civil rights and duties which is secured by Article 6 of the European Convention on Human Rights. Parliament cannot have intended that proceedings or steps taken by lawyers in order to determine or secure legal rights and remedies for their clients should involve them in "becoming concerned in an arrangement", even if they suspected that the outcome of such proceedings might have such effect.

---

99 Article 562-2-1 of the French Monetary and Financial Code provides:

> The persons referred to in § 12 of Article L. 562-1 are required to make the declaration stipulated in Article L. 562-2 when, in the context of their professional activity, they execute for and on behalf of their customers any financial or real-property transaction or when they participate by assisting their customers with the preparation or execution of transactions relating to: 1. Buying and selling real property or business concerns; 2. The management of funds, securities or other assets belonging to the customers; 3. The opening of current accounts, savings accounts or securities accounts; 4. Organisation of the contributions required to create companies; 5. The constitution, administration or management of companies; 6. The formation, administration or management of [...] trusts [...]. The persons referred to in § 12 of Article L. 562-1, when they are engaged in activities relating to the transactions referred to above, and accountants when they give legal advice [...], are not required to make the declaration provided in Article L. 562-2 when the information was received from one of their clients, or obtained on one of them, within the scope of a legal consultation, unless it took place for money-laundering purposes, or if those persons proceeded therewith knowing that their client wished to obtain legal advice for money-laundering purposes, or when they provide their professional services in the interest of that client in connection with judicial proceedings, whether that information was received or obtained before, during or after those proceedings, including advice given in relation to the initiation of such proceedings....

100 CA (Civil Division), *Bowman v. Fels* [2005] EWCA Civ 226.

11-45 In respect to arbitrators, it should be excluded that the Directive applies to them in the exercise of their jurisdictional duties. In fact, by no means could the arbitrator's mission be compared to that of assistance of a client. In addition, the obligations provided by EU Money Laundering Directives, if applied to arbitrators, would be plainly incompatible with both their independence and duty of confidentiality.

4.3. Simulated Arbitrations and Manipulation of Arbitrators

11-46 This is not to say that arbitrators should let themselves be manipulated and turned into a tool for fraud. For example, if the arbitrators realise that the arbitration has been simulated from the outset, which is to say that, in reality, there is actually no dispute, they should resign and might even – depending on the laws of the place where the "arbitration" was simulated – report the situation to the competent local criminal authorities. However, it goes without saying that in order to do so they should, have obtained very convincing evidence of the fictitious character of the arbitration, which in practice is quite unlikely to happen. A resignation of the tribunal should not, in such extreme cases, be viewed as incompatible with the provisions of law obliging the arbitrators to carry out their mission until it is completed.[101] Since the "arbitration" has been simulated from the outset, there is no real dispute and the arbitrators cannot be bound to carry out a mission which is in fact inexistent.

11-47 Fictitious arbitrations organised with fraudulent purposes may lead the parties to request the arbitrators to sign an award by consent. Such an award by consent would then consist in laundering a fraudulent contract into an apparently licit jurisdictional title. This is why arbitrators should exercise the greatest caution when accepting such a request.[102] Under the 1988 ICC Rules of Arbitration, arbitrators are bound to accept the parties' request to that effect.[103] The 1998 Rules provide that the signature of an award by consent is subject to the arbitrators accepting to do so.[104] This evolution is indeed welcome. As a

---

[101] Like Article 1462 of the French Code of Civil Procedure, which provides that: "each arbitrator shall carry out his mission until it is completed".

[102] With respect to awards by consent, see S. Lazareff, "La sentence d'accord parties aux frontières de l'arbitrage et de l'ADR", *Cahiers de l'arbitrage, Recueil, Vol. I, Ed. Gaz. Pal,* (2002) at 8.

[103] Article 17 of the 1988 ICC Rules of Arbitration:

> If the parties reach a settlement after the file has been transmitted to the arbitrator in accordance with Article 10, the same shall be recorded in the form of an arbitral award made by consent of the parties.

[104] Article 26 of the 1998 ICC Rules of Arbitration:

matter of fact, if an arbitrator has a duty to render an award, he has no obligation whatsoever to render an award by consent. He should thus be free to refuse a request to that effect, and he should be under no duty to reason his decision to do so. If the arbitrators requested to sign an award by consent refuse to do so, and the parties wish to persist in their desire to obtain such a decision, they might just replace the reluctant arbitrators[105] and try to find a more accommodating tribunal.

4.4. Criminal Law Used to Disrupt Arbitration

11-48 Arbitrators should therefore not let themselves be used as a tool for fraud. Likewise, they should not admit that criminal law be used to disrupt a lawful arbitration. Such an attempt to disrupt the arbitration can take several forms. The most direct way to disrupt an arbitration is by direct intimidation of the arbitrators, for example through threats of incrimination and even arrest. In such situations, a possible answer could be to move the seat of the arbitration to a more suitable place.[106] In this respect, it is advisable that arbitration rules evolve towards greater flexibility by permitting the institution to move the seat when local courts or authorities try to disrupt the arbitration by using extreme means.

11-49 Another, more frequent situation, is when a party files a criminal complaint and makes a motion to obtain a stay of the arbitration proceedings until the judgment of the criminal court. Such a complaint might for example relate to the forgery of documents, or simply to the existence of a fraud. In most jurisdictions, an arbitral tribunal has no obligation to stay the proceedings when a criminal investigation is pending on facts which might be relevant for the arbitration.[107] This principle was embedded by a resolution of the International Law Association adopted in 1996.[108]

> If the parties reach a settlement after the file has been transmitted to the Arbitral Tribunal in accordance with Article 13, the settlement shall be recorded in the form of an Award made by consent of the parties if so requested by the parties and if the Arbitral Tribunal agrees to do so.

105 Article 12-1 ICC Rules.

106 See, in this respect, P. Lalive, "On the transfer of the seat in international arbitration", in *Law and Justice in a Multistate World, Essays in honour of Arthur T. von Mehren* (Transnational Publishers 2002) at 515; J.-F. Poudret & S. Besson, *Comparative Law on International Arbitration* (Thomson – Sweet & Maxwell 2002) at 144.

107 In France, the rule according to which the civil judge has to stay his decision until the criminal judge's decision if the same facts are at stake is set by Article 4 of the Code of Criminal Proceedings. Case law, however, has acknowledged that an arbitrator is not bound by that principle: Paris, 23 May 2002, 20 June 2002, Cahiers de l'arbitrage, Recueil, Vol. II, Ed. Gaz. Pal. (2004) at 356-357. Moreover, the provision has recently (Article 20 of the 2007-291 Statute

11-50 If a criminal complaint is filed, the arbitrators might be called to testify before a criminal judge. In most jurisdictions, they would have to abide by such a request.[109] The only restriction to the arbitrator's duty to testify would then be the applicable rules on confidentiality. In France, for example, there is a rule which protects the secrecy of the Tribunal's deliberations, but whether this applies in the case of criminal proceedings is doubtful.[110]

11-51 Finally, a party may refuse to disclose documents during the arbitration on the basis of local regulations relating to transactions of national interest, such as arms sales.[111] Arbitrators should not, in particular when the party refusing to disclose is a State entity, be too impressed by such arguments, and may draw adverse inferences from its refusal to participate fully with the disclosure of documents.

5. … And Guardians of Good Morals in International Trade

5.1. Arbitrators as Guardians of International Legality

11-52 The relationship between arbitration and criminal law is not and should not be one of confrontation. Indeed, international criminal law powerfully contributes to the constitution of a true transnational public order, which is in turn an element contributing to the creation of an arbitral order autonomous from national laws. International criminal law is therefore part of the arbitral legal order to the same extent as trade usages and fundamental principles of international law. From this standpoint, arbitrators can be viewed as the true guardians of legality and good morals in international trade. In fact there is no

---

of 5 March 2007, see F.-X. Train, "Modification de l'article 4 du Code de Procédure Pénale", *Rev. Arb.* (2007)) been amended to the effect that the stay is no longer mandatory for the court seized of an action to vacate an award. In Switzerland, the Swiss Federal Tribunal (119 (1993) II 386), held that an arbitral tribunal has no obligation to stay the proceedings pending a criminal action. The principle of a stay in case of criminal proceedings is unknown in many jurisdictions (England, Germany, Netherlands, Portugal, Greece).

[108] ILA, Report of the 67th conference, 1996, Resolution 22, p. 32, and the debates, 618-622.

[109] In France, Article 109 of the French Code of Criminal Procedure provides that:

> Any person summoned to be heard in the capacity of a witness is obliged to appear, to swear an oath, and to make a statement….

In Belgium, Article 72 of the Code of Criminal Procedure; in Germany, Section 48 of the Code of Criminal Procedure.

[110] French Code of Civil Procedure, article 1469: "The deliberation of arbitrators shall be in camera".

[111] In France, Articles 413-9 seqs. of the Criminal Code.

doubt that the duties of the arbitrators are not only to the parties who have appointed them, but also to the international business community at large. In a worldwide marketplace, good governance, ethics and transparency are indispensable for ensuring competitors fair access to markets and a global market playing field. If arbitration were to become a safe harbour for illegality or a tool for fraud, it would not only be rejected by States, but it would also cease to be useful to the business community and, hence, to be the normal way of resolving international business disputes.

11-53 In order to understand the arbitrators' duty to sanction fraud in international trade, two conceptions should be avoided. The first is to assimilate them to national judges, and the second is to make them servants of the parties. In the first concept, arbitrators would have the duty to apply any local mandatory rule, and their awards would be closely scrutinised by national courts, leading, in practice, to their review on the merits and depriving the parties of the main benefit of arbitration, which is finality. The second concept would lead to permit the parties to fraud the State's legitimate interest to have their mandatory rules applied, thus turning arbitration into a vehicle of illegality. It is therefore necessary to conciliate the autonomy and finality of arbitration with the need to fight illicit behaviour. The only way to achieve such a balance is to distinguish parochial local mandatory rules, even when they are of a criminal nature, from universally recognised principles meant to serve the higher interests of the world community. The latter are part of transnational public policy, and arbitrators therefore have a duty to apply them regardless of the law chosen by the parties or of any rule of conflict of laws.[112] Such universal values are in fact, as the Swiss Federal Court ruled in its *Westland* 1994 judgment,[113] the true public order of international arbitral tribunals.

---

[112] E.g., an arbitral tribunal held that

> a contract instigating or favouring the corruption of public officials is contrary to transnational public policy, and if this appears to be the object of the consultancy contract, there would be no other option than to find it null and void (ICC Award 8891, Clunet 1076 (2000).

In *World Duty Free* (*supra* note 20), the arbitral tribunal held that:

> in light of domestic laws and international conventions relating to corruption, and in light of the decisions taken in in this matter by courts and arbitral tribunals, this tribunal is convinced that bribery is contrary to the international public policy of most, if not all, states or, to use another formula, to transnational public policy.

[113] *Les Emirats Arabes Unis v. Westland Helicopters*, 19 Apr. 1994, ASA Bulletin 404 (1994).

11-54 Criminal law and international criminal cooperation have powerfully contributed to the creation and development of transnational public policy. In the field of international corruption, the OECD Convention,[114] the Council of Europe Conventions,[115] the work of the United Nations,[116] and of regional bodies,[117] as well as the setting up by the World Bank of an Oversight Committee on Fraud and Corruption,[118] illustrate the international acknowledgement of the need to fight what arbitrator Lagergren called as early as 1963, "*an international evil, contrary to good morals and to an international public policy common to the community of nations*".[119]

11-55 In the field of money laundering, the work of the Financial Action Task Force and the European directives reveal a similar international consciousness. Many other examples can be given. Smuggling and piracy are certainly contrary to widely generalized conception of fair trading and good morals. If certain embargo measures, such as those taken by the U.S. against Cuba or Libya with the *Helms-Burton* or *Amato-Kennedy,* are not universally recognised, others, like those applied by the United Nations against the former regime of Saddam

---

114 21 November 1997 OECD Convention on Combating Bribery of Foreign Public Officials in International Business Transactions. See also the 1996 OECD Recommendation on Tax Deductibility of Bribes to Foreign Public Officials.

115 Criminal Law Convention on Corruption signed in Strasbourg, 27 January 1999; Civil Law Convention on Corruption signed in Strasbourg, 4 November 1999. The Council of Europe has also adopted an Additional Protocol to the Criminal Law Convention on Corruption, whereby States are compelled to adopt measures to establish as a criminal offence the fact of corrupting an arbitrator (see in this respect ASA Bulletin 3 (2006) at 449 seq.). The Organisation of American States Inter-American Convention against Corruption should also be mentioned.

116 The UN Economic and Social Council adopted in 1979 a Draft Convention to prevent and eliminate illicit payments in international business transactions, as well as a Draft Code of Conduct on Transnational Corporations. The UN Convention against Corruption was adopted in October 2003 and entered into force on 14 December 2005.

117 The 1996 Inter-American Convention Against Corruption, the 1997 Convention on the Fight Against Corruption Involving Officials of the European Communities or Officials of Member States of the European Union, the 2003 African Union Convention on Preventing and Combating Corruption.

118 World Bank President Circular on New Measures to Combat Corruption, 15 October 1998. The World Bank has also put in place guidelines for the procurement of goods and services, see Sayed, *supra* note 9 at 292-295. The WTO has on its side established a Working party on transparency in Government procurement procedures. National laws on public procurement frequently provide that competitors are bound to provide declarations that their price does not include commissions paid to third parties intermediaries. In many national laws, intermediation in public tenders is prohibited as such.

119 ICC case 1110/1963, *supra* note 8. On international corruption, see Sayed, *supra* note 9 and, from the same author, "La question de la corruption dans l'arbitrage commercial international: inventaire des solutions", 4 *ASA Bulletin* 653 (2001).

Hussein, had the nature of a transnational rule. The prohibition of drugs or human organs traffic, as well as of many other internationally recognised crimes, are also part of transnational public policy.

5.2. Self Regulation and Arbitration: The Path to the Future

11-56 Nowadays, ethics in international trade are a global concern. After the scandals that have rocked the international business community in recent years, international companies have issued ethical codes for their employees and officers in order to prevent breaches of the laws, at home and abroad. A survey carried out by Deloitte[120] found that more than 80% of US public companies have such codes, the remaining having compliance programmes as an essential component of corporate governance. This is clearly a sign that there is a growing awareness that international crime should not be tolerated. Many years ago, the International Chamber of Commerce has set up Rules of Conduct,[121] and promoted a Commercial Crime Services Bureau; the ICC has also recently launched *Fraudnet*, a network aiming at combating fraud and money laundering. The OECD has adopted non-binding guidelines for an ethical conduct of multinational companies.[122] Another significant example of this trend can be found in the *Transparency International* initiative,[123] a non-governmental organisation created by business leaders aimed at fighting international corruption. Many other private initiatives can be mentioned. Crimes like corruption and bribery are indeed a menace for the community of merchants. Bribes affect companies' profit margins. Corruption feeds itself by creating, in certain countries, a class of public officials hungry for more corruption. Public procurement procedures are distorted to the disadvantage of loyal competitors. Barriers preventing companies from entering markets are artificially created, etc.

11-57 Yet, as shown by an inquiry on the Iraqi *oil for food* program,[124] business can too easily be the victim of corrupt public officials' blackmailing. Crime in international trade needs to be fought on a global scale, and such a fight cannot be successful if it does not come from the business community itself. International criminal cooperation and self-regulation in the business community should therefore equally contribute to the development of international criminal

---

[120] International Bar News, 5 (Aug. 2005).

[121] ICC Rules of Conduct: Extorsion and Bribery in International Business Transactions.

[122] OECD Guidelines for Multinational Enterprises (Revised Version 2000).

[123] http://www.transparency.org

[124] Le Monde, 6-7 Nov. 2005: "180 entreprises françaises accusées d'avoir enrichi Saddam Hussein."

law, and international arbitral tribunals should be recognised as the natural judges of these transnational rules. No judge is better placed than an international arbitrator to sanction contracts which seriously violate *bonos mores* or international public policy. As the English Court acknowledged in *Westacre*:

> That conclusion [that the award should not be vacated] is not to be read as in any sense indicating that the Commercial Court is prepared to turn a blind eye to corruption in international trade, but rather as an expression of its confidence that if the issue of illegality by reason of corruption is referred to high calibre ICC arbitrators and duly determined by them, it is entirely inappropriate in the context of the New York Convention that the enforcement court should be invited to retry that very issue in the context of a public policy submission"[125]

11-58 The tribute paid by the English judges to arbitration is the best possible demonstration that there is no contradiction between arbitration autonomy and the need to ensure good morals in international trade.

[125] *Ibid.*

Julian D M Lew QC *

CHAPTER 12

COMPETITION LAWS: LIMITS TO ARBITRATORS' AUTHORITY[1]

1. INTRODUCTION

12-1 The right of parties to submit to arbitration and arbitrators' authority to determine disputes involving competition or anti-trust questions has long been a contentious arbitrability issue in international commercial arbitration. This is because competition law has a public policy or mandatory character in every system where there are rules aimed to protect and ensure free trade both for existing and new entrants to a specific market. For this reason, for many years it was considered that only the competent national court or authority was empowered to assess the facts, commercial behaviour and contractual arrangements which could affect, or were affected by, free competition, anti-monopoly and restraint of trade rules or legislation.

12-2 Accordingly, it was considered by many that parties could not select arbitration in preference to, or otherwise exclude, the jurisdiction of the normally competent courts from dealing with an issue involving competition law. Potentially, this had an effect even where there was a valid arbitration agreement, contained in an ordinary commercial contract, and where the competition or restraint of trade was alleged or became an issue only when a dispute between the parties arose. At this late stage in the parties' contractual relationship it was argued that the competition law allegation or implication was not arbitrable and

* Barrister and arbitrator, 20 Essex Street, London. Professor and Head of School of International Arbitration, Centre for Commercial Law Studies, Queen Mary, University of London.

1 This chapter is based on a paper given at a conference held in Athens in 23 September 2005.

L Mistelis & S Brekoulakis (eds), Arbitrability: International & Comparative Perspectives, 241-261

that the tribunal should decline jurisdiction. This contention begged the merits of the competition law allegation.

12-3 This was especially so in the early years of the European Union, which had then, and still has now, as a fundamental objective to ensure a single market in which all participants can compete freely and on a level playing field. The Treaty of Rome, the founding instrument of the European Union (then the European Common Market) sought "*to lay the foundations of an ever-closer union among the peoples of Europe*", "*eliminate the barriers which divide Europe*", "*guarantee steady expansion, balanced trade and fair competition*" and abolish "*restrictions on international trade*".[2]

12-4 In 2007, the Lisbon Treaty was signed amending and updating the Treaty of Rome.[3] Article 2(3) was amended to read:

> The Union shall establish an internal market. It shall work for the sustainable development of Europe based on a balanced economic growth and price stability, a highly competitive social market, economy, aiming at full employment and social progress...

12-5 Free competition was and is a fundamental aspect of the EU. This is recorded most specifically in Articles 81 and 82 of the Treaty of Rome as amended (previously Articles 85 and 86). These are discussed in greater detail below.

12-6 In this paper we review the circumstances and extent to which an arbitral tribunal is empowered to determine questions or a dispute which involve, or a party makes, allegations of anti-competitive or monopoly practices. In this context we deal with the follow specific issues:

- Fundamental duties of an arbitral tribunal
- Mandatory law and international public policy
- Competition law
- Arbitrability
- Scenarios for arbitral tribunals
- Parallel proceedings: arbitration tribunal and EU Commission

2 Preamble to Treaty of Rome 1957.

3 The Treaty of Rome had already been updated by the Single European Act 1987, the Maastricht Treaty 1992 and the Treaty of Amsterdam 1997.

2. Fundamental Duties of an Arbitral Tribunal

12-7 The first and principal obligation of an arbitral tribunal is to determine finally the differences and respective claims arising between the parties within the scope of the arbitration agreement.[4] In this respect, frequently, arbitral tribunals are required as a preliminary issue to determine the scope of their jurisdiction in light of the underlying contract out of which the dispute has arisen, or with respect to the authority vested in the tribunal by the arbitration agreement.

12-8 In exercising its authority an arbitral tribunal must look first to apply the applicable rules of law, both to determine their authority and to determine the issues between the parties. This law may differ in that the arbitrators' authority will depend on the agreement to arbitrate, including the law governing this agreement, the arbitration rules selected by the parties and the law (at least the mandatory rules) of the place of arbitration.

12-9 By contrast the law that governs the substantive issues between the parties will depend in large measure on the law chosen by the parties or otherwise deemed appropriate by the tribunal. Almost all national laws allow parties broad autonomy to select the national or other laws or rules to govern their contract, including general principles of law, international commercial law or *lex mercatoria.* Public international law may also be relevant and applicable in both commercial and investment arbitrations.

12-10 In the absence of the parties' choice, arbitrators define the nature of the contractual arrangement and may select a national or non-national law, or some other appropriate rules which they deem applicable or appropriate in accordance with the relevant rules for determining this issue. This direct approach comprises of the arbitrators' obligation in the first place to define what law or rules are applicable to the dispute; if no indication was made by the parties, the tribunal must directly choose the law it deems appropriate. This presumably and naturally includes competition laws where part of the applicable law or, as discussed below, where otherwise applicable. It is fully accepted that European law should be applied in the same fashion as a national law chosen by the parties, either as a

[4] Lew, Mistelis & Kröll, *Comparative International Commercial Arbitration* (Kluwer 2003) at 279-281; Final Report on the Status of the Arbitrator of the ICC Commission Working Party on this subject (P. Fouchard, Chairman), 7(1) *ICC Bulletin* (1996) at 27

national law, or as an applicable law in its own right depending on the circumstances.[5]

3. Mandatory Law and International Public Policy

12-11 As with everything, there must be some restriction to the autonomy of the parties and the authority of arbitrators. These limitations are invariably generated by mandatory law or by international public policy, although the extent and effect of these concepts leaves many issues to be discussed.

12-12 The origin of any mandatory law is fundamental to its relevance in any particular instance. Specifically, mandatory law may be applicable as part of the law chosen by the parties or by the tribunal as governing the parties' specific rights and the substantive issues in dispute. However, mandatory law can also apply as the over-riding law which regulates the transaction or some aspects of it, or as the law of the place of performance, or even the putative applicable law but for a contrary choice by the parties. This mandatory law may include directly applicable and mandatory law even in circumstances where parties have sought, by careful structuring of the transaction, or selection of the place of arbitration and the governing law, to avoid the application of such law.

12-13 Arbitral tribunals have to apply EU competition law on a mandatory basis unless it is not viewed as imperative. It is for the tribunal in each case to determine the objectives of the dispute which fall within the mandatory regulation of the EU competition law and to decide the scope of its application. Arguably competition rules have immediate or automatic application as required for the specific case. As stated by one writer:

> It may be that the international arbitrator must as a rule accept the *prima facie* application of EC competition law in accordance with its spatial and material scope, but the arbitrators may properly curtail or attenuate the full application of EC competition law in view of some other applicable legal rule of the *lex causae* or *lex arbitrii*, or in view of some other consideration, for example, one related to the specific features of international arbitration or the particular case at hand.[6]

5 N. Shelkoplyas, *The Application of EC Law in Arbitration Proceedings* (Europa Law Publishing 2003) 276.

6 P. Landolt, *Modernised EC Competition Law in International Arbitration* (Kluwer 2006) at 227.

12-14 Whilst extensively discussed, international public policy remains a vague and perhaps shadowy concept. It reflects the *"fundamental economic, legal, moral, political, religious and social standards of every State or extra-national community"*.[7] Whilst constantly evolving in any particular jurisdiction, it can be considered to include *"those principles and standards which are so sacrosanct as to require [their] maintenance at all costs and without exception"*.[8] Increasingly in recent years national concepts of international public policy have been influenced by more international factors and developed or endorsed by international institutions such as the United Nations and the European Union.

12-15 To the extent that European competition law is mandatory, it also amounts to an international public policy, at least as far as the EU member states are concerned. There can be little doubt on this basis alone that arbitrators must apply community competition law when the seat of arbitration is located in the territory of one of the Member States, or arguably if the transaction or agreement has an effect within the EU even if the arbitration has its seat outside the EU.

12-16 Merkin asserts that an arbitration award would violate public policy

> which requires one of the parties to infringe EC law, e.g., to enter into an agreement which is contrary to the competition rules in art 81 of the Treaty of Rome or to the free movement rules in arts 28 to 30 to the Treaty of Rome, and in this respect EC law is the same as any other overriding domestic law such as tax law or criminal law.[9]

12-17 Disrespectful treatment of the mandatory law or international public policy in the seat country of arbitration may result in annulment of the award by the national court of that country. EU competition law forms part of a transnational public policy which applies and must be observed when trade between the EU Member States is affected or the effect of the transaction will be felt in the EU. On this basis it has been argued that Community competition law need be applied just because the arbitration has its seat within the EU.[10]

7 Julian DM Lew, *Applicable Law in International Commercial Arbitration* (1978) at 532.

8 *Ibid.*, at 532. Quote from Chesire and North, *Private International Law* (9th ed) at 149-150.

9 R. Merkin, *Arbitration Law* (Informa Legal Publishing 2004) at no 20.11.

10 Claus-Dieter Ehlermann and Isabela Atanasiu (eds), *European Competition Law Annual 2001: Effective Private Enforcement of EC Antitrust Law* (Hart 2003) at 329. Lew *supra* note 7 at 534.

4. Competition Law

12-18 As already alluded to, competition law may be applicable on the grounds of party autonomy, arbitrators' autonomy and as mandatory rules. It may be chosen explicitly or implicitly by the parties or arbitrators as *lex contractus* or *lex causae.*[11]

4.1. EU Competition Law

12-19 The EU competition laws have a principal base in Articles 81 and 82 of the Treaty. They should be reviewed in full.

12-20 Article 81(1) prohibits specific agreements, decisions and concerted practices which may affect trade between Member States and which have as their object or effect the prevention, restriction or distortion of competition within the common market, and which

> '(a) directly or indirectly fix purchase or selling prices or any other trading conditions;
> (b) limit or control production, markets, technical development, or investment;
> (c) share markets or sources of supply;
> (d) apply dissimilar conditions to equivalent transactions with other trading parties, thereby placing them at a competitive disadvantage;
> (e) make the conclusion of contracts subject to the acceptance by the other parties of supplementary obligations, which, by their nature or according to commercial usage, have no connection with the subject matter of such contracts.'

> '2. Any agreements or decisions prohibited pursuant to this article shall be automatically void.'
> '3. The provisions of paragraph 1 may, however, be declared inapplicable in the case of any agreement or category of agreements between undertakings, any decision or category of decisions by associations of undertakings, or any concerted practice or category of concerted practices, which contributes to improving the production or distribution of goods or to promoting technical or

[11] S. Dempegiotis, "EC Competition Law and International Arbitration in the Light of EC Regulation 1/2003", 25(3) *J. Int'l Arb.* (2008) 383.

economic progress, while allowing consumers a fair share of the resulting benefit, and which does not:

(a) impose on the undertakings concerned restrictions which are not indispensable to the attainment of these objectives;

(b) afford such undertakings the possibility of eliminating competition in respect of a substantial part of the products in question.'

12-21 Under the Article 81(2), agreements violating Article 81 are automatically null and void unless exempted under Article 85(3). As described below, initially all applications for exemption had to be made to the EU Commission or come within block exemptions set down in Commission Regulations. Parties had to apply specifically for such exemption and persuade the Commission the agreement, arrangement or undertaking came within the terms of Article 85(3).

12-22 Article 82 prohibits actions by parties that dominate or control the market and which may affect trade between EU Member States. Such actions are considered *an abuse of a dominant position* and consist in particular of actions which

> '(a) directly or indirectly imposing unfair purchase or selling prices or other unfair trading conditions;
> (b) limiting production, markets or technical development to the prejudice of consumers;
> (c) applying dissimilar conditions to equivalent transactions with other trading parties, thereby placing them at a competition disadvantage;
> (d) making the conclusion of contracts subject to acceptance by the other parties of supplementary obligations which, by their nature or according to commercial usage, have no connection with the subject of such contracts.'

12-23 Under EC Regulation 17/1962 the EC Commission had exclusive powers and responsibility to enforce the Community competition law. It was the only institution with the authority to grant exemption under Article 81(3) for the strict application and effect of Article 81(1) and (2). The Courts and the tribunals had to adjourn their proceedings pending the Commission's examination of the application for individual exemption. In time it was realized that the system was over-centralised, cumbersome and inefficient.[12]

[12] *Ibid.*, at 376.

12-24 As a first stage to make things simpler for contracting parties, the Commission issued "block exemptions" to cover matters which would fall within Article 81(3). These block exemptions contained detailed pre-specified terms for specific types of contracts (e.g. distribution agreements[13], patent licenses[14]). If a contract contained these provisions it received automatic exemption from nullity under Article 81(1) and (2), and there was no need to apply to the Commission for exemption.

12-25 Subsequently, in 1999, looking to make the administration of the competition law more efficient and effective, the Commission released a White Paper acknowledging that the

> division [provided by the system] between paragraph 1 and paragraph 3 in implementing Article 81 is artificial and runs counter to the integral nature of Article 81.[15]

12-26 In this light, the EU Commission introduced new regulations which enabled the national courts and authorities to play a greater role in enforcement of the Community competition rules. Particularly, enforcement of the Articles 81 and 82 was altered by the new EC Regulation 1/2003, in force as of May 2004. It emphasized that enforcement and proper function of Community competition law requires rearrangement of the applicable exemption system. Accordingly, this new Regulation provides for de-centralisation of the system and bestowed on national courts and competition authorities the power to grant individual exemptions. (This is discussed below)

4.2. U.S. Competition Law

12-27 In the U.S. the principal antitrust or competition legislation is the Sherman Antitrust Act (or 'Sherman Act') of 1890.[16] It was enacted as "a comprehensive charter of economic liberty aimed at preserving free and unfettered competition as the rule of trade".[17] The two principal sections prohibit "contracts…in restraint

[13] Commission Regulation 2790/1999, OJ L 336/21.

[14] Commission Regulation 772/2004, OJ L 123/11.

[15] Commission White Paper on Modernisation of the Rules Implementing Articles 85 and 86 of the EC Treaty, 28 April 1999, Commission Programme No. 99/12., COM (1999) 101 final at 2, para 49.

[16] Act of July 2, 1890, ch. 647, 26 Stat. 209, as amended, codified at 15 U.S.C §§ 1-7.

[17] *Northern Pacific Railway Co. v. United States,* 356 U.S. 1 (1958) at 4.

of trade" which were declared illegal[18]; and all forms of monopoly and monopoly behavior which are stated to be a felony.[19]

12-28 The first concept to preclude anti-competitive agreements is set out in section 1 of the Sherman Act. This provides:

> Every contract, combination in the form of trust or otherwise, or conspiracy, in restraint of trade or commerce among the several States, or with foreign nations, is hereby declared to be illegal.[20]

12-29 Section 2 makes obtaining a monopoly by anti-competitive means or abusing a monopoly illegal, rather than monopoly itself. It states:

> Every person who shall monopolize, or attempt to monopolize, or combine or conspire with any other person or persons, to monopolize any part of the trade or commerce among the several States, or with foreign nations, shall be deemed guilty of a felony...[21]

12-30 Both of these prohibitions have been developed over the years through the interpretation and application by the courts and are reflected in the relevant case law. The competition law, as contained in the Sherman Act, was expanded by the Clayton Act[22] and the Federal Trade Commission Act, passed in 1914.[23]

4.3. Remedies in EU and U.S. Competition Law

12-31 In the context of this topic there is a fundamental difference in the remedies for breach of EU and U.S. competition law. The effect of breaching Articles 81 and 82 is that the agreements, arrangements, undertakings, etc are void *ab initio*, but more significantly those entities considered to be in breach may be liable for fines imposed by the EU Commission.[24] There is no remedy for an innocent party to an agreement in breach of the competition regulations or a third party injured by the wrongful competition. By contrast, an injured party's

[18] 15 U.S.C § 1.
[19] 15 U.S.C § 2.
[20] 15 U.S.C § 1.
[21] 15 U.S.C § 2.
[22] Act of October 15, 1914, ch. 323, 38 Stat. 730, codified at 15 U.S.C. §§ 12-27, 29 U.S.C. §§ 52-53.
[23] 15 U.S.C §§ 41-58, as amended.
[24] Art. 83 EC Treaty, Art. 15(2) Regulation 17/62 [OJ 1962 at 204] and Art. 23 Regulation 1/2003 [OJ L 1/16].

action in breach of the Sherman Act may be entitled to both compensatory and punitive (treble) damages.[25] It is this difference that has been one of the reasons for the different approaches to arbitrability in the two systems.

5. ARBITRABILITY

12-32 The specific question then is whether arbitrators can decide issues involving competition law, and whether there are any limitations to the authority of arbitrators.

5.1. United States: Mitsubishi

12-33 The starting point in the modern approach to this issue is the 1985 landmark decision of the U.S. Supreme Court in *Mitsubishi Motors Corp v Soler Chrysler-Plymouth, Inc.*[26] The Supreme Court there concluded that in contracts affecting international business an arbitral tribunal could determine antitrust issues and expressly rejected arguments that antitrust disputes are ill suited to the arbitral process because they require sophisticated legal and economic analysis, and are too important to be determined by arbitrators.

12-34 The dispute concerned whether an agreement for the distribution of motor vehicles in Puerto Rico violated the Sherman Act because it precluded the distributor selling vehicles outside of Puerto Rico. The parties were from the U.S. and Japan. The Agreement provided for arbitration in Japan under the rules of the Japan Commercial Arbitration Association. The agreement expressly provided that Swiss law should govern.

12-35 When a dispute arose, Mitsubishi brought an action in the United States District Court for the District of Puerto Rico seeking an order under §4 of the Federal Arbitration Act that Soler be compelled to submit to arbitration in Japan. Soler denied the breaches alleged by Mitsubishi, but counterclaimed for various breaches by Mitsubishi including that Mitsubishi had sought to divide up markets in restraint of trade and in breach of the Sherman Act.

12-36 The matter came before the U.S. Supreme Court which had to decide whether an issue involving U.S. anti-trust law could be suitably determined by an

[25] Section 15, Clayton Act, U.S.C §§ 12-27.
[26] 473 U.S. 614 (1985).

arbitration tribunal, especially one with its seat outside the U.S.. The Court first relied on the accepted principle *"that questions of arbitrability must be addressed with a healthy regard for the federal policy favouring arbitration"*[27], and that where a contract relates to international issues antitrust, claims are arbitrable provided the specific claim comes squarely within the arbitration agreement providing for disputes between parties. It based its decision on

> concerns of international comity, respect for the capacities of foreign and transnational tribunals, and sensitivity to the need of the international commercial system for predictability in the resolution of disputes require that we enforce the parties' agreement, even assuming that a contrary result would be forthcoming in a domestic context.[28]

12-37 Prior to this decision the prevailing law was that rights conferred by anti-trust law were inappropriate for determination and enforcement by arbitration. The second circuit Court of Appeal had held that

> the pervasive public interest in enforcement of the antitrust laws and the nature of the claims that arise in such case, combine to make ant-trust claims in appropriate for arbitration.[29]

12-38 The Supreme Court expressed *"scepticism"* as to the above decision. It dismissed the various arguments to support the non-arbitrability of antitrust claims. The mere fact that there may be an antitrust issue *"does not alone warrant invalidation of the selected forum on the undemonstrated assumption that the arbitration clause is tainted"*.[30] Complexity alone is not a reason to preclude arbitration and there is no evidence that arbitrators would be hostile to the application of antitrust law. "*International arbitrators are drawn from the legal as well as the business community*" and the Court presumed parties and arbitration institutions would select *"competent, conscientious and impartial arbitrators"*[31] capable of understanding and applying antitrust laws. Finally the Court held that the punitive damages/treble-damages remedy does not preclude it being sought outside an American court.

[27] *Ibid.*, at 626, referring to *Moses H Cone Memorial Hospital*, 460 U.S. at 24.
[28] *Ibid.*, at 629.
[29] *American Safety Equipment Corp v. J P Maguire & Co*, 391 F 2d 821 (1968).
[30] *Mitsubishi Motors v. Soler Chrysler-Plymouth*, 473 U.S 614 (1985), at 615.
[31] *Ibid.*, at 634.

12-39 The rationale for the Supreme Court decision was explained in the following terms:

> As international trade has expanded in recent decades, so too has the use of international arbitration to resolve disputes arising in the course of that trade. The controversies that international arbitral institutions are called upon to resolve have increased in diversity as well as in complexity. Yet the potential of these tribunals for efficient disposition of legal disagreements arising from commercial relations has not yet been tested. If they are to take central place in the international order, national courts will need to "shake off the old judicial hostility to arbitration," Kulukundis Shipping Co. v. Amtorg Trading Corp., ... and also their customary and understandable unwillingness to cede jurisdiction of a claim arising under domestic law to a foreign or transnational tribunal. To this extent, at [...] least, it will be necessary for national courts to subordinate domestic notions of arbitrability to the international policy favouring commercial arbitration.[32] (References omitted)

12-40 However, the Supreme Court established two a tiered system for correct application of the antitrust law. The first tier was the power of arbitrators to determine antitrust disputes where the parties have agreed to international arbitration. The second tier reserved the right of the courts to review the award at the post-award stage to ensure the observance of mandatory rule. The Supreme Court stated:

> Having permitted the arbitration to go forward, the national courts of the United States will have the opportunity at the award-enforcement stage to ensure that the legitimate interest in the enforcement of the antitrust laws has been addressed.[33]

12-41 The effect of this decision has been enormous for the issue of arbitrability. It removed the sacrosanct jurisdiction of national courts over antitrust issues without removing the mandatory nature of the antitrust rules. It recognised that arbitrators appointed in international disputes are capable of determining, and are often asked to determine, issues of enormous legal, factually technical and financial complexity. There is no evidence that they are less able to do so than national court judges. Quite the contrary, as arbitrators in international cases are

[32] *Ibid.*, at 634.
[33] *Ibid.*, at 638.

selected by the parties, and the nature of the dispute will often be known before the arbitrators are appointed, those with relevant skills and experience can be selected. In any event, ultimately because of the mandatory nature of antitrust law, there will in exceptional cases be an opportunity for the courts to review the decisions of an arbitral tribunal on these issues.

5.2. EU: Regulation 1/2003 and Eco Swiss

12-42 Mitsubishi had a profound effect upon those involved with European competition law, both lawyers and at the European Commission. They appear to have accepted, by actual practice and the new regulations adopted, that the policy issues expressed by the U.S. Supreme Court, i.e., that arbitrators are capable, legally and with objectivity, of determining contractual disputes where issues of competition law are raised.

12-43 Accordingly, it is clear that as a matter of principle, arbitrability of the EU competition law disputes has ceased to be an issue outside the tribunal's competence.[34] Second, the EU Commission has liberalised the regulations to allow the courts and arbitral tribunal to determine issues where competition law issues are raised with them.

12-44 Despite these changes the authority of the European Commission has not been compromised: it retains its jurisdiction to prosecute violations of competition law. By contrast, arbitrators have a clear duty to determine any competition law issue in accordance with the applicable law. The difference is that arbitrators deal with rights *inter se* between the parties; the EU Commission is more concerned with enforcing obligations on behalf of the EU and as part of its official obligations. These two jurisdictions are not competitive.[35]

12-45 Accordingly, it is now accepted that in any case where allegations relating to the infringement of the EU competition law is raised, arbitrators have the authority and responsibility to have to answer the question whether the agreement or practice violates Article 81 and 82. If the answer to this question is

[34] B. Hanotiau, "L'arbitrabilite", in *Academie de droit international de La Haye, Recueil des cours 2002* (Hachette 2003) at 296.

[35] Similar reasons were expressed in L. Radicati Di Brozolo, "Antitrust: A Paradigm of the Relations between Mandatory Rules and Arbitration – a fresh look at the "Second Look"" 7(1) *Int'l ALR* (2004) 23.

in the affirmative, an agreement, arrangements, undertakings, etc will be automatically null and void. In such circumstances, it may still fall to the arbitral tribunal to determine the issues between the parties resulting from the declared invalidity of the agreement or practice. By corollary, the arbitral tribunal cannot exercise authority that is within the exclusive jurisdiction of the EU Commission, including, in particular, imposing fines on the parties. Depending on the circumstances, it may even be appropriate for arbitrators to award remedies stipulated in the applicable law, including damages as compensation for losses incurred.

12-46 Until 2002, the EU Commission had exclusive jurisdiction to grant exemptions in appropriate cases under Article 81(3) – if they did not fall within a block exemption. Arbitrators could consider and determine whether an agreement infringed Article 81(1) – and if it so determined the agreement was and the tribunal would declare it so, it would automatically become null and void as a result of the Article 81(2). However, arbitrators could not consider and determine whether an agreement fell within the exemption under Article 81(3) that grants exemptions to the individual agreements and specific classes of agreements.

12-47 However, where there was an appropriate "block exemption" it is arguable that an arbitral tribunal could have determined whether it was applicable. Accordingly, it would have had to hear argument as to whether the facts and circumstances of the specific case fell within the requirements of the block exemption. This would not preclude one of the parties still going to the EU Commission for clearance or otherwise.

12-48 As part of the Commission proposals to modernise and make more efficient the application of Article 81(3), by EC Regulation 1/2003 it decentralised the system for application of the Articles 81 and 82. Specifically, this Regulation, along with the range of Notices,[36] granted authority to national

[36] Commission Notice on Cooperation within the Network of Competition Authorities, OJ 2004/C101/03, at 43; Commission Notice on the Handling of Complaints by the Commission under Articles 81 and 82 of the EC Treaty, OJ 2004/C 101/05, at 65; Commission Notice on the Co-operation between the Commission and the Courts of the EU Member States in the Application of Articles 81 and 82 of the EC Treaty, OJ 2004/C101/04, at 54; Commission Notice on Informal Guidance Relating to Novel Questions Concerning Articles 81 and 82 of the EC Treaty that arise in individual cases (guidance letters), OJ 2004/C101/06, at 78; Guidelines

courts and national competition authorities to apply Article 81(3) without limitations.[37]

12-49 The authority of an arbitral tribunal in light of these permissions is somewhat ambiguous. The language of Regulation 1/2003 refers solely to the national courts and national competition authorities. However, there are increasing views that even though not expressly referred to in the Regulation, as the function of arbitral tribunal is to determine disputes between parties, and as arbitrators are expected to apply EU law if applicable, arbitrators can and should exercise the powers in the same way as a national court.[38]

12-50 There is always a concern that arbitrators may determine or apply European competition law wrongly. This argument cannot be challenged as such; but arbitrators are no more likely to make errors than are national court judges. The difference is that there is an appeal on certain grounds (differing from jurisdiction to jurisdiction) from the decision of a judge to a higher court. In general, there is no right of appeal on the merits from an arbitral tribunal.

12-51 The right of arbitrators to reach decisions on European law was recognized by the ECJ in the *Eco Swiss* case.[39] In that case Eco Swiss China Time Ltd, Bulova Watch Company Inc and Benetton International NV entered into a licensing agreement permitting manufacture and subsequent sale of watches with the wording "Benetton by Bulova". The Agreement was governed by Dutch law and contained an arbitration clause providing for all disputes to be determined under the Rules of the Netherlands Arbitration Institute.

12-52 The Agreement was terminated and an arbitration award made awarding monetary compensation for wrongful termination. Benetton applied for the

---

on the Application of Article 81 (3) of the Treaty, OJ 2004/C101/08, at 97; Guidelines on the Effect on Trade Concept Contained in Articles 81 and 82 of the Treaty, OJ 2004/C101/07, at 81.

37 The Preamble to the EC Regulation 1/2003 contains, *inter alia* the following statement:

> The present system should therefore be replaced by a directly applicable exception system in which the competition authorities and courts of the Member States have the power to apply not only Article 81(1) and Article 82 of the Treaty, which have direct applicability by virtue of the case-law of the Court of Justice of the European Communities, but also Article 81(3) of the Treaty.

38 D. De Groot, "Arbitration and the Modernisation of EC Competition Law", 19(1) *European Business Law Review* (2008) 181.

39 *Eco Swiss China Time Ltd v. Benetton International NV* (Case C-126/97) of 1 June 1999, [2000] 5 CMLR 816.

annulment of the award alleging violation of Article 85 of the Treaty (currently Article 81). The application was initially rejected on the ground that it had been filed in breach of the applicable Dutch procedural rules. On appeal from the Hoge Raad, the Dutch Supreme Court filed an application under Article 234 of the EC Treaty to the ECJ requesting interpretation of the question whether:

> Arbitration tribunals are required to apply that provision [Article 81] of their own motion and whether national courts have the power to annul arbitration awards on the ground that they are contrary to the Community rules on competition.[40]

12-53 The ECJ confirmed the mandatory nature of Article 81 as a fundamental provision for the functioning of the internal Community market and importance of balancing the *"requirement to observe national procedural rules"* on the one hand, and the *"functioning of a competitive market"*[41] on the other. It concluded that

> … the national court should allow a claim for annulment of an arbitration award on the ground that it is contrary to Article 85 of the Treaty even if the national rules of procedure allow annulment on the ground of illegality only in the event of a conflict with public policy or accepted principles of morality.[42]

12-54 The effect of this decision was to recognise and affirm that national courts are entitled to review, and if appropriate annul, arbitral awards that contradict the notions of public policy.[43] The power does not depend upon the stage in the process when the allegation was raised. In the present case the party brought to the attention the issue of award's compatibility with the rules of EU competition law for the first time before the national court as a basis for the award being set aside. The court did not voice its concern as to the late stage of the allegation being raised.

[40] *Ibid.*, at para 821.
[41] *Ibid.*, at para 837.
[42] *Ibid.*, at para 837.
[43] This is what occurred in the recent decision in Tribunal de Première Instance de Bruxelles (Belgium), 8 Mars 2007, *SNF SAS v La Cytec Industrie* where the Brussels Tribunal de Premiére Instance set aside an award where it considered the remedy awarded by the Tribunal following its decision that the underlying contract violated Article 81 was inconsistent and contradictory to EC Competition law.

12-55 This decision provides protection (if such is needed) that arbitrators in the EU, or in respect of awards having effect in the EU will apply EU competition law and will do so properly. It is a recognition that arbitrators will and are obliged to apply applicable and especially mandatory rules where appropriate. Any failure to do so, or doing so wrongly, could result in the award being set aside or enforcement refused.

6. Differing Scenarios for Arbitral Tribunals in EU

12-56 As a general rule, EU competition law must be applied in cases where that law applies according to its rules. In principle, this may be arbitration proceedings taking place within or without the EU. For the reasons explained above, in all these case the EU competition law issues are arbitrable *inter partes*.

12-57 It has been suggested that the duty of an arbitral tribunal to apply EU competition law differs depending upon the origin of the parties, the subject-matter of the dispute and the place of arbitration. This law may be applicable as part of the proper law, i.e. the law which governs the substantive agreement between the parties, whether expressly chosen by the parties or chosen by the arbitral tribunal in default of party choice. It may also be applicable regardless of the proper law as mandatory law of the EU. We review various scenarios below.

12-58 The first and the simplest situation will be where the arbitration has its seat in the EU and the subject-matter of the dispute is also within the EU. In such situation to the extent that an issue of EU competition law arises the tribunal should apply it as appropriate. Whether the parties are nationals of or companies doing business in the EU is of little relevance. What matters is whether the offending agreement or arrangement has an effect on trade within the EU. This type of situation could result in an award being reviewed by a national court in light of the *Eco Swiss*.[44]

12-59 By corollary, if the arbitration has its seat outside of the EU, and the subject-matter has no relevance within the EU, then there would appear to be no relevance to the application of EU completion law even if the proper law (probably expressly chosen by the parties) is the law of an EU member state (e.g. English or French law). Here again the nationality and places of business of the

[44] *Ibid.*

parties would be of only limited if any relevance. This law only applies to transactions and agreements which has effect on trade and business within the EU.

12-60 If the arbitration has its seat outside the EU but the subject-matter of the dispute is within the EU, then, whatever the proper law applicable, it would appear the tribunal may have to consider the effect of any relevant EU competition law. Here the nationality or place of incorporation of the parties may have a greater relevance to the determination of the issue. The Tribunal Fédéral Suisse recognised the obligation of a tribunal with its seat in Switzerland to apply Community competition law (and hence its arbitrability).[45] In that case the award was annulled because the tribunal had refused to rule on the validity of the contract on the ground that it lacked jurisdiction to verify the compatibility of the contract with the Community competition rules.

12-61 A more complicated scenario is where the arbitration has its seat outside of the EU, the proper law is not the law of an EU member state, and the subject-matter of the dispute has effect in both the EU and outside the EU. In this case it will be for the tribunal to determine the extent to which, the specific EU law extends to apply outside the EU, and whether, in the circumstances, it can be applied differently to those aspects of the subject-matter of the dispute that are and are not within the EU.

7. Parallel Proceedings: Arbitration Tribunal and Commission

12-62 A practical dilemma can arise where the EU Commission opens an investigation at the same time as the tribunal is dealing with a particular issue. In general, the focus will differ even if the fundamental contractual arrangement will be the same: the rationale for the arbitration is the rights and obligations of the parties; the Commission investigation is to uphold and enforce EU competition law. The question for this parallel proceedings scenario is whether the tribunal should stay its proceedings pending the outcome of the Commission investigation.[46]

[45] Tribunal Fédéral Suisse, 28 April 1992, (1992) ASA Bulletin 368. See also: Tribunal Fédéral Suisse, 13 November 1998, (1999) ASA Bulletin 445 and 529.

[46] This dilemma is similar to the limitation on national courts and institutions which much recognise the exclusive power of the ECJ to interpret the EU Treaty: Article 234. Whilst

12-63 One important factor is the time when the tribunal was established. One party may resort to arbitration and subsequently the other party makes a complaint to the Commission seeking an investigation of the same arrangement. Alternatively, the Commission may have commenced its investigation in to a particular situation or arrangement, when one party affected exercises its contractual right and commences parallel arbitration proceedings.

12-64 There is no clear answer to the question whether a tribunal should stay the arbitration until the Commission has reported. Much will depend on the circumstances of the case, the alleged breach of the competition law and the timings of the parallel proceedings. The concern generally is to avoid conflicting decisions in public law and *inter partes*.

12-65 However, as a general rule, with respect to the first case above, there is a prevailing opinion that the tribunal should continue with its determination. This means that arbitration proceedings need not be stayed if the Commission is in a process of investigation. The tribunal has to fulfil its obligation and complete the mandate and has no obligation (or right for that matter) to seek advice from the Commission on the issue of competition law. Where an investigation is pending, even where started subsequent to the arbitration, the tribunal would need to decide whether to proceed with its mandate or await the outcome of the Commission's investigation. Ultimately, whatever the timing, and despite the risk of conflicting decisions a tribunal will have to decide whether to determine the issues before it or wait and take into account the conclusions of the Commission.

12-66 In the second scenario, the tribunal may need to determine its jurisdiction *per se,* and the difference between the issues it is being asked to determine and those being investigated by the Commission. As it is a private tribunal and not part of state machinery, it can be argued it should continue regardless of the Commission investigation. Under the Article 249 of the Treaty, national courts cannot contradict a decision of the Commission. However, as an arbitration tribunal does not perform an adjudicative function on behalf of the State it falls outside the jurisdiction of Article 249 and has no direct obligation to follow the Commission's decision.

---

arbitrators who are under an obligation to comply with the interpretation of the Treaty by the ECJ, as European law, as a private body it is not directly subservient to the ECJ.

12-67 On a pragmatic level it may be possible, before making a decision on these issues, for the tribunal to seek to co-operate and exchange information with the Commission. While arbitrators are not under an obligation to inform the Commission on the nature of the proceedings being held – there is a strong argument that the duty of confidentiality under the arbitration procedure and the arbitrators' professional regulations preclude this co-operation – it may approach the Commission with the questions of legal or factual questions relevant to the Community competition law and the nature of any investigation the Commission is undertaking.[47] It is uncertain how helpful or informative the Commission can or will be especially where it needs to keep its internal deliberations confidential and not prejudice its decision until published.

8. Conclusion

12-68 Arbitrability of competition law has ceased to be a significant issue in international arbitration. The reasons are simple. First, on a pragmatic level, international arbitration and its users have reached a level of sophistication and acceptance that arbitrators can and should determine all issues regardless of complication or content.

12-69 Second, arbitrators must apply competition law rules in the same way as they apply any other applicable law. Whatever the complication of the facts or legal issues involved, arbitrators must determine them to the best of their ability. There is no reason why competition law should be an exception to the overall duty of arbitrators. In fact, the jurisdiction or authority of arbitrators is restricted only for determinations of public law issues, such as fines or penalties due to breaches of competition law. These determinations are restricted to the appropriate court or regulatory authority which decides for the state and not *inter partes*.

12-70 Third, and this provides the regulatory authorities with some comfort, *Mitsubishi* and *Eco Swiss* established a "safety valve" to ensure that the mandatory character of competition law was maintained. This may allow the competent national courts or regulatory authorities, in certain situations, to investigate and make decisions concerning public law issues without necessarily interfering with the rights of the parties *inter se*. Further, where appropriate,

[47] S. Dempegiotis, *supra* note 11 at 388.

national courts may have the opportunity to review the competition law determinations of arbitrators in the context of challenges and applications to set aside arbitration awards or when proceedings are brought for the recognition and enforcement of awards.

*Anna P. Mantakou**

CHAPTER 13

ARBITRABILITY AND INTELLECTUAL PROPERTY DISPUTES

1. INTRODUCTION

13-1 In view of the Report of the working party on arbitration and intellectual property set up by the Arbitration Commission of the International Chamber of Commerce (ICC) in the mid 1990s,[1] this paper could also bear the title: "Arbitrability of Intellectual Property Disputes: Ten Years Later". Almost ten years ago, there was significant international, (both institutional and academic,)[2] discussion on issues regarding intellectual property dispute resolution. This activity was triggered by the initiative of the World Intellectual Property Organisation (WIPO) to create an arbitral centre, specialised, though not exclusive, in the arbitration and ADR of intellectual property issues. Ten years

* "Anna P. Mantakou Law Office" Athens, Greece; member of the ICC Court and Secretary General of Hellenic Association for Arbitration.

1 The text of the Report appears as Annex in Jacques Werner's, "Intellectual Property Disputes and Arbitration. A Comment on a Recent ICC Report", *The Journal of World Intellectual Property* (1998) 841-886.

2 See for example: Association Suisse de l' arbitrage (ASA), "Objective Arbitrability - Antitrust Disputes - Intellectual Property Disputes", 6 *ASA Special Series* (1994); David W. Plant, "Arbitrability of Intellectual Property Issues in the United States" *Am. Rev. Int'l Arb.* (1994) 11-27; Robert Briner, "The Arbitrability of Intellectual Property Disputes with Particular Emphasis on the Situation in Switzerland", *ibid.* 28-44; Jochen Pagenberg, "The Arbitrability of Intellectual Property Disputes in Germany", *ibid.* 44-53; Julian D.M. Lew, "The Arbitration of Intellectual Property Disputes", *ibid.* 110-116; Bryan Niblett, "The Arbitration of Intellectual Property Disputes" *ibid* 117-120; Judith A. Freedberg-Swartzburg, "Facilities for the Arbitration of Intellectual Property Disputes", *Hague Yearbook of Int'l L.* (1995) 69-85; P.E. Geller, "Intellectual Property in the Global Marketplace - Impact of TRIPS Dispute Settlements", *Int'l Law* (1995) 99-115; Marc Blessing, "Arbitrability of Intellectual Property Disputes", *Arb. Int'l* (1996) 191-221; a more recent overview especially for patent infringement and validity arbitrability: M.A. Smith et al, "Arbitration of Patent Infringement and Validity Issues Worldwide", *Harvard Journal of Law & Technology* (2006) 299-357.

L Mistelis & S Brekoulakis (eds), Arbitrability: International & Comparative Perspectives, 263-271

later, the international legal "landscape", in relation to the arbitrability of these disputes, has not substantially changed.

13-2 This paper focuses on what the French would call "*la problématique*" of the subject, namely setting out and highlighting the problems, rather than going into a detailed analysis of the solutions given, or, in most cases not directly given, by the various national systems on the question of which intellectual property disputes are arbitrable and which are not.

2. The Notion of Intellectual Property and Types of Disputes Involved

13-3 Intellectual property "is the branch of the law which protects some of the finer manifestations of human achievement",[3] such as technological inventions and designs rights, literary, artistic and musical creations and the related neighbouring rights, distinctive signs and trademarks employed in trade, computers' software, microchips, know-how and confidential information rights, even plant breeder's rights. The term intellectual property (IP) does not cover satisfactorily all of them, but the term has now acquired international acceptance.[4] The definition of IP contained in Article 2 (viii)[5] of the Convention Establishing the WIPO is so broad that a great variety of human activities fall into the category of IP rights. It is obvious that nowadays IP issues form part of an internationally huge economic activity. *Therefore, they are foremost property related rights.*

13-4 The variety of IP rights gives rise to various types of IP disputes. Some of them, such as disputes arising from IP licences or agreements for the transfer of IP, have a clear contractual basis; some others, such as disputes arising from

3 William Cornish and David Llewelyn, *Patents, Copyright, Trade Marks and Allied Rights* (5th ed, 2003) at 3.

4 *Ibid.*

5 "intellectual property shall include the rights relating to:
- literary, artistic and scientific works,
- performances of performing artists, phonograms, and broadcasts,
- inventions in all fields of human endeavor,
- scientific discoveries,
- industrial designs,
- trade marks, service marks, and commercial names and designations,
- protection against unfair competition,

and all other rights resulting from intellectual activity in the industrial, scientific, literary or artistic fields."

illicit copying and counterfeiting are mainly tortious and therefore there is no pre existing arbitration agreement between two parties. Some others, such as disputes in connection with ownership, validity, scope and infringement may or may not have a contractual basis. Very often issues involving, for example, validity or ownership may arise in the form of preliminary issues in the context of a dispute involving a licence agreement.[6] It has to be pointed out, though, that the lack of a pre-existing contract between the parties does not exclude the possibility of referring an IP dispute to arbitration on the basis of a submission agreement,[7] provided that the dispute *per se* is arbitrable.

3. Why Arbitrability of IP Issues is of "Special Concern"?

13-5 It has been suggested that: "On scrutiny, the special nature of IP arbitration is not really all that special."[8] I am favourably inclined towards this view, with the exception of the arbitrability issues which are, in some respects, special and could therefore prevent or restrict arbitration in some countries, mainly due to the following reasons:

1. Some aspects of IP rights are held not to be freely disposable by the parties.
2. Some types of IP rights and/or disputes are held to be within the exclusive domain of the national administrative panels and bureaus and/or national courts.

4. The Area of Possible Restrictions

13-6 The two major issues which may raise obstacles to the settlement by arbitration of certain types of IP disputes: namely, the "disposability" of IP rights and IP titles requiring state involvement, which shall now be examined:

6 See *infra* under V.

7 An agreement to arbitrate after the dispute has arisen is difficult in practice, since after the dispute has arisen the parties are often unable to agree on anything, including the method of the resolution of their dispute. In this respect, the facilities offered by the WIPO Submission Advisory Service may be proved useful. The WIPO Arbitration Center can be approached by a party and organise a meeting with the other party with a view to reaching an amicable settlement or assisting the parties in the drafting of a submission agreement. See WIPO Publication No. 445 (E) (1994) 20-22.

8 William W. Park, "Irony in Intellectual Property Arbitration", *Arb. Int'l* (2003) 451-455, 451.

4.1. Are IP Rights Freely Disposable?

13-7 Internationally, the issue of arbitrability is mainly determined by either the property nature of the claims brought to arbitration[9] or the right of the parties to an arbitration agreement to freely dispose of the subject-matter of the dispute. [10]

13-8 Whilst, nowadays the prevailing feature of IP rights is their financial nature, there is no question that these rights have also a moral aspect. The moral right of the author is linked with his personality, honour and dignity. As a result, disputes concerning the ownership or authenticity of a literary, artistic or scientific work are, according to a view much discussed in French law countries,[11] non-arbitrable because of an alleged inalienability and therefore "*non-disponibilité*" of the relevant rights. Despite the doctrinal reservations about the arbitrability of disputes relating to the moral right of the author, the French Court of Appeal, confirmed, at least once, the possibility of settling by arbitration a dispute relating directly to the author's moral right.[12] Here, the author of an English book had contractually transferred his rights to an English editor. The translation rights into French had been transferred by the editor to a French sub-editor. Both contracts contained a similar arbitration clause. The author complained about a breach of contract imputable to the French sub-editor entailing harm to the honour of the book. The Court had no difficulty in confirming the decision of the first instance court to decline jurisdiction in favour of arbitration.

13-9 Similarly, the Supreme Court of Canada, in 2003,[13] in a decision, which commentators consider as the Canadian Mitsubishi case, categorically affirmed the arbitrability of a dispute touching upon the author's moral right. The dispute concerned the interpretation of a licence agreement for the exploitation of a fictitious person Gaillou, a "cute" animated figure for children. The Supreme Court reversed the decision of the Court of Appeal of Quebec by rejecting *inter alia* the argument that moral rights are non-arbitrable. The Supreme Court

9 For example the Swiss and German model.

10 For example the French, Greek, Dutch, Italian and Spanish model.

11 See, Bruno Oppetit, "L' arbitrabilité des litiges de droit d'auteur et droit voisins", *Arbitrage et Propriété Intellectuelle* (1994) 121-131; Muriel Josselin-Gall, "Nouvelles perspectives en matière d'arbitrage - Arbitrage et propriétés intellectuelles", 105 *Droit et Patrimoine* (2002) 63-81.

12 Zeldin c/ Sté Editions Recherches : Cour d'appel de Paris, 1ère Ch., 26 mai 1993 *Revue Internationale du Droit d'Auteur* (1994) 292.

13 Editions Chouette inc. c/ Desputeaux : Cour Suprême du Canada, 21 mars 2003 : *Rev. Arb.* (2003) 473 with comments by Frédéric Bachand.

acknowledged that an artistic work constituted a manifestation of the personality of its author. It stressed, nevertheless, the fact that the Canadian copyright legislation, aiming primarily at a financial arrangement of the author's rights, did not prevent the artists from coming to an agreement with regard to their moral rights; by doing so the artists could even waive these rights and they could do so for a valuable consideration. Thus, it seems that there is a strong judicial tendency towards moral rights to be considered as freely disposable by the parties in the same jurisdictions in which the academic discussion suggests quite the opposite.

13-10 Still, there is one more case in which disputes involving IP rights may be considered as directly non-arbitrable. I refer to IP disputes arising from intellectual property rights of employees acquired during and in relation to an employment contract. In some countries, disputes which fall in the category of labour disputes may be declared non-arbitrable. In Greece, for example, if a dispute falls in the category of labour disputes, as the latter are defined by law, it cannot be referred to arbitration pursuant to an explicit provision of the Greek Code of Civil Procedure (CCP).[14]

4.2. IP Titles Requiring State Involvement

13-11 Patents and registered trademarks need typically to be registered with a public record. The acquisition and publicity of the relevant rights require the involvement of state authorities. Is this *per se* a reason to exclude disputes concerning the validity of a patent or trade mark from arbitration? In this field two major tendencies can be identified: the U.S./Swiss approach and the European Union countries approach. In the U.S., with the enactment, in 1983, of a specific statutory provision (35 U.S.C. § 294), virtually all issues concerning U.S. patents are properly subject to binding arbitration in the U.S..[15] As far as the arbitrability of trademark issues arising from a federal trademark statute is concerned, the answer is likely to be in the affirmative.[16] In this respect, Switzerland seems to be the pioneer of the liberal approach. In 1975, the Federal

[14] Article 867 of the Greek CCP renders the so-called "labour disputes" of Article 663 of the same Code non-arbitrable. By virtue of Law 2735/1999, Greece adopted, with slight modifications, the UNCITRAL Model Law on International Commercial Arbitration. However, Article 1, para 4 of the aforesaid law renders at least one category of the labour disputes provided for in Article 663 CCP *i.e.*, disputes between artisans and their clients for the works of the former, arbitrable under the Greek law of international arbitration.

[15] See Plant, *supra* note 2 at 12-15.

[16] *Ibid.* at 19.

Office of Intellectual Property held that Arbitral Tribunals are empowered to decide on the validity of patents trademarks and designs. Arbitral awards can serve as a basis for entries in the relevant Registry.[17]

13-12 Within the E.U., "disputes directly affecting the existence or validity of a registered intellectual property right are considered non-arbitrable."[18] This seems to be the situation in Greece too. Although neither court decisions nor explicit legal provisions exist in this respect, the leading opinion in Greece[19] is that disputes concerning the granting or loss of patents cannot be brought to arbitration, despite the fact that in Greece, as well as in almost all countries, all intellectual property rights may be freely disposed of by the owner. It is difficult to see the exact legal basis upon which this type of dispute is considered non-arbitrable. It seems that the fact that these rights are acquired by means of a state authority's act, classifies them automatically in the sphere of public policy, which in some jurisdictions constitutes *per se* a bar to arbitrability.

13-13 Things are rather clear in countries like Germany, where nullity proceedings fall within the exclusive jurisdiction of State Courts, such as the Federal Patent Court in Germany. It should be noted however that in Germany the granting act issued by the Patent Office is based on a substantive examination of the validity of the patent.[20] It is therefore understandable that the German legislator chose to have the whole spectrum of disputes concerning the grant or loss of the title excluded from the ambit of private justice. On the other hand, in such countries as Greece and France, where the granting act is based solely on a formal examination of the validity of the patent, the insistence on the non-arbitrability sounds contradictory: the state authority does not examine, questions such as, who is the real owner of the invention or whether the invention complies with the substantive requirements for the granting of the title, while at the same time, it claims exclusive jurisdiction of state courts on the ground that these rights touch upon the interests of the society.[21]

[17] See Briner, *supra* note 2 at 38.

[18] Julian Lew, Loukas Mistelis & Stefan Kröll, *Comparative International Commercial Arbitration* (Kluwer 2003) at 209.

[19] Anghelos Foustoucos, "The Validity of the Arbitration Agreement and its Control", *Nomiko Vima* (1992) 1366-1381 (in Greek), 1368; Thanassis Liakopoulos, *Industrial Property* (2000) 251 (in Greek).

[20] See Plant, *supra* note 2 at 48.

[21] Along the same lines see Francis Gurry, "Objective Arbitrability - Antitrust Disputes. Intellectual Property Disputes", 6 *ASA Special Series* (1994) 110-120, 116. For the Greek system of patents' examination, see Law 1733/1987 and Liakopoulos, *supra* note 19 at 211-213.

13-14 It is, therefore, submitted that disputes concerning the validity of a patent for grounds which have not been pre-examined by the state authority during the patent grant stage, should be considered as arbitrable. To be realistic, this is more likely to be admitted for disputes concerning the ownership of a patent, which are introduced in the form of an action claiming the right on the patent rather than in nullity proceedings.

13-15 The argument that this type of IP dispute cannot be referred to arbitration because an arbitral award has only *inter partes* effect and therefore cannot affect an IP right which is an *erga omnes* right is questionable. Equally judicial decisions have no *erga omnes* effect, at least in the continental jurisdictions, unless is otherwise stipulated by the law.[22] However, arbitral awards are not, in principle, deprived from a *res judicata* effect. The real question here is whether an arbitral award can serve as a basis for alterations in the Patent's registry. If the dispute is arbitrable and the arbitral award is final, then it is submitted that it can serve as a title for the Registry's entry purposes.

13-16 Two comments specifically regarding trademarks: first, in Greece, unlike for example in France, the trademark office proceeds, in the course of the registration procedure, with a substantive examination of the mark for conflicts with prior registrations. Second, in Greece, disputes concerning the acquisition, transfer and loss of rights in trademarks fall within the exclusive jurisdiction of administrative courts. Civil courts are bound by the decisions of the administrative courts and they are not entitled to decide upon these issues, not even in an incidental manner.[23] These two elements, namely the state's involvement covering all aspects of the title's validity and the disputes being of an administrative law nature, leave, in my view, no room for them to be considered as arbitrable in countries with a similar system of trademark registration.

See, however, the situation in Italian law, where it seems that the bar to arbitrability stems from a specific provision of the Law on Patents providing for the *ex officio* authority of the Public Ministry to initiate proceedings with regards to patents' validity: Aldo Frignani, "Nouveautés sur la arbitrage en matière de propriété intellectuelle et de droit des sociétés en Italie" 2 *Les Cahiers de l'Arbitrage* (2005) 30-36, 30.

22 In Italy, for example, Article 79 of the Law on Patents provides specifically for an *erga omnes* effect of the decisions on the nullity or forfeiture of patents, provided that such decisions have a *res judicata* effect. See Aldo Frignani, *ibid.* Arbitral Awards are not, in principle, deprived from a *res judicata* effect. See in this respect, Bernard Hanotiau, "L'authorité de chose jugée des sentences arbitrales", Cour Internationale d'arbitrage de la CCI, L'arbitrage complexe, 45-54.

23 Liakopoulos, *supra* note 19 at 365.

5. The Restriction-Free Area

13-17 Having examined the area of possible restrictions on the arbitrability of IP disputes, the restriction-free area becomes evident: disputes in the field of IP ownership, licences, their scope and infringements thereof are as a rule arbitrable. In practice, IP arbitration addresses principally contractual rights and obligations, breaches and infringements under licence agreements. Apart from some exceptional circumstances, [24] all issues relating to the exploitation and management and economic handling of IP rights are arbitrable.

13-18 In this context, there is only one issue of further consideration: the case where the subject-matter of arbitration includes both arbitrable and non-arbitrable IP issues. In this case arbitrators shall decline jurisdiction over the non-arbitrable issues and proceed with those that are arbitrable. The situation gets more complicated when the non-arbitrable issue is a preliminary issue for the determination of the arbitrable issue: should the arbitral tribunal stay its proceedings, waiting for the determination of a state court upon the preliminary issue? In this respect, a much-discussed decision of the French Court of Appeal in 1994, the Deco case,[25] gives some guidance. Briefly, the message is the following: in France, the question of the validity of a patent is not arbitrable. Questions pertaining to the performance and interpretation of the contract concluded in the exercise of the rights from the patent are arbitrable. An Arbitral Tribunal is not under obligation to stay its proceedings, as long as the action brought before the state court has a different subject matter than that in the Request for Arbitration. In this case, one of the parties to the arbitration had already had recourse to the "*Tribunal de Grande Instance*",[26] requesting the declaration of the nullity of the patent. According to the Court the Arbitral Tribunal was not obliged to stay its proceedings, since the dispute before it concerned, as a preliminary question, the scope of the Patent and not its validity *per se.* No need to say that the distinction is extremely delicate and it may only be dealt with by arbitral tribunals on a case by case basis.

[24] Such as Greek patents on inventions that interest the national defence, whose owners are deprived from their right to freely exploit their invention, Law 4325/1963, which raises serious issues of constitutionality.

[25] 24 March 1994: *Rev. Arb.* (1994) 515, with comments by Charles Jarosson. The Partial Arbitral Award which gave rise to the decision of the Court of Appeal in: Clunet (1992) 998.

[26] Along the same lines a 1956 decision of the Italian Supreme Court, reported by Aldo Frignani, *supra* note 21 at 31.

6. Conclusion

13-19 In conclusion, one may say that, as a rule, the majority of IP disputes are capable of being referred to arbitration. On the other hand, the variety of IP rights together with the great diversity of national legal systems with regard to arbitrability of IP disputes are factors which require the parties' extreme caution in drafting arbitration clauses involving IP issues. This is especially so regarding IP titles, such as patents and trademarks, that require the involvement of the state. Depending on the extent of the State Authority's involvement and control, the limits of arbitrability may be narrowed accordingly. Procedural issues arising from arbitral and non-arbitral claims submitted before the same tribunal, shall be most likely decided on a case-by-case basis.

Pilar Perales Viscasillas[*]

CHAPTER 14

ARBITRABILITY OF (INTRA-) CORPORATE DISPUTES

1. INTRODUCTION

14-1 Scholars dealing with arbitrability typically distinguish between objective arbitrability (arbitrability *rationae materiae*, i.e. matters that are capable of settlement by arbitration) and subjective arbitrability[1] (authority and capacity).

14-2 This chapter focuses on the objective arbitrability of intra-corporate disputes, i.e., those that arise out of the internal affairs of the corporation, rather than those arise out of contracts with other corporations. In addition the chapter is cognisant of the wider scope of objective arbitrability, especially the fact that arbitrability is an issue to be decided in accordance with domestic laws on arbitration,[2] which define arbitrability including both the subject matter of arbitration and the need of a dispute to exist.[3]

* Commercial Law Professor at University of La Rioja. The present work is written under the Research Project of the Ministry of Science and Technology (Spain) (DER2008-02244/JURI). Head of the team: Prof. Pilar Perales Viscasillas.

1 See Julian Lew, Loukas Mistelis & Stefan Kröll, *Comparative International Commercial Arbitration* (Kluwer 2003) at chapter 9. Some authors also refer to arbitrability *ratione jurisdictionis* (Kresimir Sajko, "Arbitration Agreement and Arbitrability. Solutions and Open Issues in Croatian and Comparative Law", 3 *Croatian Arbitration Yearbook* (1996) 44; and Alan Uzelac, "New Boundaries of Arbitrability Under the Croatian Law on Arbitration", 9 *Croatian Arbitration Yearbook* (2002) 140). The later also refers to arbitrability *ratione institutionis* (*ibid.* at 152 and 155).

2 The UNCITRAL Model Law on International Commercial Arbitration (1985) (MAL) is silent about arbitrability of the disputes, except in relation with the annulment of the award and its recognition and enforcement. From our point of view is better to keep a separate reference to arbitrability and to the public order, and thus not to include the former in the latter. Precisely in order to keep consistency with the 1958 New York Convention on the Recognition and Enforcement of Foreign Arbitral Awards (NYC), a proposal made during the discussion of

L Mistelis & S Brekoulakis (eds), Arbitrability: International & Comparative Perspectives, 273-292

14-3 At the same time, both the dispute and the matter capable of being object of arbitration are a component of an arbitration agreement;[4] however, arbitrability ought to be distinguished from the question of validity of an arbitration agreement.[5] The issue of arbitrability goes beyond the scope of an arbitration

---

MAL to eliminate the notion of arbitrability from Art. 34(2)(b)(i) and 36(b)(i) was rejected (see Howard Holtzmann/Joseph Neuhaus, *A Guide to the UNCITRAL Model Law on International Commercial Arbitration: Legislative History and Commentary* (Kluwer 1989) at 918 (footnote 36) and 1062). MAL does, however, deal with commercial disputes and contains in a footnote a non-exhaustive list of transactions considered commercial.
Arbitrability would be analysed by the arbitrators and the national judges, but not by the person in charge of the commercial registry, who therefore cannot deny the registration of a company on the basis of the inarbitrability of the matters contained in the arbitration clause. See: Bernardo Cremades, "El convenio arbitral", 5754 *La Ley* (4 abril 2003) 3.

3 See Art. 177.1 Swiss Private International Law (*Any dispute involving property can be the subject-matter of an arbitration*); Art. 177(2) refers to subjective arbitrability:

> If a party to the arbitration agreement is a state, a state-held enterprise, or a stated-owned organisation, it cannot rely on its own law in order to contest its capacity to be a party to an arbitration or the arbitrability of a dispute covered by the arbitration agreement;

Art. 3.1 Croatian Arbitration Law (2001): "Parties may agree on domestic arbitration for the settlement of disputes regarding rights of which they may freely dispose" (see the English translation by Prof. Alan Uzelac, in *International Handbook on Commercial Arbitration: Suppl. 39*, October 2003, annex I(B)(1) (Kluwer); and in *Revista Corte Española de Arbitraje* (2003) 455-474); and Art. 2 Spanish Arbitration Act:

> 1. All disputes relating to matters that may be freely dispose of at law are capable of being settled by arbitration. 2. When an arbitration is international and one of the parties is a State or company, organization or enterprise controlled by a State, that party may not avail itself of the privileges of its domestic law to avoid its obligations under the arbitration agreement

Translation by Fernando Mantilla at 43 *ILM* 484 (2004). There is another translation made by David JA Cairns & Alejandro Lopez Ortiz, "Spain's New Arbitration Act", 2 *Int'l ALR* (2004) 39-48. A French translation made by Shearman & Sterling LLP in 2 *Rev. Arb* (2004) at 459-479.

4 See, for example, Spanish Arbitration Act, Arts. 2.1 "All *disputes* relating to *matters that may be freely disposed of at law* are capable of being settled by arbitration" and 9.1

> The arbitration agreement, which may be in the form of a clause in a contract or in the form of a separate agreement, must express the will of the parties to submit to arbitration all or certain *disputes* that have arisen, or that may arise, *with respect to a particular legal relationship*, whether contractual or non-contractual.

5 See the confusion of the U.S. Courts, particularly after the case *First Option v. Kaplan*: Jack Coe, *International Commercial Arbitration: American Principles and Practice in a Global Context* (Transnational Publishers, Inc. 1997) 151; Lew, Mistelis & Kröll *supra* note 1 at no. 9-4, p. 188; and Alan Scott Rau, "The Arbitrability Question Itself", 10 *Am. Rev. Int'l Arb.* (1999) 287-370. Recent examples in the Anglo-American case law: *Queen's Bench Division (Commercial Court)*, 7 March 1997, XXIII YBCA (1998) 789-794; *United States District Court, Northern District of California,* 24 October 1996, XXIII YBCA (1998) 910-918, especially 917-918; *United States District Court, Southern District of New York*, 28 October

agreement, it is inherent to the power of States as to what issues are capable of being resolved through arbitration, and it is outside the will of the parties. On the other hand, the object of an arbitration clause is an issue to be decided by the will of the parties, who within the scope of issues that are arbitrable might exclude some of them. The parties cannot, however, agree to submit to arbitration disputes that are not arbitrable.

2. The Dispute: A Component of Arbitrability

14-4 Legal systems usually refer to a dispute between the parties as a component of arbitrability.[6] How to define those terms is not an easy task, but it is important at least to give some guidance, as there are important matters in corporate law disputes that might be pertinent in the decision-making process caused by an arbitrator. The terminology is thus important because it is in direct connection with the powers of the arbitrators and the need to distinguish between the arbitrators and the experts (also called expert arbitration)[7] or appraisers, who traditionally assume different roles and their decisions have a different force. Traditionally, it has been considered that arbitrators cannot fill gaps, modify contracts or resolve conflicts of interest, economics or of fact, but only to solve juridical or legal conflicts.[8]

1996, no. 96 Civ. 7817 (JSR); and *United States District Court, Southern District of New York*, 11 February 2003, no. 01 Civ. 10557 (LTS), XXVIII YBCA (2003) 1190-1195. See correctly: ICC 6474/1992, XXVIII YBCA (2003) 279-311, no. 153.

Neither should arbitrability be confused with third parties' responsibility as correctly pointed out by *United States District Court, Southern District of New York*, 16 October 1997 and 22 December 1997, 97 Civ. 5976 (DLC), XXIII YBCA (1998) 1082-1087, no. 6.

6 See Art. 177.1 PIL ("Any dispute"); Art. 3.1 Croatian Arbitration Law (2001): "settlement of disputes"; and Art. 2.1 Spanish Arbitration Act ("All disputes").

7 See Wolfang Peter, "Arbitration of Mergers and Acquisitions: Purchase Price Adjustment Disputes", 19(4) *Arb. Int'l* 491-505.

8 For French Law: Bruno Oppetit, "Sur le concept d`arbitrage", in *Le Droit des relations économiques internationals: Etudes offertes à Berthold Goldman* (1987) 229-239; Charles Jarrosson, *La notion d`arbitrage* (Libraire Generale de Droit et de Jurisprudence 1987) 147 et seq, 251 et seq, and 372:

> l`arbitrage est l`institution par laquelle un tiers, règle le différend qui oppose deux ou plusieurs parties, en exerçant la mission juridictionnelle qui lui a été confiée par celles-ci.

Also, see Charles Jarrosson, "Les frontières de l`arbitrage", 5 *Rev. Arb* (2001) 5-41 at 16-17 and 20; see Art. 1496 Civil Code of Procedure "l`arbitre tranche le litige" (Philippe Fouchard, Emmanuel Gaillard & Berthold Goldman, *Traité de l`arbitrage commercial international* (Litec 1996) no. 12). For the differences between arbitration and the expert: Cour de Cassation, 26 October 1976; Cour d'appel de Paris, 18 December 1992, 15 December 1998, 9 November 1999, 27 April 2000, and 21 December 2000 (respectively at 1 *Revue de l`arbitrage* (2001) 146-

14-5 Some modern arbitration statutes have considered expanding the concept of arbitrability and thus the power of the arbitrators by adding expressly the possibility of arbitrators to fill gaps or modify contracts, thus extending the scope of the dispute referred to arbitration by the parties.[9] If, however, the statute only refers to the traditional concept of "dispute", then it is questionable whether the arbitrability of the dispute can cover issues related to the change of the contract, or the determination of the price, for example, failing an express stipulation to that effect by the parties.[10]

14-6 Although, the concept of "dispute" is highly influenced by domestic law, in international commercial arbitration it is a notion that is in a process of evolution. From the traditional perspective where arbitrators can decide only legal conflicts, it is also admitted that the arbitrators can decide other kinds of disputes

---

150; 151-155 and 159-162; 175-177 and 178-182). Applying French Law: award ICC 7544/1995, 4 *Journal du Droit International* (1999) 1062-1066, whether the differences are clear: if the parties want a third person to solve a controversy, it is an arbitration; on the other hand, if the third person only has the mission to fix an element of the contract is an expert.
For Italian Law: Fiorenzo Festi, *La clausola compromissoria* (Giuffrè 2001) 62-70; and Espedito Claudio Cristofaro, "Arbitrato e Arbitraggio", in: *L`arbitrato. Fondamenti Tecniche*, edited by Enrico Caterini and Giovanna Chiappetta. Quaderni della Rassegna di diritto civile dirreta da Pietro Perlingieri. Napoli: Edizioni Scientifiche Italiane, 1995, pp.157-158.
For Spanish Law: Pilar Perales Viscasillas, *Arbitrabilidad y convenio arbitral: Ley 60/2003 de Arbitraje y Derecho Societario* (Thomson-Aranzadi 2005) 83 et seq.

9 See Art. 1020.4 Dutch Arbitration Act, 1 December 1986, which provides for arbitration to determine the quality or conformity of the goods; the quantum of damages or any other sum that is in arrears; as well as to fill gaps or modify contracts (see Klaus Peter Berger, *International Economic Arbitration (Studies in Transnational Economic Law)*, vol. IX. (Kluwer 1993) at 76-88); Swedish Arbitration Act (1999) admits the possibility for the arbitrators to interpret the contract and fill gaps (section 1); International Commercial Arbitration Act of Bulgaria (1988 modified in 1993), Art. 1.2, states that the arbitrators might fill gaps and supplement the contract, as well as to adapt it; and Portugal Arbitration Act of 29 August 1986 (Law no. 31/86, which entered into force on 29 November) considers that the parties might submit to arbitration not only disputes, but also issues related to the supplementation, interpretation and revision of the contract or the legal relationship that give rise to the arbitration.

10 It is not infrequent to see that in international commercial arbitration, scholars and case law pay attention to the wording of the arbitration clause in order to decide the scope of the powers of the arbitrators. The argument is not entirely correct. As pointed out before, arbitrability is out of the disposal of the parties, and thus the need to comply with the legal requirements of arbitrability is a condition and a limit for the will of the parties as expressed in the arbitration agreement.

(economic) as well as to fill gaps and modify contracts.[11] Within domestic arbitration laws, the answer might depend upon the status of the law, the legal scholars and case law.

14-7 A conservative position would lead to the conclusion that arbitrators cannot decide on the exit of a shareholder, or the determination of the price of shares in cases of appraisal rights, withdrawal, exclusion, freezing out or squeezing out transactions, mergers or dissolution, since this is not the task of an arbitrator but of an expert (in expert determination proceedings) or appraiser (*arbitrador*).[12]

14-8 An extended concept of "dispute", however, would imply the possibility for arbitrators to modify the articles of incorporation and thus to resolve disputes regarding voluntarily or forced exit of a shareholder from a corporation, as well as the determination of the price of shares. In any event, arbitrators cannot substitute the competent person, when law expressly provides for the exclusive and imperative of such person or body.[13] For example, an arbitrator would not be

[11] See Berger, *supra* note 9, "Power of arbitrators" at 282-284; Philippe Fouchard, Emmanuel Gaillard & Berthold Goldman, *supra* note 8 at no. 34 and 40-41; and René David, *L`arbitrage dans le commerce international* (Economica 1982) at 9, 31-38, 254-256, and 520-522.

[12] The conservative or traditional approach is followed by the majority of the Spanish scholars, but see: Perales Viscasillas, *supra* note 8 at 117-126; María José Carazo Liébana, *El arbitraje societario* (Marcial Pons 2005) 123 et seq.; and Bernardo Cremades, "El arbitraje societario", 5211 *La Ley* (22 diciembre 2000) 1-7. Recent reforms in Arbitration and company law are in line with this modern tendency: Art. 18 of the Law on Professional entities of 16th March 2007 (Ley de Sociedades Profesionales) includes within the scope of the arbitration clause disputes related to the withdrawal, squeeze-out and appraisal of the member's interest in the professional entity.
For Italian Law, a similar discussion: Piero Bernardini, "L`arbitrato nella riforma del diritto societario", in *La riforma del diritto societario. Atti del Convegno di studio svoltosi a Courmayeur, 27-28 settembre 2002*. Milano: Giufrfrè, 2003, p.302; and FESTI, p.163.
Different views in French scholars in regard to the determination by an arbitrator of the price of the shares. Against: Jacques Moury, "Des ventes et des cessions de droits sociaux à dire de tiers (étude des articles 1592 et 1843-4 du code civil)", *Rev. Sociétés* (juill-sept. 1997) 453 et seq.. In favour, interpreting Art. 1592 CC (Daniel Cohen, *Arbitrage et société* (LGDJ 1993) 175-177, but not in regard to Art. 1843.4 CC). Also in favour for Belgian Law in relation with Art. 31 of the Companies Act: Olivier Caprasse, *Les sociétés et l`arbitrage* (Bruylant (Bruxelles)/LGDJ 2002) 19-24.

[13] See for U.S. Law: Note, "Arbitration as a means of settling disputes within close corporations", 63(2) *Columbia Law Review* (1963) 267-289. For French Law: Cohen, *supra* note 12 at 127-134; Bernard Hanotiau, "L'arbitrabilité", in *Recueil des Cours - Collected Courses of The Hague Academy of International Law* (2002) Tome 296, (The Hague Boston London, Martinus Nijhoff Publishers, 2003) at 165-166; and Jean-Baptiste Racine, *L'Arbitrage commercial international et l`ordre public* (LGDJ 1999) 88-90. For Spanish Law: Eduardo

able to decide on the petition of a shareholder to be withdrawn from the corporation, or to decide whether a merger should take place, since the exclusive competence for doing so rests on the corporate organs or as the case might be, the shareholders meeting or the board of directors.[14] Once a decision has been adopted, i.e., whether a cause to withdraw from a corporation exists or the conditions for a merger are fulfilled, any dispute between the shareholders and the corporate bodies, for example, in regard to the existence of the appraisal right, or the price of the shares, might be resolved by arbitrators.[15]

14-9 Also a wider approach to the powers of the arbitrators would imply that they can decide situations of deadlock within the board of directors. The issue has been very controversial within Spanish law, where a traditional position has been followed and thus it was considered that it was not a case of arbitration, but of expert determination.[16]

Polo, "Introducción y ámbito de eficacia de la cláusula compromisoria en las sociedades mercantiles", 4 *Anuario de Justicia Alternativa* (1992) 88 and José María Muñoz Planas, "Algunos problemas del arbitraje en materia de sociedades mercantiles" in *Estudios de Derecho Mercantil en homenaje a Rodrigo Uría* (1978) 381-495, footnote 111.

14 See for Spanish Law: Perales Viscasillas, *supra* note 8 at 121-123, whether we also consider that the nullity of a merger is within the power of arbitrators (Art. 246 Spanish Public Corporation Act). The same conclusion for Belgian law: Caprasse, *supra* note 12 at 226-227.

15 For Spanish Law: Perales Viscasillas, *supra* note 8 at 122-123. See also for French Law: Hanotiau, *supra* note 13 at 166-168; Caprasse, *supra* note 12 at 218 et seq; Cohen, *supra* note 12 at 124. In Italy the issue is disputed particularly if the withdrawal or freezing out implies the dissolution of the corporation. See in favour: Berlinguer, *La comprometibilità*, II, at 226 et seq; Bernardini, *supra* note 12 at 302, and Andrea Pisani Massamormile, "Riflessioni in tema di clausola arbitrale e di nomina degli arbitri in materia societaria" 2 *Rivista delle società* (2000) 273-274. Against: Stefano Camilleri, "Validità delle clausole compromissorie contenute negli statuti sociali, con riferimento a quelle clausole che riservano la decisione della controversia ad organi sociali", in *L`arbitrato. Fondamenti Tecniche*, edited by Enrico Caterini y Giovanna Chiappetta. Quaderni della Rassegna di diritto civile dirreta da Pietro Perlingieri. Napoli: Edizioni Scientifiche Italiane, 1995, p.149.

16 See Resolution of the General Direction of the Registers and Notaries (Dirección General de los Registros y del Notariado) RDGRN, 27 April 1989; Polo, *supra* note 13 at 82-83 and 87-88; Silvia Gaspar Lera, *El ámbito de aplicación del arbitraje* (Aranzadi, 1998) 153; and Luis Fernández del Pozo, "Publicidad mercantil registral del procedimiento arbitral", 612 *Revista Crítica de Derecho Inmobiliario* (1992) 2035. However, there are authors that consider that it might be subject to arbitration: Carlos Suárez González, "Arbitraje y Derecho de sociedades", in *Derecho de sociedades: Libro Homenaje a Fernando Sánchez Calero* (McGraw-Hill 2002) vol. 2, at 2057; and Perales Viscasillas, *supra* note 8 at 124-126.
Similarly in Belgian Law it is arbitrable: Caprasse, *supra* note 12 at 177.
Special mention is to be done to Italian Law where Art. 37 Legislative Decree 17 January 2003, No. 5 "Definizione dei procedimenti in materia di diritto societario e di intermediazione finanziaria, nonché in materia bancaria e creditizia, in attuazione dell`articolo 12 della legge 3

14-10 Within the international treaties on arbitration, we can observe a difference in wording between the New York Convention (NYC) Art.II(1) that speaks about "differences" and the Geneva Convention Art. (I)(1)(a) [17] that refers to "disputes". Despite the dissimilarities in wording, a uniform interpretation must be achieved.[18] In any event the European (Geneva) Convention has a rather limited applicability but has been influential in the formulation of European arbitration statutes; it is the NYC where dynamic interpretation may be necessary.

3. Matters that are Subject to Arbitration

3.1. Arbitrability Defined through a General Standard

14-11 Generally speaking domestic laws consider arbitrability under general rather than exhaustive provisions. Generally, national laws provide that all rights or matters that the parties "may freely dispose"[19] or "property issues"[20] are

ottobre 2001, no. 366", published Gaceta Oficial no. 17, 22 January 2003, Supplemento Ordinario, no. 8, that within Title V (arbitration) (hereinafter Legislative Decree of 17 January 2003, no. 5 as amended by Legislative Decree of 6 February 2004, no. 37, Title V – On Arbitration) foresees the possibility of arbitration in the commented situations but only for close corporations and partnerships (see: Salvatore Sanzo, "Le riforme del diritto italiano. Il nuovo diritto societario". Commento al d.lgs. 17 gennaio 2003, n.6, d.lgs. 17 gennaio 2003, n.5, d.lgs 11 aprile 2002, n.61 (art.1). Diretto da Gastone Cottino, Guido Bonfante, Oreste Cagnasso, y Paolo Montalenti. Torino: Zanichelli, 2004, p.2996). It is not however clear whether it is a real arbitration, since the decision might be subject to appeal (Anne-Manuelle Gaillet, "Arbitration Procedures under the new Italian Company Law", 6 *IBLJ* (2005) 751). So it has been considered an "economic arbitration" (Sanzo, *ibid*, at 2996-2997).

17 European Convention on International Commercial Arbitration of 1961 Done at Geneva, April 21, 1961 United Nations, Treaty Series, vol. 484, at 364 No. 7041 (1963-1964).
Note that the UNCITRAL Arbitration Rules of 1976 use the words "dispute, controversy or claim" (see Model Clause).

18 Within the scope of The International Centre for Settlement of Investment Disputes (ICSID, see: Procedural Order no. 2 [request for provisional measures] de 28 octubre 1999, Decision of the Tribunal on Objections to Jurisdiction, 25 January 2000, Award 13 November 2000, case no. ARB/97/7, XXVII YBCA (2002) 13, no. 74-78, that defines the term "dispute".

19 See Art. 2.1 Spanish Arbitration Act (2003); Art.2 059 French Civil Code; Art. 808 Italian Code of Civil Procedure in relation with Art. 808 and Art. 1966.2 Civil Code; Art. 3 Croatia Arbitration Act (2001); Art. 1020.3 Dutch Arbitration Act; Art. 867 Greek Civil Code of Procedure; Art. 1003 Civil Code of Procedure (Luxemburg); Art. 3.1 Arbitration Act (Guatemala, 2005); Art. 3 Bolivian Arbitration and Conciliation Act; Art. 1 Peru Arbitration Act; and Art. 2 Model Arbitration Act OHADA.

20 Art. 177.1 Swiss Private International Law Act (PILA); Art. 1030.1 German Civil Code of Procedure; and Art. 1 Brazil Arbitration Law (1996).

arbitrable. Also, many statutes link arbitrability with the transaction, and thus the matters that are the object of a transaction might be also subject to arbitration.[21] These general clauses require a labour of specification and interpretation in order to assess which of the specific issues related to intra-corporate disputes are arbitrable. Although, arbitrability will vary from country to country, and even within a given country it will vary from time to time[22] since it is a concept that has changed with time, a clear principle applies with regard to its interpretation, particularly in international commercial arbitration: the principle of *favor arbitris*. The application of this principle to arbitrability means, first, that there is a general presumption in favour of the arbitrability of commercial disputes (policy favouring arbitrability),[23] including intra-corporate conflicts whether legal or economic; second, that there is a tendency to expand the scope of arbitration.[24]

[21] Belgium Law (Art. 1676.1 Code Judiciaire, 4 July 1972, Part (VI) on arbitration); Austrian Law (Art. 577 Code of Civil Procedure); Finnish Arbitration Law, 23 October 1992 (Art. 2); Japanese Arbitration Law, 2003, Law No. 138, (Art. 13.1); Swedish Arbitration Act 1999 (section 1(a)); Colombia Arbitration Law (Art. 1, Decree No. 2279, 7 October 1989); Ecuador Arbitration and Mediation Act (Law 4 September 1997, Law No. 145, Art. 1); and Venezuela Arbitration Commercial Law, 1998 (Art. 3).

[22] See for example in relation with corporate disputes in Spain: Perales Viscasillas, *supra* note 8 at 36 et seq. Under the Spanish Commercial Code of 1829, there was both a voluntarily and a mandatory arbitration for intra corporate disputes (Art. 323: "All disputes among shareholders would be settled by arbitration whether or not it has been agreed in the charter"). A forced arbitration in corporations existed also under French and Belgian Law, see: Art. 51 Commercial Code of France of 1807: "Toute contestation entre associés, et pour raison de la societé, sera jugée para des arbitres", and with identical drafting Art. 51 Belgium Commercial Code. Both rules were abrogated respectively in 1856 and 1873. See: Cohen, *supra* note 12 at 7 et seq; and Caprasse, *supra* note 12 at 145-148.

[23] See Racine, *supra* note 13 at 26; and Marta Gonzalo Quiroga, *Orden público y arbitraje internacional en el marco de la globalización comercial (Arbitrabilidad y derecho aplicable al fondo de la controversia internacional)* (Universidad Rey Juan Carlos, Servicio de Publicaciones, y Dykinson 2003) 108, footnote 341.

[24] For all: Laurance Craig, William Park and Jan Paulsson, *International Chamber of Commerce Arbitration* (3rd ed, Oceana Publications, Ind./Dobbs Ferry 1998) no. 5.07, at 60.
It is a modern tendency in arbitration laws to expand the matters that might be subject to arbitration, including sensitive areas whether commercial or not. For example, recent law reforms in Spain allow arbitration in state public contracts (Ley de Contratos del Sector Público of 31 October 2007); issues related to reclamations and complaints in matters related to equal opportunities, non-discrimination and universal access of handicapped persons (Real Decreto 1417/2006 of 1st December); in the field of consumer laws (Real Decreto 231/2008, 15th February, derogating the 1993 regulation); competition law (Law 15/2007, on 3rd July, and Regulation of 27th February 2008, and 29th February); insolvency law (Arts. 53 and 53 of the 2003 Insolvency Law), trade marks (Arts. 28 and 30 Trade Mark Law of 2001) and industrial

3.2. Arbitrability in the Context of Corporate Disputes

14-12 Very few statutes refer to arbitration/arbitrability in regard to corporations. Some of them, link arbitrability in this special field with the general standards provided in arbitration laws.[25] Others, however, consider a wider scope dealing with some of the issues that arise in the scope of corporations,[26] although sometimes limiting the scope of arbitrability to certain intra-corporate disputes or limiting the persons subject to arbitration.[27] In exceptional cases, a mandatory

designs (Law 20/2003). Also in Italy, where the modification of Art. 806 of the Code of Civil Procedure expands the matters subject to arbitration: the parties might agree on arbitration of the rights that they might freely disposed of, except as otherwise expressly prohibited by the Law. See: Decreto Legislativo, 2 February 2006 no. 40. Therefore, a legal presumption of arbitrability is now the general rule. C.f. with former Art.806 where

> the parties may have the disputes arising between them decided by arbitrators, with the exception of the disputes provided for in Articles 409 and 442, those concerning issues of personal status and marital separation and those other disputes which may not be the subject of a settlement.

25 See L 411-4 French Code of Judicial Organization, and L 411-6 where it is expressly provided for arbitration to solve "contestations relatives aux sociétés commerciales". See Louis Degos, "Les nouvelles dispositions de la loi française relatives à la clause compromissoire", 5 *IBLJ* (2001) 653-660; Philippe Marini, "La réforme de la clausula compromissoire", 32 *Le Dalloz* (2001) 2658-2634; and Philippe Fouchard, "La laborieuse réforme de la clause compromissoire par la Loi du 15 mai 2001", 3 *Rev. Arb.* (2001) 397-421.
The Dutch Arbitration Act (1986), Art. 1020.5 states that an arbitration agreement includes also agreements in the statutes of incorporation.

26 Italian Law: Legislative Decree of 17 January 2003, no. 5 as amended by Legislative Decree of 6 February 2004, no. 37, Title V – On Arbitration (Art. 34.1) states the submission of arbitration to matters that are at the free disposal of the parties, although it establishes a regime dealing with several aspects of arbitration in close corporations but not in publicly-held corporations. The rules have been subject to several critics (Giovanni Gabrielli, "Clausole compromissorie e statuti sociali", *Riv. Dir. Civ.* (January-February, 2004) 86 and 92-93; Bernardini, *supra* note 12 at 304 and 312; and Sanzo, *supra* note 16 at 2980).

27 OHADA Uniform Law on Corporations, Art. 148, which allows arbitration to solve disputes among shareholders, and shareholders and the corporation. It does not however refer to other kinds of disputes, like disputes among shareholders and the board of directors, or the disputes in case of the sale of shares, where one of the parties might be a third person. In those situations a problem of interpretation arises. But see Italian Law where the arbitration clause is binding upon the company and all shareholders, including those whose status as shareholders is disputed (Art. 34.3) and that the deeds of incorporation may provide that the clause covers disputes initiated by directors, liquidators and internal auditors (*sindaci*) or against them and, in such a case, the same is binding upon them following acceptance of their office (Art. 34.4). Legislative Decree of 17 January 2003, no. 5 as amended by Legislative Decree of 6 February 2004, no. 37, Title V – On Arbitration.
Under former Art. 631 French Commercial Code, modified in May 2001, the object of arbitration was "des contestations entre associés, pour raison d`une société de commerce". It was highly controversial whether the transfer of equity interest was arbitrable if one of the

arbitration is provided by the corporation statutes to resolve specific disputes.[28] Although these statutes refer to arbitration in corporations, as a general critique, it is worth pointing out that a comprehensive rule on arbitration for all kind of business entities is missing.

14-13 In certain countries, the interested bodies have prepared model arbitration clauses to be incorporated into the by-laws of the corporations or in the articles of incorporation. This is the case in Spain, where through the agreement of the Chambers of Commerce, the General Council of Notaries and the Bar of Public Registers, a model arbitration clause for corporations was agreed. This clause has also been accepted by Resolution of DGRN, 1 October 2001.[29] More recently, a

---

parties were not a merchant, in which case the operation was considered to be a civil transaction and thus outside the scope of Art. 631 French Commercial Code, or because one of the parties was not a shareholder. Case law, however, has lately admitted its arbitrability by considering the object of the operation – to obtain the control of a corporation – as the basis to include it under Art. 631 Commercial Code. This issue is not controversial under Spanish Law (Perales Viscasillas, *supra* note 8 at 170) nor under Belgian Law (Caprasse, *supra* note 12 at 210-212 and 224-225), and thus arbitration is possible.

28 This is the case of Finland and Sweden, where the Corporation Act foresees a mandatory arbitration to solve disputes related with squeeze-out or freezing-out transactions. See: Jouko Huhtala, Marko Hentunen and Marcus Möller, "Minority Share Redemption Disputes Between Shareholders of Finnish Limited Liability Companies", *Asian Dispute Review* (November 2004) 67 et seq; Roschier Holmberg, "Finland", in *Arbitration World, Jurisdictional Comparison* (2004) 161; and Claes Lundblad and Kaj Hober, "Sweden", in *Arbitration World, Jurisdictional Comparison* (2004) 286.

29 The Model clause states:

> 1. All company disputes which may arise between the company and its administrators or members, or between the one and the other, or between the members themselves, will be definitely settled through arbitration in Law of one or more arbitrators within the framework of the Spanish Arbitration Court of the Executive Council of the Chambers of Commerce, Industry and Navigation of Spain, in conformity with its Regulation and Statutes, which would govern the administration and appointment of the arbitrators or arbitral tribunal.
>
> 2. All the demands contesting the validity of the company's meetings or of the decisions adopted in the same meeting or the meetings of the administration board which are based upon the same nullity or annullability causes, ought to be heard and decided in the same arbitration proceeding.
>
> 3. Where the arbitration procedure relates to the validity of the company's meetings or its decisions, the Spanish Court of Arbitration will not nominate the arbitrator or arbitrators until 40 days after the date of the adoption of the meeting or the decision taken or, if any of them is subject to register, from the date of the publication in the Official Journal of the Commercial Register.

general recognition of the possibility to include arbitration clauses for intra-corporate disputes has been recognized for all kind of corporations.[30]

14-14 In many countries arbitration in corporation practice reveals that the majority of the statutes of incorporation include an arbitration clause,[31] and that the possible inclusion of an arbitration clause in the articles of association is not a contentious issue.[32] Equally undisputed is the possibility to include an arbitration agreement in other documents, such as shareholders' agreement or the regulation for the board of Directors.[33]

---

4. In the arbitration procedures relating to the validity of the company's meetings, the Spanish Court of Arbitration will fix the number of arbitrators and their appointment.

5. The shareholders by themselves and by the chartered company as future parties of the arbitration make the compromise to be bound by the arbitration award.

(Translation by the author)
See also the Model clauses for arbitration of intra-corporate disputes provided by the Arbitral Tribunal of Barcelona, Spanish Court of Arbitration, Madrid Court of Arbitration and Valencia Court of Arbitration. And the Order JUS/1445/2003, 4 June that provides for a model of articles of incorporation of a special kind of a close corporation (*Sociedad Limitada Nueva Empresa*), which includes a model arbitration clause.
Interesting also the model arbitration clause proposed by Raeschke-Kessler, that appears at Hanotiau, *supra* note 13 at 162, footnote 406. See also for the Italian practice: Gabriele Silingardi, *Il compromesso in arbitri nelle società di capitali* (Giuffrè 1979) 191-210.

30 On the 16th March 2007, the Regulation of the Commercial Registry was modified to introduce a provision where the bylaws of all kinds of corporations might include a provision on arbitration (Art. 114.2 -Sociedad Anónima – and Art. 175.2 – Sociedad de Responsabilidad Limitada-). The provision states that the bylaws might include an arbitration clause for intra-corporate disputes among the shareholders, and among them, the corporation or its bodies. Also, the new Law on Professional entities (Ley de Sociedades Profesionales) of 16th March 2007 provides the same possibility adding the inclusion of the disputes related to the withdrawal, squeezing-out and determination of the equity interest in the professional entity.

31 This is the case of Italy, where it is considered that more than 70% of the corporations and cooperatives have an arbitration clause: Silingardi, *supra* note 29 at 8 and 8-26.

32 For example in Belgium: Caprasse, *supra* note 12 at 368.

33 See Perales Viscasillas, *supra* note 8 at 198-203.
Other kinds of issues arise in regard to the arbitration clauses, but this is not a problem related to arbitrability rather a problem related to the objective and subjective scope of the arbitration clause. For example, it has been contentious whether the arbitration clauses that refer only to shareholders are enforceable against the company, the directors, liquidators or auditors, whether equity arbitration was possible, the appointment of arbitrators, the assignment of the arbitration clause, the extension of the clause and the consolidation of proceedings: see Carazo Liébana, *supra* note 12 at 217-253; and Perales Viscasillas, *supra* note 8 at 223-235.

14-15 There are several corporate issues in comparative law that we have identified as not being controversial and thus arbitrable:

- disputes in regard to the interpretation of the articles of incorporation or the by-laws;
- the existence of a restriction to the transfer of shares;[34]
- disputes in regard to the revocation of the Director of the company;[35]
- disputes in regard to the damages that might correspond to the Directors, or the quantum of their salary;
- the civil liability of the Directors;[36]
- disputes in regard to the right to vote, like those in regard to pooling agreements;[37]
- disputes in regard to the distribution of benefits;[38] and
- disputes in regard to the value of the shares.

14-16 There are, however, other matters that are controversial in regard to arbitrability and these are discussed in the next section

[34] In comparative Law: Hanotiau, *supra* note 13 at 166.

[35] See also: Hanotiau, *supra* note 13 at 165, in regard to comparative law. For Italian Law: Massamormile, *supra* note 15 at 274-275, although Bernardini, *supra* note 12 at 302; and Aldo Berlinguer, *La comprometibilità per arbitri. Studio di diritto italiano e comparato, II, Le materie non compromettibili.* Torino: G. Giappichelli, 1999, pp. 222 et seq, point out to the contrary opinion of the case law. For French Law: Cohen, *supra* note 12 at 126-127. And for Belgian Law: Caprasse, *supra* note 12 at 198-201. For Spain: Carazo Liébana, *supra* note 12 at 180 et seq.

[36] It is considered arbitrable in comparative law, see: Hanotiau, *supra* note 13 at 165. In Italy: Raffaele Teti, "La Giurisprudenza e l`arbitrato nelle società", in *L`arbitrato. Fondamenti Tecniche*, edited by Enrico Caterini y Giovanna Chiappetta. Quaderni della Rassegna di diritto civile dirreta da Pietro Perlingieri. Napoli: Edizioni Scientifiche Italiane, 1995, pp.102-103; Bernardini, *supra* note 12 at 303; and Silingardi, *supra* note 29 at 77-79. In Belgium: Caprasse, *supra* note 12 at 191-193 and 159-163. In Finland: Taivalkoski, 4 *Rev. Arb* (2003) 1401. In Spain: Carazo Liébana, *supra* note 12 at 180 et seq; and Perales Viscasillas, *supra* note 8 at 171.

[37] Hanotiau, *supra* note 13 at 166 and 168. Belgian Law: Caprasse, *supra* note 12 at 212-213. French Law: Cohen, *supra* note 12 at 108-109, and 125. In Spain: Perales Viscasillas, *supra* note 8 at 171-172.
For U.S. Law the issue is controversial: see, Note, supra note 13 (*Columbia Law Review* (1963)) at 272-275.

[38] For Spain: Perales Viscasillas, *supra* note 8 at 172. For Italian Law: Arbitral Award Chamber of Commerce of Milan, 23 September 1997, XXIII YBCA (1998) 93-96. For Finnish Law: Taivalkoski, *supra* note 36 at 1401.
It is however controversial in Belgian Law as it is considered to be an issue of public order (vid. Hanotiau, *supra* note 13 at 168). Contrary, see, Caprasse, *supra* note 12 at 214.

3.3. Limits to Arbitrability

14-17 As mentioned above the general national provisions on arbitrability need to be interpreted in order to assess whether specific corporate disputes may be arbitrable. The limits to arbitrability that apply to corporations are the classic limitations that apply to any other kind of disputes: the public policy and the exclusive jurisdiction of the national courts. However, legal systems are not in agreement as to the adjustment of those limits to specific issues in corporations.

(a) Public Policy/Mandatory Rules

14-18 As it is well known, traditionally it was held that the issues that were subject to national mandatory rules of law were not arbitrable. Unlike the field of commercial contracts where the will of the parties prevails as a general rule, in the area of corporate law, mandatory rules are prevalent. Thus, many of the important aspects of corporations were originally outside the scope of arbitration. This traditional position has been rejected in favour of a modern view of arbitrability. In modern arbitration practice, it is today clear that even if a matter is subject to mandatory rules, it might be subject to arbitration.[39]

14-19 As far as public policy is concerned and its relation to arbitrability, some arbitration laws consider that issues that are of public policy nature cannot be subject to arbitration.[40] But even in those systems, new trends are also applicable: public order is not considered any more a limitation to arbitrability, but rules of that character have to be respected by the arbitrators in order to have an enforceable award.[41] Public policy, however, in certain situations operates as

[39] *Cf* Perales Viscasillas, *supra* note 8 at 144 et seq. However, some uncertainty exists in certain areas. For example, in Spain, where the validity of the company's meeting affecting the information right of the shareholders has been considered inarbitrable due to the imperative character of such a right (SAP Barcelona, 17 February 1999; SAP Barcelona, 16 May 2003; and Auto del Juzgado de lo Mercantil de Bilbao, no. 1, 2 November 2005). However, more recent cases state the contrary: SAP Santa Cruz de Tenerife, 27 October 2006; and Auto Audiencia Provincial Barcelona, 5 March 2008.

[40] French Civil Code, Arts. 2059 and 2060.

[41] See: Racine, *supra* note 13 at 28 et seq, and 43; Walid Abdelgawad, *Arbitrage et droit de la concurrence* (LGDJ 2001) 33 et seq; Berthold Goldman, "La situation en France", in *Competition and Arbitration Law* (Institute of International Business Law and Practice, ICC 1993), 111; and Bernard Hanotiau, "L'Arbitrabilité et le favor arbitrandum: un réexamen", 47 *Clunet* (1994) 937; Philippe Fouchard, Emmanuel Gaillard and Berthold Goldman, *supra* note 8 at no. 563 et seq; José Carlos Fernandez Rozas, "Le rôle des juridictions étatiques devant l`arbitrage Commercial International", in *Recueil des Cours - Collected Courses of The Hague*

a limit to arbitrability. Whether the public order impedes the submission of a dispute to arbitration is usually a question to be decided by the law.

14-20 The validity of a shareholders' meeting (and the grounds for invalidating an assembly) is the paradigmatic example of an issue that was formerly considered to be inarbitrable because the matter is regulated by mandatory rules, as well because the matter is considered to be of public policy: the result of a dispute on the validity of shareholders meetings might affect third parties, the social interest or public interest. Also, a distinction is made depending on the type of action considered. If the action for the nullity of a shareholders' meeting is looking for the total nullity of the act, then public policy is involved and thus the issue is not subject to arbitration; whereas if it is the annulability – the act is contrary to the law or statutes of the corporation – then arbitration is possible. Today, however, a favourable approach to arbitrability is found in comparative law.[42]

14-21 Taking a comparative look, the arbitrability of a dispute relating to the nullity of a corporation is strongly. In favour of the arbitrability of that kind of dispute is Belgium,[43] Switzerland, Sweden, or U.S. In other countries, like Italy or France, the majority of the authors consider it inarbitrable, although there are

Academy of International Law (2001) Tome 290, (The Hague Boston London, Martinus Nijhoff Publishers, 2002) at 111-112; Gonzalo Quiroga, *supra* note 23 at 131 et seq; Cohen, *supra* note 12 at 117 et seq; and Caprasse, *supra* note 12 at 46 et seq.

42 An evolution of this field in Spanish Law might be seen at Perales Viscasillas, *supra* note 8 at 144 et seq. and 174 et seq. The change of view was due to a decision of the High Supreme Court of 18 April 1998:

> La impugnación de acuerdos sociales está regida por normas de "ius cogens" pero el convenio arbitral no alcanza a las mismas, sino al cauce procesal de resolverlas; el carácter imperativo de las normas que regulan la impugnación de acuerdos sociales, no empece el carácter negocial y, por tanto, dispositivo de los mismos".

See also RDGRN, 19 February 1998. For associations a similar problematic is found, see: Susana Pérez Escalona, "La impugnación de acuerdos sociales mediante arbitraje en el derecho de asociaciones: admisibilidad teórica y viabilidad práctica", *Boletín Facultad de Derecho de la UNED*, 2006, no. 28, pp.13-36.
Also in Italy: Massamormile, *supra* note 15 at 271.
It is considered arbitrable in Belgium, France, Switzerland, Austria and Germany (except if it is a listed corporation): Hanotiau, *supra* note 13 at 164; *ibid., L`arbitrabilité des litiges en matière de droit des sociétés: Liber amicorum Claude Reymond* (Litec 2004) 104. For Belgian Law: Caprasse, *supra* note 12 at 165-169.

43 Vid. Caprasse, *supra* note 12 at 155-159, rejecting the contrary opinions.

qualified exceptions that might imply a change of perspective.[44] In Spain, the issue is highly contested.[45]

14-22 The dissolution of the corporation is another subject matter where arbitrability is discussed in comparative law.[46] For example, since 1967 has been considered arbitrable under French law.[47] Recently in Finland, it has been considered arbitrable by a decision of the High Supreme Court.[48] In other jurisdictions, such as the U.S., Singapore and Spain the matter is controversial.[49]

(b) Exclusive Jurisdiction of National Courts

14-23 With regard to the exclusive jurisdiction of state courts, again an evolution process in favour of arbitrability might be seen. Traditionally it was considered that the matters that were subject to the special or exclusive jurisdiction of the Courts were not freely disposed of, and thus arbitrability was defined through that special or exclusive competence. A good example is that of a dispute on the

44 See: Racine, *supra* note 13 at 90-91 (against); and Cohen, *supra* note 12 at 142-147 (in favour), who speaks on the new developments: Cohen, *supra* note 12 at 142-147, as well as Hanotiau, *supra* note 13 at 163-164, in relation with the decision of the Cour de Cassation (Ch. commerciale), 9 April 2002, *Tolouzy c/SNC Philam*, 1 Rev. Arb. (2003) 103-114, note by Paul Didier. See also: Cour de Cassation (2ª Ch. civile), 4 abril 2002, *Société Barbot CM (SA) c/société Bouygues Bâtiment et autre*, 1 Rev. Arb. (2003) 103-114, note by Paul Didier.
For Italian Law: Fabrizio Criscuolo, "Sulla comprometibilità in arbitri della questione di nullità del contratto", in *L`arbitrato. Fondamenti Tecniche*, edited by Enrico Caterini y Giovanna Chiappetta. Quaderni della Rassegna di diritto civile dirreta da Pietro Perlingieri. Napoli: Edizioni Scientifiche Italiane, 1995, pp.133-145, contrary to the arbitrability.

45 See Carazo Liébana, *supra* note 12 at 168-170; and Perales Viscasillas, *supra* note 8 at 183-185, who are in favour.

46 See Hanotiau, *supra* note 13 at 169; and Cohen, *supra* note 12 at 141.

47 It was consider inarbitrable until the decision of the Cour of Cassation 30 January 1967 (see: Cohen, *supra* note 12 at 135-142; Hanotiau, *supra* note 13 at 169; and Racine, *supra* note 13 at 89). In Belgium it is also considered arbitrable: Caprasse, *supra* note 12 at 228-234.

48 14 May 2003, 4 Rev. Arb. (2003) 1396-1404, note by Petri Taivalkoski).

49 In Singapore, the dissolution of a corporation is inarbitrable (Michael Hwang and Rajesh C Muttath, "Arbitration in Company Matters" 5 *IBLJ* (2001) 562-563, although a recent case *Four Pillars Enterprises Co Ltd v. Beiersdorf Aktiengesellschaft* (1999) 1 SLR 737, a door is opened to arbitrability). The solution is different for partnerships (Hwang and Muttath, at 565-567), where the dissolution is arbitrable.
Doubts are expressed in regard to U.S. Law (Note, supra note 13, at 283-284 and S.S.J. Jr, "Mandatory Arbitration as a remedy for intra-close corporate disputes", 56 *Virginia Law Review* (1970 281-282); Italian Law (Silingardi, *supra* note 29 at 93-95, who is in favour); and Spanish Law (Perales Viscasillas, *supra* note 8 at 186-188, who is also in favour).

validity of shareholders' meetings, which, according to the traditional view were considered inarbitrable because of the exclusive jurisdiction of the Courts mentioned in the Corporation Act.[50] In modern arbitration practice and Law, first, it is considered that the fact that the law refers to a Court as competent to hear a certain dispute does not necessarily exclude arbitration.[51] Second, the exclusive jurisdiction of Courts is not any more a component of arbitrability than a limit, and thus issues that are of the free disposition of the parties might be considered inarbitrable where the States specially so considered by excluding its arbitrability and leaving the decision on those matters to state courts or special administrative bodies.[52]

14-24 Special mention should be made to the Council Regulation (EC) 44/2001 of 22 December 2000 on jurisdiction and the recognition and enforcement of judgments in civil and commercial matters,[53] where Art. 22(2) provides for exclusive jurisdiction of the Courts of the seat in regards to proceedings which

[50] See Spanish Public Corporation Act of 1951 (Ley de Sociedades Anónimas), Art. 70.2. And Art. 118 Ley de Sociedades Anónimas 1989. After the High Supreme Court of 18 April 1998 and RDGRN 19 February 1998, already mentioned, there has been a change in the case law and scholars and thus the reference to a competent Court does not imply excluding arbitration. See: Perales Viscasillas, *supra* note 8 at 157-160.

[51] It is also the position of French scholars: Nathalie Coipel-Cordonnier, *Les Conventions d`arbitrage et d`élection de for en droit international privé* (LGDJ 1999) 224; Racine, *supra* note 13 at 48-51 and 113; and Laurance Idot, "L`arbitrabilité des litiges, L`example français", 1 *Revue de Jurisprudence Commerciale* (1996) 11-13. For Belgian Law: Caprasse, *supra* note 12 at 123 et seq. And for Spain: Perales Viscasillas, *supra* note 8 at 149 et seq.
But see, Art. 1.1 Arbitration Act of Portugal of 1986, which considers the exclusive competence of Courts as a component of arbitrability; and Arbitration Act of Guatemala of 1995, that considers matters inarbitrable those subject to a special process.

[52] Swiss Law reveals that the exclusive competence of the Courts is a limit to arbitrability in domestic arbitration but not in international commercial arbitration. See Marc Blessing, "Introduction to Arbitration-Swiss and International Perspectives", in *International Arbitration in Switzerland: An Introduction to and a Commentary on Articles 176-194 of the Swiss Private International Law Statute*, Stephen V. Berti (ed), (Helbing & Lichtenhahn/Kluwer 2000) 173; and Robert Briner, "Article 177", in *International Arbitration in Switzerland: An Introduction to and a Commentary on Articles 176-194 of the Swiss Private International Law Statute*, Stephen V. Berti (ed), (Helbing & Lichtenhahn/Kluwer 2000) 320. The opposite solution in Croatia, Art. 3.2 Arbitration Act 2001, where the exclusive competence is a limit to arbitrability in international commercial arbitration (see Uzelac, *supra* note 1 at 147). Same solution in regard to both domestic and international commercial arbitration in Argentina, see Horacio A. Grigera Naon, "Public Policy in International Commercial Arbitration: An Argentine View", in *Comparative Arbitration Practice and Public Policy in Arbitration: ICCA Congress Series no. 3* (Kluwer Law and Taxation Publishers 1986) 330.

[53] OJ 16 January 2001, L 12/1.

have as their object the validity of the constitution, the nullity or the dissolution of companies or other legal persons or associations of natural or legal persons, or of the validity of the decisions of their organs; and Art. 22(4) that also provides for exclusive jurisdiction of the Courts in proceedings concerned with the registration or validity of patents, trade marks, designs, or other similar rights required to be deposited or registered. Whether the Regulation excludes or not arbitration is a very contentious issue among scholars.[54]

14-25 In our opinion, apart from the fact that the Brussels Regulation excludes arbitration from its scope of application, it establishes the exclusive competence of a national Court in relation to other national Courts within EU, but not in relation to arbitration. Arbitral Tribunals are not within the body of national courts and thus it is wrong to equate the former with the latter. The Brussels Regulation applies only when there is a need to distribute the competence between different national courts and thus the parties are obliged to respect the distribution of competence ordered by the Brussels regulation, but not when there is an arbitration agreement.[55]

(c) The Impact on Third Parties

14-26 A third argument against arbitration, which is particularly important in the field of corporations, considers the impact of arbitration on third parties. A dispute is considered arbitrable only when it relates to the private interest of a shareholder, whereas it is considered inarbitrable when the rights of third parties (other shareholders or creditors) are affected.

14-27 Another kind of argument considers the *inter partes* effect of the awards. The *inter partes* effect means that the decision of the arbitrators would only bind the parties in the arbitration and not third parties, i.e., other shareholders that did not participate in the process although they were parties to the arbitration

[54] See considering that the Regulation exclude the arbitrability of the disputes: Sajko, *supra* note 1 at 52; Miguel Virgos Soriano and Francisco Garcimartín Alférez, *Derecho Procesal Civil Internacional: Litigación internacional* (Civitas 2000) no. 262 and 265-266. With doubts: Lew, Mistelis and Kröll *supra* note 1 at no. 9-39, at 200 and footnote 47; more incisive, however, in relation with Art. 22.4 of the Regulation and thus excluding arbitration in regard to industrial rights (*ibid.*, no. 9-64, at 209, and footnote 78). In favour of arbitrability of the matters considered under the Brussels Regulation: Eric Loquin, "L`Exécution des sentences arbitrales dans l`espace judiciaire européen", in *Les effets des jugements nationaux dans les autres Etats membres de l`Union européenne*. Bruxelles: Bruylant, 2001, p. 166.

[55] Perales Viscasillas, *supra* note 8 at 156-157; and Uzelac, *supra* note 1 at 148-150.

agreement, or third parties that are not even parties to the arbitration agreement, such as creditors. In this case, the possibility that these other shareholders might obtain another decision, which could be contradictory to the former, or the fact that some of the decisions of the arbitrators might need to be registered in a commercial registry are considered obstacles to the submission of certain corporate disputes to arbitration.

14-28 A good example is again found in the validity of shareholders meetings where Art. 222(3) Spanish Civil Code of Procedure recognises that a decision of a Court binds all the shareholders even those that did not participate in the court proceedings. The solution then is rather simple: to recognise *erga omnes* effect to the award in the same terms as provided for court decisions under Art. 222(3) Civil Code of Procedure. Although, some other problems might arise, those do not affect the arbitrability of the dispute but rather the procedure.[56] To this regard, Italian Law is an example of the excess of the legislator by providing a mandatory procedure that constrains the arbitration process even when it is international.[57]

14-29 Further, the argument based on the impact of the arbitration on third parties is also used to deny the arbitrability in publicly held corporations, however not in privately held corporations. We cannot agree on such a

[56] In relation with the procedural obstacles, see: Hanotiau, *supra* note 13 at 158 99; Alexis Mourre, "Arbitrage, conflits de juridictions et ADR dans la résolution des litiges entre actionnaires", 3 *IBLJ* (2004) 301-302; Perales Viscasillas, *supra* note 8 at 179-183 for Spanish Law; and in relation to Italian Law: Gaillet, *supra* note 16 at 743 et seq, and Art. 35.2 of The Legislative Decree of 17 January 2003, no. 5 as amended by Legislative Decree of 6 February 2004, no. 37, Title V – On Arbitration.
To this regard, the possibility of having an arbitration *ex aequo et bono* cannot be used as an argument against company arbitration, see: Auto del Juzgado de lo Mercantil no. 1 de Madrid, 17 abril 2006; and RDGRN 4 May 2005. For Italian Law, Art. 36.1 Legislative Decree of 17 January 2003, no. 5 as amended by Legislative Decree of 6 February 2004, no. 37, Title V – On Arbitration:

> Even if the arbitration clause authorizes the arbitrators to decide *ex aequo et bono* or by an award not subject to recourse, the arbitrators must decide according to law, by an award which is subject to recourse also pursuant to Article 829, second paragraph, of the Code of Civil Procedure when, in order to decide, they have heard non-arbitrable issues or when the subject matter of the decision consists of the validity of shareholders' resolutions.

[57] See Art. 35 Legislative Decree of 17 January 2003, no. 5 as amended by Legislative Decree of 6 February 2004, no. 37, Title V – On Arbitration.

distinction, and we consider that arbitration is possible in both types of corporations.[58]

4. Future Perspectives

14-30 Arbitrability in general, and arbitrability of intra-corporate disputes in particular have evolved greatly in the last 30-40 years. Although the principle of *favor arbitris* and a policy favouring arbitrability might be considered as a general feature of international commercial arbitration, and thus the concept of arbitrability is in a process of expansion, there are still certain areas in which uniformity must be sought.

14-31 A broader concept of dispute is missing in most domestic laws on arbitration and this inevitably implies that certain intra-corporate disputes may not be subject to arbitration, as it happens with matters related to the appraisal of shares. At the same time, uniformity in many of the issues related to intra-corporate disputes that might be subject to arbitration is missing. A comprehensive rule on arbitration for all kind of business entities is missing in domestic laws on arbitration.

14-32 Different positions are found in a comparative survey as to whether certain intra-corporate disputes are arbitrable. There is a lack of consensus in regard to the dissolution and nullity of the company, the validity of shareholders meeting, arbitrability in publicly held corporations, etc. Achieving uniformity is thus a goal that must be pursued. The problems, however, are not only on the level of arbitrability; some procedural aspects also need to be analysed, like the impact of arbitration of intra-corporate disputes on third parties, issues related to the effects of the award and commercial registries, and whether equity arbitrations are allowed for this kind of dispute.

14-33 Although, the current work of the United Nations Commission on International Trade Law is the revision of the 1976 Arbitration Rules,[59] the Commission has considered arbitrability of intra-corporate disputes as well as

58 See Perales Viscasillas, *supra* note 8 at 188-194. Since this issue is connected with the securities market, we will refer to Chapter 20 of this book on arbitration and securities.

59 A/CN.9/WG.II/WP.145 and Annex I - Settlement of commercial disputes: Revision of the UNCITRAL Arbitration Rules.

other matters as future topics on the agenda of UNCITRAL.[60] This book, covering general and specific subjects of arbitrability will be of great help to the Secretary of UNCITRAL in identifying the issues to be dealt with by the working group on arbitration and conciliation with the objective to promote uniformity and predictability of this crucial issue in international commercial arbitration.

60 See Report of the United Nations Commission on International Trade Law on the work of its thirty-ninth session 19 June-7 July 2006 General Assembly Official Records Sixty-first session Supplement No. 17 (A/61/17), no. 183.

Ilias Bantekas[*]

CHAPTER 15

ARBITRABILITY IN FINANCE AND BANKING

1. INTRODUCTION

15-1 This chapter focuses on the arbitrability of banking and finance disputes, both domestic and international in character. We set out by identifying the general rule in the developed world, which favours arbitration of all contractual disputes and thereafter attempt to identify any exceptions, where applicable. We then examine statutory limitations to arbitrability in the developing world. It would be impossible to survey the legal systems of all States, thus we restrict our analysis to a representative sample, including Saudi Arabia and Gulf States, as well as India, with a view to ascertaining special rules on arbitrability stemming from Islamic traditions and jurisprudence, particularly in the banking field. In the case of the latter, we highlight the particular problems associated with bringing to arbitration disputes arising out of the payment of interest, setting out the doctrinal basis for its prohibition in Islamic law in contrast with its contemporary usage between Muslim businesses and the employment of arbitration. Moreover, the permissibility of consumer banking arbitration and the invocation of immunity in business transactions are also examined. Equally, our analysis of financial transactions is limited to only those that give rise to non-arbitrability, particularly franchise and commercial agency agreements, securities transactions, corporate disputes, warrantee and broker agreements.

* Professor of Public International Law and Associate Director, Centre for International and Public Law, Brunel University Law School.

L Mistelis & S Brekoulakis (eds), Arbitrability: International & Comparative Perspectives, 293-315

2. The Application of General Rules and Principles

15-2 It is rare for arbitration statutes to specify in detail which types of transactions and acts can never be subjected to the jurisdiction of arbitral tribunals.[1] The ambit of arbitrability in the majority of countries is delineated by reference to the general directions and injunctions of their arbitration law, the *lex specialis derogat lex generalis* principle (through which specific statutes may contain provisions that render particular acts non-arbitrable), constitutional constraints (if any) and the prevalence of courts in their interpretation of applicable laws. In the fields of banking and finance arbitrability is a pressing matter because two conflicting interests arise; on the one hand, private actors are dominant in this sphere, far more than in any other, and as a result there is certainly a desire on their part to dictate the mode for the resolution of relevant disputes. At the same time, it is not outside the purview of the State to have an interest in the regulation of the financial sector, particularly given the vulnerability of the stock markets, the lending industry, currency exchange controls, etc. and their potential detrimental and spiralling effects on the national economy and the employment sector. Equally, banking and brokerage operations are not solely limited to the financing of large industrial projects, but they also encompass the small amateur investor, the ordinary debtors (mortgages, small loans, etc), as well as the millions of individuals that deposit their monies into financial institutions. Is it really wise from the point of view of the State to allow for the settlement of disputes arising from all these relationships by means of arbitration?

15-3 In this regard, the wording of the U.S. Federal Arbitration Act (FAA) is instructive, by providing that:

> A written provision in … a contract evidencing a transaction involving commerce to settle by arbitration a controversy thereafter arising out of such contract … shall be valid, irrevocable and enforceable.[2]

15-4 It is now well established by case law that the FAA evinces a strong federal policy favouring arbitration agreements and requires courts to liberally and

[1] A limited example as to this rarity is exemplified by Section 1030(2) of the German Arbitration Act [incorporated in the Code of Civil Procedure (ZPO)], which states that: "An arbitration agreement relating to disputes on the existence of a lease of residential accommodation within Germany shall be null and void. This does not apply to residential accommodation as specified in Section 549 subs. 1 to 3 of the Civil Code".

[2] 9 U.S.C. § 2 (1988).

generously construe the scope of such agreements.[3] In fact, if doubts arise as to arbitrability, this should be resolved in favour of arbitration, irrespective of "whether the problem at hand is the construction of the contract language itself or an allegation of waiver, delay, or a like defence to arbitrability".[4] Equally, through section 1030(1) of the German Arbitration Act, arbitrability generally extends to "any claim involving an economic interest". The same is true, albeit in somewhat different language, in section 1 of the 1999 Swedish Arbitration, whereby "disputes concerning matters in respect of which the parties may reach a settlement", may be submitted to arbitration. Moreover, Article 177(1) of the Swiss Federal Private International Law Act categorically provides that "all disputes involving financial interests are arbitrable". Despite their semantic differences, the language in all of these statutes clearly demonstrates the existence of a presumption that is in favour of arbitration in all matters reflecting an economic or financial interest, irrespective of the particularities of the dispute, unless a subject-specific statute adopted after the Arbitration Act (presumably) deems otherwise. The relevant statutes exclude tacitly[5] or expressly from the scope of arbitration all those non-financial disputes, which would otherwise be exempted because of public policy considerations. Does this mean, however, that all financial matters may be submitted to arbitration? The answer is clearly negative, because of the application of the *lex specialis* and *lex posterior* rule. Section 1030(3) of the German Arbitration Act, for example, excludes from arbitration any disputes that are barred by the provisions of other statutes. This does not sit well, however, with the judgment of the German Federal Court (rendered before the introduction of the new German arbitration law in 1998), according to which recourse to arbitration is possible even where the subject matter of the dispute is governed by a mandatory law.[6] Equally, in the U.S., the presumption in favour of arbitration is inoperative where congressional intent contained in a statute or legislative history mandates solely for resolution of a particular dispute by regular courts.[7] Thus, one needs to search in the commercial statutes of his target country in order to assess whether any of these

3 *Mitsubishi Motors Corp. v. Soler Chrysler-Plymouth Inc.*, 473 U.S. 614 (1985), at 627; *Moses H. Cone Memorial Hospital v. Mercury Construction Corp.*, 460 U.S. 1 (1983), at 24.

4 *Moses Cone, ibid.*, at 24-25.

5 Section 1 of the Swedish Arbitration Act. See Per Sundin, Erik Wernberg, Sweden, available at: <http://www.globalarbitrationreview.com/handbooks/3/sections/6/chapters/45/sweden> which is taken to exclude family and criminal law matters.

6 BGHZ Judgment, 132, 279 (282-83) (1996).

7 *Shearson/American Express v. McMahon*, 482 U.S. 220 (1987), at 227.

clearly override the general presumption in favour of arbitration of financial and commercial disputes.[8]

15-5 In reality, and with the exception of a few specified commercial statutes (companies, consumers, securities), most domestic legal instruments will not contain any provision on arbitrability. There are, however, some borderline cases. Imagine, for example, a situation where a corporation has agreed with the non-corporate stakeholders of a local community in which it is operating that it will fund the founding and operation of a school in pursuit of its corporate social responsibility strategy (CSR).[9] The agreement between the parties contains an arbitration clause, which either party may seek to enforce. In such cases, it is disputable/questionable whether this agreement would relate to financial or economic activities, and whether these in fact may be subjected to arbitration. One may argue that since CSR is an extension of the corporation's governance and is not simply a charitable action, but a corporate act with a financial motive, it should be counted as an economic transaction. The problem with this approach is that it does not take into account the considerations of the social stakeholders, who clearly do not see themselves as entering into a financial transaction, apart from the inevitable contractual issues arising from a potential class-action arbitration by the multitude of individual social stakeholders, where permissible. In such cases, the presumption in favour of arbitration should not be operable and the courts must examine every case on its merits with a view to avoid disadvantaging the weaker party. In the absence of more concrete rules, an analogous application of the domestic laws of consumer arbitration would be advisable.

15-6 One final issue of general concern to the arbitrability of banking and finance matters, is the acceptance by the vast majority of developed States of the effects of the *Mitsubishi Motors* case,[10] and its extension to other financial fields other than competition. Indeed, the practice of European States[11] has followed suit and

8 See Stewart Sterk, "Enforceability of Agreements to Arbitrate: An Examination of the Public Policy Defence", 2 *Cardozo L. Rev.* (1981) 481, who, writing in 1981, noted that the statutes barring arbitrability were in their majority business-related, particularly antitrust, patents, securities, bankruptcy and liquidated and punitive damages claims, among others.

9 Ilias Bantekas, "Corporate Social Responsibility in International Law", 22 *BU Int'l L. J.* (2004) 309.

10 *Supra* note 3.

11 See for example in France, Court of Appeal (CA) Paris, 29 March 1991, *Ganz v. Nationale des Chemins de Fer Tunisiens (SNCFT)*, (1991) Rev. Arb. 478; in England, Court of Appeal, *Fiona Trust & Holding Corporation and Others v. Privalov and Others*, [2007] 2 Lloyd's Rep. 267; in

the same is true in respect of other jurisdictions, whose courts have named the *Mitsubishi* judgment as the basis for their own respective judgments.[12] The *Mitsubishi* judgment has achieved far more than liberating contractual anti-trust disputes from the limitations of regular litigation; it has, in fact, rationalised and explained the basis for subjecting the purely contractual elements of disputes to arbitration, without disrupting the public elements of such cases from the jurisdiction of civil courts and public prosecutors. Consequently, it has removed some mistrust from the arbitral process worldwide and has provided the necessary impetus for other fields of commerce, given that competition law was at the very top of those mandatory rules excluding arbitration. In the common law, at least, the *Mitsubishi* judgment and subsequent practice may have a far-reaching effect on all economic and financial disputes. Let us now proceed to examine the arbitrability of particular financial disputes.

3. Arbitrability of Disputes Arising from Securities Transactions

15-7 Securities transactions involve a variety of actors at different levels. On the one hand, they encompass contractual relationships solely between private actors through which securities are bought and sold via a securities broker. This process does not directly involve the particular corporation whose shares are traded, unless it has misrepresented its financial or other situation to the broker or prospective buyers. On the other hand, there exists a relationship between securities broker and a State, predicated on mandatory rules, whose aim it is to regulate and protect securities markets from turbulences, and, by implication, protect the investors, the corporations, their employees and the national economy. It is evident that this relationship between securities brokers and the State is destined to remain beyond the ambit of arbitrability, but this is not necessarily true with respect to the private dimension of securities transactions.

15-8 The U.S. Supreme Court has paved the way globally for releasing the private aspects of securities transactions from the restraints of civil adjudication. The adoption of the U.S. Securities Act of 1933[13] and the Securities Exchange Act of 1934[14] intended, *inter alia*, to protect the then recently-crashed stock

European Union, ECJ, 1 June 1999, C- 126/97, *Eco Swiss China Time v. Benetton International*, [1999] ECR I 3055.

12 *Quintette Coal Ltd v. Nippon Steel Co.* [1991] 1 WWR 219 (Court of Appeal of British Columbia), at 227-28; *Attorney-General v. Mobil Oil New Zealand Ltd* [1987] ICSID Rep 117, at 139.

13 15 U.S.C. §§ 77a-77bbbb.

14 15 U.S.C. §§ 78a-78lll.

market and to protect investors from securities fraud. By virtue of section 12(2) of the Securities Act, investors can recover from securities brokers any damage they suffered in cases of misrepresentation of accounts. The action is special because it is the broker that "is made to assume the burden of proving lack of scienter".[15] In order to protect the buyer/investor under such circumstances, section 22 of the Act provides for exclusive judicial jurisdiction in both federal and state courts. Moreover, section 14 of the Act, in an apparent move to further enhance investor rights, prohibits any waiver of the Act's provisions. This prohibition of waivers was for a long time interpreted as constituting a bar to arbitration generally in the relations between broker and investor, because the special right of action in section 12(2) could not be waived by the parties. It was evident, however, that this interpretation was at odds with the FAA's injunction that arbitration agreements were not to be frustrated. This position was maintained by the Supreme Court in *Wilko*, which, in reversing a Second Circuit decision, argued that the prohibition of waivers of the federal and state courts' exclusive jurisdiction rendered pre-dispute arbitration clauses and agreements void.[16] It is instructing that the Securities and Exchange Commission (SEC) at the time was understandably eager to implement the *Wilko* judgment, and by a series of Rules, declared to securities brokers that the incorporation of an arbitration clause in a contract with a buyer with the aim of binding the latter to arbitration in respect of future disputes arising out of securities transactions constitutes a fraudulent and deceptive act on behalf of the broker.[17] The gradual erosion of the *Wilko* judgment began with the *Scherk*[18] and later the *Mitsubishi*[19] judgment, which involved, *inter alia*, international securities claims, which the Supreme Court found to be arbitrable. The U.S. Supreme Court, departing from its previous jurisprudence, distinguished between domestic and international arbitration, highlighted the supremacy of party autonomy and emphasised the need to promote international commerce.[20] The nail in the coffin for the *Wilko* judgment was hammered with the judgment in *Rodriguez De Quijas v.*

15 *Wilko v. Swan*, 346 U.S. 427 (1953), at 431.

16 *Ibid.*, at 434. See Jay R. Sever, "The Relaxation of Inarbitrability and Public Policy Checks on US and Foreign Arbitration: Arbitration Out of Control?", 65 *Tul. L. Rev.* (1991) 1661, at 1670-75.

17 17 C.F.R § 240, 15c2-2a (1990). See Stephen H. Kupperman, George C. Freeman III, "Selected Topics in Securities Arbitration: Rule 15c2-2, Fraud, Duress, Unconscionability, Waiver, Class Arbitration, Punitive Damages, Rights of Review and Attorneys' Fees and Costs", 65 *Tul. L. Rev.* (1991) 1547, at 1553-55.

18 *Scherk v. Alberto Culver Co.*, 417 U.S. 506 (1974).

19 *Supra* note 3.

20 Scherk, *supra* note 18, at 515-17.

Shearson/American Express Inc.,[21] in which Justice Kennedy criticised *Wilko* as plainly incorrect, and the Court moved to allow arbitration of all claims under section 12(2) of the Securities Act, as well as any violations under the Securities Exchange Act. This judgment paved the way for the arbitrability of all securities disputes, irrespective of whether they may be designated domestic or international.

15-9 U.S. courts have, moreover, distinguished between claims of fraud invoked in respect of the entire securities transaction and claims of fraud induced with regard to the arbitration clause itself. Where the fraud relates to the entire contract, the ensuing dispute may be resolved by reference to an arbitrator, whereas, in all cases involving fraud in relation to the arbitration clause, the matter is only fit for federal courts to resolve.[22] Following the Supreme Court judgments that brought securities transactions into the realm of arbitrability, the rule in *Prima Paint* has been retained but it is now applicable also to securities fraud, misrepresentation and the full gamut of violations under the Securities Acts.[23] In a recent judgment, the Second Circuit rejected the petitioner's claim of stay for a class action securities arbitration, arguing that the parties' broad arbitration clause demonstrated their intention that the arbitrability of their claims be decided by an arbitrator and not the courts.[24] Moreover, in a surprising judgment, the U.S. Supreme Court upheld in 1995 a series of punitive damages granted in an arbitral award, notwithstanding that the agreement was governed by New York law that forbids punitive damages in arbitration.[25] The *Mastrobuono* judgment has been criticised for ignoring the parties' choice of law and Parks urges signatory parties to incorporate explicit exclusionary language in their contracts.[26]

15-10 Although an exhaustive review of all E.U. member State legislation would fall outside the narrow purview of this chapter, it suffices to say that given the broad language of all such legislation, securities transactions are generally

21 490 U.S. 477 (1989).

22 *Prima Paint Corp v. Flood & Conklin Mfg Co.*, 388 U.S. 395 (1967).

23 *Glazer v. Lehman Brothers Inc & SG Cowen Securities Corporation*, U.S. Court of Appeals Judgment (12 Jan 2005), available at: <http://www.ca6.uscourts.gov/opinions.pdf/05a0016p-06.pdf>.

24 *JSC Surgutneftegaz v. President and Fellows of Harvard College*, 2005 U.S. Dist. LEXIS 15991, (S.D.N.Y. August 3, 2005), *aff'd*, 167 Fed. App'x 266 (2d Cir. 2006).

25 *Mastrobuono v. Shearson Lehman Hutton*, 115 S Ct 1212 (1995). See William W. Park, "Arbitration in Banking and Finance", 17 *Ann. Rev. Banking L.* (1998) 214, at 234-35.

26 Park, *ibid.*, at 235.

arbitrable.[27] To the best of the author's knowledge no statute exists in the E.U. member States that serves to render securities disputes subject to the exclusive jurisdiction of regular courts.

4. The Arbitrability of Selected Financial Agreements

15-11 On the basis of our discussion on the broad language of the majority of arbitration laws in the E.U., the U.S. and other parts of the developed world, it has been shown that financial transactions and contracts thereto are generally arbitrable. Equally, it seems to be a general principle of arbitration law that the scope of an arbitration clause in one contract can extend to a dispute arising under a second contract, provided that the dispute "significantly relates" to the first agreement.[28] In *GE Capital Corp v. Union Corp et al [BancUnion Trust]*,[29] GE and BancUnion had entered into a Broker Agreement under which BancUnion would solicit customers [wishing] to obtain lease financing and then assign the leases to GE. The Broker Agreement contained an arbitration clause and applied to all transactions between the parties after the Agreement's execution, but not to separate assignment agreements entered into with respect to specific transactions. Unlike the Broker Agreement, the assignments did not contain an arbitration clause, and when GE filed a complaint against BancUnion for fraud with respect to several assignments, the latter filed a motion to stay the proceedings and compel arbitration. The Fourth Circuit Court of Appeals eventually compelled the arbitration of the fraud claims arising out of the individual assignment agreements, despite the lack of an arbitration clause thereto, on the ground that the Broker Agreement contemplated that its terms would supplement the assignments and also because following the *American Recovery* judgment, it noted that the test for the breadth of an arbitration clause is not whether a claim arose under one of the multiple agreements, but "whether a significant relationship exists between the claim and the agreement containing the arbitration clause".

15-12 Let us, now, examine those rare exceptions to the general arbitrability of financial contracts in some selected jurisdictions. It should become evident to the reader that each exception is predicated on localised financial considerations and

[27] See, e.g., *Philip Alexander Securities v. Bamberger* [1977] ILPr 73 (1996).
[28] *American Recovery Corp v. Computerized Thermal Imaging Inc.*, 96 F. 3d 88 (4th Cir. 1996), at 93.
[29] Judgment of 21 July 2005 (unpublished), available at: <http://pacer.ca4.uscourts.gov/opinion.pdf/041467.U.pdf>

perhaps a historic past during which a particular industry or class of professionals or consumers was severely disadvantaged. However, since the financial tides of most countries change rapidly and certainly the economies and professional markets of all European States have gone through rapid and wide transformations as a result of the freedom of movement and establishment, some peculiarities relating to inarbitrable contracts are, too, swept by the winds of change. An obvious example is Belgium's Distribution Law of 27 July 1961 (as amended in 1971), which subjects distributorship agreements performed in Belgium to the exclusive jurisdiction of Belgian courts[30]. In *Colvi v. Interdica*,[31] the Court of Cassation held that distributorship agreements should, in fact, be arbitrable.

15-13 In similar fashion, Article 5 of the Lebanese Law No. 34 of 5 August 1967 on the Regulation of Commercial Representation states that disputes arising out of commercial agency agreements are not arbitrable. This result was confirmed by the 9th Chamber of the Beirut Court of Appeals.[32] In a subsequent judgment by the 5th Chamber of the Lebanese Supreme Court, a distinction was made between the reference of commercial agency disputes to arbitration by means of an arbitration clause and a submission agreement (*compromis*). It is only when said disputes are submitted to arbitration through a *compromis* that they are arbitrable.[33] The rationale for this conclusion is that in the drafting of an arbitration clause within a commercial agency contract the Lebanese party has traditionally been viewed as the weakest of the two parties and with little negotiating power. The Law, therefore, was promulgated with a view to protecting the weaker party, whereas it is assumed that because the *compromis* is drafted following the appearance of a dispute, the parties are at a relative parity. Commercial agency agreements are generally not arbitrable,[34] for more or less the same reasons, throughout most of the Arab world.[35]

[30] For more on arbitrability of agency agreements see S. Kröll, Chapter 16 *infra*.

[31] Judgment No. JC04AF2 (15 Oct 2004), available at: <http:www.idiproject.com/docs/news/15102004.pdf>

[32] Judgment of 7 October 2004, available at: <http://idiproject.com/docs/news/Court%20of%20appeal.def.pdf> (in Arabic).

[33] Judgment No. 4/2005 (11 Jan 2005), available at: <http://www.idiproject.com/docs/news/Supreme%20Court.def.pdf> (in Arabic).

[34] The UAE Federal Supreme Court has held that a foreign arbitration clause in a registered commercial agency agreement is unenforceable (and therefore inarbitrable) because the Commercial Agencies Law No. 18 of 1981 (as amended by Federal Law No. 14 of 1988 and by Federal Law 13 of 17 June 2006) states that only UAE courts have jurisdiction over commercial agency disputes.

[35] Bahrain is exceptional, in that a 1998 amendment to its Commercial Agency Law abolished the statutory requirement of exclusivity for local commercial agents.

15-14 Warranty agreements are yet another area that has caused some concern in certain jurisdictions. In the U.S., some courts have been willing to entertain implied repeals to the FAA's presumption in favour of arbitration[36] in the context of the Magnuson-Moss Warranty Act (MMWA).[37] Section 2310(a)(2) of the MMWA instructs the Federal Trade Commission (FTC) to

> prescribe rules setting forth minimum requirements for any informal dispute settlement procedure which is incorporated into the terms of a written warranty.

Given that the Act does not define "informal dispute settlement", the FTC has determined that although arbitration qualifies as such, its binding nature would preclude the resolution of disputes before courts and its use should therefore be impermissible.[38] The Fifth Circuit in 2002 clarified the matter by holding that the express language of the MMWA does not override Congress's intent in favour of arbitration as manifested in the FAA.[39]

5. Arbitrability of Corporate Disputes[40]

15-15 The term corporate dispute is used in this chapter in a broad sense, with a view to encapsulate those contractual elements of the corporation that may be subject to an arbitration clause. This is broader than the general conception of corporate law as regulating the agency relationship between the principals (shareholders) and the managers. It is questionable whether a State, even a pro-arbitration one, should allow the arbitration of all disputes arising out of a corporate relationship. This is because whereas the submission of a dispute to arbitration is premised on a contract, it is unclear whether all corporate relationships are contractual in nature. However, even if one accepted that the relationship between minority shareholders and the corporation's directors and its chain of suppliers and purchasers is contractual, it would stretch the imagination

36 *Parkerson v. Smith*, 817 So. 2d 529 (Miss. 2002), at 532-537, holding that the MMWA demonstrates a clear intent to override the FAA and moreover conforms to the *lex posterior* rule; equally, in *Browne v. Kline Tysons Imps Inc.*, 190 F. Supp. 2d 827 (E.D. Va. 2002), at 831-32, it was held that the MMWA precludes arbitration, a result which was also premised on the FTC's interpretation of the Act.

37 15 U.S.C. §§ 2301-2312 (2000).

38 16 C.F.R. § 703.5(j) (2000). See Comment, Fifth Circuit Holds Magnusson-Moss Warranty Act Claims Arbitrable Despite Contrary Agency Interpretation, 116 *Harvard Law Review* (2003) 1201, at 1201-02.

39 *Walton v. Rose Mobile Homes LLC*, 298 F 3d 470 (5th Cir. 2002), at 475-78.

40 See also P. Perales Chapter 14, *supra*.

to assume that said shareholders had access to all corporate information, such that would enable them to stand at equal par with the directors and majority shareholders in the triggering of an arbitration clause. Some jurisdictions entertain these fears, e.g. India, whereas others entertain them to a lesser degree or not at all, particularly the U.S..

15-16 The fundamental starting point in any enquiry into the arbitrability of corporate disputes is certainly the existence of a contractual relationship and an enabling arbitration clause between the disputing parties. This is primarily the company's Articles of Association (or by-laws) and secondarily a host of other more limited (in scope and parties) agreements, such as shareholders' agreements, share purchase agreements and others. To the extent that the Articles of Association constitute a contract and bind every member of a corporation,[41] arbitration clauses incorporated therein subsequently bind all such persons. This is usually the case in the majority of jurisdictions. By implication, agreements that are initially extraneous to the Articles of Association, when they themselves are incorporated, attached or expressly related to the Articles, they are covered by the arbitration clause contained in the Articles of Association.[42]

15-17 We shall provide a few examples of jurisdictions that limit the scope of arbitration in respect of some corporate disputes. In accordance with Article 1020(3) of the Dutch Code of Civil Procedure (DCCP), arbitration is available only to those matters which the parties can freely dispose of. In applying this principle to claims against the validity of shareholders' resolutions, the Dutch Supreme Court had held that said resolutions on the appointment and dismissal of corporate directors and the validity of decisions adopted by corporate directors are not arbitrable.[43] Its rationale was premised on the fact that such matters are not within the free disposal of the parties because of their far-reaching consequences vis-à-vis third parties. Moreover, whereas a court judgment that voids a corporate resolution has universal effect, arbitral awards produce effects only as regards the particular parties that entertained the dispute.[44] Some authors

41 Indian Companies Act (1956), s 36; confirmed by the Indian Supreme Court (S Ct) in *Dale & Carrington Investment Ltd v. P K Prathapan*, JT 2004 (7) S Ct 434.

42 *Rangaraj v. Gopalakrishnan*, AIR 1992 S Ct (India) 453.

43 *Groenselect* case, HR (10 Nov 2006), RvdW 2006, 1005; see generally, Vesna Lazic, "Arbitration Law Reform in the Netherlands: Formal and Substantive Validity of an Arbitration Agreement", 11 *Electronic J. Comp. L.* (May 2007), available at: <http://www.ejcl.org/111/art111-16.pdf>

44 *Ibid.*

take the same view in respect of Germany, although this thesis has not been tested in court. It is maintained that it is doubtful whether a claim seeking to nullify a shareholders' resolution is arbitrable, because of the absence of a mechanism that informs all shareholders and provides an opportunity to join. If the situation was remedied in this respect, the courts may not be so sceptical about the applicability of arbitration.[45] Limitations on arbitrability on the basis of third party interests cannot be sustained where claims arise directly from a violation of the Rules of Association or any other incorporated agreement thereto. The interests of third parties are only prejudiced where a particular group of the corporation's members excludes them from a decision or transaction through the adoption of a distinct contract to which only members of the said group are parties; hence the rationale for excluding from arbitration agreements in violation of Sweden's Companies Act relating to minority shareholder rules. This is also the rationale behind non-arbitrability of disputes in relation to violation of SCA with regard to minority shareholder rules.[46] In Italy, following the adoption of two recent pieces of legislation,[47] the existence of an arbitration clause in shareholders' agreements, as well as in corporate by-laws, renders disputes arising therefrom wholly arbitrable. This is not entirely different from our other case studies, since if an agreement adopted outside the framework of the corporation's bind-all instruments, the presumption must be that disputes arising therefrom are not arbitrable.[48]

15-18 The concerns over the rights of shareholders, as third parties to agreements concluded by some shareholders or by the Board with other entities, may be resolved by permitting arbitration in order to enforce a shareholder's derivative action. The arbitrability of derivative shareholders' actions is an area that is largely unclear in comparative legal terms. In the US, if the shareholder can demonstrate a violation in respect of either a duty of care or a duty of loyalty,

45 See Erik Schafer, Germany, available at: <http://www.globalarbitrationreview.com/handbooks/3/sections/6/chapters/39/germany>

46 See Sundin & Wernberg, *supra* note 5; otherwise, the Svea CA held in 2004 that the parties to an agreement are free to arbitrate any issue that falls within their contractual freedom. *Peiker austic GmbH & KG v. SAAB Automobile Aktiebolag*, Judgment (30 Dec 2004).

47 Legislative Decree No. 5 (17 Jan 2003), Arts 34ff and Legislative Decree No. 40 (2 February 2006).

48 Article 34 of the 2003 Legislative Decree establishes that Articles of Association can establish the use of arbitration to solve disputes among members of a company, or between any member of the company itself, save for publicly-traded companies or companies whose shares are widely held by the general public. The author would like to thank Dr. Luca Cerioni for this unofficial translation and clarification of the relevant provisions.

then he or she can successfully challenge the actions of the Board in the form of a derivative suit. Such derivative suits involve a complex two-tier process through which the shareholder first sues the corporation, which thereafter proceeds to sue the entity at fault. Where the corporation is successful in its own suit, the shareholder can then satisfy his own claim. Little uniformity regards such derivative suits, as they are regulated by state, rather than federal law. In the state of New York, for example, they are permitted as long as the aim is to secure a judgment in the corporation's favour.[49] The California Court of Appeal recently held that a derivative suit brought by a shareholder whose claim was based on a contract containing an arbitration agreement between the corporation and a third entity is subject to arbitration, even though no such agreement existed between the suing shareholder and the third entity. The Court held that the suing shareholder was required to arbitrate because the causes of action sued upon belong to the corporation and not the plaintiff.[50] In India, direct as opposed to derivative shareholders' claims are not arbitrable,[51] but for different reasons than those offered in U.S. case law. Whereas in the U.S., only the corporation itself can sue for losses sustained to its assets as a result of mismanagement – including through arbitration if applicable – in India the violation of statutory rights cannot be made the subject of arbitration.[52]

6. Arbitrability of Matters Arising out of Banking Activities

15-19 Matters arising out of banking activities generally do not differ much from other financial transactions, in that they are embodied in contractual form and do not, moreover, pertain to activities over which the State may be deemed to have an overriding interest. Thus, the general rule in the developed world is that all banking activities may be subject to valid arbitral proceedings. Obviously, some exceptions to the general rule may appear from time to time, particularly where: a) in relatively smaller economies inter-banking agreements may be viewed as potentially detrimental to the stability and viability of the local economy, or; b) where investment speculators, with the collaboration of financial institutions, engage in activities that are viewed as manipulative of the local currency, even if this is an otherwise legitimate investment transaction. The author is not aware of *ad hoc* prohibitions to arbitrate disputes arising of said enterprises, but in the

49 *Eisenber v. Flying Tiger Line*, Inc., 451 F.2d 267.

50 *Frederick v. First Union Securities*, 122 Cal. Rptr. 2d 774 (CA 2002), at 779.

51 *Haryana Telecom Ltd v. Sterlite Industries Ltd.*, (1999) 5 SCC 688; Order of the Company Law Board (CLB) in C.P. No 18 (2002).

52 *Ibid.*

recent past States have resisted, some times proactively, banking transactions of this nature and a public policy constraint to arbitration under such circumstances would only be a natural consequence. In this section we are going to discuss three distinct issues relating to banking activities that give rise to arbitrability concerns. Firstly, we shall examine the arbitrability of banking disputes involving the charging of interest in the Islamic world, with a particular emphasis on Saudi Arabia – and, where applicable, comparable legal developments in other Gulf or Arab countries; secondly, consumer arbitration stemming from banking activities; thirdly, we will discuss whether the sovereign nature of certain banks, or the sovereign nature of the transaction, for at least one of the parties, renders such disputes beyond the reach of arbitral tribunals.

6.1. Arbitrability of Simple Interest in the Islamic World

15-20 Article 2 of the 1983 Saudi Arbitration Act clearly states that arbitration is permitted in disputes that may be referred to conciliation.[53] Although this general admonition may suffice in respect of family, criminal and most commercial disputes, because these are well described in both the text of the Qur'an and the *sunnah*, the exact ambit of banking disputes is in a state of limbo between classic Islamic jurisprudence and contemporary banking practice. It should be noted, moreover, in a further twist of complication, that no substantive or procedural rules of conciliation exist in Saudi legislation, apart from what is described in *Shari'a* tradition. Equally, in the Arabic language there is no semantic difference between the terms "conciliation" and "mediation" and both are translated as "*sulh*". The fundamental question, therefore, is whether banking activities are validly subject to conciliation. The matter may be classified by reference to Article 1(b) of the Saudi Banking Law of 1966, which defines "banking business" as encompassing

> the business of receiving money on current or fixed deposit account, opening of current accounts, opening of letters of credit, issuance of letters of guarantee, payment and collection of cheques, payment orders, promissory notes and similar other papers of value, discounting of bills,

[53] Royal Decree No. M/46, issued on 12/07/1403 H (1983), repealing in the process the relevant provisions of the Commercial Court Code of 1931. Reprinted in Umm Alqura Gazette, Issue No. 2969 of 22/08/1403 H (1983).

bills of exchange and other commercial papers, foreign exchange transactions and other banking business.[54]

There is a spurious omission in the definition of Article 1(b) in the form of lending activities, which are after all the primary means by which banks make profit. The Act does contain three provisions, Articles 9-11, whereby particular activities are forbidden, none of which, however, relate to lending transactions. One line of thinking views this omission as a natural consequence of the rejection of the practice of imposing interest and usury (*riba*) in Islamic jurisprudence as being *haram* (sinful), thus necessitating no particular codification for what is after all a fundamental rule of law.[55]

15-21 In *fiqh* jurisprudence, *riba* is defined as "an increase in one of two homogenous equivalents being exchanged without this increase being accompanied by a return".[56] Two types of *riba* are recognized: a) *riba al nasiah*, relating to a specified increase in return for postponement of, or waiting for, the payment, and; b) *riba al fadl*, which arises where the increase is irrespective of the postponement and is not offset by something in return.[57] It is the first of these, *riba al nasiah*, that pervades banking activities and which is therefore prohibited in most systems governed by some form of *Shari'a*. Given, therefore, that it constitutes a prohibited practice, transactions involving *riba al nasiah* are not amenable to conciliation, or to arbitration, as a result. It is not surprising, under the circumstances, that the entrepreneurial spirit of the banking sector has found other means in order to make profit and at the same time be compliant with the tenets of Islamic finance law. Islamic banking (or Islamic financing) is predicated, in the absence of charging interest, on the bank assuming the same commercial risk – or part thereof – as the borrower, reaping a profit only where the borrower himself makes a profit. Moreover, banks can only finance such projects, and share in their risk and profits, that are compatible with Islamic principles. Thus, projects relating to the production of alcohol or pornographic material may not be financed. This does not mean, however, that other *riba*-free transactions are necessarily consistent with Islamic jurisprudence, although it should be remembered that attitudes on such matters are not similar in all Muslim

[54] Banking Control Act, Royal Decree No M/5, issued on 22/02/1386 H (1966), available at: <http://www.sama.gov.sa/en/control/procedure/cofmblr/3.htm>

[55] Qur'an, 1:275.

[56] E. R. A. E. Ali, "Riba and Its Prohibition In Islam", available at: <http://islamicfinancepro.files.wordpress.com/2007/08/riba-and-its-prohibition-in-islam.pdf>, at 15.

[57] *Ibid.*

States. The general rule is that speculative agreements are void and as a result, currency futures and forward trading fall within this category of prohibited banking transactions. The same is true as regards the trading of currency as a commodity. Futures trading, on the other hand, constitute a permissible activity so long as the commodity exists at the time of the sale but is to be delivered at a future date. Where the commodity does not exist at the time of the sale, that futures transaction is void. [58] The conclusion to be drawn from the aforementioned analysis is that any banking activities involving the payment of interest, as well as other Islamic banking transactions that are incompatible with the principles of *Shari'a*, will not only be non-arbitrable, but will, moreover, be declared as void by Saudi courts.[59]

15-22 There exist two possible means by which non-Islamic banking activities may be said to be arbitrable under Saudi law. The first concerns the injunction in the Qur'an that contracts must be honoured.[60] The necessary stipulation from this injunction is that a contract providing for the payment of interest will have to be honoured, despite the prohibition of *riba* in the body of the Qur'an itself, which thereafter renders the former contract arbitrable. The result may potentially be different were a court to hold that the rule prohibiting interest trumps the *pacta sunt servanta* rule, because a different conclusion may be utilised to manipulate the legal system. The parties are obviously free to privately agree on the payment of interest, but said agreement would not be recognised or enforced by Saudi courts.[61] The Saudi government, itself, seems to have introduced an exception to the *riba*-prohibition rule by inserting a clause in a recent Gas Concession

[58] See generally, Freshfields, "Islamic Finance: Basic Principles and Structures (2006)", available at: <http://www.freshfields.com/publications/pdfs/2006/13205.pdf>

[59] Significantly, Saudi judicial practice demonstrates that in the enforcement of a foreign arbitral award in which the losing party was ordered to pay interest, the Saudi court of enforcement rejected only that part of the award that ordered the payment of interest. Diwan Almazalim Decision No 19/28 of 1399 H (1979). The decision is cited in the unpublished and draft doctoral thesis of A. Baamir (Brunel Law School), "The Arbitration and Enforcement of Banking Disputes in Saudi Arabia".

[60] Qur'an, 5:1.

[61] One way of circumventing the Saudi legal system altogether is by formulating the arbitration clause in such a way as to exclude Saudi law from the *lex arbitri* and the substantive law of the contract. In this manner, were a dispute to arise, the arbitral tribunal would not find the imposition of interest as void or illegal, as in *Islamic Investment Company of the Gulf (Bahamas) Ltd. v. Symphony Gems NV and Others*, [2002] All ER 171. See Alejandro Carballo, "The Law of the Dubai International Financial Centre: Common Law Oasis or a Mirage in the UAE?", 21 *Arab L. Q.* (2007) 91.

Agreement whereby interest is to be charged for late payment.[62] Given that the agreement provides for arbitration where a dispute arises, all matters relating to the payment of interest for delays are arbitrable. It is not entirely clear whether this is a sole exception, but it is certainly evidence that the *riba*-prohibition rule is not seen as absolute by the Saudi government and that therefore the *pacta sunt servanta* rule is not hierarchically inferior to its *riba*-prohibition counterpart. Practitioners should, however, treat these observations with caution, as they have not been tested in practice and given the conservative attitude of Saudi courts and quasi-judicial bodies, we do not expect a radical change of views any time soon. It should be noted that although the imposition of interest is prohibited in Islamic law, it is very common practice otherwise.[63] Certainly, the parties will generally rely on good faith and will not normally raise the matter before the courts![64] Finally, following the English Court of Appeal judgment in the *Beximco* case,[65] a choice of law clause in a financing contract between an Islamic bank and its borrowers that is governed by and construed in accordance with English law "subject to the principles of *Shari'a*" does not mean that both legal "systems" are concurrently applicable. Under the 1980 Rome Convention on the Law Applicable to Contractual Obligations[66] only national legal systems can be designated as laws governing a contract, a requirement which the *Shari'a* does not satisfy. In any event, the Court noted the indeterminate character of the *Shari'a* in such matters and held that even if it were applicable as a legal system, English law would not be subject to the dictates of *Shari'a*; rather, the invocation of *Shari'a* in a choice of law clause in the contract was simply an affirmation that

62 Art. 18, Gas Concession Agreement between the Kingdom of Saudi Arabia and Lukoil Overseas, reprinted in Umm Alqura Gazette, issue No. 3990 of 15/03/1425 H (4/05/2004).

63 See William M. Ballantyne, *Commercial Law in the Arab Middle East: The Gulf States* (Lloyds of London Press 1986) at 133, who argues that whereas the imposition of *riba* is tolerated in Saudi Arabia, in Bahrain, Qatar and Oman it has been expressly approved by relevant banking laws.

64 Exceptionally, Arts. 76 and 77 of the UAE Federal Commercial Transactions Law No. 18 (1993) permit a creditor to charge simple (as opposed to compound) interest, which must not exceed 12%. Some law firms warn their clients that it is by no means clear whether such an interest is compatible with Islamic law and less so if the courts will deem a dispute of this nature arbitrable. However, given the express statement of the Law and the Interpretative Decision No. 14/9 (28 June 1981) of the Constitutional Department of the Federal Supreme Court of Abu Dhabi (economic necessity requires the charging of simple interest by banks), as well as Judgment No. 245/20 (7 May 2000) of the Federal Supreme Court of Abu Dhabi (equally endorsing simple interest), disputes as to simple interest must be presumed as arbitrable in the UAE. See Hind Tamini, "Interest under the UAE Law and as Applied by the Courts of Abu Dhabi", 17 *Arab L. Q.* (2002) 50.

65 *Beximco Pharmaceuticals v. Shamil Bank of Bahrain EC*, [2004] 1 WLR 1784.

66 O.J. C O27 (26 Jan 1998, consolidated version).

the Bank conducts its operation in a particular manner, but English law would be the sole governing law. The obvious outcome for arbitrability is that although the parties would seem to want to comply with Islamic banking law – and thus render all matters relating to interest non-arbitrable – in reality the substantive matter of their dispute would be governed by English law, which lawfully subjects disputes relating to the imposition of interest to arbitration.

6.2. Consumer Banking Arbitration

15-23 So far we have provided examples of banking operations that involve large-scale financing projects in which both the bank and the borrower directly negotiate the terms of their lending arrangement. In such cases, it is the object of the loan, or the terms of the loan itself, particularly the imposition of interest, that some legislatures find offensive to their public policy and as such insusceptible to arbitration. In the present section on consumer arbitration, which will be brief, it is not the object of the loan, but the particular terms of the bank-borrower agreement that cannot be entertained in certain jurisdictions by means of arbitration. Although the bank will have provided its clients with its Terms and Conditions of consumer banking, deeming them to have accepted these, whether by activating their account, making use of the bank's services and facilities, or by signing said terms, some States consider that the borrower is at a significantly disadvantaged position vis-à-vis the bank. The general law of consumer arbitration will, therefore, apply to their mutual relations, albeit certain States may bar recourse to consumer arbitration because of the perceived vulnerable position of the consumer.

15-24 In the U.S., and in accordance with the FAA, pre-dispute arbitration clauses are permissible with respect to consumer contracts, as upheld by the U.S. Supreme Court.[67] Two exceptions apply to this broad rule; firstly, given that the right of *locus standi* before the courts has a constitutional basis, it may not be waived without express and unambiguous agreement, thus necessitating that the consumer is fully aware of the implications of the waiver.[68] This task, and the

[67] *Allied-Bruce Terminix Companies v. Dobson*, (1995) 513 U.S. 265.

[68] In *Discover Bank v. Superior Court* (judgment of 27 June 2005), 36 Cal. 4th 148, a putative class action against a credit card issuer was made for improper charges relating to late fees. The credit card issuer argued that the class action was impermissible on account of the arbitration clause, which barred customers from proceeding with their claims on a class action basis. On June 27, 2005, the California Supreme Court held that it is unconscionable under California law for a corporation, by way of a contract of adhesion, to bar customers with small individual claims from bringing or participating in a class action. On remand, however, the California Court of

onus to prove as much, befalls the bank.[69] Secondly, courts will not feel bound to uphold a pre-dispute arbitration clause that is deemed to be unconscionable. Such unconscionability will be determined both procedurally and substantively on the basis of the negotiations, disclosure of the arbitration terms, their fairness, inconvenient arbitration venue, as well as other relevant factors.[70] Where the arbitration clause is not unconscionable and the consumer is found to be fully aware of its existence and implications, U.S. courts are willing to extend arbitrability to statutory consumer protection claims brought in a bankruptcy case. In *Mintze v. American General Financial Services, Inc.*,[71] the Third Circuit held that although bankruptcy courts enjoy absolute authority over core bankruptcy proceedings but less so over non-core proceedings, "the core/non-core distinction does not … affect whether a bankruptcy court has the discretion to deny enforcement of an arbitration agreement". The lack of bankruptcy issues in *Mintze* meant that there was no inherent conflict between arbitration and federal consumer law.

15-25 In the European Union, on the other hand, under the terms of the Unfair Terms in Consumer Contracts Directive,[72] pre-dispute arbitration clauses inserted in consumer contracts will be deemed contrary to good faith where they have not been individually negotiated and subsequently any disputes arising therefrom cannot be arbitrated. This development is obviously based on the assumption that consumers will in the majority of cases be severely disadvantaged if arbitration is pursued instead of litigation, although empirical studies demonstrate otherwise.[73] Article 3(3) of the Directive refers to an Annex, which lists some terms that are deemed to be unfair. Term (q) in the Annex, which is particularly relevant to this chapter, renders unfair those terms the effect of which is to:

> Exclud[e] or hinder the consumer's right to take legal action or exercise any other legal remedy, particularly by requiring the consumer to take disputes exclusively to arbitration not covered by legal provisions, unduly restricting

---

Appeals upheld the Delaware choice of law clause in the credit card contract and found that Delaware law would allow the contractual ban on class actions.

69 See, for example, *Nelson v. Cyprus Baghdad Copper Corp.*, 119 F. 3d 756 (9th Cir., 1997).

70 See *Arnold v. United Companies Lending Corporation*, 511 S.E. 2d 854.

71 434 F 3d 222 (3rd Cir., 2006).

72 Council Directive 93/13/EEC (5 April 1993), O.J. L 95 (21 April 1993).

73 Ernst & Young, "Outcomes of Arbitration: An Empirical Study of Consumer Lending Cases" (2004), which showed that consumers generally prevailed over their adversaries. Available at: <http://www.arbitration-forum.com/rcontrol/documents/ResearchStudiesAndStatistics/2005ErnstAndYoung.pdf>

the evidence available to him or imposing on him a burden of proof which, according to the applicable law, should lie with another party to the contract.

15-26 It is not clear whether in some instances it may be permissible to insert an arbitration clause in an agreement between a bank and a consumer client. Certainly, where the arbitration clause does not wholly exclude access to courts, arbitration becomes a choice and should therefore be permissible. Equally, if the consumer was given a real opportunity to familiarise himself with the terms of the agreement and the arbitration clause, the clause then ceases to be a hidden term. It is, therefore, up to the banks to provide sufficient information, in an accessible manner to their clients, in order to avoid rendering their arbitration clause inarbitrable.

6.3. Other Procedural Bars to Arbitrability of Banking Disputes: Immunity?

15-27 When one talks of a particular dispute as not being susceptible to arbitration, this is generally so either because the subject matter is excluded by operation of the common law or statute, or simply because the particular terms of submission of certain disputes to arbitration are impermissible (objective arbitrability), as in the case of consumer arbitration. The latter constitutes, to a large degree, a permissible procedural bar to arbitration, at least in the context of the European Union. Where a party to an arbitration agreement argues that a dispute cannot be entertained by an arbitral forum because that party enjoys sovereign immunity, it is laying claim to a procedural bar to arbitration and, as a result, challenges the arbitrability of said dispute (subjective arbitrability). The matter generally arises in respect of international or mixed contracts, in which one of the parties is a sovereign State or an instrumentality thereof. In such cases, the contemporary rule in customary international law is to distinguish between those acts of States that are performed in the exercise of sovereign functions (*acta jure imperii*) from those that are merely undertaken on a commercial basis (*acta jure gestionis*). The former are by necessity protected in order to safeguard the ordinary flow of international relations; the means of protection is the granting of immunity, which serves as a procedural bar against the jurisdiction of national, but not necessarily international, courts over the acts and persons of foreign nationals acting in a sovereign capacity. *Acta jure gestionis*, on the other hand, are not covered by the rule of immunity and any transaction performed as a result may be submitted either to litigation or arbitration, if the parties have so agreed.

15-28 Loan agreements between banks and States hosting international investments are very common. Indeed, it is unlikely that a single investor, or a consortium thereof, will have the necessary funds to undertake a long-term infrastructure (such as oil and gas) project without funding from financial institutions. The banks may assume numerous functions in the ensuing contracts, whether as guarantors for the investors, or simply as financiers in a separate contract entered into solely with the investors. Where it is contractually related to the host State, and said contract contains an arbitration clause, the State party cannot claim immunity from the jurisdiction of the arbitral tribunal. The absence of immunity for *acta jure gestionis* is confirmed by its affirmation in all existing bilateral investment treaties, as well as by the terms of Article 25 of the International Center for the Settlement of Investment Disputes (ICSID) Convention,[74] which clearly does not recognise any immunity regarding the submission of disputes to arbitration,[75] and other regional multilateral investment instruments, such as NAFTA. It is also attested by the plethora of immunity statutes in various parts of the world, although it should be noted that said statutes do not produce universal effects, but only so far as they relate to the forum State.[76] Over the years, the question of what constitutes a commercial act has given rise to a consistent body of precedent and is generally determined by reference to the nature of a particular transaction and not necessarily its purpose.[77] It is quite interesting that the U.K. Immunity Act makes specific mention to financial and banking transactions, particularly

> loan or other transaction for the provision of finance and any guarantee or indemnity in respect of any such transaction or of any other financial obligation

[74] 1965 Washington (ICSID) Convention on the Settlement of Investment Disputes between States and Nationals of Other States, 575 UNTS 160.

[75] Certainly, Art. 55 of the ICSID Convention restricts the enforcement of awards by reference to applicable immunities in the country of enforcement, but said provision is not concerned with submission to arbitration.

[76] U.K. 1978 Immunity Act, s 9(1), states that:
"Where a State has agreed in writing to submit a dispute which has arisen, or may arise, to arbitration, the State is not immune as respects proceedings in the courts of the United Kingdom which relate to the arbitration."
Equally, the same is true with respect to § 1605(a)(2) of the U.S. 1988 Federal Sovereign Immunities Act (FSIA), 28 U.S.C § 1605(a)(2).

[77] See FSIA, *ibid.*, at § 1603(d).

and renders these commercial transactions not susceptible to claims of immunity.[78] Finally, it is worth mentioning that even if a State entity is found not to be immune from the civil jurisdiction of foreign courts, it is certainly immune from execution and enforcement proceedings.[79]

7. Conclusion

15-29 The examination of arbitrable matters in the spheres of banking and finance give rise to at least two distinct trends. On the one hand, developed States of the so-called Western world have liberalised their arbitration laws to such an extent that all financial and banking disputes that are contractual in nature are capable of being resolved by arbitration, at least as these relate to the parties' relationship. This is true notwithstanding that said dispute might affect third parties, as well as the interests of the State wherein it is arbitrated. These developed nations have, moreover, overcome their protectionism in certain fields of commerce, which they perceived as having the potential to disadvantage their nationals; franchise contracts were among these, but the expansion of local economies in the E.U. in favour of a wider financial community with mobility of capital, services and workers has meant that protectionism of this nature was no longer necessary.

15-30 On the other hand, some developing nations are still cautious about expanding the ambit of arbitrable disputes in the financial sector. One reason may be attributed to the vulnerability of local merchants from foreign conglomerates, and this is particularly true with respect to small States with a limited, yet healthy, economy. Another reason is associated with tradition that is impossible to part with, especially in Muslim States, resulting thus in limitations to arbitration, which in practice are flouted on a widespread scale. Nonetheless, this is not the premise of all Muslim nations. The conservative legislative approach of Saudi Arabia is not followed by the States comprising the UAE, as a result of the financial realities of the international financial and trading system. The arbitration laws of many developing countries may *prima facie* suggest that they adopt a liberal view towards arbitrability. However, given the narrow and sometimes indistinguishable boundaries between public policy and commerce in

[78] S 3(3)(b).

[79] See Art 55 ICSID Convention. Contrary to global practice, a recent ruling from the Italian Court of Cassation (Judgement No 14199 of 29 May 2008 has held that execution against a State entity in order to compensate for costs is not barred by immunity considerations. The judgment is available in Italian at: <http://www.cortedicassazione.it/Documenti/14199.pdf>.

these States, one cannot be certain in every occasion whether a particular financial or banking activity may be perceived as falling within the exclusive remit of the State or not. Arbitrability in these jurisdictions must, therefore, be approached with caution.

Stefan Kröll[*]

CHAPTER 16

THE "ARBITRABILITY" OF DISPUTES ARISING FROM COMMERCIAL REPRESENTATION

1. INTRODUCTION

16-1 In an increasingly globalized world, the existence of well functioning distribution channels is a crucial element for economic success. Already at a national level, it rarely makes economical sense for commercial entities to sell their products or services exclusively through their own personnel directly to their customers. Most entities lack the financial or personal resources necessary for an optimal market penetration; and even if these resources exist, economic considerations – such as spreading the risk – are often a strong argument for relying at least in part on independent third parties for the distribution of the goods and services. That applies *a fortiori* if goods and services are to be marketed internationally. Local representation by persons familiar with the relevant market is normally indispensable for any successful business.

16-2 There are numerous ways in which an entity can organize its commercial representation by third parties. In practice, the majority of parties either rely on the various types of commercial agents or distributors in the legal sense or operate a franchise system. [1]

16-3 Irrespective of which method of commercial representation is chosen, the principal, in general, has an interest to base his relationship with the various

* "Rechtsanwalt" in Cologne and national correspondent to UNCITRAL for Germany.

1 For the various types of commercial representation see *Schmitthoff's Export Trade: The Law and Practice of International Trade* (11th ed, Sweet & Maxwell 2007) paras 27-001 et seq.; Martinek, Semler and Habermeier, *Handbuch des Vertriebsrechts* (2nd ed, 2003) paras 214 et seq.

L Mistelis & S Brekoulakis (eds), Arbitrability: International & Comparative Perspectives, 317-350

agents, distributors or franchisees on a single model contract.[2] The transaction costs involved in negotiating and managing individual contracts with every representative would be considerable. That applies, in particular in international distribution systems, where each of these contracts could be submitted to a different law. For the same reason the principal has little interest in submitting to the jurisdiction of the home courts of its various counterparts. Consequently, in practice most distribution systems are based on a model contract prepared by the principal which may be varied slightly to take account of national particularities.

16-4 In particular, in the international arena these "model-contracts", but also contracts negotiated individually, often provide for dispute resolution by arbitration. The well known advantages,[3] in particular the expertise of the arbitrators, the avoidance of the home courts of either party and the world wide enforceability of arbitral awards, make arbitration in the area of commercial representation the preferred method of dispute resolution or at least a very popular method.[4]

16-5 However, there are a number of particular features which distinguish the various types of contracts for commercial representation from other commercial contracts. The most important one is that in many of these contracts there is an actual or at least perceived inequality of bargaining power. As a consequence the national provisions regulating the various types of commercial representation are often based on the assumption that they have to protect the agent, distributor or franchisee. As in other fields, such as labour law or consumer protection, the underlying idea of protecting the weaker party has considerable potential to limit procedural party autonomy and impose restrictions on the parties' ability to validly agree on arbitrating their disputes. The scope of these restrictions may differ between the various forms of "distribution contracts" and from country to country. It depends largely on of the weight attached to the protected interest and the particularities of the relevant market.[5]

2 See Freitag, EWiR 2000, 1061 seq.

3 For the advantages see Julian Lew, Loukas Mistelis & Stefan Kröll, *Comparative International Commercial Arbitration* (Kluwer 2003) paras 1-13 et seq.; Redfern and Hunter, *Law and Practice of International Commercial Arbitration* (4th ed, 2004) paras 1-41 et seq.

4 See Truong, *Les differences lies à la rupture des contracts internationaux de distribution dans les sentences arbitrales CCI* (Litec 2002) at 330 according to whom around 10 % of the cases filed with the ICC in the period 1985-2000 concerned distribution contracts.

5 For example, the protection afforded to the sole distributor under Belgian law, which is discussed in greater detail below, is justified by the consideration that due to the small size of the Belgian market the sole distributor is in a particularly weak bargaining position.

16-6 In the following, the three different approaches adopted in practice will be described and evaluated on the basis of examples from selected jurisdictions.

2. Arbitrability of Distribution Disputes: Still Through a Glass Darkly?!

16-7 In 1999 Jan Paulsson entitled one of his articles dealing with the issue of arbitrability under the New York Convention in general: Arbitrability, still through a glass darkly.[6] Regrettably, ten years later, the title still describes the situation very well, at least in relation to disputes arising from commercial representation. The different meanings attached to the notion of arbitrability contribute to these uncertainties. In American arbitration law a broad concept of arbitrability is used. It covers "subject matter arbitrability" as well as "contractual arbitrability".[7] Here, the term arbitrability is used in a much more restrictive way, in accordance with the notion prevailing in Europe and the New York Convention. Arbitrability, or as it is often called objective arbitrability, determines which disputes can be submitted to arbitration.[8] As will be shown in greater detail below, this type of narrow objective arbitrability should be distinguished from cases where a certain type of dispute is not excluded *per se* and in all cases from referral to arbitration, but the specific facts of a the case, i.e. the threat or the likelihood of the non-application of certain mandatory rules, renders the arbitration agreement non enforceable.

16-8 The major reason for the existing uncertainties is, that in general neither the national arbitration laws nor the special protective regulations for the various types of commercial representation explicitly address the arbitrability of such disputes. One of the few exceptions would be the new section 2 (4)(b) Federal Arbitration Act, if the Arbitration Fairness Act of 2007 were to be adopted in the U.S.. At least franchise disputes would then be clearly inarbitrable.[9] In all other cases the national laws regulating the various forms of commercial representation

[6] Paulsson, "Arbitrability, Still through a glass darkly, in: Arbitration in the Next Decade", *ICC Bulletin* Special Supplement on the Occasion of the 75th Birthday of the International Court of Arbitration at 95 et seq.

[7] For a detailed account see L. Shore, Chapter 4 *supra*.

[8] See Lew, Mistelis & Kröll, *supra* note 3 at para 9-1; Poudret & Besson, *Comparative Law of International Arbitration* (2007) para 326; Fouchard, Gaillard & Goldmann, *International Commercial Arbitration* (1999) para 532.

[9] For details see below; for the distinction see also Arfazadeh, *Ordre public et arbitrage international à l'épreuve de la mondialisation* (2005) 91 et seq.

are more or less silent on the issue. They contain primarily substantive provisions of an often mandatory nature to ensure a minimum protection of the representative. These substantive provisions are often supplemented by rules providing for the jurisdiction of the courts at the representative's place of business. Whether and how these rules affect the arbitrability of such disputes or the enforceability of arbitration agreements is not explicitly regulated. It has to be deduced from the objectives of the relevant provisions and the general principles of conflict of laws, however, which are everything but clear in the field of internationally mandatory rules, i.e. loi de police or loi d'application immediate in the French terminology.

3. The Rules on Commercial Agency as an Example for Addressing the Inequality of Bargaining Power

16-9 In principle, the contracts concluded between the principal and its various commercial representatives are contracts between two merchants, i.e., parties which are generally not considered to be in need of particular protection. Irrespective of this, many legal systems have introduced statutory provisions which are intended to protect agents, distributors or franchisees. The underlying rationale for such provisions is that the various commercial representatives are considered to be the weaker party, having less bargaining power than the principal. One argument raised to support this view is that the contracts for commercial representation are not freely negotiated between the parties. Due to the principal's strong interest in establishing a uniform distribution system, the agent, distributor or franchisee, is often only faced with the option of either accepting the contract as proposed or losing the business. The different provisions are then intended to create a level playing field to ensure minimum protection for the commercial representative. There are various means to reach these objectives. They are well evidenced by the rules on commercial agency.

3.1. Protection Afforded to Commercial Agents

16-10 A good example to provide an overview on the type of protection afforded is the EC Directive on Self-Employed Commercial Agents (Commercial Agent Directive).[10] It defines the minimum standard of protection to be granted to

[10] Council Directive 86/653/EEC of 18 December 1986 on the coordination of the laws of the Member States relating to self-employed commercial agents, Official Journal L 382, 31/12/1986 P. 0017 – 0021; for additional protection in particular concerning the exclusivity guaranteed to

commercial agents within the different Member States of the European Union. The Directive imposes on the principal a general obligation to act in good faith towards the commercial agent (Article 4), which results *inter alia* in obligations to provide certain information. Furthermore, it defines the transactions for which the agent is to receive remuneration and other details concerning the agent's commission. In particular, it provides in Article 8 that commission is to be paid not only for transactions concluded during the period covered by the agency contract but also for those concluded within a reasonable period thereafter, "if the transaction is mainly attributable to the commercial agent's efforts during the period covered by the agency contract".

16-11 Moreover, the Part IV of the Directive regulates in detail the termination of commercial agency contracts, providing *inter alia* for notice periods and the continuation of expired agency agreements. The most important protection afforded to the commercial agent in this respect is its right to be indemnified or compensated for the termination of the agency contract. The underlying rationale for the entitlement to either indemnity or damages is to compensate the agent for the loss of commission on future contracts concluded by the principals with customers acquired by the agent.[11]

3.2. Legal Status of the Substantive Rights Granted

16-12 The Directive, like most other national laws, clearly states that the parties may not derogate from theses provisions to the detriment of the agent.[12] In

---

the commercial representative see the United Arabs Emirates (UAE) Federal Law No. 18 of 1981 (as amended) Commercial Agency Law, Art. 5, 7, 23, available at http://www.government.ae/gov/en/biz/laws/forms.jsp.

[11] See Article 17 (2) which provides in its pertinent parts:

> (a) The commercial agent shall be entitled to an indemnity if and to the extent that:
>
> - he has brought the principal new customers or has significantly increased the volume of business with existing customers and the principal continues to derive substantial benefits from the business with such customers, and
>
> - the payment of this indemnity is equitable having regard to all the circumstances and, in particular, the commission lost by the commercial agent on the business transacted with such customers. Member States may provide for such circumstances also to include the application or otherwise of a restraint of trade clause, within the meaning of Article 20

[12] See for example Articles 5, 19; for a more detailed account of the "Commercial Agency Directive", see *Schmitthof's Export Trade* (11th ed, 2007) paras 27-010 et seq.

Ingmar v. Eaton[13] the European Court of Justice has made clear that the relevant provisions are not only mandatory in the sense that they may not be derogated from by contractual stipulations, but are internationally mandatory rules[14] which apply even if a different law has been chosen. In the case, the agency contract between an American principal and its UK agent for a commercial representation by the latter in the UK had been submitted by the parties to American Law. After the termination of the contract Ingmar Ltd, the UK agent, sought *inter alia* payment of damages suffered as a result of the termination of its contract with Eaton, the U.S. principal. It based its claim on the English implementation of Article 17 of the Commercial Agent Directive, which it considered to be applicable despite the choice of Californian Law in the agency contract. Under the latter no such damages would have been due. The ECJ confirmed the view that the protection granted in Article 17 is mandatory and cannot be derogated from by the parties. Invoking the purpose of the Directive to protect the agent and to harmonize the law of commercial agency within Europe the ECJ held that:

> …it is essential for the Community legal order that a principal established in a non-member country, whose commercial agent carries on his activity within the Community, cannot evade those provisions by the simple expedient of a choice-of-law clause. The purpose served by the provisions in question requires that they be applied where the situation is closely connected with the Community, in particular where the commercial agent carries on his activity in the territory of a Member State, irrespective of the law by which the parties intended the contract to be governed.

16-13 While the decision deals directly only with Article 17, the reasoning of the ECJ would apply to all other mandatory rules in the Directive which serve the protection of the agent.[15]

16-14 To what extent this also applies to comparable rules in the various national laws has to be determined in every single case. The decisions rendered and the

[13] European Court of Justice, 9 November 2000, C-381/98, *Ingmar GB Ltd v. Eaton Leonhard Technologies Inc.*, ECR [2000] I-9305 paragraph 25; for a critical comment see Verhagen, "The Tension Between Party Autonomy and European Union Law: Some Observations on Ingmar GB Ltd v. Eaton Leonhard Technologies Inc.", *ICLQ* (2001) 135 et seq.; Freitag, *supra* note 2 at 1061.

[14] The terminology varies; such rules are also referred to as "loi d'application immediate", "loi de police", "conflict mandatory rules".

[15] For this conclusion see also Verhagen, *supra* note 13 at 138.

formulation of the various laws, however, show that many of such rules will be considered to be conflict mandatory rules or even form part of the *ordre public*.[16]

3.3. Procedural Protection

16-15 The Directive does not explicitly regulate to what extent the general prohibition to deviate from the substantive provisions to the detriment of the commercial agent also affects the parties' procedural party autonomy. On the one hand the Directive only contains rules belonging to the field of substantive law and does not address procedural questions. On the other hand any protection granted under substantive law could be easily circumvented if not supplemented by procedural safeguards. In combining a choice of law clause in favour of a foreign law offering less protection, with a choice of forum clause in favour of a forum outside the Member States, which may not be bound to apply the Directive as internationally mandatory law, the application of the Directive's substantive rules could be avoided.

16-16 In light of this, some national laws on commercial agency explicitly stipulate that the courts at the agent's place of business, which are bound to apply the substantive rules, have exclusive jurisdiction. While it is beyond doubt that such rules are meant to exclude the jurisdiction of any other state court, that is less so with provisions such as Article 5 of the Lebanese Law for Commercial Agents, which provides, for example:

> Notwithstanding any contrary agreement, the Courts of the Place where the commercial representative carries on his activity have jurisdiction over the disputes arising out of the commercial representation contract.[17]

16-17 On the basis of its wording alone, it could be well interpreted to provide merely an additional head of jurisdiction, which does not exclude the jurisdiction of other state courts.

[16] See for example the law on commercial agency in the Arabian Emirates, http://www.government.ae/gov/en/biz/laws/forms.jsp; for the opposite view for the French transformation of the Directive, Cour de cassation, 28 November 2000, *Société Allium v. Société Alfin et Société Groupe Inter parfums*, Clunet 512 (2001).

[17] On the interpretation of the provision see Krüger, "Schiedsklauseln in Verträgen mit libanesischen Handelsvertretern", *IPRax* (2006) 305 seq; for a further example see Belgium Art. 4 Law of 27 July 1961 on the unilateral termination of exclusive distributorship contracts, as amended on 13 April 1971.

4. THE DIFFERENT APPROACHES TO THE "ARBITRABILITY" OF DISPUTES ARISING FROM COMMERCIAL REPRESENTATION

4.1. The Underlying Problem

16-18 The only cases of interest for the topic treated here are those in which the various substantive or procedural provisions regulating a certain type of commercial representation are of a mandatory nature. The other cases, where there are either no special rules for the particular type of commercial representation or the existing rules are non-mandatory, do not raise any peculiar problems. They may in general be referred to arbitration and the award arising from such arbitration can only be set aside or its recognition be refused if any of the existing defences are fulfilled. In general, the non-application or wrong application of such rules will not meet the high threshold of the "public policy" exception. If the parties can freely derogate from such rules it is difficult to see how the enforcement of the award could be contrary to public policy.

16-19 The situation however, is completely different if the substantive or procedural protection afforded to the commercial representative is of a mandatory character or even belongs to the *ordre public*. As mentioned above, only few of such mandatory national laws on commercial agency, distribution or franchising deal directly with their effects on the parties' ability to refer disputes relating to them to arbitration. Instead, the question has to be answered by interpreting the existing restrictions, often against the background of general principles of conflict of laws.

16-20 At least where the rules provide for the exclusive jurisdiction of a particular state court, the answer seems, at first sight, to be fairly obvious. The conferral of exclusive jurisdiction seems to exclude the arbitrability of all disputes falling within the purview of such law. The underlying rationale of such provisions is to ensure that the mandatory and protective provisions of the national law on commercial agency are applied. This would justify the extension of the exclusiveness also to arbitral tribunals, which may not be bound to apply such rules to the merits.[18] Such a conclusion however, is by no means

[18] See the decision of the Lebanese Supreme Court, Cour de cassation, quatrième chambre, 19 March 1998, reported in Clunet 877 (2001) et seq.; also Cour d'appel de Beyrouth, première chamber, 2 February 1999, reported in Clunet 877 (2001); for such a conclusion in the area of

compelling. A good example for that is provided by the interpretation of the above cited Article 5 of the Lebanese Law on Commercial Agents. Today, the conferral of exclusion jurisdiction to the courts at the commercial representatives place of business is considered to exclude the arbitrability of the disputes. In an earlier decision, however, Cour de Cassation came to the opposite conclusion arguing as follows:

> This text requires the construction of the terms 'despite any agreement to the contrary'. This only concerns an agreement on the jurisdiction of a court other than the one foreseen by this text. This cannot include an agreement to arbitrate which the law holds to be depending on the parties' intention.
>
> . . .
>
> The law has provided that the agreement to arbitrate depends on the parties, and is autonomous and sufficient in itself. Thus one cannot deny the parties' right to resort thereto, unless there is an explicit text in this respect, which cannot be found in Article 5 of Decree-Law No. 34, analysed above.
>
> . . .
>
> Agreements to arbitrate are not within the framework of the above Article 5 and, in principle, an agreement to arbitrate, just like the award stemming therefrom is not contrary to public order.[19]

16-21 In other areas of law, courts have adopted a comparable reasoning holding that that the conferral of exclusive jurisdiction on a particular state court does not affect the arbitrability of such disputes, but merely regulates the distribution of jurisdiction between the state courts.[20]

16-22 Any conclusion of inarbitrability is even less compelling where the wording of the relevant provisions already raises doubts as to the exclusive character of the jurisdiction conferred upon the courts at the representatives' place of business. And whether a general prohibition to deviate from the substantive protection granted in such laws can be considered to be an exclusion

---

insolvency see Supreme Court, New York Country, Appellate Division, 10 April 1990, 16 YBCA 663 (1991).

19 See Cour de cassation, 7 July 1988, cited by El-Ahdab, "The Lebanese Arbitration Act", 13(3) *J. Int'l Arb.* (1996) 39 (45 seq).

20 For that see Schlosser, *Das Recht der internationalen privaten Schiedsgerichtsbarkeit* (2nd ed, 1989) para 308; Münch, in: *Münchener Kommentar zur ZPO* (3rd ed, 2008) § 1030 para 32.

of arbitrability in general, or that it at least leads to the non-enforceability of the arbitration agreement in the particular case, is far from obvious.

4.2. Overview of the Approaches Adopted

16-23 The above described rules for the protection of commercial agents as well as comparable protective rules for distributors or franchisees can have different impacts on the parties' procedural freedom in relation to arbitration. What approach a particular legal system adopts, depends primarily on two factors: first, on the weight attached to the specific rules protecting the commercial representative; second, on the general attitude towards arbitration, i.e., in particular to what extent it is considered to be a means of dispute resolution providing equal protection to the parties as state court proceedings. The greater the importance of the protected interest and the more sceptical a legal system is towards arbitration, the greater will be the limitation of the parties' procedural freedom to submit disputes to arbitration.

16-24 In principle, one can distinguish three main approaches. Under the first two approaches, the restrictions on party autonomy contained in the relevant statutes on the particular type of commercial representation already affect the pre-award referral stage. The commercial representative can bring its claims in his home courts, which will not be bound to refer the parties to arbitration, either because the disputes are not arbitrable (first approach) or because the arbitration agreement is not enforceable for other reasons (second approach). By contrast, under the third approach, often referred to as the second look doctrine, the courts could only intervene at the post award stage, controlling whether the decision of the arbitrators is contrary to public policy.

4.3 The Exclusion of Objective Arbitrability of Disputes

(a) Salient Features of the Arbitrability Defence and its Position in the NYC-System

16-25 The characteristic feature of this approach is that a certain category of disputes is generally and *per se* excluded from the ambit of arbitration by being classified as inarbitrable. Systematically and on a purely legal analysis, the specific facts of the particular case are largely irrelevant.[21] As the dispute as such is inarbitrable, there is no need to examine, whether in the case at hand the commercial representative, for example, may be adequately protected by arbitration proceedings or the assumed inequality of bargaining power does not exist. Under the New York Convention (NYC), as well as under many national laws, the inarbitrability of the dispute is as such sufficient to deny, at the pre-award referral recognition of the arbitration agreement and at the post award stage, the recognition of the award. As a consequence, this approach contains the greatest restriction of the parties' procedural autonomy.

16-26 At the post-award stage Article V (2)(a) NYC stipulates, that recognition of the award may be refused ex officio if

> the subject matter of the dispute is not capable of settlement by arbitration under the law of that country.

16-27 Apart from the inarbitrability, no further requirements have to be met. The content of the award is irrelevant. In this respect, the "inarbitrability" defences under Article V (2)(a) NYC is clearly distinguishable from the "public policy" defence under Article V (2)(b) NYC, the primary focus of which is the awards content. While the inarbitrability of a dispute generally renders the enforcement of an award dealing with the dispute contrary to public policy, the structure of both defences is different. As will be shown below, this is also the largest difference between the first and the second approach, where the inarbitrability defence is not available at the recognition stage but enforcement can only be refused if it would be contrary to public policy.

16-28 At the pre-award referral stage, the assumed inarbitrability of the dispute, if understood correctly, already extinguishes any obligation of a Contracting State – i.e., its courts – under Article II (1) NYC to recognize an arbitration agreement in relation to such disputes. In practice, courts in many countries additionally or even primarily rely on the "null and void" exception of Article II (3) NYC to justify the non-referral to arbitration.[22] This is based on the widely

[21] In practice, however, most courts will - at least to a certain extent - be influenced in their findings by the facts, in particular, in areas like the present where there is little clear statutory guidance.

[22] See in particular the various Belgian decisions cited below; cf. Bernardini, "The Problem of Arbitrability in General", in Gaillard & Di Pietro (eds), *Enforcement of Arbitration Agreements and International Arbitral Awards: The New Convention in Practice* (2008) at 503 (504); Hanotiau, "What law governs the issue of arbitrability?", 12(4) *Arb Int'l* (1996) 391.

held belief that the arbitrability of the disputes affects the validity of the arbitration agreement. As has been set out in greater detail in other parts of the book, the purely procedural requirement of "arbitrability", relating to the distribution of jurisdiction between state courts and arbitral tribunals, should be distinguished from the primarily contractual questions of whether or not the arbitration agreement is valid.[23] That is even more so as the New York Convention clearly distinguishes between both questions. That is obvious at the recognition stage, where they are regulated in two different defences. But also at the referral stage, the better reading of Article II, which finds some support in Article VI (2) European Convention of 1961, allocates both issues to different paragraphs.[24] Paragraph 1 deals with the question of arbitrability and limits the general obligation to recognize written arbitration agreements to those relating to differences capable of settlement by arbitration. Paragraph 3 then defines what is meant by the obligation under paragraph 1 to "recognize" the written arbitration agreement and makes that dependent on the further conditions that the latter fulfils the normal validity requirements for contracts.

16-29 Irrespective of all differences where to allocate the "inarbitrability" defences at the Article II-referral stage, there are a number of legal systems which follow this approach in relation to at least certain types of disputes relating to commercial representation.[25]

(b) The Franchise Example: the Draft U.S.-Arbitration Fairness Act of 2007

16-30 One of the most obvious examples of such an approach, at least in relation to franchising[26] would be the U.S., if the Arbitration Fairness Act of 2007 were

[23] See S. Brekoulakis, Chapter 2, *supra* 2-58 et seq ; Arfazadeh, *Ordre public et arbitrage international à l'épreuve de la mondialisation* (2005) at 91 et seq. ; see also Lew, Mistelis & Kröll, *supra* note 3 at para 9-13.

[24] In this direction also van den Berg, *The New York Arbitration Convention of 1958* (1981) 155; Arfazadeh, *supra* note 23 at 93 et seq.

[25] See for example the Columbian decision in *Merck & Co. v. Tecnoquímicas SA* reported by Harris, "The "Public Policy" Exception to Enforcement of International Awards under the New York Convention with particular Reference to Construction Disputes", 24(1) *J. Int'l Arb.* (2007) 9 (17 et seq); for Lebanon see Cour de cassation, quatrième chambre, 19 March 1998, reported in Clunet 877 (2001) et seq.; Krüger, "Schiedsklauseln in Verträgen mit libanesischen Handelsvertretern", *IPRax* (2006) 305 et seq.

[26] While franchising is the only form of commercial representation explicitly mentioned, the general reference in no. 2 to "transactions between parties of unequal bargaining power" has the potential to apply also to other forms.

to be adopted. According to the draft bill section 2 (4) (b) FAA would then provide that:

> (b) no pre-dispute arbitration agreement shall be valid or enforceable if it requires arbitration of:
>
> (1) an employment, consumer, or franchise dispute, or
>
> (2) a dispute arising under any statute intended to protect civil rights or to regulate contracts or transactions between parties of unequal bargaining power.[27]

16-31 It is noteworthy that the draft does not explicitly declare franchise disputes to be inarbitrable but instead refers the validity and enforceability of the arbitration agreement. This terminology has to be seen against the background of the present content of section 2 FAA, the broad American understanding of the term "arbitrability" and the widely held view, that the lack of arbitrability affects the validity of an arbitration agreement. Thus, despite the wording, the reference in section 2 (4)(b) FAA has to be read to refer to arbitrability in the narrower sense as used here. According to the intention of the supporters of the draft bill, section 2 - like any other rule addressing the distribution of jurisdiction between courts and arbitral tribunals – should be applied by American courts under the *lex fori* principle relevant for jurisdictional questions, irrespective of the law applicable to the arbitration agreement.

16-32 Furthermore, the restriction to the pre-dispute arbitration agreement clearly shows that the underlying rationale of this restriction is primarily to protect the interests of the franchisee as the weaker party. Other more general interests do not play a role. In particular, arbitration is not generally considered to be an unsuitable mechanism for the resolution of such disputes. Consequently, after a dispute has arisen the parties to a franchise agreement may well submit it to arbitration.

[27] In addition, pursuant to litera (c) the arbitrators would lack the power to determine whether an arbitration agreement would be valid or not but that decision would have to be taken by the courts.

(c) The Sole-Distribution Example: The Belgian law of 27 July 1961 on the Unilateral Termination of Exclusive Distributorship Contracts

16-33 Another example *de lege lata* for at least limited inarbitrability of certain types of disputes relating to the termination of exclusive distribution agreements is provided by Belgian law. It differs in two respects from the above described draft of the Arbitration Fairness Act 2007. First, Belgian law does not explicitly declare such termination disputes to be inarbitrable, but the inarbitrability is deduced from general principles. Second, the inarbitrability of such termination disputes is, even at the pre-dispute stage, not absolute as it would be the case under the proposed American law. By contrast, arbitrability, as a requirement for jurisdiction, depends on the question of which law is to be applied.

16-34 Under Belgian arbitration law, disputes can generally be submitted to arbitration in all matters that may be the object of a compromise, i.e., where the object of the dispute is available and disposable, and where the law does not provide for an exclusion of objective arbitrability. [28]

16-35 Such an exclusion of objective arbitrability for disputes relating to the indemnification of exclusive distributors upon the termination of the distribution agreement is often read into the Law of 27 July 1961 on the unilateral termination of exclusive distributorship contracts, as amended on 13 April 1971 (Law of 27 July 1961). Pursuant to Art. 3 of the Law of 27 July 1961 the distributor is entitled to be indemnified upon termination of the distributorship. Art. 4 then provides:

> (1) The distributor who has suffered damages as a result of the termination of a distributorship contract carrying out its effect, entirely or in part, in the

[28] Belgium Arbitration Law of 4 July 1972 and considerably modified by the Law of 19 May 1998 (Belgian Gazette of 7 August 1998) in Article 1676 Code of Civil Procedure provides:

> 1) Any dispute which has arisen or may arise out of a specific legal relationship and in respect of which it is permissible to compromise may be the subject of an arbitration agreement.
>
> 2) …
>
> 3) The above mentioned stipulations shall apply without prejudice to the exceptions provided by law.

See Paulsson (ed), *International Handbook on Commercial Arbitration*, Annex I to Country Report Belgium, Suppl. 49, (April 2007).

territory of Belgium can always apply to the Belgian Courts of his or her residence or of the supplier's residence and registered office."

(2) Whenever the dispute is submitted to a Belgian court, the court will apply exclusively Belgian law.

In addition to that, Art. 6 stipulates, that the

.. articles of this law are applicable notwithstanding whatever other contrary agreement agreed upon before the end of the distributorship.

16-36 As a result, the various articles of the Law of 27 July 1961 are generally considered to be internationally mandatory provisions, i.e., "loi d'application immediate". It is also largely agreed that despite this character of the provisions, they do not form part of the Belgian public policy. [29] As a consequence, the question of the effects of these provisions on the arbitrability of disputes relating to the termination of exclusive distribution agreements has given rise to considerable and often conflicting case law.[30]

16-37 The Belgian Supreme Court dealt with it for the first time in 1979 in *Audi-NSU v. Adelin Petit.* [31] The dispute concerned the termination of an exclusive distributorship agreement between the parties falling within the scope of the Law of 27 July 1961. The agreement provided for the application of German law and contained an arbitration clause providing for arbitration in Switzerland. In the arbitration proceedings initiated by Audi-NSU in Switzerland, the tribunal held

[29] See Vermeire, "L'arbitrabilité des litiges relativs à la résiliation d'une concession de vente soumise à la loi de 1961", *Droit Fiscalité Belge*, 3 November 2004, at http.//www.droit-fiscalite-belge.com/article845.html; cf. the statement of the Advocate General in preparing the *Audi-NSU v. Adelin Petit* decision of the Supreme Court (see infra) where he said *inter alia* concerning the legal nature of the Law of 27 July 1961:

> Toutefois, et c'est en cela, que les dispositions dites "imperatives" diffèrent des dispositions d'ordre public, de telles clauses [arbitration clauses] ne sont pas illicites en soi, elles ne touchent pas aux intérets essentiels de l'Etat ou de la collectivité ou ne fixent pas, dans le droit prive, les bases juridiques sur lesquelles repose l'ordre économique ou moral de la societé, de sorte que sie le risque de pression qui pourrait etre exercé vient à disparaitre, la clause peut etre valablement conlue.

For the quote see Hollander, "L'arbitrabilité des litiges relatifs aux contrats de distribution commerciale en droit belge", in, CEPANI (ed) *L'arbitrage et la distribution commercial – Arbitration and Commercial Disputes* (2005) 27 (45); see also Cour d'appel Bruxelles, 25 April 2006, *S.R.L. Alta (Italy) v. S.A. Traches Soberac (Belgium).*

[30] For a detailed account of the case law see Hollander, *supra* note 29 at 29.

[31] Cour de cassation, 28 June 1979, *Audi-NSU (Germany) v. S.A. Adelin Petit & Cie. (Belgium)*, 5 YBCA (1980) 257 et seq.

that the termination was lawful and, applying German law, rejected all claims for compensation by Petit. Audi-NSU then tried to have that award recognized in the Belgian proceedings for compensation which Petit had initiated parallel to the arbitration. The Court of Appeal of Liège[32] refused recognition of the award on two separate grounds. First, it considered the award to be based on an invalid arbitration agreement, relating to matter not capable of being referred to arbitration. Second, it held that the enforcement of the award would be contrary to public policy being in conflict with the mandatory provisions of the Law of 27 July 1961. Due to the way the appeal against the decision was framed, the Supreme Court did not have to address directly the question of whether the recognition of awards in such termination disputes would be contrary to Art. V (2)(a) NYC, as the dispute was not arbitrable.[33] In dealing with the question of whether the Court of Appeal has sufficiently justified its finding as to the violation of public policy in the sense of Art. V(2)(b) NYC, the Supreme Court made the following statement:

> Considering that a dispute concerning the termination by the grantor of the concession under an exclusive distributorship agreement which wholly or partially concerns Belgian territory is not capable of settlement by arbitration which is agreed before the end of the contract, and which has as purpose and effect the application of a foreign law.

16-38 The case concerned the post award recognition stage at which it was clear that the arbitral tribunal had not applied Belgium law and no compensation had been awarded to the distributor under German law applied. Thus, the court did not have to deal with the question of whether and if so how the arbitrability of termination disputes is affected by the applicable substantive law.

16-39 Only in 2004 in *Colvi v. Interdica*[34] the Belgium Supreme Court finally had to deal with the effects of the mandatory provision of the Law of 27 July 1961 at the pre-award referral stage.[35] The issue was primarily whether

[32] 4 YBCA (1979) 254 et seq.

[33] Audi/NSU tried to rely on the Belgian-Swiss Convention on the Recognition and Enforcement of Judgements and Arbitral Awards of 29 April 1959 which does not contain a separate inarbitrability defence, comparable to that of Art. V (2)(a) NYC but only allows refusal of recognition if it would be contrary to public policy.

[34] Cour de cassation, 15 October 2004, *Colvi N.V. (Belgium) v. Interdica (Switzerland)*, 31 YBCA (2006) 593 para 12; Revue de Droit Commercial Belge/Tijdschrift voor Belgisch Handelsrecht (2005), pp. 488-491 with notes by M. Traest at 492-498 and Hollander at 498-504

[35] In *Gutrob Werke GmbH v. Usinorp de Saint-Hubert and Saint-Hubert Gardening*, 22 December 1988, (partly published in Journal Tribunal (1989) 458) the Court had already been faced with

arbitrability under Art. II had to be determined pursuant to the *lex contractus*, i.e. the law applicable to the arbitration agreement, or Belgian law as the *lex fori* of the court called to determine arbitrability.[36]

16-40 The dispute arose out of the termination of a sole distributorship agreement, falling within the purview of the Law of 27 July 1961 which had been submitted to Swiss law and which provided for arbitration in Switzerland. Irrespective of the latter, Colvi had initiated court proceedings in Belgium for compensation, alleging that the arbitration clause was invalid as the dispute was not capable of settlement by arbitration pursuant to Belgian law.

16-41 The Court of Appeal in Antwerp had referred the parties to arbitration, denying its jurisdiction due to the existence of an arbitration clause. It had held that at the referral stage of Art. II (3), the arbitrability of a dispute had to be determined according to the law chosen by the parties (*lex contractus*). As the Swiss law chosen by the parties considered disputes on the termination of an exclusive distributor contract to be arbitrable, the court rejected the allegation that the arbitral agreement was invalid.

16-42 The Supreme Court overruled the Court of Appeal on the issue of the applicable law. It held in this regard:

> The obligation to refer [parties to arbitration] only applies to disputes that are arbitrable. Article II (3) of the NYC does not explicitly indicate the law under which it must be determined whether the dispute is arbitrable. However, it allows the court to which this issue is submitted to test it against its own legal system, thereby setting the limits within which private jurisdiction over certain subject matters is compatible with the legal order [of that country].[37]

---

the question at the pre-award stage, but was not required to give a final ruling on the issue due to the framing of the recourse which had also already been admitted on different grounds.; for a more detailed analysis see Hollander, *supra* note 29 at 27 (33 seq)

36 While Art. V (2)(a) NYC clearly regulates that at the post award stage, the law of the enforcing court, i.e., the lex fori, applies to the questions of arbitrability, comparable explicit rules are missing for the pre-award referral stage in Art. II NYC. It only says that the obligation to enforce arbitration agreements is limited to those which cover, disputes capable of being settled by arbitration; for a summary of the discussion on the applicable law see Verbist, "Arbitrabilty of Exclusive Distributorship Agreements in Belgium: Lex Fori (and Lex Contractus)?", 22(5) *J. Int'l Arb.* 428 et seq. with further references in *supra* note 5.

37 Cour de cassation, 15 October 2004, *Colvi N.V. (Belgium) v. Interdica (Switzerland)*, 31 YBCA (2006) 593 para 12; compare: Verbist, *supra* note 36 at 428 et seq.

16-43 While that issue has been decisive for the annulment of the decision, the court also gave an *obiter dictum* that dealt directly with the question of the arbitrability. In relation to that the court stated:

> Where the parties have determined that the arbitration clause is governed by a foreign law, the state court whose jurisdiction is objected to may hold that [the dispute is not arbitrable] if this affects the public policy of its own legal system.

16-44 The explicit reference to the "public policy of its own legal system" has been interpreted in literature as a possible indication that the Supreme Court may no longer consider termination disputes under the Law of 17 July 1961 to be inarbitrable.[38] If the limitation to "public policy" in the above statement were to be taken literally, one could well argue that the provisions of the Law of 17 July 1961 do not affect the arbitrability of the dispute, as they do not form part of public policy.

16-45 However, such an interpretation is not in line with the outcome of the decision. The Supreme Court overruled the Court of Appeal, which had denied its jurisdiction. Had the Supreme Court been of the view that the dispute was arbitrable, the Court of Appeal's decision would have been correct but for the reasoning. While the referral to arbitration could not have been justified with the applicability of Swiss law, it would have been justified on the basis of Belgian law, no longer denying the arbitrability of termination disputes.

16-46 The interpretation, that the *Colvi* decision cannot be considered to constitute a change in the attitude of Belgian law towards the arbitrability of such termination disputes, is also supported by the Supreme Court's decision two years later in *Van Hopplynus Instruments v. Coherent*.[39] The dispute arose out of a distributorship agreement between a Californian company and its Belgian distributor. The agreement provided for arbitration in California under AAA rules. The Belgian distributor sued its Californian supplier in front of the Belgian courts for indemnification for the unilateral termination of the contract. The first two instances denied jurisdiction, concluding *inter alia* that at the referral stage under Art. II (3) NYC, the assessment of arbitrability is to be determined

[38] Hollander, *supra* note 29 at 44 et seq.; for such a proposition see also Cour d'appel Bruxelles, 25 April 2006, *S.R.L. Alta (Italy) v. S.A. Traches Soberac (Belgium)*.

[39] Cour de Cassation, 16 November 2006, *Van Hopplynus Instruments v. Coherent Inc.*, case No: C.02.0445.F/1, full text available at http://jure.juridat.just.fgov.be/pdfapp/download_blob?idpdf=F-20061116-7

pursuant to the *lex contractus* and not the *lex fori*. As Californian law did not contain any restrictions as to the arbitrability of such termination disputes, both courts referred the parties to arbitration. The Supreme Court held that the obligation to refer the parties to arbitration under Art. II NYC only applies to disputes which are arbitrable and that Art. II allowed the court to determine on the basis of its own law, i.e., the *lex fori*, whether a dispute is arbitrable or not. Instead of linking the arbitrability of disputes to violations of public policy the Supreme Court held:

> When, as in the case at hand, the arbitration clause is submitted to a foreign law, the court whose jurisdiction is disputed must deny a referral to arbitration, if, by virtue of its own law, the dispute may not be taken away from the state courts.[40]

16-47 Again this statement only constituted an *obiter dictum*. In principle, the *van Hopplynus* decision as well as the *Colvi* decision address directly only the question of which law applies to the issue of arbitrability at the referral stage of Art. II NYC. Irrespective of this, they can be considered to be a confirmation of the theory of limited arbitrability of termination disputes under Belgian law, which was already expressed in the *Audi-NSU* decision of 1979. Termination disputes are not *per se* inarbitrable. As long as the arbitrators have to apply Belgian law to the merits, i.e., that application of the Law of 17 July 1961 is ensured, the dispute may be referred to arbitration. Where the distributorship agreement has been submitted to a foreign law the dispute loses its arbitrability.

16-48 It appears, from the decisions, that the mere fact that the Belgian Law of 17 July 1961 is not applicable renders the dispute inarbitrable, i.e., not capable of settlement by arbitration in the sense of Art. II (1) NYC. The standard of protection afforded by the foreign law does not seem to play a role in the determination of the inarbitrability. In light of this and the classification of the Supreme Court, treating the questions as those of arbitrability, Belgium can be considered as one of the countries where certain distribution related disputes are not arbitrable. Unlike the American proposal of the Arbitration Fairness Act 2007, however, the inarbitrability is, even at the pre-dispute stage, not absolute. It depends on the law to be applied to the merits. In this respect, the Belgian

[40] French original:

> Lorsque la convention d'arbitrage est, comme en l'espece, soumise à une loi étrangère, le juge saisi d'un déclinatoire de jurisdiction doit exclure l'arbitrage si, en vertue de la loi du for, le litige ne peut etre soustrait à la jurisdiction des tribunaux étatiques.

approach has already included some elements of the second approach, taking into account the specific circumstance of the particular case, albeit in a very limited way.

5. The Likely Non-Application of Mandatory Provisions as a Ground to Refuse Enforcement of the Arbitration Agreement

5.1. Distinguishing Factors from the "Inarbitrability" Approach.

16-49 The second approach adopted in connection with arbitrating disputes relating to commercial representation differs from the above described approach in so far, as the objectives pursued by the special rules on commercial representation are not considered to render certain types of disputes inarbitrable *per se*. Instead, for every dispute falling within the purview of such provisions, it has to be evaluated on the basis of the particular facts of each case whether the arbitration agreement or the award is enforceable or not. Under the New York Convention the relevant provisions for this evaluation are at the referral stage Art. II (3) NYC and at the recognition stage primarily Art. V (2)(b) NYC.

16-50 The practical effects of these systematic differences between the two approaches become primarily obvious at the post award recognition stage. Pursuant to the first approach, even if adopted in the milder Belgian version, the mere non-application of the mandatory provisions of the forum would render the disputes inarbitrable and thus enforcement could be refused on the basis of Art. V (2)(a) NYC. Under the second approach, as the inarbitrability defence as such is not available, enforcement could only be refused by virtue of the public policy defence in Art. V (2)(b) NYC. For the latter, however, the mere non-application even of internationally mandatory provisions is not sufficient. Relevant is not which law has been applied, but whether the *enforcement* of the award would be contrary to public policy. That, however, requires more than the mere non-application of mandatory provisions. It is necessary that also the objectives underlying those mandatory provisions would be violated in an unsupportable way. For example, it may well be possible, that the tribunal did not apply the mandatory provisions of the forum, but applied a law which grants a different but largely equal protection to the commercial representative. Or, even if a lower lever of protection is attained by the application of that law, the difference may not be of such magnitude to justify the invocation of public policy. Another example is, that contrary to the assumption underlying the mandatory provisions of the enforcing state, the commercial representative in the case at hand does not require any protection because it is the economically stronger party. Instead of relying on compensation for termination, the commercial representative may have been able to agree on a higher remuneration during the term of the commercial representation. Unlike under the first approach, with its inarbitrability defences, all these case specific circumstances will have to be taken into account under the second approach within the framework of the public policy defence under Art. V(2)(b) NYC, to determine whether enforcement of the award would be contrary to public policy.

16-51 At the pre-award referral stage, the practical difference between the two approaches are often less obvious. The case specific analysis under the second approach has to be based on a projection for the future of how the arbitrators will decide the case. There is a natural tendency for courts to resort to criteria, which is easy to evaluate. As a consequence, in practice the mere threat, that the arbitral tribunal will not apply the internationally mandatory provisions of the forum, can become the decisive criterion for determining whether the arbitration agreement has to be enforced or not.

5.2. The Commercial Agent Example: § 89b German Commercial Code (HGB)

16-52 This second approach has been adopted by German courts, at least in relation to disputes arising from the termination of sole agency agreements. In addition, this German jurisprudence shows the need to differentiate between objective arbitrability on the one hand and the validity or enforceability of the arbitration agreement on the other hand.

16-53 The German arbitration law[41] contains in § 1030 ZPO a special rule defining which disputes are arbitrable. § 1030 provides in its pertinent parts: [42]

> (1) Any claim involving an economic interest ("vermögensrechtlicher Anspruch") can be the subject of an arbitration agreement. An arbitration agreement concerning claims not involving an economic interest shall have

[41] In Germany the arbitration law is contained in the Tenth Book of the Code of Civil Procedure (ZPO) and is since its revision on the 1.1.1998 largely a verbatim adoption of the UNCITRAL Model Law.

[42] Paragraph 2 excludes the (objective) arbitrability of disputes relating to the existence of a lease of residential accommodation within Germany; for a detailed commentary of the provision in English see Trittmann & Hanefeld, § 1030 paras 1 et seq., in Böckstiegel, Kröll & Nacimiento (eds), *Arbitration in Germany – The Model Law in Practice* (2008).

> legal effect to the extent that the parties are entitled to conclude a settlement on the issue in dispute.
>
> ...
>
> (3) Statutory provisions outside this Book by virtue of which certain disputes may not be submitted to arbitration, or may be submitted to arbitration only under certain conditions, remain unaffected.

16-54 It is beyond doubt that the disputes arising from the various types of contract for commercial representation involve an "economic interest" in the sense of § 1030 (1) ZPO. The exception in § 1030 (3) ZPO is interpreted narrowly and requires an explicit exclusion of arbitrability.[43] Such an explicit exclusion does not exist for any of the three types of commercial representation contracts.

16-55 The mere fact, that some of the provisions protecting commercial agents in §§ 84 et seq. HGB (Commercial Code) are considered to be internationally mandatory rules, does not affect the arbitrability of such disputes. It might have been arguable under the old arbitration law, that the international mandatory character of the provisions affected the arbitrability of a dispute, which at the time was dependant on the parties' "right to enter into a settlement on the subject matter of the disputes, can reach a settlement on the matter".[44] Under the new law such an argument is no longer tenable. The "economic interest" of the claim, which is now the decisive criterion, is not dependent on the legal nature of the provisions relevant for the claim. Consequently the legislative materials even explicitly state:

> Pursuant [§ 1030] subsection 1 first sentence any claim involving an economic interest can in the future in principle be the object of an arbitration agreement. This means, that provisions containing prohibitions to dispose, settle or renounce rights, that exist for example ...pursuant to § 89b HGB [claim for indemnification for termination of commercial agency] ...are to be interpreted in the future as not excluding the arbitrability of the underlying claims.[45]

[43] Geimer, in: *Zöller Zivilprozessordnung* (27th ed, 2008), § 1030 para 1; Schlosser, in: Stein & Jonas, *Kommentar zur Zivilprozessordnung* (2nd ed, 2002) para.

[44] § 1025 (1) pre-1998 ZPO.

[45] BT-Ducks. 13/5274, p 34, right column:

16-56 As a result, in actions arising from the termination of agency agreements, German courts are also in principle, obliged, under Art. II (1) NYC, to recognize any written arbitration agreement which is invoked by either party, since the dispute is "capable of settlement by arbitration".

16-57 Irrespective of this, in a recent decision concerning the indemnification of a commercial agent, the Higher Regional Court in Munich refused to enforce an arbitration agreement relying on the internationally mandatory character of the German law protecting sole agents.[46] The dispute arose out of a commercial agency agreement between a German agent and an American principal for the distribution of groups of semiconductors in Germany and Austria.[47] The agency agreement contained in Section 14.2 a dispute resolution clause according to which, all disputes arising out of it were to be decided pursuant to the arbitration rules of the American Arbitration Association. Section 14.3 further stipulated that all disputes, claims or court procedures were to be conducted before the State or Federal Courts in the district of Santa Clara, State of California (USA). Finally, Section 14.5 provided for the application of Californian law.

16-58 Upon termination of the agency agreement by the principal and the latter's refusal to pay any indemnification in the sense of § 89b HGB, the German agent filed a claim with the Regional Court Munich I for indemnification. In light of the arbitration clause and the choice of jurisdiction clause, the court refused to hear the case and referred the parties to arbitration.[48] On appeal, the Higher Regional Court of Munich reversed the decision, holding that the German courts have jurisdiction and remitted the case to the Regional Court of Munich for further hearing and ruling on the merits.

> Nach [§ 1030] Absatz 1 Satz 1 soll künftig grundsätzlich jeder vermögensrechtliche Anspruch Gegenstand einer Schiedsvereinbarung sein können. Dies bedeutet, dass Vorschriften über Verfügungs-, Vergleichs-, oder Verzichtsverbote, wie sie etwa nach … § 89b HGB … bestehen, künftig so zu interpretieren sind, dass eine Schiedsfähigkeit der zugrunde liegenden Anspüche nicht ausgeschlossen ist.

See also OLG Hamm, Decision of 7 March 2002, 11 Sch 1/02, where in a domestic case to appoint an arbitrator the arbitrability of the dispute was not even discussed.

46 Oberlandesgericht München (Court of Appeal), 17 May 2006, IHR (2006) 166 with note by Thume at 169 seq; see also the critical comments by Rühl, "Die Wirksamkeit von Gerichtsstands- und Schiedsvereinbarungen im Lichte der Ingmar-Entscheidung des EuGH", *IPRax* (2007) 294 et seq.; Quincke, "Schiedsverfahren und Eingriffsnormen", *SchiedsVZ* (2007) 247 et seq.

47 Later the scope of the agency was extended to Hungary, Slovenia and the Czech Republic.

48 Landgericht München I (Regional Court), 5 December 2005, 15 HKO 23703/04, full text of decision available at http://www.dis-arb.de .

16-59 The court addressed primarily the validity and enforceability of the forum selection clause and then later merely extended its findings to the arbitration clause. Relying on the jurisprudence of the German Federal Court of Justice,[49] the court held that for determining the enforceability of the forum selection clause it had to be evaluated in conjunction with the choice of law clause. Pursuant to Article 34 Private International Law Act (EGBGB – Einführungsgesetz zum Bürgerlichen Gesetzbuch) [50] the internationally mandatory character of § 89b HGB, established by the ECJ's *Ingmar* decision, makes any choice of a foreign law, derogating from the content of § 89b HGB devoid of any effect. The mandatory application of § 89b HGB, however, can only be ensured if choice of forum clauses are not enforceable, where they – operating in tandem with a choice of law clauses – could result in the non-application of §89b HGB. Thus the nature of § 89b HGB as an internationally mandatory provision of substantive law at the same time leads to a limitation of the parties procedural freedom, at least in so far as this would endanger the purpose of § 89b HGB. As a consequence of this, the court considered the forum selection clause in favour of the American courts to be non-enforceable. In combination with the choice of American substantive law, there was reasonable danger that the forum selection clause would have resulted in the non-application of § 89b HGB, as there would not have been an obligation for the American courts to apply that provision.

16-60 The court then extended these findings concerning the forum selection clause without any further discussion to the arbitration clause. It did not even mention explicitly on the basis of which provisions the refusal to enforce the arbitration agreement occurred. Instead, the court only referred to an earlier decision of the Federal Court of Justice, in which the latter had refused the recognition of an arbitration agreement in a futures transaction.[51]

[49] Bundesgerichtshof, 30 January 1961, NJW 1961, 1061 (1962); in that case, however, the court came to the conclusion that the combination of a choice of law clause and a forum selection clause both in favour of the Netherlands did not lead to the invalidity of the latter.

[50] Art. 34 Mandatory Provisions:

> This subsection [determining the applicable law and allowing for a choice of law] does not affect the application of the provisions of German law that regulate the situation by mandatory provisions without regard to the law applicable to the contract.

[51] Bundesgerichtshof, 15 June 1987, NJW 1987, 3192 et seq.; after changes in the substantive law the Federal Court of Justice, in a later cases, enforced an arbitration agreement in a futures contract concluded with an investor who had not received the necessary information and was therefore in principle subjectively incapable of concluding a futures contract. It held that the

16-61 In that case the Federal Court of Justice had based its refusal to enforce the arbitration agreement on two related but separate grounds. First, it had deduced from the internationally mandatory character of the relevant provisions, the inarbitrability of such disputes. In relation to indemnification disputes, however, reliance on this defence is no longer possible. Under the new German arbitration law, such disputes are clearly arbitrable. The second defence, which had been invoked by the Federal Court of Justice in its earlier case, was public policy under Art. V (2)(b) NYC. At the time the court had held that there might be cases where a control of the award at the enforcement stage may not be sufficient. It is of little help for an investor who wants to bring a claim against a financial institution, if it can resist the enforcement of an award rendered in favour of the latter and rejecting the investor's claim.

16-62 It can only be assumed that this argument also formed the basis of the decision of the Higher Regional Court of Munich. Systematically, this would result in the "null and void, inoperative or incapable of being performed" exception in Art. II (3) NYC as being applicable.

16-63 The standard for the non-enforceability of the arbitration agreement adopted by the Higher Regional Court in Munich, was the reasonable threat that the German provisions would not be applied. The court held that in light of the purposes pursued with § 89b HGB, it would not be required from the Claimant to establish as a fact, that the American courts would not apply the German law. In the absence of evidence to the contrary it could not be assumed that the courts in the U.S. would apply the internationally mandatory provisions of German law, despite the choice of Californian law.

16-64 With the reference to the "reasonable threat" standard, the court tried to take into account that – unlike at the recognition stage, where the state court can determine the public policy violation on the basis of an existing award – the evaluation at the referral stage is based on a hypothesis of whether, and if so how the U.S. courts would apply the German internationally mandatory provisions. By not imposing a higher standard of probability, the court also avoided the need to discuss whether the assumption relevant for the courts, that internationally mandatory provisions of a different country will not be applied, also hold true to the same extent for arbitral tribunals.

---

new protection system does not fall with in the *ordre public* regime under German law any longer: Bundesgerichtshof, 21 April 1998, BGHZ 138, 331 (336 seq.).

16-65 The decision of the Higher Regional Court in Munich shows very well the general problem of this second approach, at least at the referral stage. There, every decision has to be based on the prediction of the likely behaviour of the arbitral tribunal and not, as at the recognition stage, with the knowledge of whether the internationally mandatory provisions have actually been applied by the tribunal.

6. The "Second Look" Doctrine: Referral of all Control to the Post-Award Stage

16-66 The common feature of the two previous approaches is that the special rules for the protection of commercial representatives may already become relevant at the pre-award referral stage and prevent the enforcement of the arbitration agreement. By contrast, under the third approach, the courts will in principle refer the parties to arbitration, and only control the outcome of this arbitration, i.e., if the enforcement of the award would be contrary to public policy due to the fact that the agent, distributor or franchisee have not been adequately protected.

16-67 In other areas of law, where comparable problems arise concerning the application of internationally mandatory rules, this approach is often referred to as the "second look doctrine.[52]

6.1. Underlying Rationale of the Second Look Doctrine in the Proper Sense

16-68 The seminal decision, where this doctrine was developed, is the judgment by the U.S.-Supreme Court in *Mitsubishi v. Soler*, arising from a distribution agreement in the car industry. In the lower instances Soler tried to rely on a provision in the Puerto Rican Law, which purported to render any stipulation null and void "that obligates a dealer to adjust, arbitrate or litigate any controversy that comes up regarding the dealer's contract outside Puerto Rico, or under foreign law or rule of law"[53]. The Court of Appeal held that provision pre-empted by § 2 Federal Arbitration Act (FAA), pursuant to the latter provision only for

[52] See for example Radicati di Brozolo, "Antitrust: A Paradigm of the Relations Between Mandatory Rules and Arbitration – A Fresh Look at the "Second Look", *Int'l ALR* (2004) 23 et seq.; Baron & Liniger, "A Second Look at Arbitrability – Approaches to Arbitration in the United States, Switzerland and Germany", *Arb. Int'l* (2003) 27 et seq.

[53] Puerto Rican Laws Ann., Tit. 10, § 278b-2 (Supp.1983).

defences that could be invoked against the arbitration agreement which "exist at law or in equity for the revocation of *any contract*".

16-69 Before the Supreme Court that issue no longer played a role, the decision was primarily concerned with the arbitrability of antitrust claims. In regards to those claims, which raise similar issues to those arising from the statutory protection of commercial representatives, the court describes very well the underlying rationale of the "second look doctrine". The court held that at the referral stage the concerns associated with a possible non-application of the relevant mandatory provisions have to be considered

> ...against the strong belief in the efficacy of arbitral procedures for the resolution of international commercial disputes and an equal commitment of freely negotiated choice-of-forum clauses.[54]

In dealing directly with the potential non-application of the U.S. antitrust legislation, the Supreme Court held:

> There is no reason to assume at the outset of the dispute that international arbitration will not provide an adequate mechanism. To be sure, the international arbitral tribunal owes no prior allegiance to the legal norms of particular states; hence it has no direct obligation to vindicate their statutory dictates. The tribunal, however, is bound to effectuate the intentions of the parties. Where the parties have agreed that the arbitral body is to decide a defined set of claims which includes, as in these cases, those arising from the application of American antitrust law, the tribunal therefore should be bound to decide that dispute in accord with the national law giving rise to the claim.[55]

16-70 In the Supreme Court's view, the necessary control of the application of the American antitrust law should occur at the enforcement stage. The public policy defence in Art. V (2)(b) NYC gave the court sufficient "opportunity...to ensure that the legitimate interest in the enforcement of the antitrust laws has been addressed."[56] As a consequence, the Supreme Court refused to hear the case and referred the parties to arbitration, enforcing the arbitration agreement.

[54] *Mitsubishi Motors Corp. v. Soler Chrysler-Plymouth*, 473 U.S. 614 (631)
[55] *Ibid.* 636 seq.
[56] *Ibid.* 638.

16-71 The decision is based on the assumption that despite the parties' choice of Swiss law for their distribution agreement[57], the arbitral tribunal might apply U.S. antitrust law. In light of the parties agreement to arbitrate their disputes this likelihood is sufficient for the courts to refer the parties to arbitration. Only where it turns out, after the award has been rendered, that the tribunal did not take into account the interest underlying the mandatory provisions, the courts will ensure that these interests are enforced.

6.2. "Nullité Manifeste": The Second Look à la Française

16-72 In French law, the considerations underlying the "second look" doctrine are taken care of through the general requirement in article 1458 NCPC that at the pre-award referral stage, courts may only assume jurisdiction if the arbitration agreement is "manifestement nulle". In relation to most issues which might affect the validity of the arbitration agreements French Courts have interpreted that requirement strictly.[58]

16-73 In *Cineco v. Shure Brothers*,[59] the Court of Appeal in Paris made clear that this also applies to the question of the effects of a likely non-application of internationally mandatory provisions of French law. The dispute concerned the termination of an exclusive distribution agreement between the French distributor Cineco and the American principal Shure Brothers. The contract contained an arbitration clause in favour of an arbitration in the U.S. under the rules of the AAA and provided for the application of the law of Illinois. Upon termination of the contract, the French distributor claimed damages for the way of termination under two general, non-distribution, specific provisions, one of which it considered internationally mandatory. The French distributor submitted that due to the mandatory character of the provision, the combination of the choice of law clause with the arbitration clause would render the later "manifestment nulle" as

[57] The choice of law clause of the Sales Agreement read:

> This Agreement is made in, and will be governed by and construed in all respects according to the laws of the Swiss Confederation as if entirely performed therein.

[58] See Cour de cassation, 21 May 1997, *Renault v V 2000 (formerly Jaguar France)*, Rev Arb 537 (1997) with note by Gaillard; CA Paris, *Société A.B.S. American Bureau of Shipping v. Corpopriété Maritime Jules Vernes*, 18(12) Mealey's IAR D-1 (2003), and also in 29 YBCA 657 (2004); *cf* Lew, Mistelis & Kröll, *supra* note 3 at paras 14-55 seq.

[59] CA Paris, 2 June 2004, *SA Cineco v. Societé Shure Brothers Incorporated*, Rev Arb (2005) 675 with note by Racine at 680 et seq.

it would result in the non-application of the French Law. The court rejected that view holding *inter alia*

> Considering that the choice of law clause in the distribution contracts, submitting the question of formation and performance of the contract to the law of Illinois, does not by way of principle prevent the arbitrator from applying French Law; that consequently the recourse of Cineco based on the obvious nullity of the arbitration agreement fails.[60]

16-74 Contrary to the Higher Regional Court in Munich in its decision described above, the French Court considered it sufficient for the enforcement of the arbitration agreement that the application of the mandatory French law is not *a priori* excluded. That is, however, rarely the case. Unlike courts, arbitral tribunals can and do apply mandatory provisions which are not part of either the law chosen by the parties for the merits or of the place of arbitration.[61] Thus, only in exceptional circumstance can it be excluded that the arbitral tribunal will consider the mandatory provisions of French law, even if the arbitration takes place in a different country and the parties have chosen a foreign law to govern the merits. Consequently the requirement of "nullité manifeste" at the referral-stage has as an effect that French courts will only at the post-award stage control the application of the mandatory laws by the arbitrator.[62]

7. Evaluation of the Different Approaches

16-75 Ultimately, it is the national legislator who determines which of the three approaches described is adopted by a particular legal system for disputes arising from the various types of commercial representation. However, as the selected examples *supra* show, in most cases the relevant statutes do not directly address

60 Translation by the author; the original French text in Rev Arb (2005) 675 (677) provided:

> Considérant que les termes du contrat de distribution renvoyant les règles régissant la formation, l'exploitation et l'exécution du contrat au droit de l'Etat de l'Illinois ne font pas obstacle par principe à une application éventuelle de la loi francaise par les arbitres ; que le moyen invoqué par la société Cineco en faveur d'une nullité manifest de la clause compromissoire est en conséquence inopérant.

61 For the French view see Delvolvé, Rouche, Pointon, *French Arbitration Law and Practice* (2003) para 294; *cf* Lew, Mistelis & Kröll, *supra* note 3 at paras 17-28 et seq.; see also infra.

62 See also Racine, *Rev Arb* 680 (689) who concludes:

> L'invocation d'une loi de police francaise ne remet pa en question la validité de la clause d'arbitrage, cette loi pouvant faire l'objet d'une « application éventuelle [..] par les arbitres » pour reprendre les termes de l'arret.

the issue. Thus, courts have *de facto* a considerable discretion in applying the relevant statutes and their mandatory provisions. The guiding principle for the area of commercial representation, like any other areas of law where mandatory provisions play an important role, has been well summarized by the U.S. Supreme Court in *Mitsubishi v. Soler*. There the court stated:

> By agreeing to arbitrate a statutory claim, a party does not forgo the substantive rights afforded by the statute; it only submits to their resolution in an arbitral, rather than judicial, forum. It trades the procedures and opportunities for review of the courtroom for the simplicity, informality, and expedition of arbitration. We must assume that if Congress intended the substantive protection afforded by a given statute to include protection against a waiver of the right to a judicial forum, that intention will be deductible from text or legislative history.[63]

16-76 If the reference to "Congress" is replaced by a reference to the national legislators in general, the statement provides an adequate guideline for the courts in dealing with the relevant national rules. Thus, unless these provisions clearly state that the dispute is not arbitrable, courts should refer the parties to arbitration and limit themselves to the control of the award. There are a number of reasons which weigh in favour of the third approach, in particular, where the national law does not explicitly exclude the arbitrability of the disputes in question.

7.1. The Unwarranted Limitations of Procedural Party Autonomy under the Inarbitrability Approach

16-77 Party autonomy should be the governing principle for all types of business transactions. The parties know their own interest best, not only in relation to substance but also in relation to procedure. Restrictions to party autonomy should be limited to those few cases where they are absolutely necessary. The first approach, declaring certain types of disputes to be inarbitrable *per se* leads to unwarranted limitations of the parties' procedural autonomy. The restrictions imposed under the first approach on the parties' freedom to submit disputes to arbitration, are based on the underlying assumption that the commercial representative is the structurally weaker party which needs protection. Even if that assumption may hold true in the majority of cases, there are many cases where the relevant contracts are concluded by two commercial parties with

[63] *Mitsubishi Motors Corp. v. Soler Chrysler-Plymouth*, 473 U.S. 614 (628).

largely equal bargaining power.[64] Thus, unlike in the area of consumer protection, the complete exclusion of disputes arising from certain types of commercial representation from the scope of arbitration is not justified. If restrictions have to be imposed, they should be imposed after an evaluation of the particular case. The mere fact that the dispute may be governed by internationally mandatory rules is in itself not a sufficient ground to generally exclude its arbitrability.[65] As correctly pointed out in the above quote of the U.S. Supreme Court, by submitting to arbitration "…a party does not forgo the substantive rights afforded by the statute".

16-78 Thus, disputes arising from commercial representation should be considered to be generally arbitrable. This has the advantage that the restrictions on procedural party autonomy are limited to those cases where the objectives pursued by the internationally mandatory rules truly require them. For example, the above mentioned § 89b German HGB, granting the commercial agent a mandatory compensation claim upon termination of the agency agreement, has a dual purpose. First, it constitutes to a certain extent a payment for the services rendered. The commission due for each contract concluded during the agency agreement often does not fully reflect the services rendered. In particular the opportunities to conclude further contracts with the partners acquired through the agent after the termination of the agency contract may not be covered. Second, the compensation claim has the purpose of providing a minimum of social security for the agent during the time he is trying to acquire new principals. Both purposes could be taken into account if the evaluation of whether the dispute is to be arbitrated is taken on a case by case basis and not through the general inarbitrability of a certain class of disputes. If, for example, the agent has received a higher commission than usual to compensate him already during the lifetime of the agency contract for the goodwill acquired, there is less need to protect the agent through the compensation claim. As the objective of § 89b HGB is fulfilled irrespective of whether or not it is applied by the arbitral tribunal, there would be no need to refuse the enforcement of the arbitration agreement.[66]

16-79 It is obvious that such a case specific analysis leads to a loss of legal certainty in comparison to the first approach, where the inarbitrability of a certain type of dispute arising from commercial representation is clear from the outset.

[64] See also Verhagen, *supra* note 13 at 153.

[65] In this direction also in the context of German Law Schlosser, in: Stein & Jonas, *Kommentar zur Zivilprozessordnung* (21st ed, 2002) § 1030 para 3.

[66] See Quinke, "Schiedsverfahren und Eingriffsnormen", *SchiedsVZ* (2007) 246 (249).

However, this disadvantage is in the authors view more than outbalanced by the gain in party autonomy. Irrespective of any inequality in bargaining power, the arbitration agreement is still an expression of the parties' will.

7.2. Disadvantages of the Control at the Pre-Award Referral Stage

16-80 Those two considerations - insufficient protection of procedural party autonomy and lack of legal certainty - are also the arguments which speak against the second approach and in favour of referring all control to the post award stage.

16-81 Naturally, the uncertainties associated with the solution which allows for control already at the pre-award referral stage are greater than those associated with the third approach. The decision of whether to refer the parties to arbitration or not is based on a prognosis of whether and how the arbitral tribunal will apply the relevant provisions. Unless the mere threat of the non application of the internationally mandatory provisions of the forum is chosen as the relevant criterion, any such prognosis is fraught with uncertainties. By contrast, any control at the post-award stage is based on facts. The courts know whether the tribunal has applied the relevant provision or has at least attained the objectives pursued by the latter through other means. As already mentioned above, the really crucial question is whether the objectives pursued by a mandatory provision are attained and not whether that particular mandatory provision is actually applied. The answer to this question, however, can only be given, after the tribunal has decided the case. The fulfilment of the objectives is not necessarily dependent upon the application of the particular provision.

16-82 Moreover, only the third approach is able to take the particularities of arbitration fully into account. In court proceedings, there is a clear distinction between mandatory provisions of the forum and mandatory provisions of a foreign legal system. While the former have to be applied irrespective of the otherwise chosen law, the latter can only be applied if there is a specific empowerment for that in the national systems, which is rarely the case. By contrast, an arbitral tribunal, as stated by the U.S. Supreme Court, "owes no prior allegiance to the legal norms of particular states". Thus, the distinction of mandatory laws of the "*lex fori*" and those of a foreign state does not exist or is at least of much smaller importance. Consequently, arbitrators have less problems applying mandatory provisions of an "interested law", which is neither the law chosen for the merits, nor the law of the country where the arbitral tribunal has its seat. There are actually good arguments in arbitration for the application of such mandatory provisions where they pursue a reasonable interest and have a close connection with the dispute.[67] At least the close-connection-requirement is normally fulfilled for mandatory provisions protecting commercial representatives and the former may be as well. Consequently, unlike in court proceedings, in arbitration proceedings the choice of a foreign law does not necessarily exclude the application of the mandatory provisions of the representative's place of business, even if the place of arbitration is also in a different country. In this respect, the argument of the Court of Appeal in Paris in the above cited *Cineco* decision is convincing. As long as it cannot be excluded that the arbitral tribunal will apply the mandatory provisions of the representative's place of business, the arbitration agreement should be enforced at the pre-award referral stage.

16-83 The major objection against the second-look-approach, raised already by the minority in the U.S. Supreme Court's *Mitsubishi* decision,[68] is that there may never be the chance for a second look in enforcement proceedings. This criticism is equally true in relation to commercial representation disputes if one only looks at enforcement proceedings or setting aside proceedings. There, a second chance to look at the dispute will only occur if the principal had raised claims himself which have been awarded by the tribunal and which he wants to enforce, but which would conflict with the internationally mandatory rules protecting the commercial representative.[69] The more likely situation, however, is that the commercial representative, after a rejection of his claims for compensation by the arbitral tribunal, starts court proceedings to claim the compensation due under to the protective rule of the forum. In such proceedings the non-enforceability of the arbitration agreement could be invoked, if the previous rejection of the claims by the arbitral tribunal was contrary to public policy of the court. Due to the violation of public policy the award would also not be recognizable and consequently would have no *res judicata* effects. From the perspectives of procedural economy such an approach may appear objectionable. It creates additional expenses for the commercial representative who would firstly have to

[67] See Hochstrasser, "Choice of Law and "Foreign" Mandatory Rules in International Arbitration", 11(1) *J. Int'l Arb*, 57 (1994); *cf* Lew, Mistelis & Kröll, *supra* note 3 at paras 17-28 et seq.

[68] *Mitsubishi Motors Corp. v. Soler Chrysler-Plymouth*, 473 U.S. 614 (656 seq).

[69] For such an example in the area of franchising see the (unconvincing) German decision of the Higher Regional Court Dresden, 7 November 2007, *IHR* (2008) 119 with note by Kraayvanger. While the issue was not the non-application of internationally mandatory rules, the refusal to enforce the award is motivated by the perceived need to protect the weaker franchisee from having to arbitrate its case in a foreign country under foreign law.

go through unsuccessful arbitration proceedings before being then allowed to pursue its claims before the state courts. That however, is the direct consequence of his or her consent to arbitration. The primary objective of the mandatory provisions is to ensure a minimum of protection for the commercial representative. This objective would be attained, albeit at higher costs. Protection against such costs, however, is only a secondary objective of such mandatory provisions, if it is one at all. It should not be sufficient to override a clear agreement of the parties to arbitrate their disputes.

16-84 In principle, party autonomy should prevail. Only where important interests of higher value are affected should it be overridden. The question of whether to follow the second or the third approach boils down to the question of whether any form of threat that such interests are affected is sufficient or whether the infringement of such interests must be proven. The latter should be the relevant standard.

TABLE OF NATIONAL AND INTERNATIONAL COURT DECISIONS

All references are to paragraph numbers

Court decisions from common law systems are organised alphabetically; decisions from civil law countries are organised chronologically.

Austria

Oberster Gerichtshof, 11 November 1999, RdW 26 (2000), **9-16**

Oberster Gerichtshof, 17 April 1996, RdW 135 (1997), **9-14**

Oberster Gerichtshof, 5 June 2007, 10 Ob 29 (2007), **9-16**

Belgium

Cour de cassation, 28 June 1979, *Audi-NSU v. Adelin Petit & Cie*, V YBCA 257 (1980), **5-38, 16-37**

Cour d'appel Brussels, 4 October 1985, *Company M. v. M. S.A.*, XIV YBCA 618 (1989), **6-15, 7-59**

Cour de cassation, 22 December 1988, *Gutrob Werke GmbH v. Usinorp de Saint-Hubert and Saint-Hubert Gardening*, (partly published in Journal Tribunal (1989) 458), **16-39**

Tribunal de Commerce Brussels, 20 September 1999, *Matermaco SA v. PPM Cranes Inc et al*, XXV YBCA 673 (2000), **7-40**

Cour de cassation, 15 October 2004, *Colvi N.V. (Belgium) v. Interdica (Switzerland)*, XXXI YBCA 593 (2006), **15-12, 15-13, 16-38, 16-42**

Cour d'appel Brussels, 25 April 2006, *S.R.L. Alta (Italy) v. S.A. Traches Soberac (Belgium)*, [unreported], **16-36, 16-44**

Cour de Cassation, 16 November 2006, *Van Hopplynus Instruments v. Coherent Inc.*, case No: C.02.0445.F/1, http://jure.juridat.just.fgov.be/pdfapp/download_blob?idpdf=F-20061116-7, **16-46**

Tribunal de Première Instance de Bruxelles, 8 March 2007, *SNF SAS v La Cytec Industrie*, **12-54**

Canada

Editions Chouette inc. v. Desputeaux, Rev. Arb. (2003) 473, **3-42, 13-9**

L Mistelis & S Brekoulakis (eds), Arbitrability: International & Comparative Perspectives, 351 - 362

European Court of Justice

Egypt

England

Queen's Bench Division (Commercial Court), XXIII YBCA (1998) 789-794, **14-3**

Re Atlantic Computer Systems Plc., [1992] CH. 505; [1990] B.C.C. 859, **9-24**

Republic of Ecuador v. Occidental Exploration & Production Company, [2007] EWCA Civ 656, **10-58, 10-59**

Republic of Ecuador v. Occidental Exploration and Production Company (OEPC), [2006] 1 Lloyd's Rep. 773 **10-57, 10-58, 10-59**

Soleimany v. Soleimany, [1998] 3 W.L.R. 811, **11-9**

Syska & Elektrim SA v. Vivendi & Others, [2008] EWHC 2155 (Comm), **6-57**

Westacre v. Jugoimport [1999] 3 All ER 864, **7-40, 11-9**

Finland

High Supreme Court, 14 May 2003, 4 Rev. Arb. 1396 (2003), **14-22**

France

Cour de cassation (civil chamber), 9 January 1854, D.P. 1, 69 (1854), **3-33**

Cour d'appel Paris, 9 February 1954, D. 192 (1954), **3-33**

Cour d'appel Orleans, 15 February 1956, D. 340 (1966), **3-33**

Cour d'appel Paris, 15 June 1956, Dalloz 587 (1957), **3-33**

Cour d'appel Orleans, 15 May 1961, Rev. Arb. 188 (1961), **3-33**

Cour de cassation, 18 May 1971, *Impex v. P.A.Z. Produzione Lavorazione*, Rev. Arb (1972), **2-74**

Cour de cassation, 4 February 1986, 4 Rev. Arb. 718 (1988), **9-35**

Cour de cassation, 19 May 1987, Rev. Arb. 142 (1988), **9-35**

Cour de cassation, 7 July 1988 [unreported], **16-20**

Cour d'appel Paris, 16 February 1989, *Almira*, Rev. Arb. 711 (1989), **7-24**

Cour d'appel Paris, 29 March 1991, *Ganz v. Nationale des Chemins de Fer Tunisiens (SNCFT)*, 3 Rev. Arb. 478 (1991), **2-5, 3-34, 6-2, 15-6, 9-28**

Cour d'appel Paris, 17 December 1991, *Gatoil v. National Iranian Oil Co*, Rev. Arb. 281 (1993), **3-46**

Cour de cassation, 7 January 1992, *Siemens AG and BKMI Industrienlagen GmbH v. Dutco Construction Company (Dubai),* Rev. Arb. 470 (1992), **2-14**

Cour d'appel Paris, 19 May 1993, *Labinal v. Mors*, Rev. Arb. 645 (1993), **2-5, 3-33, 6-2, 11-17**

Cour d'appel Paris, 26 May 1993, *Zeldin v. Sté Editions Recherches*, Revue Internationale du Droit d'Auteur 292 (1994), **13-8**

Cour d'appel Grenoble, 13 September 1993, Rev. Arb. 337 (1994), **3-35**

Cour d'appel Paris, 14 October 1993, *Aplix v. Velcro*, Rev. Arb. 164 (1994), **3-22**

New Zealand

Attorney General of New Zealand v. Mobil Oil New Zealand Ltd., [1989] 2 NZLR 668, **3-22**, **3-29**

Pakistan

Hubco vs. Wapda, 15(7) Mealey's IAR (2000) (Supreme Court), **11-16**

Saudi Arabia

Diwan Almazalim Decision No. 19/28 of 1399 H (1979), [unreported], **15-21**

Islamic Investment Company of the Gulf (Bahamas) Ltd. v. Symphony Gems NV and Others, [2002] All ER 171, **15-22**

Singapore

Four Pillars Enterprises Co Ltd v. Beiersdorf Aktiengesellschaft (1999) 1 SLR 737, **14-22**

Spain

RDGRN, 19 February 1998, **14-23**

High Supreme Court, 18 April 1998, **14-20, 14-23**

SAP Barcelona, 17 February 1999, **14-18**

SAP Barcelona, 16 May 2003, **14-18**

RDGRN, 4 May 2005, **14-28**

Auto del Juzgado de lo Mercantil de Bilbao, No. 1, 2 November 2005, **14-18**

Auto del Juzgado de lo Mercantil no. 1 de Madrid, 17 April 2006, **14-28**

SAP Santa Cruz de Tenerife, 27 October 2006, **14-18**

Auto Audiencia Provincial Barcelona, 5 March 2008, **14-18**

Sweden

Svea Court of Appeals, 30 December 2004, *Peiker austic GmbH & KG v. SAAB Automobile Aktiebolag*, **15-17**

Switzerland

Tribunal Fédéral, 23 June 1992, *Fincantieri - Cantieri Navali Italiani SpA and Oto Melara SpA v M and arbitration tribunal*, XX YBCA 766 (1995), **2-5**, **2-58**, **3-37**, **6-2**, **7-24**

Tribunal Fédéral, 19 April 1994, *Les Emirats Arabes Unis v. Westland Helicopters*, ASA Bulletin 404 (1994), **11-53**

Tribunal Fédéral, 2 September 1993, *National Power v. Westinghouse*, ASA Bulletin 244 (1994), **11-23**

Tribunal Fédéral, 7 Septembre 1993 F. *S.p.A. et M. S.p.A. v. M*, 119 (1993) II 386, **11-49**

Tribunal Fédéral, 13 November 1998, ASA Bulletin 445, 529 (1999), **12-60**

Tribunal Fédéral, 28 April 1992, ASA Bulletin 368 (1992), **12-60**

United Arab Emirates

Abu Dhabi Judgment No. 245/20 (7 May 2000), **15-22**

United States

14 Penn Plaza LLC v. Pyett, 129 S Ct 1223 (2008), **8-19**

Ace Ltd. v. Cigna Corp., 2001 WL 767015, **10-7**

Action Indus., Inc. v. U.S. Fid. & Guar. Co., 358 F.3d 337, 343 (5th Cir. 2004), **3-30**

Alexander v. Gardner-Denver Co., 415 U.S. 36, 94 S Ct 1011, L.Ed.2d 147 (1974), **2-24**, **8-19**

Alliance Bernstein Investment Research & Management, Inc. v. Schaffran, 445 F.3d 121 (2nd Cir. N.Y. 2006), **8-9**

Allied-Bruce Terminix Companies v. Dobson, 513 U.S. 265 (1995), **15-24**

Allis-Chalmers Corp. v. Lueck, 471 U.S. 202, 209 (1985), **8-14**, **8-19**, **8-20**

American Manufacturing Co., 363 U.S. 564 (1960), **8-19**

American Recovery Corp v. Computerized Thermal Imaging Inc., 96 F. 3d 88 (4th Cir. 1996), at 93, **15-11**

American Safety Equipment Corp v. J P Maguire & Co., 391 F 2d 821 (1968), **12-37**

Anders v. Hometown Mortgage Services, 346 F. 3d 1024 (11th Cir. Ala. 2003), **8-11**

Apache Bohai Corp. LDC v. Texaco China, BV F.3d, 2007 WL 587233, (CA 5 Tex. 2007), **3-30**

Armco Employees Independent Federation v. AK Steel Corp., 252 F. 3d 854 (6th Cir. 2001), **8-24**

Armendariz v. Foundation Health Psychcare Services, Inc., 6 P.3d 669 (CA 2000), **8-5**

Arnold v. United Companies Lending Corporation, 511 S.E. 2d 854, **15-24**

AT&T Technologies, Inc. v. Communications Workers of America, 475 U.S. 643, 648-51, 106 S Ct 1415, 1419-1420, 89 L. Ed. 2d 648 (1986), **4-12**, **8-15**, **8-24**

Bache Halsey Stuart, Inc. v. French, 425 F.Supp.1231, 1233 (D.C. Cir. 1977), **3-11**

Barrentine v. Arkansas-Best Freight System, Inc., 450 U.S. 728, 101 S Ct 1427, 67 L.Ed.2d 641 (1981), **2-24**

Blair v. Scott Specialty Gases, 283 F.3d 595 (3rd Cir. 2002), **8-5**

Bradford v. Rockwell Semiconductor Systems, Inc., 238 F.3d 549 (4th Cir. 2001), **8-5**

Brook v. Peak Intern., Ltd. 294 F.3d 668, (CA 5 Tex. 2002), **3-30**

Browne v. Kline Tysons Imps Inc., 190 F. Supp. 2d 827 (E.D. Va. 2002), **15-14**

Buckeye Checking, Inc. v. Cardegna, 546 U.S. 440, 444 (2006), **4-7**

Certain Underwriters at Lloyd's of London v. Westchester Fire Insurance Co., 489 F.3d 580 (3rd Cir. N.J. 2007), **8-11**

Chastain v. Robinson-Humphrey Co., 957 F.2d 851 (11th Cir. 1992), **4-25**

China Minmetals Import & Export Co., Ltd. v. Chi Mei Corp., 334 F. 3d 274 (3rd Cir. N.J. 2003), **8-9**

Circuit City Stores v. Adams, 532 U.S. 105 (2001), **8-5**

Cole v. Burns International Security Services, 105 F.3d 1465 (D.C. Cir. 1996), **8-5**

TABLE OF ARBITRAL AWARDS

All references are to paragraph numbers

Awards are organised chronologically; institutions alphabetically

L Mistelis & S Brekoulakis (eds), Arbitrability: International & Comparative Perspectives, 363 - 365

ICSID

PCA

SCC

Upper Silesian Arbitral Tribunal

SUBJECT INDEX

All references are to paragraph numbers

L Mistelis & S Brekoulakis (eds), Arbitrability: International & Comparative Perspectives, 367 - 375

B

R

S

T

U

V

INTERNATIONAL ARBITRATION LAW LIBRARY

1. Moshe Hirsch, *The Arbitration Mechanism of the International Center for the Settlement of Investment Disputes*, 1993 (ISBN 07-923-1993-1).
2. Aida B. Avanessian, *Iran-United States Claims Tribunal in Action*, 1993 (ISBN 18-533-3902-4).
3. Isaak I. Dore, *The UNCITRAL Framework for Arbitration in Contemporary Perspective*, 1993 (ISBN 18-533-3573-8).
4. Vesna Lazić, *Insolvency Proceedings and Commercial Arbitration*, 1998 (ISBN 90-411-1115-8).
5. Joachim Frick, *Arbitration in Complex International Contracts*, 2001 (ISBN 90-411-1662-1).
6. Katherine Lynch, *The Forces of Economic Globalization: Challenges to the Regime of International Commercial Arbitration*, 2003 (ISBN 90-411-1994-9).
7. Christoph Liebscher, *The Healthy Award: Challenge in International Commercial Arbitration*, 2003 (ISBN 90-411-2011-4).
8. Hamid G. Gharavi, *The International Effectiveness of the Annulment of an Arbitral Award*, 2003 (ISBN 90-411-1717-2).
9. Abdulhay Sayed, *Corruption in International Trade and Commercial Arbitration*, 2004 (ISBN 90-411-2236-2).
10. Gabrielle Kaufmann-Kohler & Thomas Schultz, *Online Dispute Resolution: Challenges for Contemporary Justice*, 2004 (ISBN 90-411-2318-0).
11. Christopher R. Drahozal & Richard W. Naimark (eds), *Towards a Science of International Arbitration: Collected Empirical Research*, 2005 (ISBN 90-411-2322-9).
12. Ali Yeşilirmak, *Provisional Measures in International Commercial Arbitration*, 2005 (ISBN 90-411-2353-9).
13. Christian Bühring-Uhle, *Arbitration and Mediation in International Business*, second revised edition, 2006 (ISBN 978-9-041-12256-8).
14. Bernard Hanotiau, *Complex Arbitrations: Multiparty, Multicontract, Multiissue and Class Actions*, 2006 (ISBN 978-9-041-12442-5).
15. Loukas A. Mistelis & Julian D.M. Lew (eds), *Pervasive Problems in International Arbitration*, 2006 (ISBN 978-9-041-12450-0).
16. Julian D.M. Lew & Loukas A. Mistelis (eds), *Arbitration Insights – Twenty Years of the Annual Lecture of the School of International Arbitration, Sponsored by Freshfields Bruckhaus Deringer*, 2006 (ISBN 978-9-041-12606-1).
17. Mark Kantor, *Valuation for Arbitration: Compensation Standards, Valuation Methods and Expert Evidence*, 2008 (ISBN 978-9-041-12735-8).
18. Christoph Brunner, *Force Majeure and Hardship under General Contract Principles: Exemption for Non-Performance in International Arbitration*, 2009 (ISBN 978-90-411-2792-1).
19. Loukas A. Mistelis & Stavros L. Brekoulakis (eds), *Arbitrability: International & Comparative Perspectives,* 2009 (ISBN 978-90-411-2730-3).

www.ingramcontent.com/pod-product-compliance
Lightning Source LLC
LaVergne TN
LVHW020645300926
849161LV00004B/823